The Culture of Power and Governance of Pakistan 1947–2008

The Culture of Power and Governance of Pakistan 1947–2008

Ilhan Niaz

OXFORD
UNIVERSITY PRESS

OXFORD
UNIVERSITY PRESS

Oxford University Press is a department of the University of Oxford.
It furthers the University's objective of excellence in research, scholarship,
and education by publishing worldwide. Oxford is a registered trade mark of
Oxford University Press in the UK and in certain other countries

Published in Pakistan by
Oxford University Press
No.38, Sector 15, Korangi Industrial Area,
PO Box 8214, Karachi-74900, Pakistan

© Ilhan Niaz 2010

The moral rights of the author have been asserted

First Edition published in 2010

This edition in Oxford Pakistan Paperbacks 2011

All rights reserved. No part of this publication may be reproduced, stored in
a retrieval system, or transmitted, in any form or by any means, without the
prior permission in writing of Oxford University Press, or as expressly permitted
by law, by licence, or under terms agreed with the appropriate reprographics
rights organization. Enquiries concerning reproduction outside the scope of the
above should be sent to the Rights Department, Oxford University Press, at the
address above

You must not circulate this work in any other form
and you must impose this same condition on any acquirer

ISBN 978-0-19-906342-0

Fourth Impression 2019

Typeset in Adobe Garamond Pro
Printed on 55gsm Book Paper

Printed by Mas Printers, Karachi

To days long gone.

Contents

Preface	ix
Acknowledgements	xiii
Introduction	1
1. Imperishable Empires	20
2. Original Sins	62
3. Mandarins	89
4. Praetorians	138
5. Guardians	168
6. Diwans	210
7. Grand Seigneurs	239
Conclusion	275
Bibliography and Sources	291
Index	313

Preface

The Culture of Power and Governance of Pakistan 1947–2008, is an attempt to explain the decline in the ability of the Pakistani state to govern effectively and in accordance with its own formal constitutional parameters between the 1950s and the 1990s. The primary argument is that the mentality of the westernised ruling elite of Pakistan has steadily regressed into its pre-British form in its ways of exercising power. Thus, the state has come to be treated as a personal estate by the rulers whereby the servants of the state have become personal servants of the powerful members of the executive. This arbitrary exercise of power has reemerged as a dominant norm and undermined the institutional and psychological principles and practices inherited from the British Empire in India.

This is not a moral judgment but an empirical one that can be readily confirmed by paying a visit to almost any government office or by reading daily newspaper headlines. It is further substantiated by living memory which, though rarely enamored of British rule, concedes that the kind of routine oppression, financial corruption and violation of the law that now characterises the exercise of power at all levels in Pakistan did not characterise British India to the same extent. It is affirmed by the de-classified documents and reports in Pakistan, which practically serve as a barometer of decline from a higher to a lower level of state morality. And finally, it is conceded, at least in private, often reluctantly, but at times enthusiastically, by the servants of the state I have had the opportunity to interact with. One went so far as to declare that if we were to take away the much derided 'colonial legacy' all that we would be left with are shrines, some palaces and a few cultural and aesthetic refinements. The entire apparatus of modernity from democracy, constitutionalism, the very idea that the military ought to obey civilian authority, civil society, merit-based recruitment to public service, down to our railways and canals, are parts of the 'colonial legacy.' The same gentleman lamented that instead of trying to rationally comprehend the nature of our state and society we had become mired in surreal discourse and plunged headlong into irrelevant diatribes.

Perhaps it is almost inevitable that when a great empire declines the successor states that emerge operate under numerous handicaps. The new rulers are often poor imitations of the grand imperialists they replace. Their inferiority complexes, insecurities and neuroses condemn them to denounce imperial traditions without a clear understanding. Thus, the Maratha Confederacy and the Sikh kingdom were to the Timurid Empire what India and Pakistan are to the British Empire in India. The difference lies in the establishment by the British of the rule of law, autonomous institutions—political and administrative—that continued to function, and the decision to transfer power to successor states. Whereas the Timurid Empire suffered administrative breakdown and territorial breakup within twenty years of the death of its last great emperor, the British Empire in India managed to escape the former and mitigated the latter.

When the 'crisis of state' or 'crisis of governance' or a decline in 'the writ of the government' is discussed in Pakistan, rarely are the implications of these statements examined. To say that the quality and effectiveness of the state apparatus has declined indicates that at some point in time things were better. To lament the 'rise of corruption' in Pakistan suggests that there was a time when corruption in the form of the privatisation of public wealth and violation of laws was not as widespread. To declare that Pakistani society has 'become ungovernable' or 'anarchic' and 'violent' is to recognise subconsciously that this society was at one time governable, relatively ordered and fairly peaceful. So great, however, is our cognitive dissonance, capacity for self-deception and sophistry that we will ourselves, individually and collectively, to reject the plainly evident in favour of the contrived. And it is plainly evident that when the phenomenon of decline is discussed in Pakistan the irresistible undercurrent is that we are in fact discussing the deterioration of the quality, ethos and effectiveness of the institutions bequeathed by the British Empire in India. That the story of Pakistan's governance is best understood as a journey to an earlier governing mentality. This mentality converted autonomous institutions into servile instruments, the rule of law into the law of the ruler, and obliterated the distinction between public and private wealth and authority. Its legacy is that whereas Pakistan was a state in 1947 it gradually became the estate of the rulers and their officials much as the pre-British empires were estates of their imperial elites. Reasoned argument and debate have given way to ideological fantasies and the parroting of received wisdoms.

Trying to comprehend this process of regression and the dangers it poses to the state and society are major objectives of this study. Unless we begin to understand *why* the phenomenon of decline is so gravitational in both intensity and extent, there is no hope of it being arrested or reversed. Sadly, under the impact of irrational foreign tutelage the Pakistani elite have lost the will and perhaps also the ability to think rationally about its own predicament. Instead, enormous amounts of time and money continue to be invested in the rhetoric of national security, economic development, empowerment, conflict studies, civil society, grassroots mobilisation and the like. The prescriptions that emerge from this discourse, such as the Devolution Plan or the Access to Justice Program or various electronic governance initiatives, often aggravate problems they are originally initiated to resolve. Every few years, the older panaceas are brushed aside and new ones take their place thus enabling one set of donor-sponsored irrationalities to replace another. Witnessing this intellectual debacle unfold and examining its impact on the administration of the country one cannot help but recall Ibn Khaldun's admonishment that 'the pasture of stupidity is unwholesome for mankind.'

The unwholesomeness of the consequences of the arbitrary and delusional exercise of power was brought home painfully in 2007. As the final research and writing of the dissertation on which this book is based took place Pakistan was shaken by a series of inter-related developments. In Islamabad the Lal Masjid brigade effectively terrorised the entire city, made a mockery of the writ of the state and precipitated a full-fledged siege in the heart of the capital one residential sector away from the seat of government. In the NWFP, the provincial law minister deprecated the devolution of power to elected local governments and warned that there was no one left in charge since the abolition of the office of the deputy commissioner and the province was sinking into anarchy. Karachi found itself the scene of mob violence on 12 May 2007, while spiraling terrorist attacks left hundreds dead and thousands injured across the length and breadth of Pakistan. Baluchistan endured military intervention by the central government even as this intervention failed to secure the 'writ of the government.' The arbitrary dismissal of the chief justice, followed by a prolonged agitation led by lawyers, the declaration of emergency and purge of the higher judiciary, set the stage for further confrontation and polarisation. Finally, the assassination of Benazir Bhutto on 27 December 2007 was followed by widespread rioting in Sindh and the postponement of elections.

In their aftermath, a coalition government of former opposition parties led by the Pakistan Peoples Party has come to power. Between February and August 2008 the political parties launched a concerted campaign against President Musharraf. After Musharraf reluctantly stepped down in August, the political parties elected Asif Ali Zardari as the new president. Further confrontation between the presidency and the parliament erupted immediately and almost brought the democratic process to a premature and tragic conclusion in March 2009. In the meantime, the Taliban consolidated their control over large parts of the NWFP and threatened the rest of the country with takeover, a multitude of military operations notwithstanding.

The ouster of the Musharraf regime in August 2008 serves as a convenient marker for the present study. There is little cause for optimism and the race against time may well be lost. If, however, the new dispensation is to survive, it must be understood why earlier regimes failed. It is thus that an account of Pakistan's historical experience of governance accompanied by reflection and analysis may contribute to the amelioration of the crisis of state.

Acknowledgements

The Culture of Power and Governance of Pakistan 1947–2008, would not have been written if it were not for the hundreds of conversations I have had over the past seven years with Zafar Iqbal Rathore, a Police Service of Pakistan officer who retired as Secretary Interior. These conversations introduced me to a great number of the concepts and sources used in this book and provided rare insights into the actual working of the state in Pakistan. I have benefited greatly from Rathore's wisdom and generosity and am profoundly grateful to him.

The research and writing of *The Culture of Power and Governance of Pakistan 1947–2008,* was conducted as part of my work for a PhD in history from the Quaid-i-Azam University, Islamabad. The closest interaction that one normally has in the course of researching and writing for a PhD is with one's supervisor. I was fortunate to have begun this dissertation under the guidance of Dr Sikandar Hayat. Regrettably, his retirement from the Quaid-i-Azam University, Department of History, in September 2006, eventually precipitated a change of supervisor. Dr Tariq Rahman at the National Institute of Pakistan Studies was very generous in taking up where Dr Sikandar Hayat left off and helped me with the first revised draft of the dissertation. After the first revised draft was ready I had the opportunity of working under Dr M. Naeem Qureshi's supervision at the Department of History. Dr Tariq Rahman very magnanimously allowed me to avail this opportunity and thus I completed the second, third, and fourth, revised drafts of the dissertation under Dr Naeem Qureshi's supervision.

In spite of a repeated change in supervision, I feel that the dissertation benefited from the feedback and guidance given by three of Pakistan's most outstanding social scientists. I am, of course, particularly grateful to Dr Naeem Qureshi for seeing the dissertation through to the submission stage and to Dr Wiqar Ali Shah, the Chairman of the Department of History at Quaid-i-Azam University, for being as supportive and empathetic as he has been.

The dissertation and the present volume would have lacked substance, if it were not for Saleemullah Khan, the Director of the National Documentation Centre in Islamabad. He and his associates provided assistance and advice on finding and utilising de-classified files and reports concerning Pakistan. The Charles Wallace Trust Fellowship, Pakistan, provided timely assistance in the form of a fellowship in the summer of 2006 at the University of London, School of Oriental and African Studies (SOAS). This enabled me to examine reports and papers from British India. I am therefore indebted to Daud Ali, William Crawley and Jane Savory for their support.

I am grateful to my present colleagues at the Quaid-i-Azam University, Dr Javed Haider Syed, Dr Tanvir Anjum, Annice Mehmood, Rabia Umar Ali, Dr Farooq Dar and Fouzia Farooq for their support and encouragement. My evaluators and examiners for the dissertation, Dr Anwar Syed, Dr Ian Talbot, Dr Francis Robinson, Dr Saeedudin Dar, Dr Pervaiz Iqbal Cheema and Dr Khurram Qadir all of whom generously contributed their time, insights, criticisms, also merit appreciation.

As an academic with no direct experience of working in a bureaucratic organisation I have had to depend on the testimony and experience of those who served, or still serve, the state. I am in particular grateful to senior officers such as Ijlal Haider Zaidi, Tanvir Ahmed Khan, Inam-ul Haq, Ghiyasuddin, Ejaz Qureshi and Riaz Mohammed Khan for their valuable insight.

My friends outside academic life have also played a vital role in the research and writing process. Many have contributed their experiences of working in the public, private and social sectors and thus augmented my perspective. Others have been endless sources of encouragement. I am, therefore, particularly thankful to Ahmed Fasih, Khurram Afzal, Safiya Aftab, Jibran Riaz, Rukhsana Shama, Mohammad Suleman, Rukhsana Ashraf, Samia Khalid, and Himayatullah.

Finally, my grandmother, Sadiqa Manzoor, parents, Kamran and Nuzhat Niaz, and my sister, Nadia Niaz, provided support, enthusiasm and comments on the dissertation and the manuscript. After having profited from the assistance and support of so many, the errors and omissions that remain are solely my responsibility.

Introduction

THEORETICAL OVERVIEW

The state is a major component of historical experience. As the preeminent form of human political organisation, the state performs the essential functions of establishing and sustaining order and collecting taxes. Every state must carry out these two functions with reasonable effectiveness or else it fails and anarchy ensues. States also have to negotiate with the social context in which they operate. Of all forms of the state the continental bureaucratic empire is the most widespread and for much of history was also the most successful.[1]

In continental bureaucratic empires the ruler either exercised universal proprietorship over the land and moveable assets or aspired to do so and was thus hostile to the free accumulation of private property. In this sense, the entire country was the personal estate of the ruler. Many of these empires grew too large, populous and complex for the ruler and his leading warriors to manage directly even when they monopolised armed force and controlled food production.[2] Expansion concentrated wealth in the ruler's hands and made it possible for him to sustain further territorial acquisitions[3] and indulge his aesthetic sense. The ruler, of course, did not want to share power with the local leaders his conquest had forced into submission. It was in this context that in the fourth and third millennia BC a class of servants[4] that exercised sovereignty in the ruler's name across the administrative sub-units of the empire emerged.[5] Although the details of this class varied from one continental bureaucratic empire to another, the essential features were nearly everywhere the same.[6]

A most important feature was that the servants of the state derived their powers from the sovereign at the centre and enforced his proprietorship over the country. In the context of Sumer we find that the *en* by 2500 BC 'was the leader of the bureaucracy' and made decisions concerning scribes and officials divided into over a hundred specialised functions as enumerated in official texts.[7] In Egypt scribes were the instruments of the pharaoh's rule and through them his will was made manifest.[8] Senior officers were recruited from the scribe class, a special college was maintained at the capital to train these generalist administrators, and enterprising young men were advised to enter the pharaoh's service in this capacity:

> In Egypt scribes were not only amongst the elite, they knew it, and said so plainly. 'Be a scribe,' ran the advice, 'it saves you from toil, it protects you from all manner of labour.' 'Be a scribe. Your limbs will be sleek, your hands will grow soft. You will go forth in white clothes, honoured with courtiers saluting you.' And many a senior figure in the state included 'scribe' amongst the accumulated titles of his curriculum vitae.[9]

The Chinese mandarins are perhaps the most famous example of administrative elites and China was for over a millennium the continental bureaucratic empire *par excellence* blending into a remarkably coherent whole, Confucian ethics and ideology and Legalist politics and administrative practice. Though the size of the bureaucratic elite varied from ten thousand to thirty thousand depending on the dynasty in question, entry into its ranks was controlled by a competitive examination held every three years. Candidates were allotted roll numbers, sat in cubicles, and had to answer questions from subjects such as history, law, ethics and the classics. The final test was conducted by the emperor himself whose many functions included that of the chief examiner.

The effectiveness with which these servants executed their master's orders determined their merit in the eyes of a competent ruler. The recruitment, promotion, and transfers of these servants were subject to the ruler's will though in many continental bureaucratic empires a First Minister, Royal Council, or Grand Vizier, handled routine work.[10] The lives, property, and honor of the servants of the state were at the mercy of the ruler. Disobedience and inefficiency often entailed catastrophic consequences and so long as the ruler was competent his servants reacted to his demands with servility and an inordinate desire to please. Since the ruler considered the entire land his personal estate, his demands were often arbitrary and entailed the dispossession, enslavement, coercion, or liquidation, of many of his subjects.[11] In this manner the arbitrary power of the ruler over his servants translated into the arbitrary power of the state over society.

A concentration of armed force, universal proprietorship and a ruling class of servants, was complemented by a state religion or ideology. Again, while the details of this ideocratic complex varied, the basic features remained more or less constant. The ruler was regarded as either divinity incarnate or as a reflection of divinity. The official priesthood and intelligentsia held their positions at the ruler's pleasure. Their salaries, privileges and terms of service depended upon the ruler's will. Their principal task was to project the pronouncements and actions of their ruler as sublime and infallible manifestations of the divine will.[12] Consequently, opposition to the ruler was considered both treason and sacrilege. Often the judicial officers of continental bureaucratic empires were recruited from the priestly class. The abject dependence of this class upon the ruler safeguarded his arbitrary power, provided legitimacy, and brought a modicum of predictability to the administration of justice. The theoretic emphasis on order, obedience and tradition, combined with the reality of routine excesses and arbitrariness, promoted an atmosphere of intellectual rigidity and moral flexibility. Occasionally, a radical despot or religious movement would change the state religion or ideology without altering the ideocratic orientation of state power. In this event, after a brief period, the new belief system would either be reduced to the status of the old having changed only the rhetoric of power, or a competent conservative ruler would succeed and restore the old beliefs. In any case the ideocratic nature of the continental bureaucratic empire remained essentially unchanged.[13]

In more recent times various 'utopian projects' driven by 'totalitarian' and authoritarian movements took root in continental bureaucratic states confronted with the challenge of modernisation.[14] These movements, often using ideological and pseudo-scientific rhetoric, in many ways 'represented a reversion to ancient and primitive times when deity and ruler were one.'[15] Perhaps the greatest of the misconceptions spread by these movements was that their motivations and ideologies existed autonomously of cultures of power and historical experiences. Soviet Russia with its Stalinist horrors and wastage of human life was far removed from the Marx-inspired Labor party in England or the social democracies of northern and western Europe.[16] From these and other historical experiences it appears that cultures of power bend and break ideologies but are rarely bent or broken by them.[17] Changes in rhetoric and rationalisation do not translate into more just or better governance.

The total sum of relations produced by the operation of continental bureaucratic empires produced an arbitrary and ideocratic culture of power that encompassed the behavioral patterns manifested by the ruling class in the exercise of power and the reactions of the ruled with regard to exposure to the state apparatus. Cultures of power do, of course, vary but in all continental bureaucratic empires their inherent propensity is towards extreme arbitrariness that proceeds from the nature of the state itself. Arbitrariness, centralisation, and ideological delusions, are reinforced by historical experience and broad environmental conditions.

The great weakness of continental bureaucratic empires is their overdependence on the quality of the central executive or, in more sophisticated cases, the ruling corporation.[18] Prolonged exposure to arbitrary rule produces failed societies characterised by atomisation, apathy, fatalism, mutual distrust, risk-aversion and extreme greed. These societies are servile when the state is strong and ungovernable when the state is weak. Since the prevalent culture of power causes both the ruler and his servants to see the country as a personal estate, as soon as the former weakens the latter carve out personal estates for themselves accelerating movement towards administrative breakdown and political anarchy.[19] When a new ruler emerges the same pattern manifests itself and the petty bureaucratic estates are fused by violence and conspiracy into a single grand estate. Alternately, chaotic conditions can continue for decades or centuries until sufficient external force is applied by new imperial elites.

STATEMENT OF THE PROBLEM

Pakistan's sixty years of independence have been characterised by great instability, repeated recourse to extra-constitutional methods, and a high level of arbitrariness in the conduct of the state apparatus. The main objective of the present study is to explain *why* the Pakistani state thus far has failed to exercise power in a manner consistent with the dignity, prosperity and security of its citizens and act in its own enlightened self-interest. The explanation proffered rotates on three principal axes.

The first is philosophical and examines Pakistan as a continental bureaucratic empire and an administrative state in which the predominance of the executive function is a structural as well as a normative imperative. The second axis is empirical and describes the *actual* exercise of power by the ruling elite through the administrative institutions and instruments. The third assesses the impact the exercise of power by the elite has upon the effectiveness, quality and ethos of the state apparatus, as well as the reaction of society.

In terms of the theoretical framework several central themes relating to cultures of power and governance in Pakistan have been integrated into the study. The most important are the high levels of arbitrariness in decision-making and execution and the overriding propensity to treat the state as a personal estate. An equally strong tendency amongst rulers is that they treat the servants of the state as personal servants. The servants of state, in turn, carve out their own networks of patronage and try to achieve a measure of personal security and aggrandisement. In this environment policy making is far removed from realities on the ground and a high level of cynicism prevails alongside intolerance of original thinking and criticism.

The empirical basis of the theorisations enumerated thus far comprises the actions, reflections, desires and reform efforts of the ruling elite over the past sixty years. This elite, it must be borne in mind, for most of Pakistan's history can be equated with the administrative elite. It is thus important to discuss the development of political and administrative habits and the cultivation of state morality during Ancient/Medieval/British periods in the subcontinent's history in the context of their relevance to Pakistan's governance. An important qualitative difference exists between the British Empire in India and its development of autonomous institutions under laws and earlier empires and the resultant tensions in Pakistan's culture of power and governance. The roles of the political leadership vis-à-vis the state apparatus, the higher bureaucracy and judiciary, the law and order and financial administrations, the military interventions in the state apparatus and its relations with the other arms of the executive and American/American-inspired tutelage on the culture of power and governance in Pakistan act as important empirical markers.

The assessments that flow from the theoretical and empirical inputs reflect upon the direction of Pakistan's administrative history, governance and culture of power between 1947 and 2008. All the important administrative functions of the state inclusive of law enforcement, taxation, area administration, local government, health, education, infrastructure, etc., have been simultaneously politicised and privatised. There has been a consistent erosion of merit, probity, regularity, trust and internal discipline, in the management of the state apparatus. The intellectual and moral qualities of Pakistan's administrative class have registered a steady decline under the impact of politicisation, privatisation and the arbitrary and unenlightened political and bureaucratic leadership. American tutelage and funding has significantly contributed to the delusional tendencies of the Pakistani ruling elite. The reformers have either failed to understand Pakistan's underlying structural imperatives or having understood failed to translate their ideas into practice. The greatest damage done was by reforms that misunderstood Pakistan's problems and were put into practice. The state has slowly but steadily become ineffective while the society has become increasingly ungovernable. Pakistan appears to have developed an unenlightened, highly arbitrary and delusional culture of power and instead of building upon the positive aspects of the British imperial legacy and rolling back its negatives has in effect reversed the positives and exacerbated the negatives.

Scope of the Study

The time period covered by the present study encompasses the first sixty-one years of Pakistan's history (1947–2008) and terminates with the resignation of Pervez Musharraf, Pakistan's most recent military ruler, in August 2008. It also goes into the background as the need arises to explain or elaborate upon significant and relevant aspects of cultures of power and governance in other times and places. Within these sixty-one years of Pakistan's history greater attention is paid to years of change, upheaval and reforms. It appears that the Pakistani state apparatus undergoes bursts of reformative activity and reassessment at five to ten year intervals. These intervals in part reflect the alternation of regimes and provide a fairly sound basis for tracing and explaining the development of Pakistan's culture of power and its impact on governance.

In spatial terms the study is multi-focal. The effort is to examine those areas of the country where changes affecting Pakistan's culture of power and governance took place. Thus, examples from East Bengal/East Pakistan, the centre, and the other provinces are drawn upon to carry the narrative and interpretation forward. Within this a serious limitation, which is in part reflective of Pakistan's culture of power, is that the central government and state apparatus are preeminent. Thus, the seat of government and administrative power occupy a spatially dominant position. Even at the provincial and local levels administration and politics are defined with reference to the centre under both democratically elected and undemocratic regimes.

In structural terms the scope of the study is primarily limited to the executive function. This limitation is not particularly constrictive as the executive function accounts for about nine-tenths of the state's activities. Thus, within the executive functions the leadership, civil service, military, justice system, financial administration, local government and the rise and growth of corruption, are singled out for examination. The study is not as concerned with the intentions, policy statements, and rhetoric of reformers and politicians, as it is with the actual performance, structure, ethos and culture of power of the Pakistani state from 1947 to 2008.

SIGNIFICANCE OF THE STUDY

There is perhaps no human activity that has the ability to have greater positive or negative effect on the psychological and material conditions of life than governance.[20] Appreciating how and why we were and are governed is vital to the improvement of the quality of life. In continental bureaucratic empires the servants of the state determine in large measure the quality and effectiveness of governance. The executive function builds infrastructure, maintains order, collects taxes, assigns rights in land, regulates capital and labor, provides agricultural subsidies and even legislates by ordinance and exercises magisterial and quasi-judicial powers in many cases. It accounts for nine-tenths of the state's activities, past and present and thus the executive function determines more than any other the credibility of the state as a whole in continental bureaucratic states such as Pakistan. The internal discipline, organisation and quality of this function are of central importance to governance and the overall wellbeing of society.

For instance, in order to reduce carbon emissions to prevent or mitigate global warming, a state must employ inspectors, supervisors, adjudicators, statisticians, record-keepers, secretaries, technicians, training staff and general administrators. Since controlling carbon emissions involves regulation of motorised vehicles and factories, enforcement falls to the area administration. If the enforcement staff is recruited with little reference to their competence, paid poorly, given powers to fine violators and register cases under laws and are promoted and transferred whimsically, the state will have merely added another layer of corruption, venality and inefficiency. It will have also wasted taxpayers or borrowed money and not achieved much on the ground. Merely passing laws in the local, provincial, or national assemblies, or judicial activism, or civil society staging protests, however well-intentioned, will not, to continue with our example, lead to the enforcement of pollution controls on carbon emissions.

A state is part cognition, part organism and part machine. There is a chain of cerebral, organic and mechanical reactions that needs to occur in order to translate any policy or law, be they for mass murder or the protection of animal rights,[21] into effects felt on the ground. This study's significance is that it dissects, describes, and explains the functioning of the cognitive-biomechanical apparatus of Pakistan. Any serious attempt to try and reform governance in Pakistan or other developing countries must take into consideration the history, culture, and ethos of the state apparatus. Unfortunately, reforms have centred either on politics and development planning or such trivial curiosities as youth parliaments and gender sensitisation seminars that serve to waste taxpayers' money or borrowed funds that mortgage future generations. The exercise of state power is an existentially serious activity, perhaps the only one that requires wisdom, strength, and good fortune, including the wisdom and strength to take advantage of good fortune in preparation for harder times, in equal measure. By explaining the exercise of state power in Pakistan it is hoped that the present study will generate further research on the subject and lead to greater understanding of our collective and worsening predicament which, in turn, is a necessary prerequisite for its amelioration.

METHODOLOGY

The present study tries to deal with facts and patterns of behavior and the structures that modify them when people are placed in positions of power. Consequently, the approach adopted is primarily analytical with a strong element of interpretation. In trying to provide a rational explanation of a widely felt phenomenon that has touched almost everyone's life in Pakistan, this study is oriented towards explaining 'why' things are the way they are in the context of Pakistan's culture of power and governance.

There is also a strong quantitative component within the main narrative, especially in sections that cover the financial administration, corruption, or in some cases the justice system. It is particularly useful to trace the rise in the growth of corruption, for instance, in the public perception through surveys past and present carried out by the state as well as non-government agencies. It also helps to quantify the costs of corruption and wastage on the national finances or bring home the amount of time wasted in delay, indecision, and inefficiency by the criminal justice system. These facilitate the task of explaining the price Pakistan has paid for its crisis of governance and the arbitrary culture of power that holds sway over the apparatus, its political masters, and ordinary citizens. Together, the employment of qualitative and quantitative methods work to reinforce the narrative and help guide the interpretation and explanation of events and behavior that is the study's major objective.

REVIEW OF THE LITERATURE AND SOURCES

The major sources upon which this study draws include the declassified cabinet record held by the National Documentation Centre and Cabinet Secretariat Library in Islamabad, private papers, interviews, state reports and publications, as well as memoirs, books and academic studies. An important drawback in the published sources about Pakistan is that their focus is primarily on politics or policy and the sources upon which they are themselves based are the public statements and posturing of important players.[22] When it comes to memoirs or other 'first hand' accounts practically all of them engage in self-justification and generalise from personal experience. It is interesting to contrast their perspectives with the official record or with assessments made by the commissions and committees constituted to submit reports on the administration during their periods of association with the political executive. For instance, there is a general tendency amongst the civil servants and military officers to idealise the Ayub Khan period and denigrate the Bhutto era.[23] They also tend to focus on politics and rarely try to explain the underlying causes of the state's behavior hanging on to much of the information that makes them privileged insiders.[24] Others, such as Mubashir Hasan, blatantly try to transfer the responsibility onto others by arguing that they never had power to begin with.[25] What is intriguing about Mubashir Hasan's assertion is that there was probably no civilian government other than Jinnah-Liaquat Ali Khan which wielded greater power than the Bhutto regime from 1971-1977. Every aspect of national life, from the nationalisation of services and industries to the drastic administrative changes and purges of the bureaucracy, indicate that the civilian government of which Mubashir Hasan was a prominent member (finance minister) wielded very real power.

Between the history of politics and the politics of history[26] little effort has been made to explain the actual behavior of the state apparatus and the structures through which power has been exercised in Pakistan. What has been attempted is by way of 'development' or 'democratic' change/ transformation and is heavily influenced by American patronage and tutelage. Thus, for instance, *The Post-Colonial State and Social Transformation in India and Pakistan, Pakistan Authoritarianism in the 1980s* and *Politics and the State in Pakistan* remain content with an analysis of policies and politics.[27] There is some attempt in the latter to probe beneath the surface, but the broad thrust is towards contextualising the state in a political framework. A core problem with the academic discourse in and about Pakistan is that it seems to take the Second World War as the starting point and the post-colonial state is interpreted in light of received wisdoms such as democracy, economic development, national security,[28] and other devices churned out by American-financed academic industries. Even those who oppose this trend do so from a Marxist or Islamist perspective and are thus also the recipients of tutelage. This is understandable but as it is subsequently demonstrated the impact these alien discourses have had on the ability of the state to think and act rationally has been tragic. Related to this is failure to grasp continuities amidst change, exceptions such as Mohammad A. Qadeer's *Pakistan: Social and Cultural Transformation in a Muslim Nation* notwithstanding, or appreciating the role of the state, as opposed to politics, in historical process.[29] While researching Pakistan's culture of power the official record was found to be immeasurably more helpful than the published sources. Therefore, while appreciating the perspective and insight of other writers this dissertation relies primarily on the declassified record. It may also be fit to mention that many of the earlier writers on Pakistan's politics did not pay much attention to the structure or ethos of the administrative institutions.

In terms of the National Documentation Centre holdings the entire declassified record on governance has been consulted and is included in the Bibliography and Sources. In addition to these files some fifty important reports and summaries on different aspects of the state apparatus have been consulted from the Cabinet Secretariat Library and the National Documentation Centre. Since this study is addressed to public servants and academics in Pakistan great care has been taken to ensure that the inferences drawn are grounded in the official record of the state itself. This serves the added research purpose of revealing the self-perception of the rulers and their diagnostic abilities even as it sheds light on their inability to act effectively to retrieve the situation. It is hoped that this study by bringing forward such a large concentration of primary sources, many of them never used before and certainly not in such abundance, will stimulate interest and further inquiries. For example, one of the most remarkable insights into the intellectual potential of the Pakistani elite is S. K. Dehlavi's 'Report on the Administrative Law & Courts in England, France, Germany, Switzerland, Italy, Holland, Belgium, Sweden & Spain.'[30] In a period of about four months a Pakistani generalist administrator produced a report of immense complexity on an ostensibly technical issue in a lucid manner and successfully addressed the development of executive accountability in Europe on a continental scale. In the course of the report the role of executive legislation in England in undermining parliamentary power and the neatly compartmentalised theories of rule of law, administrative law and the Council of State in France, as well as the efforts made with greater or lesser success in other European countries to make the administrative institutions, i.e. the executive function, accountable before the rule of law are discussed.[31] The report also compares favourably with the works produced by foreign consultants on Pakistan and falls in the same category as the landmark 1986 report submitted by the committee constituted by the government to study corruption or the papers and summaries prepared between 1981 and 1985 by the Establishment Division. It shows that *if* an effort had been made early on Pakistan could have developed an autonomous and rational understanding of its predicament.

The background sections within the narrative for the British Empire in India are based upon sources consulted at the School of Oriental and African Studies (SOAS) library, the Senate House Library and the British Library (BL) in London. These libraries were consulted thanks to the sponsorship of the Charles Wallace Fellowship Trust for Pakistan in the summer of 2006. Published translations of classical texts on statecraft and administration and a diversity of scholarly inputs on other cultures and civilisations have also been utilised.

Some of these include well-known published primary sources such as the *Jinnah Papers*[32] or the *Transfer of Power* volumes,[33] the *Arthashastra* and *Ain-i-Akbari* and more recent works such as *Corruption and the Decline of Rome*,[34] *Identity and Violence*,[35] and *Indian Summer*.[36] In terms of the historical discipline this study is inspired and affected by a large number of works of macro-history that do not necessarily find their way into the main text or references. Perhaps the most significant of these are by Ferdinand Braudel and include *A History of Civilizations*[37] and the capitalism trilogy comprising *The Structures of Everyday Life*, *The Wheels of Commerce*, and *The Perspective of the World*.[38] Other important influences include C. A. Bayly's *The Birth of the Modern World*,[39] Arnold J. Toynbee's *A Study of History*,[40] and Quentin Skinner's historical study of humanism and neo-Romanism in early modern Europe titled *Visions of Politics*.[41]

CHAPTER OUTLINE OF THE STUDY

In addition to the Introduction, Conclusion and Bibliography and References, the present study is divided into seven chapters:

- **Chapter One: Imperishable Empires**, provides the historical background to the present study and traces the rise and fall of

major continental bureaucratic empires in the subcontinent as well as their contribution to the culture of power of the region.
- **Chapter Two: Original Sins** examines the first few years of Pakistan's independence and identifies some of the critical fissures that opened up. It also highlights the decline of the political leadership and the rise of a governing corporation of civilian and military officials.
- **Chapter Three: Mandarins** is essentially about the civil service and higher bureaucracy in Pakistan. The mandarins were the officials who ruled imperial China and were recruited through a competitive examination. They provided the state with its bureaucratic leadership and served the emperor not only as administrators but also as political agents, governors and conciliators. In many respects they resembled in ethos, corporate profile and influence, the higher bureaucracy of Pakistan, especially its civil service component from 1953 to 1969. As the civil service was the premier institution of the British Empire in India and, relative to the other institutions inherited by Pakistan, it was the best developed, its performance is of great relevance to the quality of governance.
- **Chapter Four: Praetorians** is about the military and its role in providing leadership to the state apparatus. The Praetorians were the elite imperial guard of the Roman Empire and were stationed outside Rome after the fall of the republic in 27 BC. After the succession of competent emperors ended in AD 180 the imperial guard assumed political control. This chapter also examines how Pakistan's senior military commanders have perceived the state and its administration and identifies the characteristics of the Pakistani praetorian's mindset. It also studies the impact of military interventions on the administration of the country and the role that it has played in Pakistan's administrative decline.
- **Chapter Five: Guardians** is about the justice system in Pakistan with particular emphasis on the higher judiciary and the police. It examines how the Pakistani state apparatus has discharged the principal function of maintaining law and order.
- **Chapter Six: *Diwans*** is about the financial administration of Pakistan. The *diwans* were the senior revenue officials in pre-British India and exercised tremendous power often independently

of the governors. In this chapter the nature of tax collection in Pakistan, the quality of the institutions that collect the state's revenues, and their impact on the overall performance of the state, are addressed.

- **Chapter Seven: Grand Seigneurs** addresses the role of corruption in Pakistan. The term Grand Seigneur was used by Europeans to refer to the Ottoman Sultan. One of the facets of the Ottoman statecraft that impressed the Europeans as being very different from their own experience of governance was that the sultan was the proprietor of the entire empire. From this difference in principle flowed differences in attitude, administrative structure and public ethos. A peculiar feature of this ethos was that away from the emperor's watchful eye, his officials in their more limited capacities imitated their master's propensity to treat the state as personal estate. This chapter examines the proprietorial attitude of Pakistan's rulers and public officials towards the state and the impact that this has had on the effectiveness and credibility of the state. It also examines the public perception of corruption and tries to quantify the costs of corruption in Pakistan.

NOTES

1. For a more thorough treatment of the culture of power of the subcontinent as a whole see Ilhan Niaz, *An Inquiry into the Culture of Power of the Subcontinent* (Islamabad: Alhamra, 2006; Second Edition, 2008).
2. One of the major underlying themes of human history has been that '...the difficulty of framing autonomous states on one ethnic basis, against the gravitational pull of cultural or economic attraction (as well as disparities of military force) has been so great that empire (where different ethnic communities fall under a common ruler) has been the default mode of political organisation throughout most of history. Imperial power has usually been the rule of the road.' John Darwin, *After Tamerlane: The Global History of Empire since 1405* (London: Penguin Books, 2007), 23.
3. One of the most expansive and successful of these empires was Achaemenid Persia (c.600 BC-300 BC). At its height it was organised into twenty satrapies each required to remit a predetermined tribute to the central government. One of the most important sources of revenue was the gold submitted by the Indian territories of the empire. This sprawling dominion controlled, directly or indirectly, territory stretching from the Indus to the Sahara. It was held together by the imperial army, royal slaves, and a remarkable system of intelligence and communications. The

physical manifestations of the Persian communications system were the couriers and their resting places that dotted the imperial highways. Herodotus immortalised the imperial servants who acted as the empire's central nervous system: 'Nothing mortal travels so fast as these Persian messengers...Along the whole line of road there are men stationed with horses, in number equal to the number of days which the journey takes...these men will not be hindered from accomplishing at their best speed the distance which they have to go, either by snow, or rain, or heat, or by the darkness of night.' Herodotus, *Histories*, trans. George Rawlinson (Hertfordshire: Wordsworth Editions, 1996), 649. Thousands of years later, in Pahlavi Iran (1925-1979), the Shah of Iran's dreaded secret police, SAVAK or the *Sazman-i-Etelaat va Amjiniat-i Keshvar* (National Information and Security Organisation), employed some sixty thousand officials out of a total state bureaucracy of seven hundred thousand and counted as much as one-third of the adult male population as its informers. Robert Fisk, *The Great War for Civilisation: The Conquest of the Middle East* (London: Harper Perennial, 2006), 120-1.
4. For the most part the terms 'royal servant', 'imperial servant', 'the ruler's servants' or 'servants of the state' are used to refer to what would today be called bureaucrats or public servants.
5. The transition from tribalism and chiefdoms to continental bureaucratic empires was driven by demographic growth, competition for resources, and the need to organise for defense and environmental control. The Sumerian *en, ensi* and *lugal*, Egypt's pharaohs, and China's kings and emperors were thus '...distinct from the chiefs who went before them in their capacity to make laws and to command a bureaucracy.' Geoff Mulgan, *Good and Bad Power: The Ideals and Betrayals of Government* (London: Allen Lane, Penguin Books, 2006), 18. Most of these 'early states' behaved 'like criminal enterprises' and were driven by hunger for arable land, women, slaves, and precious metals and stones. Ibid., 18-19.
6. The Seljuk first minister Nizam al-Mulk Tusi elaborates numerous ways in which the ruler can use spies, reporters, slaves, and other agents to ensure proper supervision of tax-collectors and ministers, the proper training of secretaries and pages, and other officers of the state and slaves of the ruler. See Hubert Drake, trans., *The Book of Government or Rules for Kings: The Siyasatnama or Siyar al-Muluk of Nizam al-Mulk* (London: Routledge and Kegan Paul, 1960).
7. Mulgan, *Good and Bad Power*, 19.
8. The pharaohs had divided Egypt's arable land into units given to cultivators in exchange for rent which, in turn, was the state's principal source of revenue. Herodotus, *Histories*, 159.
9. Barry J. Kemp, *Ancient Egypt: Anatomy of a Civilisation* (London: Routledge, 2002), 111.
10. In Ancient Egypt, for instance, the Overseer of the King's Documents and the Overseer of the Grand Mansions (royal residences) were some of the most important high officials. The pharaoh depended on them to run the scribal state and manage his household. Nigel Strudwick, *The Administration of Egypt in the Old Kingdom: The Highest Titles and their Holders* (London: KPI Limited, 1985), 176, 181 and 199-201.
11. Herodotus provides a stimulating insight into the suffering that the construction of the Egyptian pyramids probably entailed. Cheops, the builder of the greatest

pyramid, is said to have shutdown the temples and imposed compulsory labor on the entire population. Approximately one hundred thousand laborers were organised to work in three-month shifts. The pyramid-building frenzy lasted over a century and left the world with some of its most inspiring ancient monuments. That said, 'The Egyptians so detest the memory of these kings that they do not much like even to mention their names.' Herodotus, *Histories*, 169-171.

12. 'The religious traits associated with kingship in a variety of global cultures are of course common, but none more so than the belief in the monarch as mediator between the social order and a higher cosmic superhuman reality.' W. M. Spellman, *Monarchies: 1000-2000* (London: Reaktion Books, 2001), 13.

13. The experience of the Arabs during their imperial period under the Umayyad (660-750) and Abbasid (750-1258) dynasties is a case in point. In both cases the Arabs adopted the administrative practices and techniques of the continental bureaucratic empires they had defeated in war. By the mid-700s the Arab Empire had 'developed an impressive bureaucracy unlike any contemporary state in the Christian West....' The 'staff of salaried professional clerks (*kuttabs*)' were responsible for maintaining 'records of income and expenditure and lists of those who served in the army and their rates of pay. Furthermore, the clerks who worked in the offices (*diwans*) were all laymen....' This 'bureaucracy expanded even as the frontiers of the empire contracted, and by the beginning of the tenth century, against a background of chaos and disintegration, one of the clerks, Qudama ibn Ja'far (d. 948), produced a manual of administration which described the whole apparatus in exhaustive detail.' Hugh Kennedy, *The Court of the Caliphs: When Baghdad Ruled the Muslim World* (London: Phoenix, 2005), 35. The pillars of Abbasid power were the salaried military and civilian bureaucracy, much as had been the case with the Umayyads. Indeed, Abbasid rule 'looked very much like the Umayyad one it replaced, but with different people in charge.' Ibid., 21., The Umayyad state structure and culture of power were inherited or borrowed from the continental bureaucratic Sassanid Persian and Byzantine empires.

14. Michael Burleigh, *Earthly Powers: Religion and Politics in Europe from the Enlightenment to the Great War* (London: Harper Collins Publishers, 2005), 2.

15. Ibid.

16. George Orwell, writing in the *Observer* on 23 May 1943, reflected that '...if common ownership is ever established in Britain' it could never be of 'the continental Marxist type.' George Orwell, *Orwell: The Observer Years* (London: Atlantic Books, 2003), 13-14. Writing about Marxism in Russia on 15 February 1948, Orwell noted that Marx expected a numerically overwhelming proletariat overthrowing a small group of exploiters. In Russia, however, the communist revolution took the form of the 'seizure of power by a small body of classless professional revolutionaries' who proceeded to establish '...the dictatorship of a handful of intellectuals ruling through terrorism.' Ibid., 72-3. Those who overthrew the czar's autocratic rule were themselves products of an arbitrary, ideological, and proprietorial culture of power, and, if anything, the aggravated insecurities and pretensions of the revolutionary 'vanguard' made them far more arbitrary than the czars had ever been.

17. One of the 'terrible' paradoxes that utopian projects and the ideocratic delusions that sustain them is that 'the ardent and often sincere desire to combat evil' has

generated and does generate 'evil on a grander scale.' Philip Zimbardo, *The Lucifer Effect: How Good People turn Evil* (London: Rider, 2007), 9. Evil itself is linked to power and *'consists in intentionally behaving in ways that harm, abuse, demean, dehumanize, or destroy innocent others-or using one's authority and systemic power to encourage or permit others to do so on your behalf.'* Ibid., 5.

18. A contemporary example of such a corporation is the French Great Corps of the State recruited through the elite National School of Administration (for social sciences) and Polytechnic School (for the sciences).
19. The intermediate stage of which is sometimes described as *muluk al-tawa'if* or *parakandeh shahi*. That is rule by gangs or warlords with little effective central control. Michael Axworthy, *Empire of the Mind: A History of Iran* (London: Hurst & Company, 2007), 36.
20. Some of the most serious reflection on this aspect of social experience took place in eighteenth century France. Voltaire argued that the nature of government, religion, and education, in that order, determined the human condition. Montesquieu emphasized the role of the natural environment, while Rousseau argued that '...no people would be other than the nature of its government made it.' Henry Steele Commager, *The Empire of Reason: How Europe Imagined and America Realized the Enlightenment* (London: Widenfeld and Nicolson, 1998), 109-110.
21. Nazi Germany opted to do both. In his first few months as chancellor, Hitler 'signed no fewer than three separate laws providing for the protection and proper treatment of animals....' Andrew Roberts, *Hitler and Churchill: Secrets of Leadership* (London: Phoenix, 2003), 7.
22. Some examples of political memoirs include Ayub Khan's *Friends not Masters* (Lahore: Vanguard, 2000) and Sherbaz Khan Mazari's *Journey to Disillusionment* (Karachi: Oxford University Press, 1999). The former is from a position of authority the latter reveals the opposition perspective. Both are concerned with politics and leadership, not with an understanding of the state. The former is useful however for comprehending the military's perception of politics and administration especially when squared against the official record of the cabinet and the numerous commissions and reports of the period. Other important examples in the context of the military's understanding of politics and administration include; Khalid Mahmud Arif, *Working with Zia: Pakistan's Power Politics 1977-1988* (Karachi: Oxford University Press, 1995) and Gul Hasan's *Memoirs* (Karachi: Oxford University Press, 1993).
23. Roedad Khan, *Pakistan a Dream Gone Sour* (Karachi: Oxford University Press, 1997).
24. Sajjad Ali Shah, *Law Courts in a Glass House: An Autobiography* (Karachi: Oxford University Press, 2001).
25. Mubashir Hasan, *The Mirage of Power: An Inquiry into the Bhutto Years 1971-1977* (Karachi: Oxford University Press, 2000).
26. Lawrence Ziring, *Pakistan: At the Crosscurrents of History* (Lahore: Vanguard, 2004); Ian Talbot, *Pakistan: a Modern History* (Lahore: Vanguard, 1999); Rafique Afzal, *Pakistan: History and Politics 1947-1971* (Karachi: Oxford University Press, 2001), and Hamid Khan, *Constitutional and Political History of Pakistan* (Karachi: Oxford University Press, 2001), are some of the more recent additions to this genre.

27. S.M. Naseem and Khalid Nadvi, eds., *The Post-Colonial State and Social Transformation in India and Pakistan* (Karachi: Oxford University Press, 2002); Craig Baxter and Syed Razi Wasti, eds., *Pakistan Authoritarianism in the 1980s* (Lahore: Vanguard, 1991), and Mohammad Waseem, *Politics and the State in Pakistan* (Lahore: Progressive Publishers, 1989).
28. Veena Kukraja and M.P. Singh, eds., *Pakistan: Democracy, Development and Security Issues* (New Delhi: Sage Publications, 2006) is one of the many manifestations of the South Asian obsession with the fashionable and the inability of the academic elite to develop its own empirical categories for rational discourse.
29. One serious attempt to grasp the nature of continuity and change in Pakistan is Mohammad A. Qadeer, *Pakistan: Social and Cultural Transformation in a Muslim Nation* (London: Routledge, 2006). Qadeer emphasizes competing influences such as modernisation, indigenisation and Islamisation and observes that there are major disconnects in terms of an underdeveloped, if not regressive non-material culture, between the public and private spheres and imagined versus experienced culture. These disconnects have grown in part due to the failure of the state to maintain standards and order in practically every sphere ranging from education to law and order.
30. S.K. Dehlavi, 'Report on the Administrative Law & Courts in England, France, Germany, Switzerland, Italy, Holland, Belgium, Sweden & Spain' (Rome/Islamabad: Ministry of Foreign Affairs/Constitutional Commission, 1961).
31. Dehalvi observed that in Britain there had been a tremendous expansion in executive legislation through statutory rules and orders. In 1920, against eighty-two Acts of Parliament, there were eight hundred and twenty such executive orders. Ibid., 5-7. Taken along with the rapid growth of executive departments at the local and central levels the British state apparatus was for the most part only nominally under parliamentary control. In order to bring the system back under parliamentary control the British, in the late 1950s, were contemplating the introduction of administrative law on the French pattern. France, which had a vastly more developed executive function than Britain, had taken steps to bring its ever-expanding state bureaucracy under the rule of law relatively early in its modern history. One of Napoleon Bonaparte's greatest innovations was the Council of State, founded in 1799, to hear complaints against the administration and restrain the arbitrary exercise of executive power. Ibid., 28-29. The Council of State, which acted as an apolitical semi-judicial institution, had, over many years, accumulated great prestige. It influenced nominations and promotions within the civil service, checked political interference and punished officials who broke the law. It thus helped ensure that in spite of prolonged periods of political instability the French state continued to function efficiently.
32. Z.H. Zaidi, ed., *Quaid-i-Azam Mohammad Ali Jinnah Papers: Prelude to Pakistan, 20 February—2 June 1947*, vols. I-XV. (Islamabad: National Archives of Pakistan, 1993-2007).
33. N. Mansergh and E.W.R., Lumbey, eds., *Constitutional Relations Between Britain and India: The Transfer of Power*, vols. I-XI (London: Her Majesty's Stationery Office, 1970-82).
34. Ramsay MacMullen, *Corruption and the Decline of Rome* (New Haven: Yale University Press, 1988).

35. Amartya Sen, *Identity and Violence: The Illusion of Destiny* (New York: W.W. Norton and Company, 2006).
36. Alex Von Tunzelmann, *Indian Summer: The Secret History of the End of an Empire* (London: Simon & Schuster, 2007).
37. Ferdinand Braudel, trans. Richard Mayne, *A History of Civilizations* (New York: Penguin Group, 1995).
38. Ferdinand Braudel, trans. Sian Reynolds, *Civilization and Capitalism 15th-18th Century* (London: Phoenix Press, 2002-2003). One of the most sophisticated and balanced analyses that have emerged over the past century is that of the Annales school in France. The late Ferdinand Braudel, a leading exponent of this school, focused attention on mentality, and the persistence of continuity amidst economic change over the past five hundred years. One of the most important concepts is that of 'Worldtime' which 'might be said to concentrate above all on a kind of superstructure of world history: it represents a crowning achievement, created and supported by forces at work underneath it, although in turn its weight has an effect upon the base.' Ferdinand Braudel, *The Perspective of the World: Civilization and Capitalism 15th–18th Century* (London: Phoenix Press, 2002), 18. When one considers '…the great subcontinent of India: draw four lines-along the coast of the Coromandel, the Malabar coast, from Surat to Delhi and from Delhi to the delta of the Ganges. You have now enclosed India in a quadrilateral. Only the edges of this quadrilateral can really be said to have lived at the same pace as the outside world…Worldtime applied primarily to such axes of activity.' Ibid. Returning to the theme of continuity and change Braudel adds that '…a country develops because it is already developing, because it is caught up in a movement already underway which helps it. So the past always counts. The inequality of the world is the result of structural realities at once slow to take shape and slow to fade away.' Ibid., 50.
39. C.A. Bayly, *The Birth of the Modern World: 1780-1914* (Oxford: Blackwell Publishing, 2004).
40. Arnold J. Toynbee, *A Study of History*, abridged in two volumes by D. C. Somervell (New York: Dell Publishing Co., 1978).
41. Quentin Skinner, *Visions of Politics* (Cambridge: Cambridge University Press, 2002).

1 Imperishable Empires

1.1 Continental Bureaucratic Empires and the Culture of Power of the Subcontinent: Ancient India, 2000 BC–AD 1000

There is a strong probability that the Indus Valley civilisation was a continental bureaucratic empire.[1] The broad environmental conditions conducive to the emergence of hydraulic civilisations along the Nile and in Mesopotamia are found in the Indus region—aridity, plains bounded by natural obstacles such as mountains, deserts, and plateaus and a ready source of fresh water that doubled as a communications system.[2] The exploitation of this environment required the capacity to mobilise and organise labour on a large scale, a food distribution system, and a strong central authority. By 2250 BC this central authority appears to have exercised effective control over the hydraulic heartland of the Indus River Valley and exerted influence through commerce and diplomacy as far as the Oxus and northern India. Communications within the core territories of the Punjab and Sindh were waterborne. Larger than its contemporaries in Egypt and Mesopotamia, the Indus Valley civilisation manifests several signs of centralisation.

The most important is the Indus civilisation's urban development. In a much later scenario Ibn Khaldun emphasised that urban centres 'with their monuments, vast constructions, and large buildings' required 'united effort and much co-operation.'[3] Given the exertion and sacrifices required, people 'must be forced and driven to build cities.'[4] Either the 'stick of royal authority is what compels them' or 'reward and compensation' on such a large scale that only such an authority could furnish, are necessary.[5]

In the context of the Indus Valley civilisation, which covers an area that stretched from Gujarat to the Punjab with a presence as far as the Oxus and the Makran Coast of Balochistan in present-day Pakistan, the cities displayed a striking degree of uniformity. Each city drew upon an agricultural hinterland for food and resources. The production and distribution of these certainly involved scribal intervention on the Egyptian pattern. The regimentation, orderliness and size of the cities also point to the existence of a powerful central authority that operated through a class of appointed servants. These bureaucrats were presumably responsible for managing the agricultural cycle, maintaining order, collecting taxes and supervising large-scale construction activities such as fortifications, baths and granaries. The economic and social status of the bureaucracy corresponded to its power and privileges. The rulers of what is sometimes described as the Harappan[6] Empire, were possibly legitimated by a homogenising religion or ideology. Until, however, the writings of the Indus Valley civilisation are deciphered, we must confine ourselves to the statement that it was probably a continental bureaucratic empire that manifested substantially the same ideocratic and arbitrary culture of power as its contemporaries.

For the Aryan period evidence is more forthcoming. In the sixth century BC continental bureaucratic empires emerged in the Ganges river valley. Able to mobilise resources and manpower more effectively than tribal republics or petty chiefdoms, the continental bureaucratic empire outfought other less centralised and arbitrary forms of the state.[7] By the fourth century BC the Nanda dynasty had brought much of the northern plain under its control and fielded an army two hundred thousand strong. In or around 320 BC the Nandas were overthrown by their former army chief, Chandragupta Maurya, in collusion with Kautilya his wily councillor and other elements disaffected by Nanda oppression and harshness.

It is to Kautilya that posterity owes a remarkable and holistic account of the exercise of state power in Ancient India.[8] At the heart of the absolutist *Arthashastra*[9] State was the ruler who was advised 'A king can protect his kingdom only when he himself is protected from persons near him, particularly his wives and children.'[10] Few moral relationships could exist in this culture of power. Princes, compared to crabs, vipers, and fighting rams, are a great danger to the ruler and thus 'It is better to kill them quietly if they are found wanting in affection.'[11] Queens and other members of the royal household were to be kept perpetually under surveillance by spies.[12] All those with access to the king were considered covetous of his throne. This was perfectly understandable as the king was often a usurper and his arbitrary powers generated immense fear, resentment, and greed amongst his subordinates. As long as the king, who was 'the embodiment of the state,' employed 'without hesitation, the methods of secret punishment' against real or perceived enemies, the calculus of fear and greed produced servility.[13] The instant the royal resolve or capability to inflict punishment was perceived, accurately or inaccurately, to falter the same calculus produced rebellion.

The Mauryan ruler was the universal proprietor and 'The metropolitan area was under a highly centralised system of administration.'[14] The ordinary cultivator paid rent to the imperial treasury. The servants of the ruler were paid cash salaries and granted lands as revenue assignments. The official priesthood and other recipients of imperial largesse also received revenue assignments in land. Land was held by cultivators as long as they paid taxes and by imperial servants during their period of employment. The ruler owned or controlled hydraulic infrastructure, settled villages as insular caste-bound units, and maintained an excellent network of royal highways complete with state-owned caravanserais. Merchants laboured under the perpetual threat of confiscation, their trade regulated, their organisations subservient to the state, and their profits and prices fixed by bureaucrats.

The management of the sprawling Mauryan estate, which at its height stretched from Bihar to the Oxus, necessitated its division into administrative sub-units. The smallest unit was the village. Ten villages made a sub-district. Twenty sub-districts (two hundred villages), made a district. Two districts (four hundred villages) constituted a division. Finally, two divisions (eight hundred villages) made a province. Cities were organised into four divisions further divided into multiple wards. At the centre, some three dozen ministries and departments performed functions as diverse as the maintenance of order, tax collection, regulating trade and industry, espionage, prostitution and enforcing detailed rules and regulations for those who washed clothes for a living.[15] Every task was entrusted to a salaried bureaucratic hierarchy whose members were recruited, promoted, transferred or liquidated at the ruler's will with the *adhyakshas* or department heads answering directly to the emperor. Kautilya warns aspirants to official posts: 'Service under a King has been compared to living in a fire. A fire may burn a part of one's body and, at its worst, all of it; but a King may either confer prosperity or may have the whole family; including wives and children killed.'[16] Consequently, an intelligent officer makes 'self-protection his first and foremost concern.'[17] This goal was best achieved through complete obedience in action, word, emotion, and thought, for the royal presence in the form of spies was everywhere, sensitive to the slightest indications of dissent.

The effectiveness and grandeur of the state depended upon the intellect and work ethic of the ruler and his appointed servants. Of every twenty-four hours, the ruler was to spend separate ninety-minute periods to review reports on defence and finances, grant audiences, receive revenue and make official appointments, draft correspondence and consult with spies, inspect military forces, confer with his defence chiefs, manage secret agents, discuss matters of state with senior officers and appoint spies, respectively. In addition to these twelve hours of regular work, an additional six hours were devoted to secret deliberations and security-related matters. The ruler who stood at the heart of the *Arthashastra* bureaucratic machine was supposed to work eighteen hours a day and so set an example for his servants to follow.

It was in the ruler's own interest that his servants, absolute servility assumed, were recruited, transferred, and promoted on merit. Candidates for public office underwent tests of *dharma* (morality and law), *artha* (finance and worldly affairs), *kama* (recreation and aesthetics), and courage. A candidate who excelled at every test was appointed to the emperor's personal staff as a palace official. Those that excelled at morality and law received judicial, police, and district management postings. Demonstration of superior excellence in *artha* netted appointments in the financial administration. Success in recreation and aesthetics secured postings in the recreational establishment responsible for managing brothels, training musicians, and the like. Excelling in the test of courage was the path to the ruler's personal bodyguard and intelligence service. Candidates that failed every test retained hope, if the ruler so wished, of appointments in the departments of mines, forestry, elephants, or workshops.

Salaries ranged from forty-eight thousand *panas* (silver pieces) a year for the royal councillors, guru, priest, defence chief, crown prince, queen, and queen mother, to four thousand to twelve thousand *panas* a year for the bureaucratic middle order that comprised, among others, governors, auditors, and comptrollers, to three thousand to five hundred *panas* for a lower order that included district officers, brothel managers, local spies, and village headmen. Between the apex and the middle order was a grade of high palace officials paid twenty-four thousand *panas* a year. Beneath the officer grades subsisted an amorphous mass of petty clerks, runners, peons, and menial workers, all paid small but regular cash salaries. The civilian side of the apparatus was complemented by a vast standing military establishment estimated as high as six hundred thousand strong, organised on the same bureaucratic principles, and paid regular salaries.

Controlling this leviathan was no easy task. It was to sustain the state machinery that extensive economic controls had to be introduced lest the cost of living undermine the purchasing power of public sector salaries and encourage officers to abuse their authority. A system of regular correspondence between the palace and the districts combined with royal inspections enhanced the ruler's control of his servants. The most effective instruments of royal control were spies. Royal agents installed in covers as varied as senior officers, innkeepers, wandering ascetics and poison specialists disguised as cooks in the households of royal servants, reported to the king and his senior officers. The objective of the pervasive intelligence apparatus was not to prevent corruption. This was recognised as impossible given the size and complexity of the Mauryan Empire. Rather the aim was instilling in the hearts and minds of royal servants fear of their master's omniscience and omnipotence. In so doing, corruption (that is stealing from the sovereign) would be reduced and any adverse impact on the ruler's writ minimised.

The ideocratic complex of the Kautilyan continental bureaucratic empire comprised the familiar combination of an official religious establishment and a bureaucratic intelligentsia. The ruler assumed the mantle of divine sanction and thus tongues that committed sacrilege and treason by speaking ill of him were to be ripped from their indiscreet owners' mouths. Religious ceremonies imbued the ruler and his servants with an aura of cosmic significance, as did the employment of *pandits* (learned Brahmins) in the judicial service.[18] In the districts and cities holy men, gurus and tricksters, all on the royal payroll, projected the ruler's infallibility and divine attributes, and worked with spies, who found out and secretly punished the dissatisfied. When the last of the great Mauryan rulers, Ashoka, converted from Hinduism to Buddhism, the state religion also changed. However, while the rhetoric of the state changed, the structure of the ideocratic complex did not—a Buddhist bureaucratic intelligentsia and official priesthood were created.[19] The ideocratic complex continued to reflect the use of the ruler's arbitrary powers for self-justification and self-aggrandisement and while Ashoka was proclaimed the 'Beloved of the Gods'[20] the officers of *dharma* or *dharma-mahamattas* 'appear to have been powerful officers with special privileges, possibly fully aware of their role in propagating an imperial ideology.'[21] The hollowness of Ashoka's proclaimed pacifism and Buddhism is evidenced by the sequence of events:

> ...the greatest of the Mauryan emperors, felt remorse and adopted Buddhism *after* he had bloodily 'pacified' most of the subcontinent stretching up into Afghanistan, and was ensconced as the unchallenged *chakravartin* (the supreme hegemon), in other words, he renounced violence only *after* he had done away with all conceivable threats to himself and his realm.[22]

After the disintegration of the Mauryan Empire in the second century BC the subcontinent broke up into numerous kingdoms and principalities each governed on the principles of the Kautilyan continental bureaucratic empire. In the fourth century AD another great continental bureaucratic empire under the Gupta dynasty emerged. A series of wars brought much of the subcontinent under Gupta rule by the fifth century. The core of this empire was the old Maurya heartland. Its capital, Pataliputra, was the old Mauryan capital. The Gupta rulers proclaimed themselves god-kings, exercised universal proprietorship, and brought the country under the direct rule of their appointed servants distributed across the administrative sub-units of the empire. The key figure was the *visayapati* (district officer), who controlled rights in land and performed executive and judicial functions. Village headmen were official nominees and the state undertook extensive hydraulic projects to increase yields from agriculture and settle new villages on an insular caste basis. The state monopolised armed force, mobilised labour on a vast scale, minted currency in gold, and possessed an official priesthood and bureaucratic intelligentsia that mythologised the past, preached the virtues of obedience, and projected the ruler as a divine, infallible, being. After the Gupta Empire fragmented in the sixth century the new states that emerged modelled themselves on the same pattern regardless of size. From the smallest Rajput principality to medium-sized successor kingdoms, the same combination of universal proprietorship, militarism, reliance on appointed servants, and divine sanction, prevailed.

The continental bureaucratic empires of Ancient India manifested an ideocratic and arbitrary culture of power similar in many respects to continental bureaucratic empires in other parts of the world. The country was the personal estate of the ruler. The micro-management of this estate was entrusted to a complex and vast bureaucracy subject to the ruler's arbitrary will. An official priesthood and bureaucratic intelligentsia, both dependent on the ruler's favour for pay and privileges furnished the illusion of legitimacy. All wealth, status, and honour flowed from the ruler's will and could, therefore, be arbitrarily withdrawn. An extensive network of reporters, agents, and spies, kept the ruler informed and silently visited retribution upon those guilty of thinking, speaking, or acting, against the *chakravartin*. A large military establishment organised on bureaucratic principles stood at the ready to restore order, respond to emergencies, expand territorial frontiers, and punish rebellious tributaries.

Society was deliberately atomised by the state into sub-political, insular, caste-based units placed in direct contact with officers representing the overwhelming powers of the central state. The Mauryan state, for instance, 'took the precaution of keeping its peasants unarmed.'[23] Society responded with servility when the state was strong and with rebellion if the state was perceived to be weak.[24] Successful rebellion, however, led to anarchy and the rise of warlords and petty tyrants who were even more arbitrary, capricious, and unenlightened. The Indian society simply lacked adequate horizontal or vertical power associations capable of creating an organic political order when the external force of the imperial state dissipated. After many centuries of breakdown, an apathetic and brutalised society was, once again, brought under the direction of a *chakravartin*. The new order, however, was basically a replica of the old and endured only so long as the intellectual and moral qualities of the rulers remained high. This, however, was often the product of luck or circumstance and if the war of succession that often followed the death of a ruler failed to produce a competent heir, the state would fail and society would be left at the mercy of master-less, fragmenting, arbitrary, and remorselessly selfish, bureaucratic instruments. Kautilya warned that in the absence of a *chakravartin*, there was a real danger of a foreign invader successfully conquering the subcontinent and establishing an empire of his own. Six centuries after the fall of the Guptas, the Turks invaded a subcontinent convulsed by conflict and emerged as the supreme hegemonic element by the mid-thirteenth century.

1.2 Continental Bureaucratic Empires and the Culture of Power of the Subcontinent: The Delhi Sultanate, 1206-1526[25]

The Turks were a tribal people on the margins of civilisation that came into West Asia and North Africa as military slaves of the Arab Empire. In the mid-800s the Abbasid ruler, Mu'tasim, established an imperial guard 'a few thousand strong but tough, disciplined and devoted to their master' comprising only Turks.[26] By the late-800s AD the Turks established themselves as the ruling class of a fragmenting Arab Empire.[27] Like the Arabs before their imperial ascension, the Turks had no experience of ruling a bureaucratic state. Again, like the Arabs, once the Turks acquired power they quickly absorbed the ideocratic and arbitrary cultures of power of the continental bureaucratic empires that fell under their sway. At a more formal level this transition meant the adoption and practice of Ancient Persian conceptions of statecraft. It is perhaps no coincidence that the Turks identified more readily with Ancient Persian precepts than with those maintained by their former Arab masters. At any rate, the significance of Turkish assimilation into a Persianized culture of power was that before they ventured into the subcontinent they, like the states of the subcontinent, exercised power in the ideocratic and arbitrary manner common to continental bureaucratic empires.

The core organisational principle of the Delhi Sultanate was the universal proprietorship of the sovereign. The test of a sultan's strength was his ability to enforce his universal proprietorship. Ghiyathudin Balban, through a policy of terror and confiscation, brought his fellow slaves under control. Allaudin Khalji confiscated the properties of his predecessors' servants, converted their revenue assignments or *iqtas* into crown land, and confiscated all privately-held property, inclusive of charitable endowments and lands granted as gifts.[28] Similar acts of mass-confiscation characterised the reigns of later sultans. The inherited insularity, apathy, and atomisation of Indian society helped the sultans establish their arbitrary rule. Village headmen became the sultan's highway watchmen or were often forbidden from possessing arms or horses, kept in a sub-political role, and subject to beatings and confiscations. Property in the form of capital was similarly under the ruler's control. Leading merchants were compelled to live in the vicinity of the capital. A network of market superintendents, reporters, and spies regulated prices and profits, with violators punished mercilessly with torture and confiscation. The sultan owned his own manufacturing establishments that converted taxpayers' money into luxuries, such as robes of honour (hundreds of thousands of which were doled out each year), handicrafts, luxuries, and weapons. Merchants required official permits, licenses, and passports, and existed at the sufferance of the sultan and his servants.

The sheer size of the Delhi Sultanate meant that the ruler had to rely upon appointed servants to do his bidding. These servants, be they judges, tax collectors, military governors, or city magistrates, were granted *iqtas*, or transferable revenue assignments in land, in exchange for their services. The central government comprised a royal council, ministries for revenue, local administration and communications, war, and markets, plus departments for justice, agriculture, river navigation, canals, land clearance, subsidies, and the navy. The sultanate was divided into provinces, divisions, districts, villages, and urban areas, each administered through a hierarchy of appointed servants or local notables dependent on the sultan's favour.

Like Achaemenid Persia, the Delhi Sultanate made extensive use of slaves to fill administrative and military posts. Indeed, the first sultans were slaves themselves. In the early thirteenth century the sultan owned about fifty thousand slaves. By the late fourteenth century the sultan owned nearly two hundred thousand slaves. In addition to these slaves thousands of migrants from Persia, Central Asia, and the Arab world poured into the subcontinent seeking employment in the sultan's service. It was not uncommon for half or more of a sultan's high officials to have been born outside the subcontinent. Within the subcontinent, the sultans sometimes elevated people of meagre background to high offices. Slaves, being the property of the sultan, were often imported from abroad and also of humble origins, and so owed everything to their master. Moreover, as the slaves were equal to each other they sought to preserve that equality even if it entailed perpetuating their own servitude. Foreigners, often well-educated and from families with traditions of state service, were driven into the subcontinent by the Mongol advance or lured by the prospect of enrichment. Either way, they depended on the sultan for survival in their adopted home. The elevation of lower class or caste locals similarly guaranteed their dependence upon the ruler as it alienated them from their own groups and antagonised those with better pedigrees. The greatest advantage of this system was that the sultan's arbitrary power, if wielded effectively, could rapidly and without encumbrance operate through a bureaucratic elite that was talented, hardworking, and unquestioningly obedient. The greatest disadvantage was that the bureaucratic class was highly heterogeneous, atomised, lacked moral relationships, and, in the absence of a strong ruler capable of inspiring fear, simply fell apart into thousands of rival petty estates.

In order to maintain control of this estate the sultans had two formidable weapons at their disposal—the army and spies. As with the Mauryas, the size of the Delhi Sultanate's armies under competent rulers is estimated between three hundred thousand and six hundred thousand. Even if we accept the lower estimate, the cost of maintaining such a large standing armed force on fixed salaries placed immense strain on the economy. Like the Mauryas, the sultans used a combination of economic controls and regulations to keep prices and shortages in check. Unlike the Mauryas, the sultans did not appoint a permanent army chief and, instead, performed that role personally. Repeated failures of dynastic succession meant the territories of the Delhi Sultanate had to be re-conquered every two generations. When not engaged in re-conquest, the army expanded the frontiers of the sultanate and quelled internal rebellions.

Spies and reporters were used for a diverse range of functions. The most important was providing the sultan with an independent source of information. Regular reports coordinated by the postmaster general, were delivered through an impressive courier-relay system.[29] Ibn Battuta recounts how at Multan his party stopped for a routine inspection by the intelligence service.[30] Normally, the journey from Multan to Delhi took 'fifty days march but when the intelligence officers write to the sultan…the letter reaches him in five days' by the postal service.'[31] Besides regular reports, spies were employed in the households of the sultan's closest relations and senior-most officers, given undercover assignments in the administration and military, investigated the full extent of officers' assets, pried into household expenses of ordinary subjects, watched markets, and even wandered as beggars and mendicants. There prevailed an 'atmosphere of perpetual suspicion and distrust' in which 'spies and reporters poked their noses into everyone's private business.'[32]

The Delhi Sultanate was an eminently ideocratic enterprise. The ruler styled himself the Shadow of God and disobedience to him was equated with disobedience of the divine will. The punishment for speaking against the sultan was death. An official priesthood and bureaucratic intelligentsia paid from public funds and grants in land, dispersed across a country with an overwhelming Hindu majority, and thus abjectly dependent upon the sultan, provided him with adulation and the illusion of legitimacy. From the class of Muslim clerics and scholars were drawn the judicial officers (*qazis*) responsible for settling disputes unrelated to the administration. The sultan appointed the *qazis* and their decisions could be appealed to the sultan who changed, countermanded, or confirmed them as he saw fit. The sultan personally dispensed justice, as did his governors, according to their caprice. Many sultans pursued a policy of destroying Hindu temples and converting them into mosques, albeit with varied zeal. The idea was to humiliate the gods of the Hindus and so demonstrate that divinity was on the side of the sultans and their loyal servants. Elaborate and lavish court ceremonial, on the Ancient Persian pattern, complete with prostration and ground kissing, served to dramatize the distance between the ruler and his subjects, 'was highly artificial and reveals anything but a virile and healthy environment.'[33] By the mid-fourteenth century, Sufi orders were brought under the patronage and control of the state.

The Delhi Sultanate was a continental bureaucratic empire that periodically rivalled in extent and powers its Gupta and Maurya predecessors. The sultan was the universal proprietor, sanctioned by divinity, and operated through a hierarchy of slaves and servants. So long as the sultan was intelligent enough to wield the instruments at his disposal effectively his arbitrary sway prevailed. As soon as the ruler proved incompetent or indecisive he would be overthrown. If the period of disorder did not quickly produce a competent successor the central administration, which 'was practically the only unifying force in the country,'[34] collapsed and anarchy ensued. The sultan ruled only so long as he was successful:

> ...one little disaster, one chance defeat, and the whole fabric of the state broke down. Under such a scheme of government, the masses of people, already living in intellectual isolation, became ever more indifferent to the fortunes of their monarch and the political destiny of their kingdom.[35]

The culture of power of the Delhi Sultanate manifested the same arbitrariness, bureaucratisation, militarism, lack of trust within the ruling class, ideocratic delusion, perpetual surveillance, and contempt for private property as the *Arthasastra* State. The differences were in the formal organisation of the state, the dominant idiom, lifestyle, and rhetoric used by the rulers to convince themselves and others of their perfection. Like the Hindu rulers the sultans ultimately failed to heed Kautilya's warning of the presence of great outsiders. In 1526, a force of Chingezi Turks and disaffected Afghans under the leadership of Babur, including blood relatives of the incumbent sultan whose pharonic pretensions dwarfed his capabilities, defeated the decaying Delhi Sultanate. This inaugurated the Timurid, or, as it is more popularly known, the Mughal, empire.[36]

1.3 Continental Bureaucratic Empires and the Culture of Power of the Subcontinent: The Timurid Empire, 1526-1707

Though established in 1526, it took the Timurid Empire thirty-four years to emerge as the largest and most powerful of about twenty states in the subcontinent. From 1564 to 1591 the Indo-Gangetic plain was brought under Timurid rule and by the first decade of the seventeenth century the empire pressed with some success into the Deccan and peninsular India. When Akbar the Great (1556-1605) died, the Timurid Empire stretched from Kabul to Bengal and from Kashmir to the Deccan. Akbar's three great successors, Jahangir, Shahjahan, and Aurungzeb, provided a century of strong governments.[37]

In the classical tradition of continental bureaucratic empires the basic principle of the Timurid dominion was that the entire country was considered the personal estate of the ruler.[38] The sheer size of the estate meant that if the ruler wished to manage it without sharing power he would have to rely upon an imperial bureaucracy distributed across administrative sub-units. These sub-units, in the early 1600s comprised twelve provinces, one hundred divisions, and about three thousand districts. The imperial bureaucracy of the Timurids were known as *mansabdar*s or office holders, and the system through which they were recruited, promoted, transferred, and remunerated, was known as *mansabdari*. The *mansabdar*s were organised into a hierarchy of grades starting at twenty and going up to seven or ten thousand. Remuneration consisted of salaries and revenue assignments in land or *jagir*s. Given the rank of the officer, he maintained a specified number of heavy cavalry.

The size and complexity of the central financial administration and the wealth and privileges of the warrior-bureaucratic elite were almost without parallel. While in Persia and Turkey there was only one principal treasurer appointed to the royal court 'here in India, the amount of revenues is so great, and the business so multifarious' that twelve royal treasurers were needed to help the emperor manage his finances.[39] Each of the emperor's one hundred workshops had its own treasurer bringing the total to about one hundred and twelve in all.[40] In 1647, when the annual revenue of the empire stood at two hundred and twenty million rupees, the four hundred and forty-five *mansabdar*s of grade five hundred and above accounted for 61 per cent of total revenue, while the sixty-eight princes and nobles at the top accounted for some 37 per cent of total revenues.[41] When Yamin-ud-Daula, a prominent provincial noble based in Lahore, died in November 1641 and imperial officers took account of his possessions, his estate was assessed at twenty-five million rupees[42] inclusive of three million rupees in jewels, twelve and a half million rupees in cash, and three million rupees in jewels.[43] At that time, the Safavid Shah of Iran had an annual income of twenty-four million rupees.[44] Great wealth was also the source of great insecurity for the emperor was 'himself the heir of all the *Omrah*s, or lords, and likewise of the *Mansabdar*s, or inferior lords, who are in his pay.'[45] When an officer fell from royal favour or died his possessions were seized by the emperor's agents and confiscated. This practice was the logical outcome of the ruler being the 'proprietor of every acre of land in the kingdom, excepting, perhaps, some houses and gardens which he sometimes permits his subjects to buy, sell, and otherwise dispense of, among themselves.'[46] As transfers were frequent, and confiscation assumed, imperial officers extorted 'as much as they could from the peasantry without any concern for the economic future of the areas temporarily under their control.'[47]

Local notables, such as *zamindar*s, *chaudaries*, and even Rajput princes, were confirmed in their possession of land, served either as *mansabdar*s or under the direction of imperial officers and could be expropriated if they misbehaved. Merchants operated under numerous restrictions, were subject to arbitrary confiscation, and city magistrates appointed guild leaders. To protect themselves and secure better terms, many merchants sought the patronage of imperial officers in exchange for sharing profits. This protection racket was a lucrative source of illegal income for the warrior-bureaucratic ruling class who abused its powers to amass great trading fortunes.[48]

Controlling imperial servants and through them the country was no easy task notwithstanding the apathy and atomisation of society. The Timurids relied principally on their military machine to maintain order and collect taxes, one of the advantages of the *mansabdari* system being that it allowed for the dispersal and flexible use of military power. The size of the military establishment is, however, open to question. If we go by Abul Fazl's figures, the total numerical strength of the military, including the heavy cavalry, musketeers, royal guard, and auxiliaries maintained by local notables, comes to an incredible four million four hundred thousand.[49] Based upon these figures and the total revenue demands of the Timurid Empire, which amounted to between one-third and half of the Gross National Product, as many as twenty-six million people may have depended directly and indirectly upon the military for their livelihood and produced a fearfully strong military-agrarian complex.[50] In the royal stables, for instance, there were seventeen categories of servants.[51] Another estimate is that by the mid-seventeenth century the total number of paid soldiers was about one million.[52] Of these soldiers the emperor kept enough of the best troops in his own hands and those of the royal princes, and retained the most important *mansabdar*s at the imperial court. The general trend was that so long as the emperor was strong, rebellions by local notables, imperial servants, or disgruntled peasants, were crushed. Logic and a measure of enlightened self-interest dictated that the Timurid warrior-bureaucratic elite unite against their arbitrary overlord and gain a measure of personal and collective security.

This eventuality was prevented by the heterogeneous and alien nature of a ruling class that comprised Turks, Mongols, Uzbeks, Persians, Arabs, Rajputs, Marathas, Afghans, a smattering of Indian Muslims and a few exceptional Hindus. Turks, Persians and Afghans accounted for 60 per cent of the imperial higher bureaucracy between 1595 and 1678, Rajputs 13 per cent and Indian Muslims 13 per cent.[53] Many of the imperial officers were of mean origins and had been raised quite suddenly to high office, and were thus completely dependent on royal favour. Many were foreigners and lacked knowledge of local conditions. Even after experience was acquired, the system of regular transfers combined with the imperial bureaucracy's preference for living in the cities and sending agents and soldiers to collect revenue from *jagir*s, a process that can be described ineloquently but effectively as absentee-parasitic-bureaucratic-landlordism, ensured that the rulers remained strangers to the land they governed and looked down upon their subjects as intrinsically inferior creatures.[54] Intense rivalries between ethnic and religious groups meant that the rebellion or disobedience of one noble, or group, provided others the opportunity to gain their master's favour at the upstart's expense. Even a moderately intelligent ruler could manipulate the calculus of fear and greed to keep his demographically diverse apparatus in line. However much the imperial servants feared their master, they knew that if one of their own seized power he would assert his universal proprietorship and redistribute assets amongst his favourites.[55]

In 1560, for instance, when word got out that Akbar was upset with his guardian and tutor, Bairam Khan, 'all men turned their backs upon him and their faces towards the Emperor' in 'the hope of receiving dignities and *jagir*s suitable to their condition.'[56] About twenty years later, Akbar, having raised Khwaja Mansur, a former clerk in the imperial perfumery department, to the post of *diwan* (revenue minister),[57] threw him in jail upon receiving complaints of his pettiness and obstructionism.[58] After a while, Akbar relented and restored Khwaja Mansur to his ministerial post. Soon, letters fell into Akbar's hands indicating Khwaja Mansur was disloyal. His anger fanned by nobles dissatisfied with Khwaja Mansur, Akbar ordered his arrest and execution, which were immediately carried out. After the execution, Akbar decided to have his 'confidential servants' investigate the letters, which were proved to be forgeries.⁵⁹ Akbar 'regretted the execution' but didn't pursue the matter further.⁶⁰

Another vital instrument of control were 'confidential servants' or reporters, spies, informants, and secret operatives. Each district had its news-writer whose job it was to report everything of note that occurred in a district. At the centre, fourteen 'zealous, experienced, and impartial' imperial secretaries summarized reports, prepared accounts, handled routine correspondence, and performed other vital paper work.⁶¹ Away from the emperor's watchful eye, in the provinces and districts, the news-writers often opted for mutually beneficial collusion and concealment with local officers.⁶² One can imagine that diligent reporters were unpopular with the local governors and given the latter's military powers, exposed to considerable risks.

Spies and informers were thus necessary for providing the emperor with more reliable information. These agents were deployed to check the household expenditures of royal subjects, infiltrate the harems of nobles and report political and personal information, spy on the royal princes, check accounts, investigate cases, prevent rebellions or at least provide early warning, and report on military efficiency. The postmaster general acted as the head of the formal and informal system of correspondence carried by a courier-relay system. To be on the safe side, the Timurids employed spies to spy on other spies, known as *harkara*s. Pervasive suspicion meant ordinary subjects and state servants resorted to concealment and theft as and when possible. The former lived in studied indigence and buried their valuables in the ground and in wells. The latter spent lavishly and secretly hoarded ill-gotten wealth knowing that sooner or later it would be investigated and the emperor would confiscate the uncovered amount. So, the logic was, to steal so much that even if most assets were confiscated enough was left to maintain the family until another one of them became an imperial servant. Given the Timurid preference for fair-skinned foreigners, however, chances of imperial employment declined with each succeeding generation.

The ideocratic complex of the Timurid Empire consisted of an official priesthood and a bureaucratic intelligentsia. The state paid subsidies to religious establishments, regular stipends to religious scholars, and employed the Muslim priestly class as judges much as the Delhi Sultanate did. The ruler was divinely sanctioned and so to oppose him was blasphemous and treasonous. Although great attention has been paid to Akbar's infallibility decree and creation of a royal religious cult based on emperor and sun worship (*Din-i-Ilahi*), taking imperial rhetoric seriously obscures the underlying arbitrary power of the sovereign.[63] There was nothing new in the infallibility decree extracted as it was from a servile, cynical, and worldly official priesthood. Since ancient times the rulers of the subcontinent assumed the mantle of infallibility. The creation of a new religious cult or legitimating ideology was also not without precedent. Allaudin Khalji and Mohammed bin Tughluq contemplated founding religions. In ancient times, Ashoka changed the official religion, which subsequently alternated between Buddhism and Hinduism, depending on the ruler's personal inclination. That Akbar chose not to spread his religious cult beyond the military and bureaucratic elite does not alter the fact that, ultimately, it was his choice.

Akbar's successors drifted towards an increasingly orthodox ideocratic complex characterised by the wanton desecration of hundreds of Hindu temples, the culmination of this process was reached under the last great ruler, Aurungzeb who, like his predecessors, used religion for political ends and to cloak himself in an aura of divinity and infallibility. Part of this policy was to employ religious scholars and judges, normally at the base of the Timurid power pyramid, in financial and administrative posts. This led the lay nobles to bemoan the emperor's reliance on abjectly servile 'hypocritical mystics and empty-headed scholars.'[64] Much like the consultants and development experts that clog the arteries and numb the minds of continental bureaucratic empires in the developing world today, 'these men are selling their knowledge and manners for the company of kings' and 'to rely on them was,' and is, 'neither in accordance with the divinely prescribed path, nor suited to the ways of the world.'[65] Indeed, 'these men are robbers in every way' and '(As the saying is), the finances are given over to the Qazi and the Qazi is satisfied only with bribes.'[66] Lavish court ceremonials involved the circulation of tens of millions of rupees of gifts every year, and emphasised the ruler's universal proprietorship even as it legitimised bribery.[67]

Society's response to the Timurid imperial machine was even greater insularity and apathy. As the Timurid Empire extracted more resources out of a stagnant economic base in pursuit of military glory and monumental extravagance, flight from the land, concealment, and rebellions became more common. By the 1670s and 1680s there were indications that order in the vicinity of Delhi and Agra had begun to break down. The atomisation of society meant that when the external force holding the country together waned the results were anarchy, bloodshed and spiralling arbitrariness and confusion. The end came swiftly for the Timurid Empire. After Aurungzeb's death in 1707 the succession of competent rulers failed. Wars of succession and dislocation at the centre caused fragmentation, spread anarchy, and invited foreign invasions. By 1721 the central government ceased to be effective. In the 1730s and 1740s local officers carved out kingdoms for themselves. In 1764, the last vestiges of Timurid power vanished with the British victory at Buxar. The dynasty survived as British dependents until 1857 though its effective power barely encompassed the palace grounds at Delhi.

The Timurid continental bureaucratic empire is matched only by the Mauryas in terms of territorial extent and centralization. The rulers of this empire were the servants of the emperor, organised into a bureaucratic hierarchy recruited, transferred, and liquidated at the ruler's will. The ruler was also the universal proprietor and legitimised by his preferred interpretation of divinity. The bureaucratic classes also served as the academic elite while scholars and priests depended on imperial patronage. Within the Timurid omni-estate all wealth, status, and position, emanated from the favour of the ruler and his servants. To keep his flocks and shepherds in line, the emperor employed military coercion and espionage on a vast scale. The Timurid Empire, as its megalithic textual remains indicate, was essentially a government that operated by correspondence, remote decision, and, so long as the ruler was capable, outward respect for complex bureaucratic routine.

The arbitrary powers of the sovereign pre-empted moral relationships from developing even within the ruling family. The emperors' brothers, sons and relations revolted repeatedly. Akbar's son and successor, Jahangir, revolted and had Abul Fazl murdered. Jahangir's son, Khusrau, revolted against his father but failed, was imprisoned and three hundred of his partisans were impaled outside Lahore. Shahjahan's third son, Aurungzeb, who, in a series of campaigns, defeated and killed his fellow royal princes, imprisoned the aging emperor. Imprisonment and exile were the fates of Aurungzeb's own sons. In 1707, upon Aurungzeb's death, a war of succession failed to produce a competent ruler capable of living for several decades and the heterogeneous and conspiratorial nature of the imperial warrior-bureaucracy combined with the apathy of the ruled, caused the empire to fragment into hundreds of petty bureaucratic estates, exponentially increasing the levels of arbitrariness, mismanagement, corruption and insecurity. Eventually, out of the maelstrom of wars of Timurid succession a new power willing and able to unify the subcontinent emerged.

This new power was Britain, or, more precisely, the British East India Company. The British possessed a culture of power anomalous even by European standards that found formal expression in the State of Laws. After the British conquest of Bengal in 1757 it remained to be seen if the British culture of power so admired by Enlightenment thinkers such as Voltaire and Montesquieu, could reform the ideocratic and arbitrary culture of power of the subcontinent. The State of Laws and the continental bureaucratic empire were set to confront each other. Far more was at stake in this struggle than the future of India or the validity of philosophical liberalism. At stake was the idea of the alterability of the human condition in relation to the exercise of state power so central to the Enlightenment and the Revolution. After thousands of years history was about to offer a choice.

1.4 THE ANGLO-SAXON ANOMALY AND THE STATE OF LAWS

The environmental setting in which the State of Laws evolved was relatively poor, isolated, and quite literally, at the margins of civilisation. Britain lacked agricultural resources, and it was not until the Roman conquest of the first century AD that civilisation reached its shores. Till the Roman withdrawal three centuries later, Britain was governed as an imperial province. After the barbarian invasions of the fourth and fifth centuries, which brought the Anglo-Saxons to Britain from Germany, the island was overrun and descended into chaos. It took more than four centuries and the threat of Viking attack for the Anglo-Saxon nobles to realise the necessity of some form of central leadership. Under Alfred the Great (871-99) the country was governed with the advice and consent of the *witena gemot* (council of the wise) and the *folkmoot* (semi-annual gathering of freemen).

The successful Norman invasion of England in 1066 resulted in the establishment of military feudalism and a strong monarchy. The Norman rulers dispersed the Anglo-Saxon aristocracy and replaced it with nobles from Normandy. These nobles were considered tenants by the ruler and owed him military service which, if not properly fulfilled, could result in the confiscation of their lands. An important feature of the Norman system that militated against the ruler's universal proprietorship was that the estates were normally held for life and stood to be inherited by the eldest son. The Norman nobility also maintained order, dispensed justice, and collected taxes, from their estates. Over time, the Norman nobility developed a strong proprietary interest, made long-term investments in developing trading centres and towns on their own initiative, secured a local power base, and, through marriage and enculturation, ceased to think of themselves as foreigners. Royal focus, distracted by continental entanglements ranging from relations with the French monarchy to the Crusades, failed to fathom accurately the growing power of what soon became an Anglo-Norman aristocracy.

The attempts made at circumventing the power of the aristocracy by rulers like Henry II (1154-1189) actually decreased their own arbitrary powers over the long-term. For example, Henry II constituted royal courts that administered the Common Law assisted by juries of twelve freemen. His objective was to draw litigants away from the manorial courts. The Common Law judiciary, however, became one of the champions of a limited monarchy. Later attempts to manipulate judicial power in order to enhance royal control, such as the Nottingham Declaration and crisis precipitated by Richard II (1377-1399), the High Commission employed by James I (1603-1625) and the Court of the Star Chamber used by Charles I (1625-1649) to enhance royal power by intervening against aristocrats in their disputes with peasants, ended in defeat for the monarch. Indeed, royal efforts to use the judiciary were an admission of executive weakness and indicated the absence of centralised means of administrative control.

If circumvention proved futile, confrontation brought disaster. Practically all attempts by the executive to impose centralised control failed and actually provoked important groups to establish autonomous institutions, most famously the Lords and the Commons, to deter further efforts. In 1215, for instance, King John tried to compel his nobles to join a royal expedition to re-conquer Normandy, which was lost to France in 1204. In order to finance the expedition King John vigorously collected taxes, imposed fines, and abused his powers of escheat and wardship. He also relied on favourites from Normandy and raised a mercenary army which, complemented by feudal levies, was to invade Normandy. The aristocracy, wary of the king's grasping and arbitrary ways, and fearful of what might happen if the army were turned upon them, rebelled. They managed to catch the king off-guard and extracted from him the Great Charter (*Magna Charta*) of 1215.

This charter limited the powers of kings in important areas. The king could not interfere in property-related matters. The appointment of local officials was formally entrusted to the local governments dominated by the aristocracy. Free subjects could not be arbitrarily thrown in jail and had the right to trial by jury. Additional taxes and customs could not be levied on towns and cities and their privileges and exemptions were confirmed. The king could not demand additional funds beyond those derived from the royal lands without the consent of the lords and the higher clergy. Mercenaries were to be disbanded and foreign favourites sent home. The state, in other words, was not the personal estate of the ruler. Lawful opposition was possible, even expected, should the king try to govern the country as his personal estate. The law 'was an independent power,' an autonomous institution, to which the ruler was accountable.[68]

Between 1215 and 1688, the monarchy, the Church, the Lords, the Commons and the judiciary, engaged in a complex struggle for power. While the alignment of these institutions changed, broadly speaking, the parliamentary and judicial institutions overcame the executive and ecclesiastical combination. At a cognitive level the State of Laws rested on the twin realisations that 'There is no liberty, if the judiciary power be not separated from the legislative and executive'[69] and 'If the legislative power was to settle the subsidies, not from year to year, but forever, it would run the risk of losing its liberty, because the executive power would no longer be dependant.'[70]

Our survey thus far has indicated that the broad direction of historical development favoured the emergence of continental bureaucratic empires. Variations in organisation, sources of power, and social responses reflected differences in degree. The main characteristics were, and are, nearly everywhere the same. A fundamentally different form of the state and with it a very different culture of power did emerge on the margins of the civilised world. This state was the State of Laws. The culture of power of this State of Laws was characterised by the existence of lawful and effective means of defying the sovereign, the prevalence of autonomous institutions, the rule of law, and private property. The soil in which this anomaly grew was England and, eventually, her overseas dominions of settlement. Alexis de Tocqueville, a contemporary of the Marquis de Custine[71] who travelled in the opposite direction to the United States found,

> The English colonies—and that was one of the main reasons for their prosperity—have always enjoyed more internal freedom and political independence than those of other nations; nowhere was this principle of liberty applied more completely than in the states of New England.[72]
>
> ...All the general principles on which modern constitutions rest, principles which most Europeans in the seventeenth century scarcely understood and whose dominance in Great Britain was then far from complete, are recognised and given authority by the laws of New England; the participation of the people in public affairs, the free voting of taxes, the responsibility of government officials, individual freedom, and trial by jury—all these things were established without question and with practical effect.[73]

Each of the laws and mores identified by de Tocqueville were brought over from England. In England, however, aristocratic and class privileges placed limits on the representative principle. In the dominions of settlement where no such feudal undergrowth existed the result was faster movement towards greater representation and self-government. It was not until the twentieth century that England made the final transition from aristocratic liberalism to representative democracy as practiced in its dominions of settlement.

Most notions of constitutionalism, civil liberties, and the rule of law, are derived from the historical experience of governance of the English and their dominions of settlement. Through the medium of the British Empire aspects of the State of Laws were exported to many parts of the world. British prosperity and military superiority were admired and envied by many in the bureaucratic states of continental Europe. Some of these continental bureaucratic empires attempted sincerely but with limited success, like France and liberal-conservative Italy in the nineteenth century, to incorporate some of the habits and practices associated with the State of Laws. Others, like Bismarck's Germany, were cynical and created a representative façade to obscure despotism. Some states, like Russia, openly held the State of Laws in contempt and resisted all attempts to share power with the executive. One of the greatest challenges to the State of Laws as a historical phenomenon came in 1757 with the advent of the British Empire in India after the East India Company defeated Nawab Sirajud Daula of Bengal at the Battle of Plassey and established indirect rule through puppets. India, however, had long been governed by continental bureaucratic empires. It was also too densely populated to become a dominion of settlement along the lines of Canada and Australia and in spite of domestic pressure the British authorities did not encourage emigration to India as a matter of policy.

1.5 CONTINENTAL BUREAUCRATIC EMPIRES AND THE CULTURE OF POWER OF THE SUBCONTINENT: THE BRITISH EMPIRE IN INDIA, 1757-1947

As the ascent of the British Empire in India through craft and coercion to supremacy has already been dealt with exhaustively in other sources, we limit our survey to those indicators most relevant to the continental bureaucratic empires and their ideocratic and arbitrary cultures of power. It was not inevitable that the remorselessly avaricious rule of the East India Company in Bengal would be brought under parliamentary regulation. The constitutional problem with such intervention, the horror stories and enriched 'nabobs' emanating from Bengal aside, was that the Company was a chartered body. Consequently, the Company had a lawful sphere of autonomy ceded to it by the sovereign that could not be arbitrarily interfered with. Even as evidence mounted of criminal incompetence and rampant corruption between the conquest of Bengal in 1757 and the first regulation acts a generation later, the Company's chartered status protected it. The British State of Laws was full of chartered bodies such as the hundreds of privately owned turnpike trusts that built and operated the country's road system to the City of London. Parliamentary power and legitimacy originated in the Great Charter of 1215 that was reissued thirty-eight times. An attack on the lawful autonomy of the Company would rouse other chartered bodies to rally to its defence to protect a legal principle from which, arguably, their liberties and that of the country at large, were derived. Fortunately for the Company's Indian subjects, the costs of fighting wars combined with manifest administrative ineptitude brought the Company to the verge of bankruptcy. In 1772, the Company's liabilities, at nine million pounds, far outweighed its assets, estimated at five million pounds. Parliamentary intervention took place in the context of the Company's request for public funds to avert collapse. In exchange for a bail-out, the government received regulatory powers that created a governor-general, a council of officials appointed by the British cabinet, and a reduction of the annual dividend from 8 to 6 per cent.

Under the new framework Warren Hastings, a company official with decades of experience in India, became the first governor-general (1774-85). Hastings, an aspiring *chakravartin*, was primarily concerned with making the Indian tradition of arbitrary rule effective and expanding the Company's territories. Like other Indian rulers, he amassed a considerable personal fortune, patronised scholars, and used whatever means necessary, including extortion, to maximise his powers. His relationship with his council was, at best, ambivalent, and very often hostile. With the Supreme Court at Calcutta, constituted by the Bengal Judicature Act of 1781, and initially headed by his class fellow and friend, Justice Impey, Hastings had a better relationship. Hastings's tenure was important in two respects as far as the culture of power is concerned.[74] The first was that after Hastings the post of governor-general went almost exclusively to British aristocrats and reflected the realisation that continental bureaucratic empires can only be governed from the palace—the counting house mentality being utterly ill-suited.[75] Having said that, few in England understood the problems Hastings faced 'in constructing the framework of civil administration from want of local knowledge, from the inefficiency of a refractory and corrupt Civil Service, and the venality of native officials.'[76] The second was in part a consequence of this lack of understanding and entailed Hastings's impeachment in a trial which dragged on for nine years.

On 4 April 1786, Hastings was charged with 'sundry high crimes and misdemeanours.'[77] If convicted, Hastings faced the death penalty. On 1 May, Hastings began his defence by asserting, only as an arbitrary ruler could, that his decisions were 'invariably regulated by truth, justice, and good faith' when the logical choice was to plead necessity of state and show some contrition.[78] On 1 July 1787, Edmund Burke, the leader of the campaign against Hastings, thundered: 'I impeach him in the name of the people of India, whose laws, rights, and liberties he has subverted, whose properties he has destroyed, whose country he has laid waste and desolate.'[79] Burke's impassioned plea on behalf of a collective ('The people of India') that did not exist, and of rights and laws and liberties that had no indigenous variant in India, must not obscure the 'nuggets of truth' in the accusations or the deeper implications of this rhetorical flourish.[80] The accusations were based on Hastings's arbitrary exercise of power and established the earthly accountability of the supreme executive. That such arbitrariness and excess were the norm in India did not matter. It was in principle wrong and every English officer of the Company was responsible for upholding the state morality of the British State of Laws whilst in India.

Actually doing so was the task of Hastings's liberal-aristocratic successor, Lord Cornwallis (1785-93). A product of the Enlightenment, Cornwallis believed that operating an efficient despotism on indigenous principles was morally and politically unacceptable as 'The principle of despotic government is subject to a continued corruption, because it is even in its nature corrupt.'[81] For Cornwallis 'the essence of the problem was to limit government power and so prevent its abuse.'[82] The judicial powers of the boards of revenue and collectors were taken away even though his closest advisors, such as John Shore, argued in favour of a strong district executive as the Indians 'being accustomed to a despotic authority should only look to one master.'[83] Secret inquiries were launched into the illegal activities of the Company's servants and despite the difficulties inherent in trying to prosecute white collar crime, by February 1787 the Advocate General was moving against the corrupt.[84] Cornwallis refused to exercise his discretion in order to favour candidates for official appointments simply because they were backed by the monarch or leading aristocrats.[85]

The sovereign ended his universal proprietorship and vested it in the local landlords, or *zamindars* in the hope that an aristocracy would gradually emerge. In each district of Bengal the district judge was given control of the police and received greater status and pay than the collector. The armed retainers of the *zamindars* were disbanded and Indians removed from offices of importance. Officers were discouraged from accepting presents and, if they were ever placed in a situation where they couldn't refuse, the gift was made over to the public treasury, and examples were made of corrupt officers. Cornwallis made it clear through word and deed that he did not see the country as his personal estate and that the government machinery and servants of the state were beholden to the law. The greater reliance on Europeans was justified on the grounds that Indian officials were greatly influenced by their superiors' character and competence and thus 'under an active collector of scrupulous integrity, all gross abuse of powers' was often prevented.[86] Cornwallis and his acolytes thought that by 'giving the landholders a permanent establishment in their possessions' a number of advantages would be reaped.[87] First, the landlords would secure 'the benefit of future improvement' and save and invest more wisely and so contribute to a general increase in the level of economic prosperity.[88] Second, the landlord would naturally contrast the security and assured importance granted by the British with their immeasurably more 'precarious' condition under Indian rulers.[89] Third, this would gain their attachment to British rule and provide it with a broader social base especially in the countryside. Cultivating the landed elite was vital given that it was dangerous to 'over-rate the advantages...from a favourable disposition on the part of the peasantry' which, in India, 'pass with the land from ruler to ruler, with scarcely any consciousness of the change.'[90]

To make the law more effective and clear, Cornwallis began the process of codification.[91] Cornwallis's successors, Sir John Shore (1793-1798) and Lord Wellesley (1798-1805), continued along the classical liberal trajectory by expanding the scope of property rights, leaving dispute settlement to the judicial power, and limiting the executive function to the bare minimum required to maintain order and collect taxes.

The Cornwallis system did not work as planned. The judicial power was too slow, alien, and expensive to be the central element of the administration. By 1824, there were nearly one hundred and twenty-four thousand cases in arrears in Bengal alone.[92] It took time for the British to realise that whereas back home the 'grandest and most expensive undertakings' could 'be left to individual enterprise or the excitement of public spirit', the 'opposite duty' fell upon their shoulders in continental bureaucratic empires such as India where an arbitrary culture of power had over centuries substantially crushed both.[93] Here it was expected that the rulers and their servants would provide the initiative, resources and organisation, necessary for 'the construction and maintenance of works of great public utility.'[94] Learning from Indian history, it was increasingly appreciated that its sovereigns had 'long been in the practice' of providing agricultural loans, manufacturing subsidies, building hydraulic and communications infrastructure, maintaining the intelligentsia, as well as ensuring order, collecting taxes, and defending the realm.⁹⁵ Continental bureaucratic empires, in other words, were ruled from palaces, not counting houses, and the ethos of leadership and management in such states were inspired by princely, not mercantile, values.⁹⁶ This was a point that Wellesley asserted with effect when he argued that the East India Company's officials 'could no longer be considered as the agents of a commercial concern' and must conduct themselves as the 'officers of a powerful sovereign.'⁹⁷

The *zamindars*, deprived of their coercive powers, relied on loans to finance their indolent and lavish lifestyles. When they were unable to repay the loans, their lands were auctioned. The result was the emergence of a new class of absentee-merchant-landlords based in large measure in Calcutta who, much as the parasitic Turco-Persian *zamindars* they dispossessed, did little to improve agriculture. Furthermore, territorial and demographic expansion placed immense strain on a system that was structurally deliberative. By 1815, the British Empire in India had forty million subjects. Forty years later, it had about one hundred and fifty million with even more difficulties to grapple with.⁹⁸

In opposition to the Cornwallis program emerged the Munro school.⁹⁹ Munro and his supporters critiqued the Cornwallis system on two major points. The first concerned the transfer of proprietorship from the state to the *zamindars*. This had proved ineffective, if not counterproductive, because the *zamindars* could not shake off their cultural hangover from the Timurid period. Research into the tax records of Indian states annexed by the British indicated that in many places the earliest known revenue settlements were made with peasants and villages.¹⁰⁰ It also made sense that villagers and kinship groups, provided a predictable arrangement, would make a greater effort to improve their lot than *zamindars* accustomed to a life of extortion and ease. Thus, the state should transfer property rights to peasants or villages and settle revenue with them directly.

The second line of criticism addressed the role of the executive function in continental bureaucratic empires. The Cornwallis system relied on judicial power to settle disputes. While Montesquieu would have applauded this decision as a vital step towards a State of Laws, the

Munro school argued in favor of making the executive function superior to the judicial. This was necessary because over centuries Indians had become accustomed to arbitrary rule through appointed servants. The number of disputes and the difficulty of applying standards of proof meant that the Cornwallis system bred inertia, confusion, and diluted the effectiveness of the state. It led to widespread abuses as landlords continued to resort 'to nothing but arbitrary demands' enforced on the tenants 'by stocks, duress of sorts, and battery of their persons.'[101] Meanwhile, the local moneylender greatly aggravated 'the evil by his own usurious practices' which drove both landlord and peasant to desperation.[102] Unlike the peasant who had no one to appeal to as the collector lacked the authority to redress his grievances and the judiciary was too remote, complex, and expensive, the moneylender had the means to move the courts for protection and engage in litigation, often frivolous, to secure his interests. The judicial approach to governance in a continental bureaucratic empire thus raised the cost of securing justice and was unintelligible to the vast mass of rural society. A strong executive presence was needed to negotiate the rural minefield.

Eventually, the views of the Munro school prevailed and were accepted by William Bentinck, Governor General of India from 1828-1835. Bentinck became convinced that the separation of judicial and revenue powers had led to 'inefficiency, misrule, and injustice.'[103] The courts were simply overwhelmed at all levels, the detentions of prisoners under trial were being illegally extended, while the one person to whom ordinary people could appeal, and from whom the wealthy and powerful had anything to fear, the district collector, lacked the authority to settle problems as and when they occurred.[104] Bentinck was certain that if things continued as they were the British Empire in India would be very short-lived. His dire observation, on 10 December 1828, put the situation in perspective:

> ...if I were obliged to draw an inference from the facts and reports which each council brings more or less before us, as well as from the information received out of doors, I am afraid that I should be obliged to say, that the administration of civil and criminal justice, if not a complete failure, was so defective and inefficient as to demand our instant and most serious attention.[105]

Given Bentinck's realism, proposals for a drastic reorganisation of the district administration met with approval at the highest levels.

Starting in 1829, India was reconstituted as a hierarchy of administrative sub-units (provinces, divisions, districts, sub-districts) ruled through a hierarchy of collector-magistrates with supervisory powers over the police (commissioners). Each district was small enough to be personally inspected by its commissioner. The commissioners acted in the classical generalist tradition of other continental bureaucratic empires and directed nearly all the activities of the British Empire in India. They were also the academic elite of the empire and expected to engage in substantial abstract and practical thinking in relation to the state. Their salaries and privileges, though laughable by Timurid standards, were, in absolute terms, enough to secure an upper middle-class living in Britain. The thousand to one thousand five hundred members of the Indian Civil Service (ICS) were the functional equivalent of the Timurid Empire's five hundred senior-most *mansabdars*.

Unlike the cosmetic differences between the pre-British continental bureaucratic empires, important features of the British State of Laws and culture of power seeped into the British Empire in India. The organs of the state, be they the civil service, police, customs or the forestry department, were constituted under laws that could not be arbitrarily changed. Second, the recruitment, transfers, promotions and discipline of public servants were merit-oriented and conducted autonomously of the sovereign. Thus the officers were not the personal servants of the governor-general and could lawfully oppose and campaign against approved policy provided they did so through reasoned argument. Third, the cohesion and *esprit de corps* of the state service was remarkable when compared to the atomised and self-seeking nature of earlier bureaucratic elites.

Comparable developments took place in the relationship between the armed forces and the sovereign. Since ancient times, the military was an intensely political institution. The officers were the personal servants or slaves of the ruler. Should the ruler show any weakness, he would be confronted with insurrection and rebellion. There was no theoretical or practical distinction between the civil and military power. The British understood that the actual basis of their power and of all states, but imperial states in particular, was the ability to apply force effectively.[106]

However, it was in the interest of the rulers themselves 'that Government should disguise, as much as possible, the principle of its support.'[107]

The idea that men with weapons should obey unarmed servants of the law, which is the essential distinction between the rule of force and the rule of law, would have elicited nothing but contempt from pre-British rulers. Many rulers rose from the military to supreme power and thus it was simultaneously the deadliest instrument of arbitrary power and the greatest source of danger to the ruler. Their unique culture of power guided the British response to the same danger faced by rulers of continental bureaucratic empires for millennia.[108] The solution was to insulate the military from politics and quite literally create a parallel political dimension within which the recruitment, transfers, promotions, and discipline of officers and enlisted men would take place through an autonomous institutional process. While concerns had been raised before the 1857 revolt, which began as a mutiny in the Bengal Army, it was not until after such a trial by fire that more comprehensive policies were laid down. It was imperative that the military be separated from all civil functions, such as policing and taxation, and constituted as a full-time professional force governed by a combination of seniority and merit.

Finding this balance between the seniority and merit systems, then, as now, proved a difficult and controversial task. It was decided to strike a compromise and promote European officers primarily on the basis of seniority in order to prevent the exercise of patronage by the government and create certainty within the officer corps.[109] However, 'the promotion of Native commissioned and non-commissioned officers' was to be based primarily on efficiency rather than seniority.[110] Even those who disagreed with these decisions and argued for a system based solely on efficiency were constrained to admit that 'security against favouritism and jobbery' could only be achieved through the seniority system.[111] That said, the peasant communities and castes of northern India were to be the principal recruitment base for the army within which 'castes should be placed upon a perfect equality.'[112] The Bengal Army, moreover, was too numerous and its 'fixed and most undeserved position of superiority with the Government of India' after the revolt was forfeit.[113] The system worked because the formulation of strategy remained in the hands of a combination of British parliamentarians and civil servants, which thus left the armed forces to focus solely on developing their operational proficiency in relative isolation from Indian society.

The ideocratic complex of the British Empire in India also manifested substantial differences from earlier empires. The most obvious was the freedom to criticise the rulers. The most important was the secularism of the state.[114] There was a bureaucratic intelligentsia but there was no official priesthood. Individual members of the apparatus did patronise Christianity and missionaries, but the consistent effort of the state was to place as much distance between itself and religion as possible.[115] The experience of the 1857 uprising by units of the Bengal army, which was fuelled by belief in a Christian missionary conspiracy, drove this particular point home. In Britain and India missionaries came in for considerable criticism 'which amounted in some quarters to the charge that missionary provocation was the primary cause' of the rebellions of 1857-58.[116] By the 1880s, 'most British officers had reverted to the habit of their predecessors of the 1820s in regarding missionaries as, at best; absurd; at worst subversive.'[117] Even those officers who remained sympathetic to the cause of Christian proselytising in India began 'avoiding any direct association with missionary publications or with public debates.'[118] After 1857, as advised by prominent Indians, such as Sir Syed Ahmed Khan, the founder of Muslim modernism in India, some aspects of Indian court culture, such as durbars, and the distribution of prizes and honours, were revived.[119] On the whole, British India was remarkably devoid of the kind of ideocratic complex and behaviour characteristic of other continental bureaucratic empires.[120]

Self-government and the institutions required to sustain it was in many respects the great project of the British Empire in India and the ultimate test of the exportability of the British State of Laws. The process began in the early nineteenth century in Calcutta, Madras, and Bombay. From 1850 to 1893 steady progress was made in local government institutions. The first four decades of the twentieth century saw the extension of the representative principle to the centre and the provinces in British India and the Indianisation of the civil service and military officer corps. In the course of applying the representative principle to the higher tiers of the state, such as an Imperial Advisory and Legislative Council (1909), or debating the relative merits of elections as opposed to nominations for local government, a sustained process of consultation and dialogue with Indians and Englishmen of all shades of opinion unfolded. A retired assistant commissioner, Raja Aurungzeb Khan, told the district commissioner of Jhelum in 1907 with reference to the input asked by the government about the desirability of establishing advisory and legislative institutions at the central level:

> No Sahib, consult us by all means, but do it secretly. It is not right to put people in opposition to Government. I will tell you the truth. The Sarkar is well meaning...but it has made two fatal mistakes.
>
> First it has given education to people unfitted for it; second, it has put the tenants above the land-lords. Now it wishes to put the *kamins*[121] above itself. The Sarkar should never be a defendant.[122]

Narindra Nath, the deputy commissioner of Gujrat (Punjab), advised the government to consider questions of political economy and social change in framing its policy observing that 'the enormous value attached to proprietary rights in land' was of 'recent origin' and a departure from the pre-British period when 'Husbandry was looked down upon as an inferior occupation.'[123] Furthermore, 'Indian society' was 'rapidly changing' and just as the 'India of today is very different from India' a generation earlier, another couple of decades 'may see changes in economic and other conditions which it is difficult to foresee.'[124] At the other end of the subcontinent another civil service officer posted in East Bengal, Babu Hari Charan Das, warned that the representative principle would wreak havoc upon 'The Indian—nay the Asiatic—idea of Government' which 'is that it derives its sanction from the Creator of the Universe.'[125] On balance, while many expressed reluctance about the viability of the representative principle, consciousness of the phenomenon of change and the need for the state to adapt and develop without, however, compromising on the performance of its core functions, prevailed. By the 1920s many people with experience or power, if not both, would have agreed that it was 'absurd to suppose that a handful of foreigners from across the seas can continue to rule indefinitely hundreds of millions of Orientals on the patriarchal lines pursued, with no essential modification.'[126]

Although the turbulence wrought by the two world wars and a global economic depression accelerated the demise of the British Empire, its legacy in the subcontinent was different in important respects from previous empires. The country was no longer the personal estate of the sovereign. The officers of the state, military and civil, were not personal servants of the ruler. The state was secular and almost anti-ideological in its ethos and laws. Representative institutions and a culture of constitutionalism and lawful opposition were in place, albeit in an underdeveloped form at the centre. A substantial body of politicians had emerged many with decades of experience in local, provincial, and national affairs. The higher judiciary inspired confidence while the lower judiciary, though overburdened, kept the wheels of justice spinning at a tolerable pace.

Post-imperial writers have fixated on individual acts of brutality and oppression, such the siege of Delhi in 1857, the Amritsar massacre at Jallianwalabagh in 1919, the Mopilla Uprising of 1921, or the numerous flare-ups along the turbulent Indo-Afghan frontier. These atrocities are worthy of condemnation and ideally should not have taken place. Compared, however, to other imperial powers, such as the Belgians in the Congo or the French in Indo-China and Algeria, the Russians in Central Asia and Eastern Europe, the Spanish in Central and South America, or the Japanese in China, British imperialism was astoundingly restrained. It is perhaps precisely to this restraint that the British owed their imperial success for it made possible collaboration and led many subject peoples to participate in the imperial project.[127] Certainly, the kind of systematic violence employed by the British Empire in India's contemporary imperial formations was not engaged in by the British in India. Some of the greatest innovations instituted by the British were lawful opposition, agitation politics, and civil disobedience. These acted to release pressure, prevented armed insurrection and revolution, and ensured that while the British transferred power in August 1947, the change of regime did not fundamentally and immediately alter the nature or composition of the state. India and Pakistan had a choice between continuing along the path of legal democracy and building upon the institutions and habits bequeathed by the British or reversion to ideocratic arbitrary rule.[128]

1.6 The End of the Beginning

In the preceding survey of the nature of state power in the subcontinent several important features merit recapitulation. First, the dominant form of the state in the subcontinent was the continental bureaucratic empire. Second, the culture of power of continental bureaucratic empires whether ruled by Hindus, Turks, or Europeans, exhibited high levels of arbitrariness. Third, under British rule serious and sustained efforts were made to reform the nature of the state in the subcontinent. The motivation for such reform came from the contradiction between the British experience of the state at home and the profoundly different reality found in India. This, in turn, evolved into a gradual movement towards the establishment of a State of Laws in India that, however, incorporated many features of the continental bureaucratic empire. The objective of this synthesis was to establish a state that could achieve and sustain effective constitutional government along representative lines on a continental scale[129] and potentially establish a truly 'imperishable empire' of reason, laws, and state-morality.[130]

It is to this effort more than anything else that the fact of Indian constitutional government owes its survival to the present day. Pakistan was far less fortunate in terms of the quality and quantity of its imperial inheritance and beset with such profound problems and challenges to its very existence that its founding fathers committed a number of errors that substantially altered its trajectory. Many of these errors were committed out of a combination of inexperience, expediency, desperation and at a subconscious level, the reassertion of the subcontinent's ideocratic and arbitrary culture of power. It is to these original sins that we now turn.

NOTES

1. A thought provoking theory is found in Aitzaz Ahsan's work on Pakistani national identity. Seeking to identify the causes of the Indus Valley civilization's extraordinarily static and uniform nature combined with the absence of architectural evidence of royalty, he contends that probably 'Fundamentalist priests and dogma held sway over the Indus cities.' Thus 'there was no initiative, no science, no invention' during the period of Indus ascendance. Aitzaz Ahsan, *The Indus Saga and the Making of Pakistan* (Lahore: Nehr Ghar Publications, 2001), 30.
2. Herodotus reveals that Menes, the first pharaoh (c.3200 BC), 'raised the dyke which protects Memphis from the inundation of the Nile' and that these waterworks, thousands of years later in his own time (c. 450 BC) when Egypt was a satrapy of Achaemenid Persia, were '…guarded with the greatest care by the Persians.' Herodotus, *Histories*, 155-6.
3. Ibn Khaldun, *The Muqaddimah (An Introduction to History)*, trans. Franz Rosenthal, ed. N. J. Dawood (London: Routledge and Kegan Paul, 1978), 263.

For Ibn Khaldun, the terms 'dynasty' and 'state' were synonymous for 'A state exists only insofar as it is held together by the dynasty; when the dynasty disappears the state collapses.' Ibid., xi.
4. Ibid., 263.
5. Ibid.
6. Harappa was one of the most important cities and located at the centre of the Indus Valley civilization.
7. Karen Armstrong goes so far as to describe the monarchical states such as Magadha and Kosala as 'modern kingdoms' with 'streamlined bureaucracies and armies' loyal to the monarch. They were thus 'far more efficiently run' than the tribal oligarchies and aristocracies. Karen Armstrong, *Buddha* (London: Phoenix, 2002), 20.
8. Different versions and editions of Ancient India's compendium on statecraft include: Kautilya, *The Arthashastra*, trans. L. N. Rangarajan (New Delhi: Penguin Books, 1992); Kautilya, *Arthashastra* trans. R. Shamasastry's (Bangalore: Government Press, 1915); and B. P. Sinha, *Readings in Kautilya's Arthasastra* (New Delhi: Agam Publishers, 1976). Kautilya was the prime minister to Chandragupta Maurya, the founder of the Maurya Empire, about 320 BC.
9. The *Arthashastra* is often 'mistakenly believed' to be 'a text on Hindu political thought.' This is highly misleading given that Kautilya is not concerned with presenting a philosophy of government. In fact, the treatise is 'a text-book on administration in a monarchical state.' Romila Thapar, *Cultural Pasts: Essays in Early Indian History* (New Delhi: Oxford University Press, 2005), 411.
10. Kautilya, *The Arthashastra*, trans. Rangarajan, 154.
11. Ibid.
12. Ibid.
13. Ibid., 157-8.
14. Thapar, *Cultural Pasts*, 430.
15. Kautilya, *The Arthashastra*, trans. L. N. Rangrajan, 246.
16. Ibid., 205.
17. Ibid.
18. A somewhat analogous class of priests known as the Magi existed in Achaemenid Persia. Their functions were the enforcement of religious orthodoxy and providing the rulers with legitimacy. They enjoyed a relatively privileged position in Persian society. Axworthy, *Empire of the Mind*, 10. Sassanid Persia, which lasted from the third to the seventh centuries AD and ruled more or less the same territories as its Achaemenid predecessor, maintained a theocratic establishment of some twenty-five thousand salaried priests and ecclesiastical officials. David L. Lewis, *God's Crucible: Islam and the Making of Europe, 570 to 1215* (New York: W. W. Norton, 2008), 20.
19. In his edicts Ashoka entrusts 'officers' and 'rural officers' as well as 'rural chiefs' to assemble the people and explain to them the principles of Buddhism and the new thinking. Thapar, *Cultural Pasts*, 427.
20. Ibid., 436.
21. Ibid., 434.
22. Bharat Karnad, *Nuclear Weapons and Indian Security: The Realist Foundations of Strategy* (New Delhi: Macmillan, 2002), 325. In this groundbreaking and informative work, Karnad demolishes most popular notions of Hindu-Indian

pacifism, and Gandhian and Nehruvian idealism. One of the lessons that can be drawn from Karnad's work is that a remarkably large section of the Indian ruling class, came to believe its own lies and, consequently, placed severe constraints on the Indian 'will to power' and pursuit of national interests. It also confused the expression of desire or intent and the receipt of praise with real achievement and the accumulation of power and respect.

23. Thapar, *Cultural Pasts*, 227.
24. The intermediate forms of resistance included renunciation, flight, 'philosophical acrobatics', migration, violating existing caste regulations and joining another sub-sect. Ibid., 213-32. The nature of the dissent itself indicates that the relative power of the state was significant. One might also consider that the ability of a rural and caste-ridden society to resist a determined armed minority keen to impose demands on it in the form of taxes and compulsory service would not be very great.
25. The term 'Sultanate' is a bit misleading. The Delhi Sultanate was a succession of dynastic states that rose and fell between 1206 and 1526. The dynasties were the Shamsids (Slave Dynasty), Ghiyathids, Khaljis, Tughluqids, Sayyids and the Lodhis. Most of these dynasties had only one great ruler under whom the Delhi Sultanate exercised effective control of the Indo-Gangetic plain and penetrated the Deccan. The total period of effective central authority for the Delhi Sultanate is about a century and a half. However, the maximum total period of continuous, effective, rule from a single centre is about sixty years (1325-88).
26. Kennedy, *The Court of the Caliphs*, 214.
27. Mu'tasim then moved the capital from Baghdad to Samarra: 'The new regime was established in Samarra, and the new army and the bureaucracy were moved there. Mu'tasim was now master in his own capital, surrounded by the troops who owed everything to him. Baghdad with its turbulent inhabitants and vigorous commercial life, was well out of the way. He could not have realized how this isolation in the middle of his troops would make Samarra a prison and ultimately a death trap for his successors.' Ibid.
28. Peter Jackson, *The Delhi Sultanate: A Political and Military History* (Cambridge: Cambridge University Press, 1999), 241.
29. This system, of Ancient Persian origin, was extensively employed by the Arab imperial states. The second Abbasid ruler, Mansur, 'relied heavily on an organisation called the *barid*. This is usually translated as 'post', but though it did carry official correspondence its remit ran much wider. The agents of the *barid* operated in every city and district a sort of alternative government structure, reporting directly to the caliphs on the behaviour of the governor, the *qadi* or judge and such mundane but important matters as the movement of prices of essential commodities.' Kennedy, *The Court of the Caliphs*, 15. When Harun al Rashid, the Abbasid ruler immortalized in the *Arabian Nights*, died in 809 at Tus, some 1900 kilometres from the capital, Baghdad, the news was transmitted through the *barid* and arrived at the imperial palace in eleven or twelve days. Ibid., 85.
30. Ibn Battuta, *Travels in Asia and Africa 1325-54* (London: Routledge and Keagan Paul, 1929; reprint Lahore: Services Book Club, 1985), 181.
31. Ibid.

32. K. A. Nizami, ed., *Politics and Society During the Early Medieval Period: Collected Works of Professor Mohammed Habib,* vol. 2 (New Delhi: Peoples Publishing House, 1981), 369-70.
33. K. M. Ashraf, *Life and Conditions of the People of Hindustan* (New Delhi: Munshiram Manoharlal, 1959), 77.
34. Ibid., 2.
35. Ibid., 36.
36. Babur was a descendent of Amir Taimur, who led the second wave of Mongol invasions. These invasions, in the late fourteenth and early fifteenth centuries, devastated the Muslim world. In 1398-99, The Timurid armies conquered and sacked Delhi, a blow from which the sultanate, then undergoing dynastic failure, never truly recovered. After Taimur's death in 1405, his empire disintegrated into hundreds of petty despotisms. The first Timurid Empire drew it strength from two major groups of imperial servants. The war machine was administered by the nomadic Turco-Mongol warrior elite whose tribal rivalries were manipulated in order to ensure loyalty to Amir Taimur. The settled districts, cities, towns and trade routes were managed by a Persian or Persianized bureaucracy. By balancing and encouraging rivalries within the imperial apparatus and employing an extensive network of spies and couriers on the classical Persian pattern, Amir Taimur made his will prevail over all others. He *was* the system and 'power was exercised personally, rather than through institutions.' Justin Marozzi, *Tamerlane: Sword of Islam, Conqueror of the World* (London: Harper Collins, 2004), 204-5.
37. Akbar can be credited with leading the Timurids to paramount power status in the subcontinent. Ishtiaq Husain Qureshi, *Akbar: The Architect of the Mughul Empire* (Karachi: Ma'aref Limited, 1978). More recent research into the 'documentary evidence' has 'only tended to confirm and underline the standard propositions about the elements of centralisation and systematisation' in the Timurid Empire. M. Athar Ali, *Mughul India: Studies in Polity, Ideas, Society and Culture* (New Delhi: Oxford University Press, 2007), 87-8.
38. During the reign of Humayun (1530-56) the Timurids experimented with sharing different provinces amongst the royal princes instead of plunging into a fratricidal civil war. The consequences for the Timurid dominion were almost fatal as dissension between the brothers crippled the state and led to humiliation and exile at the hands of the Afghan Sher Shah Suri (1540-45). Ultimately, Humayun had to defeat his brothers and lead a re-conquest of northern India, which was, at the time of his death in 1556, still far from complete.
39. Abu'l Fazl, *A'in-I Akbari,* trans. H. Blochmann, 65.
40. Ibid.
41. Irfan Habib, *Essays in Indian History: Towards a Marxist Perspective* (New Delhi: Tulika, 1995), 97.
42. Standard silver currency units.
43. Inayat Khan, *Shahjahan-nama,* trans. A. R. Fuller, eds., W. Begley and Z. A. Desai (Delhi: Oxford University Press, 1990), 282.
44. Ibid., 232.
45. François Bernier, *Travels in the Mogul Empire: AD 1656-1668,* trans. Irving Brock, revised and improved edition, Archibald Constable (London: Archibald Constable and Company, 1891; reprint, Karachi: Indus Publications, n.d.). 204.

46. Ibid.
47. Tapan Raychaudhuri and Irfan Habib, eds., *The Cambridge Economic History of India*, vol 1, *c1200 to c1750* (Cambridge: Cambridge University Press, 1982), 173.
48. M. Athar Ali, *The Mughal Nobility Under Aurungzeb* (New Delhi: Asia Publishing House, 1970), 155-6.
49. Abul Fazl Allami, *A'in-I Akbari*, trans. H. Blochmann (Calcutta: Calcutta Madrassah, 1873; reprint, Lahore: Sang-e-Meel Publications, 2003), 225.
50. Raychaudhuri, *The Cambridge Economic History of India*, vol 1, *c1200 to c1750*, 179. The total revenues are estimated at 130 million rupees under Akbar, 220 million rupees under Shahjahan, and 380 million rupees during the later half of Aurungzeb's reign.
51. Ibid., 181.
52. Abraham Eraly, *The Last Spring: The Lives and Times of the Great Mughals* (New Delhi: Viking, 1997), 815.
53. Athar Ali, *Mughul India*, 68.
54. This point is driven home by Yoginder Sikand. He argues that the local converts to Islam were regard as *ajlaf* by the Muslim elite, or *ashraf*, in pre-British India. Until the decline of Turco-Persian imperial power in the eighteenth century the *ashraf* didn't even consider it possible for the 'Natives' to become *real* Muslims. Yoginder Sikand, *The Origins and Development of the Tablighi-Jama'at, 1920-2000: A Cross-country Comparative Study* (New Delhi: Orient Longman, 2002).
55. Ibn Hasan notes that 'In the absence of any constitutional body or permanent authority in the state to control and supervise the administration, the only guarantee to avert, check, or overcome the dangers to the Empire, and to ensure smooth working of the administration, was the vigilance of the ruling monarch.' Ibn Hasan, *The Central Structure of the Mughal Empire and its Practical Working up to the Year 1657* (Karachi: Oxford University Press, 1967), 85.
56. Nizam-ud-din Ahmed, *Tabakat-i-Akbari*, trans. Sir H. M. Elliot (n.p. 1871 reprint; Lahore: Sind Sagar Academy, 1975), Book I, 86.
57. At the provincial level two officers of equal importance, the provincial revenue ministers and provincial governors, headed the financial administration and order apparatus, respectively. Both officers were often rivals and reported upon each other to the emperor.
58. Nizam-ud-din Ahmed, *Tabakat-i-Akbari*, Book II, 89.
59. Ibid., 96.
60. Ibid.
61. 'Keeping records is an excellent thing for a government; it is even necessary for every rank of society. Though a trace of this office may have existed in ancient times, its higher objects were but recognized in the present reign.' Abul Fazl Allami, *A'in-I Akbari*, trans. H. Blochmann (Calcutta: Calcutta Madrassah, 1873; reprint, Lahore: Sang-e-Meel Publications, 2003), 245.
62. Bernier, *Travels in the Mogul Empire:* AD *1656-1668*, 231.
63. 'No dignity is higher in the eyes of God than royalty; and those who are wise, drink from its auspicious fountain…royalty is a remedy for the spirit of rebellion, and the reason why subjects obey. Even the meaning of the word Padishah shows

this; for *pad* signifies stability and possession, and *shah* means origin, lord.' Abu'l Fazl, A'in-I Akbari, trans. H. Blochmann, 58.
64. Athar Ali, *The Mughal Nobility Under Aurungzeb*, 99.
65. Ibid.
66. Ibid.
67. 'In *Asia*, the great are never approached empty-handed. When I had the honour to kiss the garment of the great Mogol *Aurung-zebe* (Ornament of the Throne), I presented him with eight *roupies*, as a mark of respect; and I offered a knife-case, a fork and a pen-knife mounted in amber to the illustrious *Fazal-Khan*...a Minister charged with the weightiest concerns...on whose decision depended the amount of my salary as a physician.' Bernier, *Travels in the Mogul Empire: AD 1656-1668*, 200.
68. Simon Schama, *A History of Britain: At the Edge of the World? 3000 BC-AD 1603* (London: BBC Worldwide Ltd., 2000), 162.
69. Charles de Secondat, *The Spirit of Laws* (New York: Prometheus Books, 2002), 152.
70. Ibid., 160.
71. 'Tocqueville, believing the strength of American democracy to lie in its local institutions, travelled almost exclusively in the provinces, greatly neglected the organs of the central authority, visited Washington only briefly, towards the end of his journey, and with only perfunctory interest. Custine, coming to a country where power was centralised as nowhere else in the Christian world, quite properly and naturally confined his attention largely to the capital city, the court, and the central apparatus of government.' George F. Kennan, *The Marquis de Custine and his 'Russia in 1839'* (London: Hutchinson, 1972), 19.
72. Alexis de Tocqueville, *Democracy in America*, trans. George Lawrence, ed., J. P. Mayer (New York: HarperCollins, 2000), 39.
73. Ibid., 43.
74. Hastings's own motto may as well have been 'When in India, do as the Indians do.'
75. In 1895, Winston Churchill, on his first visit to the United States was struck by the superior quality of communications in New York as compared to a rather unimpressive currency: 'The communication of New York is due to private enterprise while the state is responsible for currency: and hence I came to the conclusion that the first class men of America are in the counting houses and the less brilliant ones in the government.' Martin Gilbert, *Churchill: A Life* (London: Minerva, 1990), 57. In continental bureaucratic empires, which account for the overwhelming preponderance of human historical experience, the equation between the 'palace' and the 'counting house' was precisely the opposite.
76. G. W. Forrest, ed., *Selections from the State Papers of the Governor-General of India*, vol I, *Hastings* (London: Constable & Co. Ltd., 1910), 161.
77. Conor Cruise O'Brien, *The Great Melody* (London: Minerva, 1993), 351.
78. Ibid., 354.
79. Ibid., 376.
80. Jeremy Bernstein, *Dawning of the Raj: The Life and Trial of Warren Hastings* (London: Aurora Press Ltd., 2000), 166.
81. Montesquieu, *The Spirit of Laws*, 115.

82. Eric Stokes, *The English Utilitarians and India* (New Delhi: Oxford University Press, 1982), 4.
83. A. Aspinall, *Cornwallis in Bengal* (New Delhi: Uppal Publishing House, 1987), 24.
84. Ibid., 16-17.
85. Ibid., 30.
86. *Selection of Papers from the Records at the East India House Relating to the Revenue, Police and Civil and Criminal Justice under the Company's Governments in India*, vol I (London: E. Cox and Son, 1820), 59.
87. Ibid., 15
88. Ibid.
89. Ibid., 16.
90. Ibid., 26.
91. The Cornwallis Code of 1793.
92. Stokes, *The English Utilitarians and India*, 152.
93. *Selection of Papers from the Records at the East India House Relating to the Revenue, Police and Civil and Criminal Justice under the Company's Governments in India*, vol I, 65.
94. Ibid.
95. Ibid.
96. Lawrence James, *Raj: The Making and Unmaking of British India* (London: Abacus, 2003), 153.
97. G. B. Malleson, *Administration of British India under Lord Wellesley* (New Delhi: Daya Publishing, 1988; original edition, 1889), 102.
98. Niall Ferguson, *Empire: How Britain Made the Modern World* (London: AllenLane the Penguin Press, 2003), 56.
99. Thomas Munro, a collector, and later governor of the Madras Presidency.
100. H. H. Dodwell, ed., *The Cambridge History of India*, vol. 5, *British India 1497-1858* (Cambridge: Cambridge University Press, 1921; reprint, New Delhi: S. Chand & Company (Pvt.) Ltd., 1987), 470.
101. *Selection of Papers from the Records at the East India House Relating to the Revenue, Police and Civil and Criminal Justice under the Company's Governments in India*, vol. I, 211.
102. Ibid.
103. C. H. Philips, ed., *The Correspondence of Lord William Cavendish Bentinck: Governor-General of India 1828-1835*, vol. I, *1828-1831* (Oxford: Oxford University Press, 1977), xxv.
104. Ibid., xxv.
105. Ibid., 111.
106. *Selection of Papers from the Records at the East India House Relating to the Revenue, Police and Civil and Criminal Justice under the Company's Governments in India*, vol II (London: E. Cox and Son, 1820), 187.
107. Ibid.
108. In the Punjab the collapse of Timurid authority facilitated the rise of the Sikhs, a military brotherhood professing a blend of Islam and Hinduism. During the eighteenth century the Sikh *khalsa*, or army of the pure, gained prominence and successfully challenged the Afghans and Timurids for control of the Punjab.

During the early nineteenth century, under the leadership of Ranjit Singh, the Sikhs established a kingdom with its capital at Lahore that was strong enough to defeat the Afghans and check British expansion. The *Khalsa Sarkar* was a single-mindedly military government devoid of many of the cultural refinements of its Timurid predecessor. Even the most sympathetic reading of events leaves little doubt in this regard. See for instance Khuswant Singh, *Ranjit Singh: Maharaja of the Punjab* (New Delhi: Penguin Books India, 2001; original edition, 1962).
109. *Report of the Commissioners Appointed to Inquire into the Organisation of the Indian Army, Together with the Minutes of Evidence and Appendix* (London: Her Majesty's Stationery Office, 1859), xi.
110. Ibid., xi.
111. *The Indian Army Commission Report of Major General Hancock* (London: Her Majesty's Stationery Office, 1859), 14-16.
112. Ibid., 27-8.
113. Ibid., 30.
114. The Company's Charter required it to 'protect' Indians 'in the free exercise of their religions' and was interpreted by its officials as a mandate for 'non-interference' in religious affairs. Avril Powell, *Muslims and Missionaries in Pre-Mutiny India* (Surrey: The Curzon Press, 1993), 80.
115. Indeed, the East India Company and its officials feared 'the consequences of allowing would-be missionaries' access to the parts of India under British rule. The missionaries often harped on 'the sinfulness and vanity of all other religious paths' and were thus guaranteed to offend Hindus, Muslims and other religious communities in India. Ibid., 76.
116. Ibid., 283.
117. Ferguson, *Empire*, 155.
118. Powell, *Muslims and Missionaries*, 284.
119. David Cannadine, *Ornamentalism: How the British Saw Their Empire* (New York: Oxford University Press, 2001), 89-90.
120. Over the past forty years there has been a consistent attempt to read a great many things into the British Indian state's attempts at acquiring knowledge about its subjects. The broad thrust of the argument made is that in conducting censuses or compiling gazetteers at the local or regional levels the British somehow defined Indians into new categories that ossified into political identities. Thus, the 1871-72 census of India is taken as the starting point for the development of a distinctly 'Muslim' or 'Hindu' identity because people in India were asked to indicate their religious affiliation. Given the religious complexity and fractiousness of Indian society it was only logical that the British would want to know the number of people of different faiths in territories under their control. The idea that the British could impose identities on ancient and deeply ingrained religious and cultural traditions borders on the absurd especially if one is familiar with these traditions. A recent example of this line of inquiry is Alex Padamsee's *Representation of Indian Muslims in British Colonial Sources* (New York: Palgrave MacMillan, 2005).
121. Indicates a low caste, normally a worker or tradesman, such as a barber. Also used as an insult and to indicate inferior status.

122. *East India (Advisory and Legislative Councils)* Vol. II, Part II, *Replies of the Local Governments, Enclosures XXI to XXX to Letter from the Government of India, No. 21, dated the First of October 1908* (London: His Majesty's Stationery Office, 1908), 78.
123. Ibid., 81.
124. Ibid.
125. Ibid., 47.
126. Evan Maconchie, *Life in the Indian Civil Service* (London: Chapman and Hall, 1926), 251.
127. Following the end of the European imperial age the post-colonial states that emerged 'found it natural to base their political legitimacy on the rejection of empire as an alien, evil and oppressive force.' Marozzi, *After Tamerlane*, 23. The rejection of empire rarely had much substance given that nearly all the post-colonial states were empires in their own right with a miniscule elite ruling a diverse multitude of ethnicities and religions.
128. In Africa, the colonial state was far lighter on the ground than in India. In effect Africa was left 'to the mercy of commercial or settler interests' whose rapacity and ignorance were an embarrassing contrast to the probity and efficiency of the Indian administration. Ibid., 315-16.
129. For a comparative perspective, see Larry Siedentop, *Democracy in Europe* (London: AllenLane the Penguin Press, 2000). Particularly relevant is Chapter I 'Democratic Liberty on a Continental Scale?', 1-24.
130. Macaulay's speech in the House of Commons on 10 July 1833. Later, as the Law Member of Bentinck's council, Macaulay advised the government not 'to leave the natives to the influence of their own hereditary prejudices,' stop spending money on publishing works in Arabic and Sanskrit for which there was hardly any market demand, and reorient public education towards instruction in English and the vernaculars. C. H. Philips, ed., *The Correspondence of Lord William Cavendish Bentinck: Governor-General of India 1828-1835*, vol. II, 1832-1835 (Oxford: Oxford University Press, 1977), 1409-12.

2 Original Sins

2.1 Ascension

The founding of new states is a difficult and morally compromising process. Rarely have new states emerged without the extensive employment of force and guile. Those who aspire to rule the new creation are not typically actuated by altruism. More often, it is the hunger for power, acute insecurities, opportunism, cynicism and at best, enlightened self-interest that guide such endeavours. In an age of public opinion, aspiring elites may employ religious or ideological rhetoric to give their public pronouncements emotional resonance amongst the people in whose interests the great national liberation project is launched.[1] Communities, parties, movements and states, like individuals, 'hide behind egocentric biases that generate the illusion that' they are somehow unique or motivated by higher purposes than their antecedents and adversaries.[2] In effect such 'self-serving protective shields allow us to believe that each of us is above average on any test of self-integrity.'[3] Behind these masks lurks the actual motivating force which is cupidity or the combination of 'avarice, greed' and 'the strong desire for wealth or power over another.'[4]

In the subcontinent the experience of British rule made a critical contribution to the creation of the westernised elite.[5] In 1900, for instance, the University of Calcutta, with eight thousand students, was the largest in the world. The westernised elite was drawn from Hindu, Muslim, Sikh, Parsee and such other communities that existed and its members had a great deal more in common with each other than they did with the traditionalist members of their own communities.[6] Some of the more important commonalities included an identification of progress with the industrialisation of Europe, the use of the English language, the practice of law, and a desire for a greater share in the exercise of state power at all levels. Collaboration with the British coexisted with constitutional opposition, demands for greater reforms and civil disobedience.⁷ While Englishmen may have been amused by the cultural pretensions of this elite and its claim to national leadership, it was with them that the British Empire in India negotiated, and it was to them that greater power and responsibility were transferred between 1909 and 1947.

Having established a national space for the western educated elites of all communities,⁸ the British hoped that the administrative unity of India would in time allow it to become a more organic and composite national state that would also prefer to remain within the British Empire. As wars, economic depression and recurrent internal and international crises between 1914 and 1945 sapped the vitality of the British Empire and called into question its survival, a struggle for imperial succession began. The British themselves were compelled by circumstances to 'reconsider many of their assumptions about India' and accelerate 'their projected timescale for political advance'.⁹ This process of reassessment increased the power and influence of the educated Indians for 'In the paid services of the Raj, Indians were crucial-from the 150,000 Indian troops, the majority of policemen, to those who manned the courts and the lower echelons of the civil government.'¹⁰ After 1919, in British India, Indian ministers exercised control over a number of provincial subjects which were gradually expanded in response to demands. The steel-frame of the Raj, the ICS, had over three hundred and fifty Indian officers against about nine hundred Europeans by 1929. Even without the Second World War and the granting of independence in 1947, by the mid-1950s Indians would have reached the highest ranks in the official hierarchy (secretaries, generals and inspector-generals). Along with the Indianisation of the administration and services 'A recognizably modern, continental style and structure of politics was the arena in which were played out the issues of Imperial governance' as Indian society underwent considerable change.¹¹

However, like the sons of the Timurid rulers, the westernised elites produced by British rule fell out amongst themselves as soon as the ruling power's hold became shaky and visibly weak. The rise of Muslim nationalism and the demand for Pakistan were particularly clear manifestations of this phenomenon. In the 1900s and 1910s Muslim political leaders sought, and to some extent secured, special reservations and safeguards for their community. With the advent of organised provincial politics in the 1920s and 1930s, Muslim leaders bargained pragmatically along provincial lines. With the outbreak of the Second World War the Muslims became 'aware that provincial strategies might prove inadequate when the British devolved power at the continental level.'[12] As had happened so many times before, either one element would prevail and the empire would hold, or an inconclusive outcome to the succession struggle would lead to fragmentation, the re-emergence of warring states, and the intervention of 'great outsiders.' The inability of the Congress leadership to appreciate in time the seriousness of the situation combined with the insecurity-driven but relentless and effective campaigning of the Muslim League set the stage for the division of the British Empire in India along communal lines. The westernised Muslims had little faith in the conversion of their Hindu counterparts to the secularism and liberalism they espoused given the reality of escalating communal violence and majoritarian chauvinism. The Hindu leadership could neither forgive nor forget the original sin of the eight centuries of Turco-Persian and Afghan 'Islamic' domination that had preceded British rule. For the Muslims, August 1947 marked the end of a century and a half of British imperial rule. For the Hindus, August 1947 marked the end of a millennium of imperial subjugation.

The amount of time and energy expended by the Indian and Pakistani intelligentsias in reliving the controversies surrounding the liquidation of the British Empire in India and its partition along communal lines is indicative of a number of critical failings. Neither the Indian nor the Pakistani elite seem to understand that states are not judged by how they are born. States are judged by how they live and die. The leadership and intelligentsia on both sides of the divide have demonstrated a profound shallowness and a near inability to grasp that the real test of an elite's mettle lies in transcending the almost invariably sordid circumstances in which states emerge and rising above the recriminations, sorrows, and compromises that the process entails. Of the two states, however, Pakistan faced a far more taxing set of challenges.

The westernisation experience of the Anglo-Muslim leadership was far inferior to its Hindu counterpart. This was partly reflected by the astonishing fact that only in the United Provinces did the Muslim community have a share in the total number of graduates proportionate to their population (around twelve per cent). The territories of what would become West Pakistan had come under British rule in the 1840s. Direct British control was exercised in the settled districts of the Punjab,

North-West Frontier Province (NWFP), and Sindh. Politics in these regions were dominated by Muslim landlords with Hindus more or less monopolising industry and commerce.[13] Across a thousand miles of Indian territory lay East Bengal, the rural backwater of united Bengal. On the administrative side, by 1947, there were only a hundred and one Muslim civil servants in the All-India Services (AIS) and merely four Muslim military officers (out of over six hundred) of the rank of Lt. Colonel in the army.[14]

Even if the westernisation experience of the Anglo-Muslim leadership had been superior to its Indian nationalist counterpart, partition generated pressures and contradictions of its own. The process was carried out in great haste and it was not until 3 June 1947 that the British finally acquiesced and made the necessary plan public, though even then the boundaries were yet to be determined. The partition had enormous consequences for Pakistan at both the central as well as the provincial levels. At the central level, Pakistan would need to set up a new federal capital (Karachi was chosen) in great haste wherein the institutions of a federal government would be established from scratch. At the provincial level, the two most populous provinces, the Punjab and East Bengal, would be carved out of their united antecedents along communal lines. This meant that East Bengal, home to over half of Pakistan's population, would need a new capital city. The sparsely populated territories that now comprise Balochistan were an assortment of directly administered territories and strong points, tribal areas and princely fiefdoms, held together by force of arms and imperial machinations. Balochistan, however, accounted for some four-tenths of West Pakistan's territories, bordered Iran and Afghanistan, and enjoyed proximity to the Persian Gulf. An Indian National Congress government still ruled the NWFP and a referendum had to be conducted to determine its status vis-à-vis Pakistan. The Punjab was plunged into communal warfare with millions displaced and hundreds of thousands killed. Moreover, the establishment of Pakistan's federal capital at Karachi meant that the Sindh government, itself presiding over a refugee crisis of no mean proportions, was turned into a refugee in its own right and had to make room for the central government. War with India over Kashmir combined with an insecure émigré leadership added to the initial problems. Thus, Pakistan had to establish centres of administration where none existed before. The new edifice, moreover, had to be raised from the leftovers, spare parts and poorly tested materials thrown into the ruling party's hand by chance, the haphazard division of assets and circumstance.

Religious rhetoric and symbolism had played an important role in the pan-Islamic, separatist and Pakistan movements led by the Anglo-Muslim elite. The British rule had substantially deprived the Muslim theological establishment (judges, teachers, readers collectively referred to as *ulema*) of 'their privileged position in state and society.'[15] The land grants and stipends that sustained them were withdrawn while knowledge of Arabic, Persian, religious law, and traditional medicine, were rendered obsolete or became irrelevant as prerequisites for state service.[16] The Anglo-Muslim elite was inspired by a humanistic worldview and sought to reinterpret Islam in the light of scientific advances, industrialisation, and new political and economic paradigms such as liberalism and communism. This elite was in direct competition for jobs, patronage and political representation with its equivalents in other communities and it felt threatened by Indian nationalism suspecting it to be a cover for the establishment of 'a majoritarian Hindu utopia.'[17] Certainly the growth of extremist Hindu movements such as the Arya Samaj (1875), the Hindu Sabha (1909), the Hindu Mahasabha (1915), the Hindu Sangathan (1921-22), the Rashtriya Swayamsevak Sangh (1925), the abundant use of religious symbolism by 'Mahatma' Gandhi, and the behaviour of the Congress ministries in the provinces (1937-39)[18] caused considerable disquiet. Critically, conservative Hinduism had a much easier time reconciling with European-style territorial nationalism and incorporating a sense of victimisation, 'conspiracy theories and a never-ending sense of threat to Hinduism, which was equated with the nation.'[19]

The Anglo-Muslim elite faced a far more complex situation. Since the British had deprived the *ulema* of status and basis for wealth, and established a secular state, conservative Muslims felt threatened by both the British imperialists as well as the 'creatures of colonial rule, the western educated Muslims.'[20] Very few traditionalists believed that Jinnah, Liaquat and the other westernised Muslims wanted to establish the kind of traditionalist Islamic society desired by the *ulema*.[21] This perception was validated by 'Jinnah's undermining of the Shariat Application Bill of 1937' as well as his role in the Dissolution of Muslim Marriages Bill of 1939, which were a harsh lesson for conservative opinion as to where Jinnah stood.[22] In their desire to fight the British and the modernist Muslim 'infidels', conservative Muslims and movements, such as the Deobandis, reconciled with the concept of composite nationalism articulated by the Indian National Congress (INC).[23]

To a growing section of the Anglo-Muslim elite the danger to the Muslim community came not from the British, whose power was in visible decline after the First World War, but to post-British dispensation. The administrative unity of India, from this perspective, was the product of the extraordinary exertions of the British imperial class. The Muslim separatists feared that when this elite withdrew power would, under a democratic dispensation, be captured at all levels by the majority Hindu community. The Congress was not, in their opinion, sincere in its professions of secularism and under democratic cover caste Hindu interests would dominate as soon as the British left. The only line of argument which was likely to resonate across the length and breadth of Muslim India was that Islam was in danger and to save it a separate homeland (or homelands), ought to be carved out of India comprising those areas where Muslims were in a majority. The rhetoric combined with Jinnah's towering prestige and the imminence of British departure worked wonders. In the 1946 elections the All-India Muslim League (AIML) trounced its electoral opponents and secured some nine-tenths of both the popular Muslim vote and seats. Those swayed by the rhetoric were seeing in the ambiguous Islamic rhetoric and rhythmic sloganeering what they wanted to see. The neurotic response of the Congress and nationalist press, which dubbed the 1940 Lahore Resolution as the Pakistan Resolution, lent substance to Jinnah's carefully prepared shadows. The price paid was an escalation of communal discord and religious fervour, both of which spun out of control by the end of 1946.[24]

The Anglo-Muslim elite that successfully prosecuted the Pakistan demand suffered from many important handicaps. Its westernisation experience was qualitatively and quantitatively inferior to the leaderships of other Indian communities in general but the Hindus in particular. Whereas India already existed, Pakistan's executive agencies would have to be put together at the central and provincial levels amidst tremendous chaos. Further complications arose from the nebulous and contradictory nature of the Pakistan demand itself, even within the

Muslim League—that Ch. Zafarullah Khan, a prominent Ahmedi, and Maulana Shabbir Ahmad Usmani, a leading Deobandi dissident, found themselves in its leadership testifies to this. The religious rhetoric and communal violence generated a dynamic of its own, while the migrations and slaughter cleared the ground for a new society and economy to emerge along with a new state. India's implacable hostility, in many respects a continuation of pre-partition debates, exacerbated contradictions.

Faced with these challenges, Pakistan's new rulers responded along certain lines the impact of which can still be felt today. First, the siege situation from within and without convinced the central government to concentrate as much power as possible in its own hands. Second, in order to legitimise this appropriation of authority, increasing emphasis was laid on the centre's monopoly of competence with regard to development work and the ideological nature of the state. Third, as power became more centralised and the rhetoric more audacious, the elected politicians progressively lost their cohesion and will to make policy and supervise its execution. Into this vacuum entered 'the establishment', a coterie of senior bureaucrats and military officers. Collectively, these original sins, products as much of accidents and circumstances, as of idiosyncrasies, represented the first steps towards the reassertion of an arbitrary, delusional and ultimately self-destructive culture of power.

2.2 In the State of Siege

On 10 January 1949, Francis Mudie, the governor of the Punjab, complained in an exasperated tone to prime minister, Liaquat Ali Khan that the Punjab's chief minister, the Nawab of Mamdot '...has, to everyone's knowledge, defeated the Centre, even the Qaid, every time that they have intervened and the feeling is growing that the Centre is powerless even when the Government is hopelessly corrupt and the administration paralysed.'[25] The governor continued that 'No questions of policy are even contemplated', it was almost impossible to get routine work out of the way, while the services were increasingly demoralised, the ministers were interfering in the administration and becoming 'more and more rapacious.'[26] Rivalries within the Muslim League were spiralling out of control, while Mamdot was characterised as 'lazy, inefficient and a liar' whose 'main interest in the administration is to obtain possession of evacuee land' and 'his brothers have done very well indeed' out of such allotments.[27] Mamdot's followers were bound to him by expectations of patronage and would ditch him if he fell from power.[28] The provincial government was employing 'corrupt officers because they are the willing tools' of the chief minister to 'the neglect or worse of honest officers.'[29] The governor warned that if this is allowed to continue 'democracy will be discredited to such an extent that it will inevitably sooner or later be overthrown.'[30]

In response to this and other pleas the centre imposed Section 92-A, dismissed the Mamdot ministry, and constituted a Council of Advisers answerable directly to the centre via the governor. By 30 May 1949, there was 'a marked improvement in the standard of administration', extensive touring by the government ministers was taking place and the provincial revenue agencies had launched a drive to collect overdue taxes yielding an additional ten million rupees in its first month.[31] Having said that, the governor had himself warned earlier that Section 92-A was at best a temporary measure and could not offset the 'feeling that the League is not only corrupt, but totalitarian' and the likelihood that it would lose in a free and fair election.[32] Those ousted by the centre's interference soon wormed their way back into the mainstream and launched effective attacks upon the governor and administration whom they sought to dislodge owing to his refusal to assist government candidates in the forthcoming elections.[33] Mudie was thus forced out. His resignation was accepted on 9 July 1949. Eleven days earlier, Ambrose Dundas, the NWFP's governor, had received the acceptance of his resignation. He had informed the prime minister that 'I do not think you know how tired I am',[34] and warned that due to the absence of effective central control 'a great deal now goes on of which I disapprove and which I think to be bad policy, bad for the Province and bad for Pakistan.'[35] The state was 'not doing nearly so well as appears on the surface, and I like it less and less.'[36] Dundas was successful in convening tribal *jirgas* and ensured that practically all the tribes ratified 'new treaty-based settlements between them and the Pakistan government on the colonial model.'[37] In April 1948, the contribution of the tribes to the war effort against India in Kashmir elicited thanks from Jinnah and resulted in 'the withdrawal of all regular army presence...from the region.'³⁸ One of the major incentives for the tribal leaders, chieftains and princes was 'the ratification of their authority' by the new government.³⁹ That the Pakistani government had teeth was demonstrated by its use of air power against the Fakir of Ipi in 1948, and the bombardment of hostile tribal forces on the Afghan side of the border in 1949.⁴⁰

The warnings and admonishments delivered by the last Englishmen to rule the subcontinent reflected the crisis raging within the state. The NWFP had already experienced the dismissal of its government by the centre in August 1947. Baluchistan had already experienced the first of many military actions launched by the centre in the shape of the operation against the Kalat State on 22 June 1948. In other regions, such as Bahawalpur State and Sindh, central intervention through overt and covert means was alternately invited and condemned by local leaders eager to settle scores with each other. East Bengal was simmering with discontent over the national/official languages controversy. Kashmir was the scene of direct military confrontation with India.

In the context of refugee rehabilitation, the Punjab's governor informed the centre that the most galling fault of the Muslim League ministers was 'their refusal to cooperate with the Pakistan-West Punjab Refugee and Rehabilitation Council or even to attend its meetings, unless they have some personal axe to grind.'⁴¹ Of the three committees under Punjab government ministers formed to deal with different facets of the refugee crisis only one 'has sent us any proceedings at all.'⁴² In exasperation, the governor advised in favour of greater central control so as to secure a coordinated and uniform response to the refugee crisis and 'of removing this problem…from local politics and personalities.'⁴³ Indeed, serious consideration needed to be given to effective concentration of power at the centre 'and a restoration more or less to what used to be the position before the 1935 Act introduced more or less complete provincial autonomy.'⁴⁴

The refugee crisis was but one component of the state of siege. As over ten million brutalised and suddenly impoverished people streamed into and out of Pakistan, crises loomed on multiple fronts. India, believing Pakistan to be a temporary visitor, did whatever it could to hasten Pakistan's departure. Stores and equipment were held up, funds were handed over only upon Gandhi's intervention, water and currency disputes combined with direct military pressure on West Pakistan, almost overwhelmed the new state. In East Bengal, the centre's desire to make Urdu the language of national communication raised a storm of controversy. Across the Durand Line, Afghanistan, egged on by India, claimed Pakistani territory up to the Indus and earned the distinction of being the only country to vote against Pakistan's entry to the United Nations. Religious parties, many of whom had opposed the creation of Pakistan, such as the Jamaat-i-Islami (JI), began opening their franchises in the Muslim homeland and agitated for its conversion into a priestly state. Communist agitation and desire to bring about a revolution in Pakistan added to the anxieties of the Muslim League leadership. Navigating the ship of state through this storm was a tremendous undertaking.

As the challenges to its executive authority emerged and became more complex, the central leadership sought refuge behind Jinnah's transcendental prestige and charisma. As things stood, Jinnah was the governor-general and the president of the Constituent Assembly. Already, on 30 December 1947, the central cabinet adopted a convention that aimed at fusing Jinnah's personal authority, standing, and popularity, with that of the government's. At the cabinet meeting the ministers,

> ...were all agreed that the Quaid-i-Azam's presence was the greatest factor making for the stability and progress of the State...no question of policy or principle should be determined and decided except at a meeting of the Cabinet to be presided over by the Quaid-i-Azam...in the event of any difference of opinion between the Cabinet and the Quaid-i-Azam latter's decision should be final.[45]

A minister enthusiastically added:

> ...that it would be recalled that as soon as the Cabinet was sworn in on the 15 August, the Ministers had made it known to the Quaid-i-Azam that they did not wish him to be only a constitutional Governor-General. The people looked to the Government as the Quaid-i-Azam's Government.[46]

Jinnah observed that 'It was entirely for the Cabinet to decide' what issues should be brought to his attention and asserted 'that he had not the slightest intention of taking the decisions himself.'[47] Moreover, 'only questions of policy' should be brought to his notice and no one would or could 'dispute that democracy was the ideal to be aimed at.'[48] The cabinet unanimously approved the convention and stipulated that Jinnah 'will be entitled to call upon the Secretary-General or the Secretary of any Ministry to furnish him with any information he might require and they shall be bound to do so.'[49] The convention was declared 'personal to the Quaid-i-Azam' and was to last 'until the final constitution of Pakistan' comes into force.[50]

In passing this convention the Muslim League government created a number of damaging precedents. First, the convention obsequiously acknowledged that the Muslim League drew its strength from Jinnah and felt his sanction to be vital to the formulation of policy. Second, it represented the first legitimisation of extra-constitutional authority and Jinnah had himself pointed this out in the course of the discussion concerning the convention. Third, it enabled the governor-general to directly commune with the senior levels of the civil service without reference to the cabinet. Fourth, it made it appear that the government was of a personal, not institutional nature. And finally, it represented a reversal of the direction that constitutional development in the subcontinent had taken over the past generation in making the executive more accountable to the other branches of the state. On 11 August 1947, Jinnah had declared that the legislature was the real sovereign and had all the power and authority. By 30 December 1947, the leading members of that same legislature had elevated the governor-generalship and Jinnah's person to a sovereign position. Although Jinnah's personal status and contribution may well have been above reproach, the precedent of reordering constitutional norms to aggrandise the transient occupants of the highest offices in the country became, and remains, an enduring feature of Pakistan's culture of power.

Sitting in Karachi the central government saw provincial politics as an interminably discordant enterprise. An effective medium was needed to execute the will of the central government and preserve the state. 'The larger interests of the State' necessitated that the most important services which materially affected 'the lives of the people', specifically the Civil Service of Pakistan (CSP) and the Police Service of Pakistan (PSP), 'should be used to promote homogeneity and a common outlook.'[51] Care had to be taken to strike a balance between knowledge of local conditions and loyalty to the centre. It was felt that the provincial governments were generally not up to the task of making policy in their own sphere of competence and too prone to confusing politics with administration to supervise and execute policies made either by themselves or by the centre. This was unfortunate because practically everything that materially affected the well-being of the citizens, ranging from law and order and land revenue, to health, education, local government, and public works, was supposed to be under control of the provincial governments. As the crises continued and the centre became increasingly disheartened by the manner in which even the most routine functions, such as collecting water-rates, or the most vital to the survival of the state, such as managing the refugee problem, were subordinated to politics, greater emphasis came to be placed on centralisation.

The provincial governments themselves reinforced the centre's perception by alternately appealing to and defying central intervention. In the context of the Sindh-Khairpur irrigation dispute, for instance, the prime minister was advised that nothing less than direct personal 'intervention could bring about a just and fair settlement between the contending parties.'[52] The prime minister was also urged to display a firm attitude so that settlement could be reached.[53] The provinces, even as they failed to resist the centre's taking over of the right to collect sales tax and its abolition of the provincial petrol tax, berated the centre for failing to provide funds for development and for favouring certain areas, such as the Punjab and urban Sindh, over others, such as rural Sindh and East Bengal.

The fact was that the centre did pay more attention to the Punjab owing to the severe dislocations endured by that province. Of the nearly seven million refugees to pour into West Pakistan, four million four hundred thousand arrived in the Punjab.[54] The task of resettling the refugees on agricultural land was entrusted to the deputy commissioners operating under the central Ministry of Refugees and Rehabilitation in their capacity as District Rehabilitation Officers. Their performance was remarkable and with a total of less than a hundred officers working round the clock some nine-tenths of the refugees had been resettled by 1949 on rural properties.[55] At no stage in this entire exercise did order completely breakdown for any length of time and the police matched the performance of their colleagues in the civil service and rescued some forty-thousand abducted women. Sindh's governor, communicating with the governor-general in 1952, shortly after the imposition of Section 92-A, observed that 'it is the Services who are really responsible for the good or bad government of a country.'[56] The governor also felt that the centre 'should for some time' allow the provincial governments control over their administrations as most of the officers even from the purely provincial cadres who were being appointed and transferred by the centre 'did not pay so much regard to the Provincial administration as they should' and looked directly up to the central government.[57]

The centralisation of revenue collection referred to above was justified on the grounds of heavy defence spending, the need to rapidly develop an industrial base to increase total revenues and conserve foreign exchange, the insufficiency of existing sources of revenue, and the prospect of heavy deficits.[58] In addition to taking over sales tax and relieving the provinces of the petrol tax and agricultural income tax, the centre appropriated 'the full discretion to increase the customs and central excise duties and to retain the whole of the proceeds.'[59] The idea that gained ground at the centre was that the provinces could be induced to give up their control over the raising and collection of revenue, especially from growing sources such as taxes on consumption of goods and services, 'if we agreed to share the proceeds with them on a basis to be worked out because they would then be relieved of the opprobrium of levying' the taxes themselves.[60] Evidently, the provinces did not realise that the opprobrium of raising funds on their own, or self-taxation, was the essence of self-government, without which all the rhetoric about provincial autonomy was a meaningless exercise in political semantics. For the central government, its finance minister, Ghulam Muhammad, effectively summarised the nature and extent of the siege and the desperate situation faced by the centre, which, in turn, justified such measures as had to be taken, in his budget speech for 1947-48:

> I also wish to emphasise that formidable as the lack of industrial development is by itself the situation has been rendered more difficult by the manner in which partition has taken place. Quite apart from the patent inequities of the Boundary Award which has materially affected our economy, the process of partition has resulted in India remaining in full possession of all the privileges, facilities and institutions vital to the economic and financial well being of a nation, while Pakistan has to build up everything from scratch, and that too with its limited resources.[61]

One of the most effective mechanisms of administrative and fiscal centralisation was state-sponsored economic development. The speed with which the centre moved to take charge of economic development was remarkable given the other challenges it faced. By April 1949, the Ministry of Economic Affairs constituted an Economic Policy Branch integrating planning and supervision.[62] Already, some one hundred and forty-three development schemes were under examination and fifty-one were being processed for approval.[63] An Industrial Finance Corporation was started with capital of thirty million rupees to execute schemes with the assistance of provincial governments in order to facilitate 'private enterprise.'[64] Between April and September 1949, proposals for one hundred and eighty-nine schemes were received, of which ninety-one were approved at a projected cost of more than six hundred and fifty million rupees to be spent over five years.[65] Of this amount, some two hundred and thirty-six million rupees were marked for East Bengal.[66] It is remarkable to behold a central government located in Karachi determining the extent of financial help to the Holy Family Hospital in Rawalpindi, building spinning mills and a paper mill in East Bengal, taking acute interest in bamboo production, promoting the wool industry and sheep rearing in the pastoral expanses of Baluchistan and the NWFP, or, for that matter, setting up a Mycological Herbarium in the environs of the capital.[67] The initial experience gained from the development exercise reinforced the centre's growing sense of its monopoly of competence and confirmed the perception that the provincial governments, for all their rhetoric, had no real interest in improving the lot of the people of Pakistan:

> ...the Governments of East Bengal and Sind have not made use of the Central Government's offer of development schemes. Consequently, no progress at all has been made in respect of the development schemes pertaining to which loans were sanctioned to East Bengal. Sind has proceeded slowly with the Lower Sind Barrage Project. Even the Governments of Punjab and NWFP who drew the loans offered to them during the last two financial years have not made full use of the money at their disposal.[68]

Indeed, the Punjab spent only thirty-three per cent of its allocation for 1948-49 and 25 per cent in 1949-50, while the NWFP spent 33 and 26 per cent of its allocations for the same years, respectively.[69] The centre concluded that 'The performance of Provincial Governments has thus been rather disappointing. At the same time, none of these Provincial Governments have reported any real difficulty which may have held up the progress of any Provincial schemes.'[70]

We can thus see in action the principal mechanism by which fiscal and administrative centralisation combined with development planning by remote agencies took shape well before the first mission of the International Bank for Reconstruction and Development (IBRD) to Pakistan arrived at Karachi on 14 February 1950.[71] The state of siege and the imperatives to which it gave rise justified the centre's assumption of the right to collect taxes from what were provincial sources of revenue. The central government encountered remarkably little resistance for the provincial politicians either did not understand the link between self-taxation, however unpleasant, and self-government, or were too busy undermining the local governments and playing politics with everything they could lay their hands on. Even in those areas of their direct concern, the politicians failed to demonstrate the will or ability to sit down and formulate policy, oversee its execution, and make adjustments as necessary. The central government made this process easier by offers of loans, development assistance, and a share of national finances. Once the provinces became dependent on central allocations and disbursements their secretariats lost control over the projects in question while planning, financing, and supervision, were drawn into central hands. When this process failed to yield the expected results, the centre concluded that the provinces were utterly ill-suited to constructive activity and further centralisation occurred. The availability of foreign sources of funding from 1950 onwards further strengthened the hands of the centre for the provinces could not raise loans on their own from abroad. Rapid import substitution industrialisation determined the centre in a country where nine-tenths of the people lived by subsistence agriculture, was the key to saving foreign exchange and building up a tax base to meet defence needs. Defence expenditures owing to the conflict with India were a serious burden and consumed on average about six-tenths of government expenditure during the first decade of Pakistan's existence.

Purchases of military equipment, the search, initially futile, for foreign allies, and the prioritisation of defence needs may have given the new state a sense of purpose and some confidence relative to its truculent neighbours, but it did little to assuage the political insecurities of the Muslim League's leadership. Jinnah's death in September 1948 deprived the Muslim League of its moral and psychological anchor. Faced with growing dissensions within the ranks and the challenge of traditionalists who, having by and large opposed the creation of Pakistan, reinvented themselves as Pakistan's moral custodians, as well as the communists, the Muslim League leadership led by such luminaries as Liaquat Ali Khan, Zafarullah Khan, Ishtiaq Hussein Qureshi and Maulana Shabbir Ahmad Usmani, took to redeploying the religious rhetoric of the Pakistan movement.[72] The deviation from Jinnah's express desire that Pakistan ought not to be a priestly or theocratic state was substantial and the Muslim League leadership turned its back upon Jinnah's eminently sound advice given in his address to the Constituent Assembly on 11 August 1947, in his capacity as its president:

> ...everyone of you, no matter to what community he belongs, no matter what relations he had with you in the past, no matter what is his colour, caste or creed, is first, second and last a citizen of this State with equal rights, privileges, and obligations...
> ...We should begin to work in that spirit and in course of time all these angularities of the majority and minority communities...will vanish.
> ...You are free; you are free to go to your temples, you are free to go to your mosques or to any other place or worship in this State of Pakistan. You may belong to any religion or caste or creed that has nothing to do with the business of the State...We are starting with this fundamental principle that we are all citizens and equal citizens of one State. The people of England in course of time had to face the realities of the situation and had to discharge the responsibilities and burdens placed upon them by the government of their country and they went through that fire step by step. Today, you might say with justice that Roman Catholics and Protestants do not exist; what exists now is that every man is a citizen, an equal citizen of Great Britain and they are all members of the Nation.
> Now I think we should keep that in front of us as our ideal and you will find that in course of time Hindus would cease to be Hindus and Muslims would cease to be Muslims, not in the religious sense, because that is the personal faith of each individual, but in the political sense as citizens of the State.[73]

In March 1949, the Muslim League pushed through over the opposition of all the non-Muslim members of the Constituent Assembly in attendance, the Objectives Resolution, which declared:

> Whereas sovereignty over the entire universe belongs to Allah Almighty alone and the authority which He has delegated to the State of Pakistan, through

its people for being *exercised within the limits prescribed by Him* is a sacred trust....

Wherein the principles of democracy, freedom, equality, tolerance and social justice *as enunciated by Islam* shall be fully observed...

Wherein the Muslims shall be enabled to order their lives in the individual and collective spheres *in accordance with the teachings and requirements of Islam as set out in the Holy Quran and the Sunnah*...[74]

The *ulema* were not pleased with the fact that in the Objectives Resolution the elected representatives had appropriated the right to legislate for themselves. The *ulema* contended, not illogically, that a parliament dominated by the laity had neither the knowledge, nor the moral prerogative, for the interpretation of the laws and traditions of Islam. The Objectives Resolution reopened the debate on sovereignty and citizenship, alienated the minorities and opposition, and whetted the appetites of the *ulema*, whose ranks had swelled due to the migration of many of their counterparts from India.[75] Thanks to a network of seminaries, which numbered one thousand and seventy-four and had over eighty-five thousand pupils at the secondary and higher levels in East Bengal alone, in addition to innumerable mosques spread across the length and breadth of the country,[76] the *ulema* were able to exert considerable pressure on the government. Indeed, 'the traditionalists, by their simplistic emphasis on the formal classical apparatus of an Islamic state, couched their message in general terms so that it had the capacity of being widely understood. This put them at a considerable advantage over the modernists.'[77]

The JUI-P (Jamiat-Ulema-i-Islam, Pakistan) declared that as Islamic law is perfect and complete only qualified interpreters were needed.[78] Other clerics demanded that non-Muslims be declared *dhimmis* (protected subjects of an Islamic state without full citizenship) while Maulana Abdul Hamid Badayuni insisted that that the non-Muslims be barred from the army and judiciary.[79] Maulana Mohammed Ibrahim Chisti complained of the 'fuss' about democracy and minorities and the unnecessary 'emphasis upon Western concepts.'[80] The relatively more sophisticated Maudoodi, acknowledging the possibility of delegation of authority by God, pointed out that some parts of the Sharia could be altered, but only by experts in Islamic law and traditions.[81] In the debate over the Islamic provisions of the constitution, the modernists contended that 'The *Ulema* were intolerant of criticism' while the latter retorted 'that no criticism could, indeed, be tolerated against the fundamentals of Islam.'[82] There was, and is, an almost universal tendency amongst politically active 'doctors of religion' to equate dissent with heresy, define politics 'in dictatorial, not democratic terms', and thus stifle reasoned argument in public life.[83] The ultimate weapon in the hands of the forces of 'obscurantism and religiosity' was the constant threat 'of excommunication.'[84] The medievalisation of public discourse had found a fresh momentum.

On 7 August 1950, Sindh's governor communicated his vision for the 'budding nation of Pakistan.'[85] It was imperative that the Pakistani public, eighty-five per cent of them Muslim, be instructed by the state to live in accordance 'with the true Islamic way of life.'[86] In order to achieve this objective, 'the general policy of our education should be revised,' religious instruction made compulsory at school, and Pakistan 'must have a portfolio for religious affairs in the Central Cabinet.'[87] A proper Islamic education was the solution to all of Pakistan's problems.[88] These views met with a sympathetic hearing as the commerce and education minister had already communicated his analysis of the subject to the prime minister on 19 September 1949:

> The existing system of education, with its alien background, coloured by Hindu and Christian ideas, is so foreign to the spirit of our ideology that, for so long as it continues, it cannot be expected to produce men and women who would realise the value of the Islamic way of life and would make loyal and zealous citizens of Pakistan.[89]

In order to produce the new Islamic man and woman, 'we have to draw up the syllabus for every subject on the basis of Islamic ideology.'[90] A new national history was needed to uncover the providential nature of Pakistan's emergence as was some kind of Islamic research centre.[91] The provinces were incapable of managing things and so 'The Central Government should assume direct responsibility for the general planning and coordination of education in all fields.'[92] However, it was 'important to bear in mind' the rather distasteful 'presence of the Hindu community in East Bengal' that constituted about one-third of that province's population.[93] The caste Hindus were 'wedded to the Bengali language' and represented 'the hard core of resistance to the changes which we wish to introduce on the basis of our educational ideology.'[94]

Neither these ideocratic longings nor repressive legislation such as the Public Representative Offices Disqualification Act (PRODA) or the Public Safety Act (PSA) improved the fortunes of the ruling Muslim League. There was a failed communist-inspired coup[95] and a successful attempt on Liaquat Ali Khan's life in 1951. In March 1952, the interior secretary, G. Ahmed, submitted a note on the internal situation to Khwaja Nazimuddin, the new prime minister (1951-1953). The interior secretary reported 'a noticeable loss of public confidence in the Government' which was universally seen as 'weak and, except at certain levels, far from competent.'[96] The public mood indicated that Pakistan was 'on the downgrade internally' since Liaquat Ali Khan's death.[97] Political and provincial disharmony had increased everywhere and while the only major trouble had occurred in Dhaka, the capital of East Bengal, which necessitated army deployment, 'an undercurrent of restlessness' pervaded the federation.[98] The Muslim League, notwithstanding its dubious success in the recent Punjab elections, had 'lost considerable ground', fractures had 'developed everywhere' while the party machinery, never particularly efficient, had ground to a halt.[99] The cause of the malaise was the mindset of the politicians and their medieval attitude towards the acquisition and exercise of power:

> The present idea of their obligations in the minds of most Members of the legislature seems to be either to seek advantage from the Government for themselves or their friends and relatives, or to advertise and exploit the supposed grievances of their constituents. Explanation and defence of Government policy and of its point of view on current problems do not find a place among the responsibilities of Party leaders and Members of the Legislature belonging to the Muslim League.[100]

While the politicians at all levels used and abused the state as a personal estate, the provincial leaders had, additionally, adopted 'an intensely parochial line irrespective of the interests of the country' or the central government, or even their own parties.[101]

The 'communist virus' had been checked by the government's actions following the uncovering of the Rawalpindi Conspiracy, though it remained fairly virulent in parts of the urban East Bengal, particularly the University of Dhaka.[102] That said the greatest threat to Pakistan, which was spreading confusion and anxiety 'in the minds of the general public' was 'the parrot-like repetition by politicians of the slogan that

Pakistan is an Islamic State.'[103] This kind of rhetoric was 'fraught with considerable danger' and being 'fully exploited by the enemies of Pakistan to discredit it abroad as well as by the obscurantist elements inside the country.'[104] The impression 'among the intelligent section of the people' was 'that talk of an Islamic State on part of the politicians' was merely a 'device to keep themselves in power.'[105] The politicians seemed 'to be banking on reactionary forces for political support' which risked Pakistan 'degenerating into the primitive levels of certain countries in the Middle East.'[106] This suspicion had gained widespread acceptance due to 'the ease and freedom with which it has been possible for orthodox Mullahs to make Pakistan a happy hunting ground.'[107] Mosques and seminaries throughout Pakistan were being used to preach 'superstitious and unenlightened religiosity' without any check, and it seemed that the state was 'pandering to orthodoxy.'[108] The politicians were playing a very dangerous game by trumpeting Islamic ideology and 'raising expectations which, because they vary according to the prejudices and predilections of individuals or groups, would be impossible to fulfil.'[109] It was ultimately suicidal for the modernist Muslims, whom the traditionalists considered infidels, to pursue such a course of action and 'there should be less talk of Islamic ideology and no encouragement whatever of orthodoxy in any shape or form.'[110]

In effect G. Ahmed's advice boiled down to two principles. First, the politicians should discipline themselves and stop treating the state (*sarkar*) as their hereditary personal estate (*watan-jagir*). Second, they must stop playing games with the religious fundamentalists for short-term political benefit. If they failed to do so then they risked their own future as the leaders of Pakistan and made it more likely that the country would degenerate into sectarian schism, violence and administrative breakdown. The politicians did not take heed, but at least we know now that they were not ill-advised by the servants of the state. In the 1951 elections in the Punjab, the Muslim League used the state machinery and allied with the Majlis-i-Ahrar and Jamiat-Ulema-i-Islam, Pakistan (JUI-P), and secured a suspiciously heavy mandate in the province. Mian Mumtaz Daultana became the chief minister and was elected unopposed. His party members, however, soon plunged into speculation, hoarding, and wreaking havoc upon the food distribution system in order to manipulate prices in their favour as many of them were powerful landlords. The Ahrars thought it an opportune moment to renew their campaign to have the Ahmedis[111] declared non-Muslims. Soon, agitation spread in the province. Both Daultana and Nazimuddin encouraged the agitation. The former believed he could use it to put the centre on the defensive and rally the provincial Muslim League behind himself, while the latter thought he could render his government above questioning or challenge by manipulating orthodox Islamic sentiment. By the end of July 1952, the Punjab Muslim League had voted two hundred and sixty-four against eight in support of the agitators' demand and Section 144, reluctantly imposed by Daultana in parts of the Punjab on the insistence of the Inspector-General Police, Qurban Ali Khan, was lifted. Nazimuddin tried to one-up the Punjab Muslim League and constituted an Islamic Advisory Board in which the *ulema* were invited to come and give their advice to the Basic Principles Committee of the Constituent Assembly. It was hardly surprising that the consequences for the politicians as a body as well as for the country were not long in the coming and proved disastrous and almost irretrievable.

2.3 THE FALL

For senior administrators such as G. Ahmed and Qurban Ali Khan, the senior military commanders such as the Commander-in-Chief General Ayub Khan, the Area Commander Lahore, General Azam Khan, and senior bureaucrats turned politicians, such as Ghulam Muhammad, Ch. Muhammad Ali and Iskander Mirza, the turn of events was cause for extreme concern. Indeed, no two religious scholars agreed 'as to the definition of a Muslim' and by accepting the point of view of any one sect or scholar or school, one automatically became an infidel according to all the other definitions.[112] It was a dangerous game to play in a diverse society like Pakistan for while today it was the Ahmedis, tomorrow, perhaps, it could be the Ismailis, or the Ahl-i-Hadith, or mainstream Shias, or the Deobandis or Barelvis, to say nothing of what would happen to the ten million plus Hindus in East Bengal, or the Parsi community of Karachi and Quetta.

By March 1953 the agitation had spun out of control. In the ensuing riots some three hundred were killed. On 6 March, martial law was imposed in Lahore and the agitation crushed within hours. Daultana's ministry was dismissed and martial law remained in force for two months during which time everything from a crackdown on lawless elements to a public cleanliness campaign were conducted. On 17 April 1953, Ghulam Muhammad, governor general since Liaquat Ali Khan's assassination, dismissed Nazimuddin's government under Section 10 of the provisional constitution even though the prime minister had recently proven his majority by passing the budget.

Nazimuddin's dismissal was Pakistan's first successful coup. Emboldened by the ease with which it was pulled off, Pakistan's senior civil servants and military commanders, took it upon themselves to restructure the nation and the state to produce uniformity, discipline, and progress. The question remained whether Pakistan would be a civilian bureaucratic dictatorship supported by the military or a military dictatorship supported by the civilian bureaucracy. Either way, invertebrate and self-seeking politicians would be welcome to join the officially patronised party and help keep up constitutional and democratic pretences. Within two years of Nazimuddin's dismissal the Constituent Assembly, the provinces of West Pakistan, and the higher judiciary, would fall before the application of executive power. 17 April 1953, thus marked the point at which Pakistan's politicians lost control of the administrative and military machine crafted under the leadership of Jinnah and Liaquat Ali Khan to enable Pakistan to survive in a state of siege. Except for brief and tragic interludes[113] control would not be restored to elected politicians. The mandarins and praetorians were now in control of the palace, the former more visibly than the latter. It is therefore to the ethos, evolution and structure of the civilian bureaucracy, in particular its elite cadres, that we now turn.

NOTES

1. Perhaps the most comprehensive study undertaken of the use of religious and ideological symbols as instruments of mass mobilisation is M. Naeem Qureshi's *Pan-Islam in British Indian Politics: A Study of the Khilafat Movement, 1918-1924* (Leiden: Brill, 1999). Qureshi excavates the origins of the Ottoman Empire's ideocratic pretensions and explains with painstaking detail both the power and the limitations of the use of Islamic symbols for the purpose of generating popular support. Yet, in the final analysis, Qureshi found Pan Islam to be a mirage.
2. Zimbardo, *The Lucifer Effect*, 5.
3. Ibid.
4. Ibid., 4.

5. For more on the formation of this elite and its perpetuation after 1947 in Pakistan see Tariq Rahman, *Language Ideology and Power: Language-learning among the Muslims of Pakistan and North India* (Karachi: Oxford University Press, 2002).
6. A point that is driven home in Sikandar Hayat, *The Charismatic Leader: Quaid-i-Azam Mohammed Ali Jinnah and the Creation of Pakistan* (Karachi: Oxford University Press, 2008). Hayat demonstrates Jinnah's aloofness and alienation from the mainstream Indian Muslim culture. Relying upon Weber's alternate perspective on charisma, which maintains that a true charismatic leader possess rationality, sobriety and the ability to incorporate his charisma into institutions, Hayat argues that Jinnah was in fact a charismatic leader. Jinnah's charisma was eventually incorporated in the new state of Pakistan.
7. For more on the complexity of the Pakistan movement see Sikander Hayat, *Aspects of the Pakistan Movement* (Islamabad: National Institute of Historical and Cultural Research, 1998). Hayat examines the Muslim nationalist position as an exercise in mobilisation that contained mutually contradictory long-term objectives. It was successful owing to the qualities of leadership, charisma, and technical competence of M. A. Jinnah.
8. The space very slowly expanded to include some female leaders as well. For more see Dushka H. Saiyid, *Muslim Women of the British Punjab: From Seclusion to Politics* (London: MacMillan Press Ltd., 1998).
9. Judith M. Brown, 'India' in Judith M. Brown, ed., *The Oxford History of the British Empire* Vol. IV, *The Twentieth Century* (Oxford: Oxford University Press, 1999), 426.
10. Ibid., 424-5.
11. Ibid., 429.
12. Ibid., 435.
13. The economic backwardness of the Muslims was reflected in the value of assets abandoned by them in India at partition estimated at about one billion rupees. Assets abandoned by Hindus and Sikhs in Pakistan were estimated at five billion rupees. Given that an almost equal number of people fled to either side of the new international boundary the discrepancy shows the per capita economic superiority of the non-Muslims. Kuldip Nayar and Asif Noorani, *Tales of Two Cities* (New Delhi: Lotus Collection, 2008), 39.
14. Hasan Askari Rizvi, *The Military and Politics in Pakistan 1947-1997* (Lahore: Sang-e-Meel Publications, 2000), 45.
15. Francis Robinson, *Islam, South Asia and the West* (New Delhi: Oxford University Press, 2007), 59.
16. Ibid.
17. Jyotirmaya Sharma, *Hindutva: Exploring the Idea of Hindu Nationalism* (New Delhi: Penguin Books, 2006), 2.
18. Ibid., 7.
19. Ibid., 10.
20. Robinson, *Islam, South Asia and the West*, 61-2.
21. Ibid., 86.
22. Ibid.
23. Maulana Abul Kalam Azad, *India wins Freedom* (New Delhi: Orient Longman, 1988), 208-248. Azad was president of the Congress in 1923 and from 1940-

1946. After independence he became India's federal minister for education and served till his death in 1958.
24. By June 1947, the Muslim League had raised a force of nearly a hundred and forty thousand national guards. The Congress and its allies has raised a force of about one hundred thousand. The Hindu fundamentalists, however, outdid both Muslim separatists and Congress nationalists and armed more than one hundred and ninety thousand. B. B. Misra, *The Indian Political Parties: An Historical Analysis of Political Behaviour up to 1947* (Delhi: Oxford University Press, 1978), 611-612.
25. National Documentation Centre, Islamabad. Folder Six, 1949. File No. 2(2)-PMS/49, Government of Pakistan, Prime Minster's Secretariat, 'Correspondence with the Governor, West Punjab', 4.
26. Ibid., 7.
27. Ibid.
28. Ibid., 9.
29. Ibid.
30. Ibid., 7.
31. Ibid., 67.
32. Ibid., 152-3.
33. Ibid., File No. 2(6)-PMS/49, Government of Pakistan, Prime Minister's Secretariat, 'Resignation of Sir Francis Mudie', 252.
34. Ibid., File No. 2(8)-PMS/49, Government of Pakistan, Prime Minister's Secretariat, 'Retirement of Sir Ambrose Dundas', 265.
35. Ibid., 269.
36. Ibid.
37. Sana Haroon, *Frontier of Faith: Islam in the Indo-Afghan Borderland* (London: Hurst & Company, 2007), 181.
38. Ibid., 182.
39. Ibid., 183.
40. Ibid., 187-190.
41. National Documentation Centre, Islamabad. Folder Three, 1948. File No. 2(2)-PMS/48, Government of Pakistan, Cabinet Secretariat, Prime Minster's Secretariat Branch, 'Correspondence with the Governor of West Punjab (Ref. Rehabilitation of Refugees)', 22.
42. Ibid., 38.
43. Ibid., 24.
44. Ibid., 25.
45. 1947, File No. 21/CF/48, Government of Pakistan, 'Adoption of Convention by the Cabinet', 1.
46. Ibid., 3.
47. Ibid., 2-3.
48. Ibid., 2.
49. Ibid., 5.
50. Ibid.
51. National Documentation Centre, Islamabad, Folder Five, 1949. File No. 3(4)-PMS/49, Government of Pakistan, Prime Minster's Secretariat, 'Correspondence with the Hon'ble Minster for Interior, Information and Broadcasting', 133.

52. National Documentation Centre, Islamabad, Folder Twelve, 1950. File No. 7(1)-PMS/50, Government of Pakistan, Prime Minster's Secretariat, 'Correspondence with the Chief Minster of Sind—Sind-Khairpur Irrigation Dispute', 217.
53. Ibid.
54. 1949, File No. 20/CF/49, Government of Pakistan, Cabinet Secretariat, Cabinet Branch, 'General Summary of the Policy and Progress of Resettlement of Muslim Refugees on Evacuee Lands in West Pakistan,' 6.
55. Ibid.
56. National Documentation Centre, Islamabad, Folder Nineteen, 1952. File No. 2(3)-PMS/52 Pr. III, Government of Pakistan, Prime Minster's Secretariat, 'Correspondence with the H. E. the Governor of Sind', 60.
57. National Documentation Centre, Islamabad, Folder Seventeen, 1952. File No. 1(1)-PMS/52, Government of Pakistan, Cabinet Secretariat, Prime Minster's Branch, 'Correspondence with the Governor General of Pakistan', 48.
58. 1947, File No. 224/CF/47, Government of Pakistan, Cabinet Secretariat, Cabinet Branch, 'Readjustment of the Tax Structure Between the Centre and the Provinces', 1.
59. Ibid., 2.
60. Ibid., Cabinet Meeting, 24 December 1947, Case No. 217/33/47, 1.
61. Ibid., 'Speech of the Finance Minister', 1.
62. 1948, File No. 150/CF/48, Government of Pakistan, Cabinet Secretariat, Cabinet Branch, 'Half Yearly Summary of the Ministry of Economic Affairs', No. 69 (5), EA/Admin/49, November 1948-April 1949, 1.
63. Ibid.
64. Ibid., 1-2.
65. Ibid., 'Half Yearly Summary of the Activities of the Ministry of Economic Affairs for the Period April 1949 to September 1949', 1.
66. Ibid., 2.
67. Ibid., 1.
68. Ibid., 'Half Yearly Summary of the Activities of the Ministry of Economic Affairs for the Period October 1949 to March 1950', 3.
69. Ibid.
70. Ibid., 4.
71. Ibid., 6.
72. See for instance the *Constituent Assembly Debates*, 12 March 1949 (Karachi: Pakistan Publications, 1949), esp. 90-94 concerning the adoption of the Objectives Resolution referred to below.
73. Mohammed Ali Jinnah, 'Presidential Address to the Constituent Assembly of Pakistan', 11 August 1947, in Khurshid Ahmed Khan Yusufi, ed., *Speeches, Statements and Messages of the Quaid-i-Azam*, vol. iv, 1946-48. (Lahore: Bazm-i-Iqbal, 1996), 2602-6.
74. My emphases. See, *Constituent Assembly Debates* 12 March 1949, (Karachi: Pakistan Publications, 1949) 90-4.
75. Freeland Abbot, *Islam and Pakistan*, (Ithaca: Cornell University Press, 1968), 186.
76. Khalid B. Sayeed, *Political System of Pakistan* (Boston: Houghton Mifflin Company, 1967), 167-8.

77. Inamur Rehman, *Public Opinion and Political Development in Pakistan 1947-1958* (Karachi: Oxford University Press, 1982), 38.
78. Golam W. Choudry, *Constitutional Development in Pakistan*, (London: Longman Group, 1969), 48.
79. Ibid.
80. Ibid.
81. Allen McGrath, *The Destruction of Pakistan's Democracy*, (Karachi: Oxford University Press, 1996), 68.
82. Rehman, *Public Opinion and Political Development in Pakistan 1947-1958*, 23.
83. K. K. Aziz, *Pakistan's Political Culture: Essays in Historical and Social Origins* (Lahore: Vanguard, 2001), 116-117.
84. Ibid., 127.
85. National Documentation Centre, Islamabad, Folder Nine, 1950. File No. 2(3)-PMS/50, Government of Pakistan, Prime Minster's Secretariat, 'Correspondence with the Governor of Sindh', 21.
86. Ibid.
87. Ibid.
88. Ibid., 22.
89. Ibid., File No. 3(4)-PMS/50, 'Correspondence with the Hon'ble Minister for Commerce and Education', 202.
90. Ibid.
91. Ibid., 203.
92. Ibid., 213.
93. Ibid., 209.
94. Ibid.
95. See National Documentation Centre, Islamabad, Folder Twenty-Two, 1953. File No. 23(34)-PMS/53, Government of Pakistan, Cabinet Secretariat, Prime Minster's Branch, 'Judgment in the Rawalpindi Conspiracy Case.'
96. National Documentation Centre, Islamabad, Folder Twenty-One, 1952. File No. 3(5)-PMS/52, Government of Pakistan, Prime Minster's Secretariat, 'Correspondence with the Hon'ble Minster for Interior and States & Frontier Regions,' 72.
97. Ibid.
98. Ibid.
99. Ibid.
100. Ibid., 74.
101. Ibid.
102. Ibid., 76.
103. Ibid., 77.
104. Ibid.
105. Ibid.
106. Ibid.
107. Ibid., 77-8.
108. Ibid., 78.
109. Ibid., 80.
110. Ibid., 81.

111. A religious sect that claims to be Muslim but denies the finality of the Prophethood. It was founded by Mirza Ghulam Ahmed (1835-1908) who claimed to be a prophet in his own right. Most Sunni and Shia Muslims believe the Ahmedis to be non-Muslims because of this deviation.
112. Mohammed Munir, *From Jinnah to Zia* (Lahore: Vanguard Books, 1980), 46-7.
113. 1972 to 1977 was a period of rule by an elected civilian government that exercised effective power over the state apparatus. Arguably, Nawaz Sharif's second term as prime minister from 1997 to 1999 could also be counted as a period of substantive rule by an elected government. Sharif enjoyed a two-thirds majority in the lower house and successfully dislodged the president, chief justice, and army chief, and replaced all three with his own favourites. His attempt to remove Musharraf from the post of army chief precipitated a military coup. In each case the elected civilian executive failed to understand when to stop.

3 Mandarins

3.1 IMPERIAL NOMOCRACY

The pre-British continental bureaucratic empires were organised along three key principles. First, the entire country was the personal estate of the ruler and thus the servants of the state were the ruler's personal servants. Second, the rulers were legitimised by divine sanction or official ideology that equated opposition with treason and blasphemy. Third, ultimate decision-making powers in all affairs, be they administrative, legislative, political, military, social, or economic, were concentrated in the hands of the supreme executive. Although this was the structure of the state and society that the British inherited in the course of their conquest of India, they made certain changes inspired by their own anomalous culture of power that found formal expression in the State of Laws and Enlightenment-inspired notions of order, progress and liberalism. These changes significantly altered the ethos and orientation of the central state in the subcontinent and reflected the British realisation that in continental bureaucratic empires it was the quality of the officer corps of the state that determined the quality of governance.[1]

The British Indian state was an imperial nomocracy.[2] Successive acts and charters had increased the powers of the British Parliament over the East India Company between 1770 and 1833. After 1858, the Secretary of State for India acted as the cabinet's representative to the India Council, a body of senior officials with ultimate responsibility for government in India. Some of the more energetic viceroys, such as Curzon, felt aggrieved by the restrictions imposed upon them but all had to submit ultimately to its oversight. A critical aspect of parliamentary control was that Indian accounts were laid before parliament annually and it appointed auditors as well.[3] The viceroy, six regular members, and the commander-in-chief of the Indian army as an extraordinary member, constituted the vice-regal council within which the majority ruled subject to executive veto.⁴ This council normally met once a week with its attention focused on issues of an inter-departmental nature, matters of policy, and important routine business, such as budgeting.⁵ Present at these meetings were the secretaries of the concerned departments. They not only prepared the ground for the meetings but gave advice, took note of decisions and were responsible for implementation.⁶ Their autonomy and integrity were guaranteed by the fact that they were from the covenanted Indian Civil Service owing their appointments to the secretary for state, not the viceroy, and thus substantially immune to executive whimsicality. They were also the leaders of a vast and varied administrative machine and the members of this elite corps were rotated between the centre and one province in the course of their careers. Their familiarity with the condition of the people of the country combined with their importance as revenue collectors and magistrates made them especially qualified to actually advise the political executive on what course of action to follow. This was particularly useful for the governor generals and most of their council members were often British politicians or nominees of Parliament with little experience of governance in a bureaucratic state. The broad principle of administration was that the centre would lay down the policies and general outline of important measures and leave the provincial administrations 'to fill in the details by rules drafted by themselves, but approved by the Government of India.'⁷

From 1853 onwards the civil service was recruited through open competitive exams, which completely superseded the system of nomination by powerful patrons. Curiously enough, the attempt to apply this principle to the civil service in England generated tremendous opposition. Stafford Northcote and Charles Trevelyan had urged the establishment in England along Indian lines 'competitive examinations and a central board for recruitment to all home departments.'⁸ Opposition to this scheme at the highest levels delayed its implementation in England until 1870 when:

> The Queen grumbled and, unusually in this phase was not brought into line on Gladstone's side by Prince Albert. 'Where is the application of the principle of public competitions to stop?' she asked apprehensively, perhaps influenced by Lord John Russell's view that the 'harshly republican scheme was as hostile to the monarchy as it was to the aristocracy.'⁹

The application of this 'harshly republican scheme' drew flak from many quarters. The opponents of the competitive recruitment system argued that academic brilliance was no guarantee of morality and physical fitness.[10] The competition system 'induced a man to regard his appointment as a right which made him not so manageable in public service' as compared to those 'who received appointment as a gift.'[11] The exam did not test 'culture' and allowed the 'crammer' to replace the nominee who allegedly knew how to govern by virtue of aristocratic instinct.[12] This nostalgia for the old system of patronage and pretension was utterly vitiated by the reality on the ground:

> These young men, nominated in London under an outworn system of patronage, and once in Calcutta apparently under no official pressure to apply themselves to study, were signally failing to acquire a knowledge of the relevant Indian languages and laws, without which they would never do their jobs effectively. Fifty-six of the most recent batch in training had failed their examinations.[13]

The competition system, though it took time to work out the technical problems, was fundamentally sound. While the patronage system produced three or four unfit candidates for one or two good ones, the reverse could be said of the competition system.[14] The candidates who came through the competition were less extravagant, worked harder, and were more eager to perform.[15] Later, when the age limit was raised and graduates filled the ranks of the civil service, the tirades launched against 'crammers' and 'bookworms' were replaced by fulminations against the 'know-alls' who did not know how to deal with people.[16] On balance, competitive recruitment generated a much higher median quality of civil servant, fewer duds and as many genuinely gifted administrators.[17]

The ICS was the apex administrative cadre and exercised general control over a bureaucracy that was by the 1840s substantially Indianised at the middle and lower levels. Specialised services and departments existed for public works, health, education, policing, and certain kinds of taxation. The ICS members were expected to be generalists as well as experts on a diversity of subjects including law, history, politics, economics, local languages, ethnography, etc.[18] They were also required to act as collectors of land revenue, magistrate, supervise the police and coordinate the activities of other departments. At several levels, ranging from local governments to the central government, they also played a quasi-political role, suggesting, advising and actively participating, in the formulation of policies. They were also academics who compiled, edited, translated and authored invaluable historical, ethnographic, legal and literary works.

Perhaps the ultimate function of the ICS was to set not just the intellectual but also the moral standard within the state. Not only did the ICS officers 'have to be incorruptible' they also 'had to be above suspicion.'[19] In what was perhaps the ultimate manifestation of the British effort to instil the dual notion into the servants of the state that they were not agents of private enterprise, the spirit of which was intrinsically incompatible with public service, and that the country was not their personal estate, the ICS was held to the highest standards:

> They were not allowed any interest, however innocent, in any commercial venture that might affect their professional conduct. If you were the Chief Secretary in Madras, your son could not own a coffee plantation in the presidency; if you were Political Agent in a native state, your relatives could not buy property there.[20]

Failure to comply resulted in disgrace, censure, suspension, and premature retirement. The high *esprit de corps* ensured that questionable behaviour was quietly but effectively punished. In contrast to the loud and ineffective accountability meted out arbitrarily by earlier (and subsequent) rulers, the system worked:

> At his retirement dinner in 1898 Sir John Edge remarked that during his years as Chief Justice of the Allahabad High Court he had received over a thousand letters, usually anonymous, abusing the ICS. Yet not one of them had suggested 'even covertly that any member of the Covenanted Civil Service had acted from any corrupt motive in any matter.' With this omission the authors of the anonymous letters had thus paid a great if unintended compliment.[21]

Such standards could not, of course, be maintained throughout the apparatus and the lower and middle ranks of the bureaucracy did continue to peddle influence, take bribes, and generally make life as miserable as possible for their real or perceived enemies. However, for many Indians the district officer was a paternalistic figure to whom one could appeal for redress and of whom one ought to be respectful and fearful. At the same time, the fact that the most powerful person in the district was a servant of the law, recruited through an open competition, educated in a university or a college, and normally from a middleclass or upper-middleclass background, was a remarkably progressive feature of the British rule.

British Indian imperial nomocracy, however, was not democratic even though it provided the administrative foundations upon which a more representative order could be built in a continental bureaucratic empire. That it took as long as it did to develop these representative institutions must be understood in terms of the age. Victorian Britain was not a democracy and it was not until the late nineteenth century that most men got the right to vote.[22] It took till 1911 for the House of Lords to lose its power to veto taxation legislation and till 1928 for women to get the vote. One cannot with any pretence of objectivity accuse the British of failing to introduce a system of representative government in India that did not exist in their own country in the form taken for granted today until the last twenty or thirty years of their imperial rule.

In introducing the representative principle into the Indian environment, the great challenge was to Indianise the covenanted services while ensuring that the politicians elected at the local, provincial, and central levels, respected the statutory relationship between themselves and the servants of the state.[23] This relationship was that the politicians ought to frame policies and supervise while civil servants advised and executed. By 1933, the provincial services were almost entirely Indian in composition, while the All-India Services were about one-third Indian. The travails of the years that followed had a negative impact on Indianisation and while provision was made for the special induction of Muslim candidates, the quota was not made with Pakistan in mind. Thus, in 1947, while the situation at the provincial levels was tolerable at all-India level, the situation in the covenanted services left much to be desired.

3.2 A Few Civil Servants

Eleanor Roosevelt remarked in the course of her 1952 visit to Pakistan that she had 'the impression that a small number of senior civil servants' were 'quietly working themselves to death.'[24] Indeed, in the five years since independence four out of the thirteen secretaries had suffered coronary thrombosis and evidently a 'secretary to the Government of Pakistan' was 'not a good life insurance risk.'[25] Tragically, even as Pakistan's civil servants worked themselves to ill-health and incapacitation, the first of many blows upon the prestige, culture, and integrity, of the services had already landed. Justice Muhammad Munir, chairing Pakistan's first pay commission, declared:

> We do not think it to be a right policy for the State to offer such salaries to its servants as to attract the best available material. The correct place for our men of genius is in private enterprise and not in the humdrum career of public service where character and a desire to serve honestly for a living is more essential than outstanding intellect. We cannot, therefore, prescribe our pay scales with the object of attracting to public service all the best intellect in the country.[26]

Although the reflections of the first pay commission would be repeatedly disavowed by many subsequent commissions and reports the fact was that none of them succeeded in restoring the pre-independence situation as far as the remuneration of senior civil servants was concerned. It would, however, take a generation for the real impact of this kind of thinking to be felt upon the apparatus as a whole.

In the immediate aftermath of partition the higher bureaucracy was given the task of reconstituting the executive apparatus of the state. This task was entrusted to an initial corps of about one hundred and sixty civil servants, including about forty British officers who stayed on, a few till the early 1960s. Of the Muslim officers, about half had served less than ten years and a mere handful qualified for senior positions. In effect, this meant that assistant and deputy commissioner rank field officers found themselves elevated to senior positions where their input on policy was required. Though ailing, Jinnah directly addressed civil servants on half a dozen occasions between October 1947 and August 1948.

There is little evidence that indicates Jinnah 'aimed at reforming the bureaucratic order inherited from the British Raj.'[27] Jinnah wanted to retain the positive features of the British period which included an 'apolitical, neutral and independent' civil service.[28] The politicians and bureaucrats would have to work together and respect each other's lawful autonomy and role in the state.[29] Moreover, Jinnah appreciated the role of the bureaucracy as an integrating agency 'in a country where regional values persisted.'[30] On 14 April 1948, at the Government House Peshawar, Jinnah informed the assemblage that whereas ministers and governments came and went the bureaucracy must stay on and thus constituted 'the backbone of the state.'[31] The weight borne by this backbone and the speed with which it managed to restore order, taxation, and communications, and even begin working on long-term development plans was stunning:

> Approximately 74 positions above the rank of assistant secretary had to be filled in the provincial secretariats of Pakistan but only 22 Muslim provincial service officers had held such posts before, and it is doubtful if more than three-quarters of them were available to Pakistan. These facts speak more effectively than the explanation. Most developing states have faced the trauma of independence with acute shortage of administrative skill, but at least most states had inherited a national entity which merely changed its status from colony to sovereign nation. Pakistan had to create *de novo* a state from two culturally disparate, physically separate, strife-torn areas. The odds against success were enormous. To have constructed a nation for several years with about 50 experienced government officials of reasonable maturity in policy-making positions is a singular tribute to both the British administrative heritage and Muslim perseverance.[32]

The centre moved quickly to set up a civil service academy at Lahore in 1948 and began the induction of fresh CSP officers at a rate of twenty-five per year, laying great emphasis on their training. In addition to one year at the academy, the new entrants spent a year abroad at an English university and upon return spent another year being trained in the field, after which they became eligible for postings. Unfortunately, the 'most important bulwark of ICS training—meticulous field training under an able deputy commissioner—collapsed under the pressure of greater urgencies' and the shift of emphasis in favour of development.[33]

These limitations and exigencies notwithstanding, by 1955, it was through this nucleus of about two hundred civil service officers plus about a hundred from other services of similar or greater competence (rising to about four hundred from CSP plus a hundred others by 1962-1963) that the elite executive culture of the British imperial nomocracy was preserved and transmitted to the public services at large. These services, by 1963, totalled some one million employees of whom about five thousand were officers.[34]

Extraordinary promotions combined with illegal demands for patronage by politicians, who had the power of transfer over officials and could inflict significant harm on the peace of mind and finances of subordinates, led to serious problems. Sometimes pressure was applied in order to victimise other politicians. Writing to the prime minister on 13 February 1948, the governor of the Punjab stated:

> Another very bad case of a different kind that has come to my notice is the treating of Khizar Hayat as an evacuee and the allotment of his *zamindari* rights in Montgomery to someone. This was done by the *tehsildar* on the orders of the DC. Whether the DC received orders from someone else I do not know, but he and Mamdot are very close as you know. Hence the indifference with which he treats Government orders.[35]

On 30 March 1948, the governor informed the prime minister of 'considerable apprehension' in the services about their protection against arbitrary treatment by politicians.[36] Arguing in favour of autonomous public service commissions appointed without ministerial input, the governor observed that in countries like Pakistan 'a democracy can function only if there is a strong and independent civil service.'[37] It was imperative, and in the politicians' own interest, that 'the tenure and conditions of service of members of the Commission, and to a lesser extent, of the staff of the Commission' be 'excluded from the Ministerial field' for otherwise, threats, pay cuts and changes in the tenure of members could 'compel the members to do what' powerful members of the government wanted or resign.[38] Unless this was done, the government's attempts to secure the autonomy of the public service commissions 'by providing for nomination by the Governor-General would be illusory.'[39]

Two months later, the governor brought to the prime minister's notice another case that illustrated the importance of administrative autonomy from political interference. In this case, members of the District Muslim League in Mianwali were threatening Manzur Ali, a Provincial Civil Service (PCS) treasury official to perjure himself 'before the Election Tribunal' that was 'considering the Election-Petition of Nawab Mian Muhammad Hayat Qureshi against Mian Sultan Ali.'[40] Manzur Ali was 'a very competent officer' with a good service record.[41] In the 1946 elections Qureshi had lost to Sultan Ali by a margin of over four thousand votes, and subsequently levelled charges of official misconduct against the civil servants involved in making the arrangements. After an inquiry, the allegations were dismissed as baseless. Soon after independence, the case was reopened with ministerial backing and Qureshi demanded that Manzur Ali pressure Sultan Ali to give up his seat. If Manzur Ali refused, he would face suspension, humiliation and dismissal from service.[42] Sadly, this kind of behaviour, though ultimately self-defeating, was increasingly becoming the norm amongst politicians:

> As for the local gentry, it has unfortunately become habit with Khan Amir Abdullah Khan, Chairman, District Board, Mianwali, and Malik Fateh Sher of Dullewala, in the Bhakkar Sub-Division; to make frequent recommendations in cases on behalf of their clientele. From their behaviour I suspect that these gentlemen are not only politically benefited, but otherwise too. Their recommendations are also generally couched in a language smacking of arrogance which might be enough to influence inexperienced officers. Both are prominent office-bearers of the District Muslim League.[43]

A significant problem for civil servants was that many applicants would come to them with letters endorsed by politicians, in some cases even chief ministers and governors. These applications would ask for special consideration or respect or action to be given/taken upon the issue addressed. These ranged from admissions to academic institutions, employment in some government job, financial assistance and so on. In some cases the application was legitimate and dealt with favourably. This created the impression that the application was approved due to political endorsement. Many times the applicants would be turned away empty-handed, sometimes courteously, sometimes rudely, but often with reserve and aloofness. This created the impression that the civil servants were obstructive and instead of being servants of the people were acting as rulers (*naukarshahi*). In many cases the politicians would sign applications without even reading them and then lay the blame on the civil servants if it did not meet with a particular criteria. To put it differently, the politicians, who naturally wanted to please their clients and supporters, generally said 'yes' to the applications brought before them. The civil servants in general, but especially the CSP and PSP, more often than not had to say 'no'. Rather than genuinely working towards improving their constituents by framing sound policies and overseeing their execution, the politicians laid blame on the civil servants, while those rebuffed thought the civil servants were arrogant and unresponsive.

The essential problem was that the politicians did not appreciate the gravity of their predicament and the seriousness of their role. Making sound policies and laws to anticipate the needs and guide the development of a society undergoing rapid change is an immeasurably difficult task. If such a task were taken up seriously by politicians they would not have had the time or energy to engage in the politics of patronage. Equally, it was most dangerous for the politicians to be consistently demonstrated as intellectually and morally inferior to the servants of the state with whom they were in intimate contact and to whom they were supposed to provide leadership. Once the administrative and military machine became conscious of its own strength and managed to occupy senior political positions there could be no going back. Fortunately, the training of the British period and the state morality that it bequeathed prevented the rising governing corporation of civil servants and military officials from physically exterminating the political class. Indeed, from April 1953 onwards, this governing corporation tried to preserve the semblance of constitutional democracy even as it assumed greater control of the nation's foreign, defence and domestic policies.

3.3 THE GOVERNING CORPORATION

Between April 1953 and March 1969, Pakistan was ruled by a governing corporation that drew the bulk of its intellectual and moral strength from the Civil Service of Pakistan, the higher echelons of the military, and elements within the judiciary sympathetic to it. It was during this period that the first American advisors arrived in Pakistan and urged the state to reorient itself towards democracy and economic development. Apparently oblivious to the fact that by then the politicians and representative democracy had been eclipsed by the governing corporation, these consultants urged Pakistan to accept the imperatives of the new age that had dawned with the American discovery of the Earth post-1945:

The basic problems surrounding present day administration in Pakistan arise largely from the fact that an administrative system born as an instrument of colonial policy has been carried over with but few modifications and utilised as the machinery for democracy...

The colonial system of government was probably fully satisfactory as an instrument for assuring public order, the swift administration of justice, the prompt collection of taxes and the maintenance of land records...

The major weakness of the present administrative system with respect to national development stems largely from the fact that Government is still substantially directed to the law and order function in its organisational, procedural, personnel and fiscal aspect.[44]

Another wilfully ignorant benefactor authoritatively declared that 'All proposals for organising the public administration must be tested in the crucible of their effectiveness in strengthening the institutions of democratic self-government.'[45] The 'most important guarantee of democratic institutions and representative government' was the 'strength of the religious sentiments of the Pakistani people.'[46] Sadly, Pakistan's civil service was 'living in the past'[47] and had 'a long road to travel' both 'intellectually and emotionally' to adjust 'to the fact that democratic self-government is politically-controlled government.'[48] Politicians were the servants of the sovereign people for 'to be elected and re-elected they must secure votes' which must be 'cast by citizens.'[49]

These were more than mere words especially after American assistance and consultants became a regular feature of the post-1954 administrative landscape. By 1960, law, which used to occupy about three-fourths of the curriculum at the Civil Services Academy, was reduced to about one-third to make way for development subjects.[50] Thanks to American largesse, between 1954 and 1963, some '1200 officers have had direct contact with American public administrative technology'.[51] Given that the CSP cadre ranged between two hundred and five hundred officers[52] and that the total number of officers from all services combined was around five thousand by the mid-1960s, it meant that about one in five officers was directly exposed to American tutelage. Braibanti noted with transparent satisfaction that 'the most noteworthy characteristic of American-induced administrative training in Pakistan is the manner in which it has become accepted at the highest level of government, attracted some of the best talent, and has been absorbed by the elite cadre.'[53]

While foreign advisers insisted upon democratic development and the economic imperatives of the age, the governing corporation proved unable to bring a semblance of order to politics in the country. To the centralist bureaucratic mind, the turbulence and endless shifting of loyalties at the provincial and national levels were utterly repugnant. Something had to be done to stabilise the façade without, however, sharing real power with the politicians. In 1955, the decision to merge the provinces and territories of West Pakistan into One Unit with its capital and secretariat at Lahore was taken and implemented. The provincial assemblies were compelled to dissolve themselves through threats, intimidation and unethical incentives. The constitution was then pushed through the second Constituent Assembly which had equal representation for East and West Pakistan (forty each) acquiesced to the principle of parity between the two provinces as the basis for a unicameral legislature. The formula was put into effect by Muhammad Ali, formerly secretary-general to the federal government, subsequently prime minister. The hope was that One Unit in West Pakistan plus inter-wing parity would allow for greater administrative and national cohesion, a more powerful state and a more disciplined set of politicians.[54] The thinking was that 'Any territorial or other changes that would imperil national unity and solidarity and promote provincial, regional or local loyalties in preference to the supreme loyalty to the State should be out of the question, particularly in the formative years of our history.'[55] One Unit was the inevitable consequence of the 'essential oneness and indivisibility of West Pakistan' generated by a 'common historical heritage, a uniform pattern of agricultural economy, dependence on the same water and power resources and deep cultural and social affinities of the people living in the province.'[56] The idea was that units, such as districts and divisions, even if artificial, become stable over time through a 'natural process of association.'[57] The administrative confusion that transferring many established centres of administration to Lahore entailed was compounded by the fact that 'When postings of Secretaries for West Pakistan were considered, it was found that there were not enough officers of the requisite seniority [fourteen years of service] to fill all the posts.'[58]

The trouble was that it proved rather impossible to discipline the politicians—they could not be demoted, transferred, or controlled by writing stiff notes (if for no other reason than that they were not likely to bother reading what came their way). They could be disqualified under PRODA but then as soon as they became useful again the ban on them would be relaxed. The politicians also chafed under the domination of the governing corporation and did what they could, by way of transfer and denunciation, to put the administration on the defensive. The bureaucrats, for their part, were drawn into politics and interfered in areas that could safely have been left in the hands of political protégés. Finally, the conditions that had made possible the emergence of a governing corporation, namely the disintegration of the Muslim League and the absence of credible national political leadership, also ensured that no matter which factions or groups were rotated in and out of office, none succeeded in providing a semblance of governmental stability. One Unit in West Pakistan merely meant that provincial politics became more acrimonious and polarised between its proponents and opponents as the now defunct smaller provinces and regions tried to gang up against the Punjab's domination.

By 1956, the Muslim League has reached an advanced stage of disintegration and its members were defecting to the new officially patronised Republican Party. In August, the prime minister tried to patch things up, but in the meeting of the Coalition Parliamentary Party his own party members refused to attend if defectors to the republican camp were allowed to participate. On 8 September 1956, Muhammad Ali resigned the premiership, which was the sensible thing to do, given that he was a creature of the establishment and had no political legs of his own to stand on now that the president, Iskander Mirza, had ditched him. Bringing in H. S. Suhrawardy, a leading Bengali politician, as prime minister on the condition that he would leave foreign affairs and defence in Mirza's hands did little to stabilise the situation. While in the opposition, Suhrawardy had condemned the 1956 constitution for denying provincial autonomy, but after he became the prime minister he held that it granted all the autonomy ever desired. Suhrawardy, like nearly all Pakistani politicians, lost sight of the damage done to their collective reputations and interests by their opportunistic abandonment of the powers of argument for the arguments of power. Soon enough, his wings on matters of domestic policy were clipped, his commercial and agricultural proposals undermined by Mirza and his republican allies. Forced out of power in October 1957, Suhrawardy's successor, I.

I. Chundrigar lasted barely two months and was replaced by Firoze Khan Noon, the former premier of the Punjab.

Noon had not been much of a success in provincial politics and his ministry in the Punjab had ended disastrously. Towards the end divisions in his cabinet were 'having an adverse effect on the administration as various factions in the Party were using 'Government officers for political purposes.'[59] The governor was, consequently, authorised to take countermeasures.[60] A few days later, the interior minister informed the cabinet that Noon's ministry, now dismissed, 'had decided to allot land to all Major-Generals in the Army, all Deputy Commissioners in the Punjab or their relatives and most of the members of the legislature' and also wanted to extend this facility to the higher judiciary.[61] The total value of this land grab designed to placate members of the governing corporation and its political front-men was valued at over three hundred million rupees.[62] By October 1958, twenty-six out of eighty members of the national assembly had ministerial rank and more were expected to be added. Nevertheless, the opposition was gaining ground and it was likely that the clients of the governing corporation would lose the elections scheduled for March 1959. Chief Justice Muhammad Munir, in total disregard of his status as impartial adjudicator, advised President Mirza to hold the elections, let chaos take over and then proclaim an emergency.[63] Mirza, however, felt that his chance of remaining president after the elections was about 5 per cent.[64] He therefore decided to abrogate the constitution, declare martial law, and nominated Ayub Khan, the army chief for seven years at this point, as the Chief Martial Law Administrator (CMLA). Three weeks later, Ayub Khan overthrew Iskander Mirza and assumed dictatorial powers. A new era, full of danger and opportunity, for the governing corporation, had begun.

3.4 The Noble Sarkar

The civilian bureaucracy adjusted rapidly to Ayub Khan's leadership. Many of its senior members had known Ayub for years and had worked closely with him since he became army chief in 1951. There was undeniable improvement in the efficiency of the administration as politics receded into the background. Of the one thousand three hundred civil servants dismissed, retired, or disciplined by administrative tribunals, a mere thirteen were from the CSP cadre, and fifteen from the PSP cadre. Ayub, however, deprived the CSP of a year of training at a British university, effective from 1959-60, in favour of shorter courses that degenerated into junkets at American institutions. The impact of this change took several years to be felt for by 1960 all but one of the three hundred and thirty-two CSP officers had received British university component of their training. That said, Ayub had a tremendous amount of respect for the higher bureaucracy, especially the CSP, and relied on their advice and assistance. He also used them in a political role, as part of the Basic Democracies scheme, and effectively placed his faith in their ability to deliver both order and progress. There was remarkably little opposition to the regime until 1964, which prudently decreed that military courts were to 'be of a limited number and should only deal with serious offences arising out of anti-state, anti-Martial Law and smuggling activities' while 'All other cases should be tried by the civil courts.'[65]

Ayub felt disheartened by the fact that 'people in Pakistan expected the Government to do everything' which 'was not a healthy attitude'.[66] People, in particular those in the rural areas, should 'do some 'self-help' work' inclusive of 'improving communications, digging and repairing water channels, running poultry farms, gardening' and the like.[67] Back 'in the old days' these activities were undertaken 'by the villagers under the direction of the District Magistrate.'[68] However, since 1947, political governments had through political interference and arbitrary transfers 'deprived the District Magistrate of all his authority and initiative.'[69] It was imperative that immediate and suitable steps be taken 'to restore the authority and initiative of the District Magistrate' so that 'he would be in a position to undertake this job as in the old days.'[70] Ayub's Basic Democracies were, under the commissioners, required 'to continually stimulate people's interests in the general advancement and development of the country' and were perfectly in consonance with his 'general concept' for the central government which was that it should be stronger and more effective but also leaner in terms of size.[71]

Indicative of Ayub's faith in the CSP was the composition of the Administrative Reorganisation Committee constituted by his government on 12 December 1958, 'To review the organisational structure, functions and procedures of the Ministries and Departments as well as coordination between different tiers of the government'.[72] The chairman was G.

Ahmed while the members were A. R. Khan (CSP, Secretary Establishment), H. A. Majeed (CSP, Secretary Finance), N. A. Faruqui (CSP, Secretary Industries), M. Khurshid (CSP, Secretary Defence), Hamid Ali (CSP, Secretary Health), and M. Ayub (CSP, Director, Pakistan Industrial Development Corporation).[73] The committee had the temerity to launch a frontal assault upon the Bureau of National Reconstruction (BNR) set up in December 1958 to project the policies of the government and 'develop a character pattern essential for the creation of a national outlook.'[74] The secretaries asserted that the BNR was redundant given that it performed tasks already under the direction of the Ministry of Information.[75] It was recommended that the BNR's staff be reduced by half and it be reconstituted as a research wing of the Ministry of Information.[76] Subsequent to the submission of the report in 1960 the BNR faded into obscurity and does not figure in the declassified files of the Ayub regime.[77]

The CSP exercised a vice-like grip over practically all tiers of government and by 1964 nine out of ten secretaries at the centre, nearly seven out of ten secretaries in the provinces, and three out of four divisional commissioners, were drawn from its ranks.[78] What this meant was that policy planning at the centre, coordination with the provinces, and execution at the local level, were effectively in the hands of the CSP. From the Planning Commission and industrial development corporations, to public sector corporations (thirty-six of them by 1965), to the local governments, this elite within the elite came to exercise transcendental control of the state apparatus. When, in 1962, a batch of CSP trainees were sent to Kakul for military training they 'protested so vehemently and exerted such political pressure that the scheme was abandoned.'[79] The trainees objected that they were much older and better educated than the military cadets and that military discipline was useless insofar as their careers were concerned.[80] This episode provided 'an index of the immense power and prestige of the CSP. Under a martial law regime, a group of some twenty-five young men, ordered to military training for a few months, succeeded in having this training scheme abandoned.'[81]

Under the Basic Democracies scheme, deputy commissioners effectively became district governors that performed not only a multiplicity of administrative functions but also acted as political representatives for the president. Ayub's local government system depended on the 'District Officers' initiative, leadership and advice' which imparted 'vigour to all the development plans of the district.'[82] The commissioners were the 'strategic link' between the *sarkar* (state) and the *awam* (people), acting as exponent, interpreter, mediator, as well as executor, of the sovereign's will.[83] It was up to the CSP officer 'to employ all his resources of intelligence, tact, and skill in human relation to get optimum co-operation' and 'set a high example of work and conduct to inspire his colleagues in other Departments' as well as the 'members of the public to be associated with the processes of Government.'[84] The CSP *was* the living embodiment of what in earlier ages was referred to as the noble *sarkar* and like the high-ranking *mansabdars* or *omrahs* of the Timurid Empire it was they who acted as sub-sovereigns in the ruler's name.

At a synoptic level the CSP played a critical and little understood role. Its strong corporate identity combined with deployment at the key levels in practically all tiers and departments of the state enabled it to form a buffer between the rulers and ruled and an umbrella under which the less prestigious and weaker services and specialists could operate. During military rule this function assumed even great importance as the CSP prevented, to a large extent, the exposure of civil society to direct contact with military personnel. As an extension of the same role, it also allowed all but the very senior layer of generals from being exposed to the corrosive effects of politicisation and ensured that the policy of insulation was able to continue at the day to day level. This aspect of the CSP's role was appreciated by the Constitution Commission established by Ayub Khan, which argued that the 'demarcation that has been kept up all along' and inherited from British India between the civil and military functions of the state 'should not be departed from.'[85] The Constitution Commission elaborated:

> Parleys and discussion, which are the methods to be adopted by a civil officer in dealing with the mass of the people, are not expected of a member of the Armed Forces, who has to deal only with those who have, by a course of discipline, become really subordinate to him. A...Commissioner, on the other hand, cannot regard the people of his district in the same manner. He has to deal with them with great tact...From this point of view, his work is far more difficult than that of an officer in the Armed Forces of a corresponding rank. The very fact that an average military officer, when confronted with a question of complexity involving discussion of respective

rights, would normally exclaim that he is a soldier and has no time or inclination for a debate, indicates the difference in the points of view of the services.[86]

Evidently, Ayub Khan agreed with the Constitution Commission and the induction of military officers into the CSP against a 5 per cent quota was terminated by 1963.

The importance of the CSP was reinforced by the preference it received as the first choice in the public service examinations. About 80 per cent of the aspirants put the CSP as their first choice, between ten and 15 per cent put the Pakistan Foreign Service (PFS) as the first choice, while a negligible percentage opted voluntarily for the remaining services. Sadly for itself, the CSP failed to play a proper leadership role vis-à-vis the rest of the bureaucracy. Instead, it assumed an odious air of superiority that was simply not justified by the actual differential between its own competence and that of the other services. Indeed, many members from the other services were demonstrably superior to their counterparts in the CSP, while specialists felt aggrieved by the fact that they had practically no chance of rising to the top within their respective departments. Often enough, secretaries drawn from the CSP in charge of specialised departments of which they had little understanding or knowledge, took credit for the output of the specialists under them. As the CSP came to play a political role in manipulating the Basic Democracies, which Ayub Khan made the Electoral College for the presidency, their impartiality and prestige suffered. The first serious rumblings of corruption in the higher bureaucracy, and of systematic nepotism, even at the most exalted levels, began to be heard. More ominously for the health of the governing corporation, an intra-bureaucratic polarisation between the CSP and non-CSP, already evident before 1958, intensified. Prominence was a double-edged sword.

The Pay and Services Commission of 1959-1962 constituted under the chairmanship of Supreme Court Justice, A. R. Cornelius, voiced the opinions of those who fell outside the CSP cadre. While lauding the British administrative heritage and attributing to its liberal and constitutional tendencies the pre-emption of totalitarianism in the subcontinent, the Commission hit hard at the CSP. It asserted that the privileges, higher pay, accelerated promotions, and near monopoly of policy, coordination, and key executive positions across the board were great discrepancies as it was 'wrong to suppose that the latter [specialists] have either inferior education or lower intellectual capacity.'[87] Given changing circumstances the inferior position of all these services was far less acceptable and that 'the concept of a 'governing corporation" should continue to be adhered to was cause of 'great discontent and discomfiture' in the specialised cadres.[88] Furthermore, now that economic development was the primary function of the state, the old law and order approach was obsolete and with it the generalist CSP was part of a colonial hangover. Indeed, '...the hope of the administration of the future lies in the 'administrative technocrat" a professional 'equipped with intellect, education, and ability to conceive of a plan of development, with the aid of modern techniques and machinery.'[89]

Even in the areas where the CSP were expected to exercise control and leadership (land revenue, magistracy, supervision of police), the system was patently prone to injustice. In the context of land revenue, the staff under the commissioner in his capacity as collector 'carries the entire burden of that administration', but, as they belonged to the Class II (support staff), or Class I (Provincial Civil Service), they 'cannot aspire to the post of Collector.' The work was almost entirely theirs but credit went to the commissioner.[90] In the case of the magistracy a similar situation prevailed:

> The trial of cases, and the management of a file of cases are tasks which involve expenditure of time and attention to detail...For these tasks the District Magistrate of today simply has not the time, and the result is that they are performed by the Magistrates under the guidance and control of the Additional District Magistrate, who is a senior member of the Provincial Service. But the post of District Magistrate is available, in the ordinary way, only to the members of the CSP, and is occupied normally by comparatively junior members, with some 3 years to 10 years of service. Here again, there is denial of justice. The group of men, constituted into a service, who carry on the entire work, are denied the headship, even in this respect, in the district.[91]

The commissioners' supervision over the police lead to numerous conflicts and the need for the retention of all these functions 'in a single person, who was the agent of the ruling power' was no longer a valid approach now that 'the strength of the administration is derived from the people.'[92] The Commission recommended the separation of the collectorship and magistracy, placing each under its own head, and the end to the domination of the secretariat posts by the CSP.[93] In a remarkable rhetorical flourish indicative of the degree to which American tutelage had infected the services, the Commission asserted that the supremacy of the law and order, public security, and land revenue administration, as the primary functions of the state, which were concomitant with the superiority of the ICS and IPS steel frame, were decidedly passé:

> Law and order and public security must take, in Pakistan, the same position among the public affairs of the country as they occupy in other free countries, that is to say, not unimportant, but at the same time, not of super-eminent importance, so as to confer the status of rulers upon their officers. Something of that super eminence lingers on by the exclusive recognition of these two services as All Pakistan Services.[94]

While the Pay and Services Commission of 1959-1962 operated under a large number of misconceptions, bore the undeniable mark of irrational foreign tutelage, misunderstood the French administrative system which it upheld as a model for Pakistan, and took law and order, public security, and land revenue administration for granted, the response of the CSP was equally misguided. Instead of taking heed that the nearly five thousand officers in specialist and technical cadres wanted a place in the sun and should be brought on board through timely concessions, the Commission's findings were shelved. In a sense, the CSP failed to appreciate that time was not on its side and that it ought to try and manage its decline. The fact was that there was simply too much to do and the tour de force of the first decade could not reasonably be sustained. Moreover, the CSP's power was increased and the cadre was converted into the backbone, nerve centre, and limbs, of the Ayub regime. This led to the 'politicisation of the services...Professionalism, competence and honesty, which were the hallmark of the British system, started giving way to cronyism, pliability, and dishonesty—both intellectual and financial.'[95] The rot had started at the top with senior officers going 'to any length to please their superiors in order to remain near the seat of power.'[96] By 1969, the CSP had abdicated its leadership role to such an extent that its representatives on the Working Group on the Reorganisation of the Public Service Structure in Pakistan withdrew and submitted a separate report.

The remaining members of the working group, unsurprisingly, dismissed the CSP as a relic of the nineteenth century and regurgitated all the by now stock arguments made by foreign experts that the basic function of the state was development for which technocrats were required.[97] And indeed, development expenditures had risen from four hundred million rupees for the financial year 1951 to ten billion rupees in financial year 1968-69.[98] This massive increase in government expenditure, ironically enough, fuelled both lopsided growth, inflation, and inter-wing disparity, which combined brought down the Ayub regime. Ayub's overthrow at the hands of his handpicked army chief, Yahya Khan, and the protest movement launched against him by political parties and agitators did not lead to any improvement. What followed was the break up of the country, the ascent of Zulfikar Ali Bhutto's Pakistan People's Party (PPP), and the unprecedented medievalisation of the state. Ayub Khan's resignation on 25 March 1969, made him the first, and most prominent, casualty of the massacre.

3.5 THE MASSACRE

Unlike Ayub Khan, Yahya Khan thought that the state could be operated on the same principles as the military. After assuming power, Yahya shifted the centre of administration from the presidency and federal ministries to General Head Quarters (GHQ) and established a Chief Martial Law Administrator's (CMLA) Secretariat staffed by military personnel. Underneath a lieutenant general, who headed the CMLA Secretariat, were two brigadiers. Below the brigadiers were officers of various ranks and designations. The cabinet assembled by the new regime comprised an assortment of political non-entities with Cornelius the solitary figure of national standing and repute in it, though he merely damaged his credibility through this association. Although a CSP officer continued to serve as the presidential secretary, he was out of the loop in most sensitive matters. The president and his advisers were convinced that Ayub Khan had been deceived and manipulated by the higher bureaucracy, especially the CSP, which took all the credit for the achievements of the regime and dumped all the blame on the military. Now, the military would assume direct control of the administration through the deployment of hundreds of military officers in the supervisory positions and take full credit for 'sorting out' the mess the nation found itself in.

Amongst the first to be sorted out were three hundred and three senior civil servants. Though given a chance to defend themselves before tribunals, all these officials were purged, not necessarily for the abuse of power, but for their proximity, real or perceived, to Ayub Khan. Adding insult to injury, secretary and joint secretary level officers found themselves at the receiving end of peremptory commands by military officers of inferior seniority and rank. The Yahya regime's 'parade ground style'[99] and cavalier handling of national affairs 'alienated the bureaucracy, which in any case was marginalised by the martial law administration.'[100] The civil service, 'thereafter, remained a passive critic of the regime, whose set-backs evoked sardonic jokes and derisive comments in civilian circles.'[101]

By April 1970, the great achievement of the governing corporation, One Unit in West Pakistan, was dissolved, and out of it the four provinces that presently comprise Pakistan constituted (or re-constituted). The other marvel of political engineering pieced together by the governing corporation, parity between East and West Pakistan in the national assembly, was done away with, and decisions about provincial autonomy were to be taken up by elected assemblies in the near future. Moreover, it would take a simple majority to effect changes in the constitutional set up after the December 1970 elections. Yahya's strategic mind had countenanced three contingencies:

> ...first, the most optimistic situation forecast by all the intelligence agencies was that no single party would gain an absolute majority in the National Assembly. This would enable the regime to manage a coalition of reasonable parties and personalities. Second, if such a coalition did not emerge, or if it did prove recalcitrant, the President could exercise his powers to reject the Constitution framed by the National Assembly; the Assembly would then stand dissolved and fresh elections could then be indefinitely postponed. Third, as a last resort, martial law could be revived with full force, if the first situation did not materialise and the second option was found impractical.[102]

The price paid by the country for this remarkable exercise in self-deception was that in the December 1970 elections the secessionist Awami League secured a near monopoly of seats in East Pakistan enabling it to command over one hundred and sixty seats in a National Assembly of three hundred and thirteen seats. In West Pakistan, with over eighty seats, the Pakistan People's Party emerged victorious. Having already been defeated politically, and in response to unmistakable signs that the Awami League was preparing for rebellion, the meeting of the new assembly was postponed and finally, in March 1971, a military crackdown began. The failure that followed, agonisingly well-documented and discussed in the declassified portions of the Hamood-ur-Rehman Commission's report, led to the secession of East Pakistan, and the transfer of power by Yahya to Zulfikar Ali Bhutto and the PPP on 20 December 1971. The next five and a half years provided a sordid reminder of the veracity of the dictum that life is rarely quite so bad that it cannot get worse.

Between 23 December and 30 December 1971, the chairman of the National Press Trust, the senior editor of the *Pakistan Times*, the chairman of PIDC, and the managing directors of Progressive Papers and the National Shipping Group, were dismissed under Martial Law Regulation (MLR). MLR-114 Removal from Service Regulation was soon unleashed on thousands of unsuspecting and substantially innocent civil servants. MLR-114 did not allow the accused the right of defence, something that Ayub and Yahya, the former sincerely, the latter as a mere formality, had conceded. Vaqar Ahmad, the Cabinet and Establishment Secretary, testified in November 1977 that when he advised in favour of a show cause notice for those about to be dismissed Bhutto informed him 'that he did not believe *in the Anglo-Saxon sense of justice* and his Revolutionary Government would not accept any such suggestion.'[103]

On 5 February 1972, Vaqar Ahmad asked the other secretaries to give him names of the corrupt and those reputed to be corrupt within nine days.[104] Excluding the Ministry of Finance, where the minister, Mubashir Hassan, took a keen personal interest and sent one hundred and six names, the rest yielded a mere twenty-seven.[105] Bhutto was not pleased and so Vaqar Ahmad added two hundred and forty-five names on his own initiative while the Special Police Establishment when squeezed yielded a mere eighty-eight names with the qualification attached that in some cases investigations were in the preliminary stages.[106] Bhutto demanded more sacrifices even though with Yahya Khan's purge a few years earlier, it was highly unlikely that more than a fraction of those already rounded up were guilty of anything more than making personal calls from their official phones. The governors of the Punjab, Sindh, and the NWFP, along with Ghulam Mustafa Jatoi, all PPP leaders, were entrusted with the task of finding 'necks that fitted the noose.'[107]

On 12 March 1972, 'about 2000 public servants, who had normally attended office earlier in the day, heard on Radio/TV that they had been dismissed or removed from service, or reduced in rank, because they were corrupt, or inefficient, or both.'[108] Six days later, over five hundred officers of the provincial services were dismissed or retired.[109] On 18 April, twenty-four judicial officers and, two days later, eight Intelligence Bureau (IB) officers, were dismissed.[110] The negative public reaction led the government to allow review petitions but of the nearly eighteen hundred received the bulk 'were never scrutinised' though exceptions were made 'in the case of a few fortunate ones for whom recommendations were received from Mrs Bhutto, Ministers, MNAs, MPAs or the like.'[111]

The 1973 Constitution did away with the security of tenure of public servants. Under the Civil Service Act of 1973, 'a civil servant was totally deprived of the security of tenure the moment he rose above the level of Joint Secretary' which was precisely the point at which autonomy and security were most sorely needed.[112] A politically connected subordinate could easily overpower his superiors while the insecurity of the senior servants affected their impartiality and professionalism in dealing with both politicians and administrative subordinates. In the disciplinary code no mandatory inquiry into alleged misconduct was required if the investigating officer so determined.[113] The national and provincial assemblies could institute public service commissions which were now, at a statutory level, at their mercy:

> The Public Service Commissions were reduced, in effect, to mere shadows of their former selves. The Federal Public Service Commissions Act, 1973, prescribed no qualifications for the members. It empowered the President, that is, the Federal Executive, to terminate the appointment of a member before the expiry of his term of office, and left the Commission with practically no function besides the conduct of tests and examinations. Its consultative functions did not extend to disciplinary matters.[114]

Meanwhile, the purges continued. On 19 August 1973, eight secretaries, one additional secretary, and seven joint secretaries, were arbitrarily retired without any noting on their case files—evidently the orders had been issued verbally.[115] In January 1975, two secretaries, three additional secretaries, four joint secretaries, and one deputy secretary, were retired in a similar manner.[116] In 1976, a fresh batch of victims, one hundred and seventy-four in number, was identified by the Federal Investigation Agency (FIA) and Vaqar Ahmad issued the necessary orders and notices on 16 October.[117] Bhutto, according to Khaqan Mahmud, then Special Secretary in the Cabinet Division, wanted two hundred names for this particular purge.[118] In the run-up to the 1977 elections 'Letters were written to the Chief Ministers of the Provinces that they should prepare lists of persons who would be appointed to posts of DSPs, Inspectors, Sub Inspectors of Police, Tehsildars and Naib Tehsildars.'[119] Bhutto wanted to carry out another purge of officers in May 1977 though this was pre-empted by events.[120] In concluding his statement, Vaqar Ahmed raised a question and answered it in a manner that Timurid *mansabdar*s, slaves of the sultans, and servants of the ancient Indian monarchs, would have readily related to: 'Before I conclude I must answer a question which is asked that why did I continue to serve in this environment. I was afraid that I would become a suspect and it is known what happened to suspects.'[121]

In part fulfilment of his pledge to 'break the back of the CSP', Bhutto instituted a number of administrative reforms. One of these was the Lateral Entry Scheme, which, at least in theory, would allow for the induction of highly qualified personnel at senior levels as the need arose. At the higher levels (officers plus senior-most support staff in Grade 16 and above), five thousand four hundred and seventy-six inductees were absorbed, with about two thousand eight hundred at the centre and the rest in the provinces.[122] Bhutto wanted to create a body of officials personally loyal to him and abjectly dependent on his favour for their elevation.[123] Through them, the career bureaucrats could be controlled and marginalised. As lateral entrants of the 'requisite type and qualification' could not be found in a manner consistent with the principles of merit and ethics, arbitrary methods were used to secure inductions.[124] Many of the candidates were simply political nominees with little idea of what was required of them as public servants. Others were outright in their malevolence towards, and contempt of, their colleagues and subordinates and felt themselves immune to the rules and regulations; in the contravention of which they had been recruited. Most were demonstrably inferior to those recruited by the old system. Of course, a few were genuinely outstanding. By 1976, the discontent, rivalries, and demoralisation, had gotten so out of hand that Bhutto decided to transfer the lateral entry scheme to the Federal Public Service Commission (FPSC) and fixed a 10 per cent quota for such recruitment. These tactical concessions did not mask Bhutto's inability to tolerate autonomous institutions or restrain him from issuing 'direct orders to Provincial Ministers and officials.'[125] The tone for the entire administration was set by the prime minister's handling of 'his home District of Larkana, which he made a Division' and where 'senior officials took orders from no other person.'[126]

While arbitrary dismissals, appointments, and transfers, reduced the higher bureaucracy into a quasi-medieval instrument, the formal changes in the structure of the services, their remuneration, and nomenclature, shattered its flexibility and adaptability. Drawing inspiration in part from foreign authorities and in part from the 1970-1972 National Pay Commission[127] the principles of unity, equality and functionality were adopted. The old system had about six hundred and fifty scales of pay spread across four classes. Class I was for officers, II for higher support staff, III for lower support staff, and IV for menial/unskilled employees. This was dismissed as being elitist and colonial, and a Unified Grading Structure with twenty-two the highest (secretary) and one the lowest grade (peon) tied to a standardised national pay scale that consciously tried to bring about equality between the higher and lower ranks was adopted. The inspiration, evidently, came from the United States with its eighteen grades of civil servants and Lord Fulton's committee in Britain, which advocated a similar system. The British tried the system at a few levels but soon abandoned it and reverted to their earlier system.

The problem was that the standardisation of grades masked great chaos, wastefulness, and complexity. Yes, there were eighteen grades in the United States, but there were over nine hundred positions classified under a General Schedule. Within the ranks candidates competed for jobs as vacancies arose and were advertised nationally. 'Such a job-oriented system has no concept of promotion, seniority, or transfers' with some civil servants getting stuck while others managed to jump around.[128] Moreover, in the United States, grades five through eighteen were for officers while there was no uniform pattern with several services, such as the foreign or postal services, 'run on a career pattern', with individual states reserving powers to adjust the pay scales.[129] About a fifth of civil servants left the public sector each year for the private sector, leading to a fluid environment within the public services with continuous intake of fresh personnel.[130] Its manifest theoretical deficiencies aside, the entire reform exercise of the 1970s was vitiated by the lack of serious considerations given to its implementation by the reformers:

> Our authorities could appreciate the requirements of a changeover from the career structure to a Unified Grading Structure. The responsible functionaries of Establishment Division were unaware of its full implications and the academics associated misled by a superficial knowledge of the working of this system in the USA...In producing a 'unified grading structure' with such flourish, no time was wasted on comprehending the complexity or details of the American system.[131]

The situation was further 'aggravated by the framers through their lack of working knowledge of the provincial administration.'[132] The provincial administrations were bewildered by instructions that made no sense and 'failing to get a satisfactory response to their pleadings, decided to ignore the reforms almost completely.'[133] The impact on the ethos of the civil service, already straining under the remorseless arbitrariness of a government whose leader pursued vendettas against junior officers caught smoking off-guard as he passed by was tragic:

> The naïve application of some aspects of a Unified Grading Structure in the absence of a job evaluation of posts did away with the earlier discipline where the availability of a vacant post was a pre-requisite for recruitment and promotion. The administration went on a spree in notifying appointments in terms of 'grades' with little regard to vacancies. Most civil servants genuinely believed it to be a new game without rules and harboured expectations of getting higher and still higher grades.[134]

Whereas under the old system the 'vertical ranking of posts' was 'almost self-evident' within each individual service and 'horizontal equivalence' relative to other services was irrelevant, the new system introduced rigidity, distortion and grade consciousness.[135]

The change of the services into occupational groups was the other measure pushed through during the Bhutto-era administrative reforms.

Thus, for instance, the CSP was renamed the District Management Group (DMG), the PFS as the Foreign Affairs Group (FAG), the PSP as the Police Affairs Group (PAG), and so on and so forth. While some of the new names would have no doubt appealed to Bhutto's sense of humour, the manner in which they were constituted was typical of his regime's transparent contempt for law as well as his propensity for arbitrariness. Indeed, 'the creation of these Groups had no legal backing...most were constituted through office memoranda disregarding the rules and in some case, even the constitutional provisions governing the services.'[136] The Tribal Areas Group (TAG) was created through a letter of the Secretary Establishment.[137] The Police group was brought into existence through a one page office memorandum.[138] The Secretariat Group was 'created through a note from the Additional Secretary Establishment Division to the Establishment Minister.'[139] The DMG was 'the solitary Group which evoked some correspondence and discussion' which recognised its pre-eminence and indicated that it was 'to include a hard core of handpicked and loyal persons and its control was to vest totally in the Federal Government.'[140] Vaqar Ahmed actually argued in favour of prime ministerial nominations to the DMG in order to 'develop a class of loyal civil servants' drawn from the 'Powerful and influential families and sections in the countries' that could be 'through this device, controlled.'[141]

The challenge of leadership was indeed control and it was here that the final element of Bhutto's administrative strategy came into play. The politicians as well as the bureaucrats 'were controlled through a system of corruption, made possible by the nationalisation of large and medium', and eventually small, concerns.[142] Broadly speaking, 'The objective was to weaken and corrupt the various vested interests or groups through so-called reforms and corrupt practices.'[143] Related to these were the fuelling of inflation by the government's populist measures and the employment of more and more people in the public sector. This put the squeeze on the salaries of government employees many of whom found themselves in direct control of productive assets. The government in turn took to rewarding its employees, like a regressive medieval state, in kind rather than cash. The general relaxation in routine accountability and oversight, combined with periodic purges created an atmosphere of tension and insecurity in which rationality dictated corruption and apathy. There was little incentive to be honest or hardworking, let alone both, if the government routinely bombarded its servants with illegal demands and then purged the ranks with brutal indifference to procedure, norms of justice, and, indeed, guilt or innocence. Civil servants, 'likely to be pilloried whatever they do' sank as a collective 'into apathy and time serving' and the PPP government left in its wake 'an ill paid and demoralised bureaucracy' which had lost both 'its earlier efficiency' and integrity.[144]

It was perhaps poetic justice that Bhutto's attempt to create an even more powerful bureaucracy that was loyal to him and deeply entrenched in every area of national life backfired. Bhutto inspired fear in his subordinates as no other Pakistani ruler had. So afraid were his servants that in the March 1977 general elections they went out of the way, even beyond Bhutto's instructions, in trying to secure a favourable outcome. The results gave the PPP over a hundred and fifty seats against the opposition Pakistan National Alliance's (PNA) thirty-six seats. When in 1970 the opposition had been divided into a dozen small parties and the PPP had won a substantial majority it was understandable. Under the First Past the Post (FPTP) election system, the single candidate with the largest number of votes would win the contest in the constituency in question. By the same token, with practically all the other parties united against the PPP, it would have been difficult for the government to secure more than a simply majority. In the opposition rebellion that followed it seemed as if Pakistan was once again poised on the brink of a civil war, this time along political rather than ethnic lines. Against this backdrop, Bhutto's handpicked army chief, Ziaul Haq, with the support of the opposition parties, staged a coup on 5 July 1977. It was now up to those who had survived the massacre, often through sheer luck, to pick up the pieces of what was just a decade earlier enviously regarded as one of the finest administrative states in the developing world.

3.6 All the King's Horses and all the King's Men

What had been destroyed could not be restored by men of as limited vision and intelligence as Ziaul Haq and his chief whip Ghulam Ishaq Khan. It was not that they were ill-advised. Indeed, the Zia era stands out in terms of the wisdom, insight, and diagnostic capacity of the higher bureaucracy as evidenced by Ijlal Haider Zaidi's summaries and exhortations, the philosophic and self-critical perspective of the 1986 Committee for the Study of Corruption,[145] or the synoptic and yet immensely detailed, *Government and Administration in Pakistan*.[146] The principal achievement of this period (1977-1988) was stability. Flowing from this, there was a partial restoration of the earlier ethos; no purge of officials was carried out, technical improvements were made in the training of officers, a quantitative evaluation system, and de facto security of tenure for most senior executives. The higher bureaucracy benefited from Zia's willingness to listen to and learn from his subordinates about, for instance, the difference between the political states of North America, Britain, and Australia, and the administrative states prevalent in nearly all other parts of the world. Equally important was Zia's refusal to blindly try and undo the administrative reforms of the 1970s and his effort to try to make them work as best as possible.[147] The administrative consolidation was made possible in part by Zia's ability not to get easily offended as well as a willingness to reward loyalty with trust and the retention of the services of his closest associates. Zia also regarded the higher bureaucracy in general, but the DMG in particular, as representing the ablest members of the state and society, and though a military quota against vacancies was established, the total number of inductees was negligible.[148]

Zia was also quite comfortable with the centralising tendencies of his predecessors. While the higher bureaucracy recovered some of its 'relative autonomy of ethos and structure'[149] the paramount importance of the secretariat[150] was vigorously asserted. All told, the executive function of the state comprised forty-one divisions, six secretariats, and numerous attached departments, subordinate offices, corporations, etc., bringing the total number of components to two hundred and sixty-eight.[151] In the federal government, of one hundred and twenty thousand employees, about ten thousand, or 8 per cent, were officers in grades seventeen through twenty-two.[152] Whereas in 1947, a secretary, corresponding to grade twenty-two, drew a monthly salary of four thousand rupees and a peon, equivalent to grade one, drew fourteen rupees a month, in 1981 the former drew a maximum monthly basic pay of eight thousand four hundred rupees while the latter drew eight hundred and sixty rupees per month.[153] Thus, since independence, the pay of the officers had doubled or trebled, while the pay of the lowest staff had increased sixty fold. This emphasis on equality was a natural outcome of the 1972-1973 reforms and meant that while previously the officers were well-paid and the lower staff poorly paid, now everyone was poorly paid and dependent upon the provision of housing, transport, plots of land, and subsidized utilities, by the state. The reduced financial independence of the higher bureaucracy made them more corrupt, servile, and inefficient:

> In fact many of the past controversies like 'generalist versus specialist' have been overtaken by events. They are in any case peripheral to the stark reality: the continual erosion in real pay and pension may soon divide the civil services between the corrupt and the destitute. The latter may even now be no exaggeration for many of our pensioners. In the circumstances, attainment of professional excellence remains a goal only for a small and shrinking circle. This is reflected even in our intake: government service as a career hold little attraction for bright persons and the new amongst them who join, do so for the wrong reasons.[154]

It was highly 'unusual for any government to advertise its preference for the mediocre' as the first Pay Commission had done.[155] Successive regimes, including Zia's own, 'failed to anticipate the graver dangers of mediocrity succumbing to greed.'[156] The attempts to economise, equalise, democratise, and functionalise, produced 'neither economy nor efficiency' where both would have been better achieved through a combination of proper remuneration, due prestige and challenging work.[157] In a developing country it was even more important for the state to draw the best into its ranks for while in the morning a civil servant 'may be explaining the objectives of his organisation to a foreign expert' later that same day he may 'find himself explaining policies to a venerable gentleman mentally living in the 11th century.'[158]

Pakistan's rulers were 'carried away by the slogans denigrating the law and order arm' and lauding development.[159] They failed to understand, as did many civil servants, that an independent country experiencing rapid and often unwholesome socioeconomic change needed 'even more stable law and order conditions' than 'the subjects of a colonial power.'[160] The assertion of national sovereignty as well as the fulfilment of the duty of the state to provide basic social and economic services was inextricably linked to the rigorous and progressive collection of taxes.[161] While the core functions of the state were neglected and left to fend for themselves within the framework of an increasingly dysfunctional nineteenth-century psychological and material infrastructure, tens of billions of rupees were pumped into development without appreciating the need for proper and effective supervisory and inspectorial controls.[162] While, for instance, the population of the territories comprising Pakistan quintupled between 1901 and 1981, 'The administrative units, especially in the Punjab and Sind' remained more or less the same even as new regulatory functions stretched the administrative resources to the breaking point:

> The results are there for all to see. The general administration is gasping for breath and may collapse unless urgent and imaginative steps are taken to resuscitate it. The development administration is in no better shape notwithstanding the generous financial inputs.[163]

The consequences of this cavalier treatment of the essential functions of the state were most tangibly felt in the countryside where, in the 1980s, some seven-tenths of the population still lived. Land revenue administration and agricultural management were areas of state activity with which 'more people came into contact...than with any other.'[164] And yet, they had hardly ever been discussed as vital areas of administration in their own right.[165] The Committee on Revitalisation of Revenue Administration observed:

> It is generally felt, both in public and government circles, that the Revenue Administration has deteriorated a great deal during the last twenty to thirty years. We found enough evidence to confirm this view...it is largely attributable to the prolonged neglect of this vital area of administration by the Government itself.[166]

Rural folk routinely faced delay, inefficiency, corruption and the tyrannical behaviour of petty officials[167] with occasional appeals to the increasingly deskbound commissioners who simply did not have adequate time to invest in land revenue administration. Indeed, land revenue administration, like law and order, 'seems to us to be *passé*', 'status-quo', and 'anti-development.'[168] Neglect has meant that 'at any given time in most villages, there would be scores of cases of disregard of law resulting in ejectments, grabbing of facilities, misuse of credits, etc.'[169] The reaction of people to the state machinery in the rural areas varied from 'total submission, even to illegal demands' to 'cold imperviousness' with practically no cooperation and understanding.[170]

The irony was that whereas since independence 'the district and divisional administrations' had become far more powerful in terms of the patronage and resources at their disposal,[171] they had also become more arbitrary, personalised, and corrupt. Indeed, no event could 'occur in the district of which it' was 'not the duty of the Deputy Commissioner to keep himself informed and supervise its operation where necessary.'[172] The district administration was now 'a rural development administration' with DMG probationers sent to the Pakistan Academy of Rural Development to be trained in the latest administrative techniques.[173] The elected local councils established by Zia were practically powerless against the bureaucracy which, especially its DMG component, acted 'as the eyes and ears of the Government and the Secretariat Departments.'[174] Unfortunately, the relative stability[175] of the Zia era was not used to push through any substantial systemic changes and with his death in a mysterious plane crash in August 1988 a greatly weakened and compromised political class formally reassumed control of a bureaucracy that desperately needed creative and strong leadership.

3.7 THE FINAL ASSAULT

It got neither. Instead, for eleven years (1988-1999) the system floundered for lack of leadership and little attention was paid to its improvement. Not even its pay scale was revised after 1994. In the mean time, different parts 'of the country were being administered by the whims and idiosyncrasies' of local notables 'whose sole aim was to perpetuate themselves in offices of benefit.'[176] Members of the national and provincial assemblies 'were allocated their own quotas for jobs' leading to unabashed cronyism at the middle and lower levels.[177] The already serious problems of delinquency, incompetence and pliability spiralled out of control while 'a clique of corrupt courtiers' enveloped those exercising power in Pakistan's increasingly 'medieval ruling culture.'[178] These influence peddlers 'became the link between the rulers and the ruled' and were embedded in the 'network of patronage' arising out of an electoral system that was, and is, 'basically clannish'.[179] The marginal recovery in terms of the 'neutrality, independence and non-partisanship of public services' made under Zia collapsed in the face of unrestrained political patronage.[180] The 'persistent interference from the elected representatives' in the transfers and promotions of officials high and low allowed 'unscrupulous and dishonest bureaucrats' to rise and reinforced a pervasive 'culture of corruption.'[181] Such arbitrary acts eroded to a very considerable extent the 'autonomy of all departments' and adversely impacted the district administration.[182]

While elected representatives eagerly 'helped themselves to public funds and assets' and ignored 'any rule of law or moral probity' the administrative machinery became ineffective.[183] Across the length and breadth of the country 'authority seems to have eroded under the weight of the prolonged politicisation' of the higher bureaucracy.[184] The state's failure 'in its most basic and minimal task: providing security of life and property to its citizens'[185] understandably fuelled a crisis of confidence:

> The administrative decline has left citizens without the kind of order, security, and justice they had previously been used to. At this institutional level too, the system has become unresponsive to public needs, and therefore dysfunctional. The collapse of law and order in many parts of the country is the most deleterious but inevitable consequence of this weakening of administrative efficiency.[186]

Both the PPP and Pakistan Muslim League (PML-N) governments engaged themselves in the 'often senseless removal of officers from posts rendering them Officers on Special Duty (OSD) for long periods.[187] Out of turn promotions to personal favourites, such as Nawaz Sharif's decision shortly before he was overthrown to promote his Additional Secretary Foreign Affairs to full secretary rank and send him as ambassador to Washington, combined with more systematic attempts, such as Benazir Bhutto's Placement Bureau (1989) meant to circumvent established procedures for induction, further demoralised the bureaucracy. Such 'arbitrary actions generated a lot of resentment'[188] and increased the reluctance of officials to take decisions at their own levels. One could say that honest and competent officers were regularly shuffled to unimportant posts while the pliant and corrupt were routinely rewarded with important assignments where they could be of use to the ruler. The result was that civil servants who had the capacity to be good administrators were denied the opportunity to gain experience in important assignments while those granted such opportunities saw themselves as personal servants of the rulers and were not oriented towards performing their lawful functions. The damage done to the state was two-fold in that individuals who should not have been trusted with important positions were given a free hand while those who could have served properly gained relatively little exposure. Thus most of Pakistan's capable civil servants do not know how to run the administration for lack of experience while the servile sycophants who are often entrusted with important offices have no little inclination or aptitude for serving the state.

Iqbal Akhund, a former diplomat who served as Benazir Bhutto's National Security Adviser described what he saw during her first term as premier:

> Ministers were besieged in their homes from morning to night by petitioners, job-hunters, favour-seekers, and all and sundry. It was the same inside the National Assembly, where every minister's seat was a little beehive with members and backbenchers hovering around and going back and forth with little chits of paper. How the ministers ever got their official work done is a mystery, but in any case policy took a back seat to attending to the importunities of relatives, friends, and constituents.[189]

The cavalier attitude towards policy-making manifested itself in the cabinet's response to a policy paper prepared by the Ministry of Labour on overseas employment. The cabinet ministers were least interested in applying their minds to questions of policy and focused on the employment of a thousand temporary workers for the annual pilgrimage to Mecca and assigned government parliamentarians quotas of twenty jobs each.[190] Benazir Bhutto was personally inclined to favour those who had made sacrifices during the Zia years but the amount of pressure for patronage was so great that the new government behaved in a manner that was 'unmitigated even by the pro-forma respect for rules and regulations shown by the regular bureaucracy.'[191]

Nawaz Sharif was particularly notorious for his propensity to 'rule by verbal order' and 'monarchical-style of governance.'[192] Combined with his lack of a proper body of advisers 'publicity' prevailed 'as substitute for policy.'[193] His immediate successor, Moeen Qureshi, Pakistan's interim prime minister in 1993, frankly admitted that the 'Government was being used as an instrument of political patronage' and 'being run as a feudal estate rather than as a representative government.'[194] The World Bank executive turned interim premier, however, betrayed his meagre understanding of what a state is and ought to do when he described the highpoint of his term as the increase in utility prices and biggest disappointment as his 'inability to have done as much as I would have liked to, for women.'[195] Soon after his departure things continued as before with arbitrary transfers and endless politicking combined with clever tactical decisions bringing the administrative system to its knees:

> In many ways it appears that Pakistan has reached a stage of institutional exhaustion…In spite of a large number of over-staffed departments at the federal and provincial levels, *ad hocism* reigns supreme…As one goes down to the district and local level, one finds that the government hardly exists.[196]

Arbitrary 'changes in the tenure of officers', uneven and over-rapid promotions without reference to merit, greatly 'reduced the level of professional maturity and experience' of the higher bureaucracy.[197] One of the clearest indicators of the 'sharp decline in the intellectual calibre of the civil servant'[198] was that the district officers 'no longer' prepared 'literature of great historical and administrative value like the District Gazetteers, Settlement Reports, and Codes of Customary Laws' and stopped 'doing extensive field work.'[199] Under a succession of political governments the 'power exercised by politicians, feudal lords' and other influential persons had a 'baneful' impact on the administration.[200]

In this administration, the DMG, owing to the continued concentration of land revenue, magisterial, and police supervisory powers, became the pre-eminent instrument through which national and provincial politicians exercised power in their constituencies. These politicians were by and large hostile to elected local councils, which died natural deaths in the early 1990s. This meant that in many ways, while the district administration had to please a few hundred more powerful politicians, it did not have to submit to the caprices of thousands of local representatives or take them on. Interestingly, even without the reservation of posts, the DMG's importance in the eyes of politicians was resented by the other services. The perception that it was the key component of the higher bureaucracy continued to persist and was at least in part validated by reality on the ground.

As Pakistan edged steadily towards bankruptcy, theocracy, and state failure, the military was called in. In the mid-1990s it was used to restore the writ of the state in Sindh. In the late-1990s it was tasked with the carrying out of the census and the collection of electricity bills. This was a key indicator that the civil administration had failed even in the performance of its simplest functions. Thus, when the military took over on 12 October 1999, it faced a new challenge. Not only were the political institutions exhausted, as had happened before in the 1950s and 1970s, but this time, the administrative institutions were also running on vapour. Previously, the military had relied extensively on the services, support, and guidance of the higher bureaucracy, which in many ways mitigated the severity of military rule and prevented the armed forces from being drawn excessively into the administration. This time, however, the praetorians decided that the mandarins were beyond redemption and decided to assume direct control of the administration:

> The civil service is effectively controlled by the DMG. The group has close relations with international donors...Other groups in the public administration chafe under the control of one group and would welcome a democratisation of civil service structure. The end of the domination of the bureaucracy by one group is a necessary pre-condition for the attainment of administrative power by the Army and the creation of conditions for national reconstruction.[201]

Indeed, the higher bureaucracy led by the CSP/DMG served as the great administrative restraint on military rulers and was able to assert its intellectual and moral superiority time and time again, often for good, sometimes for ill, over their counterparts in the military. Yahya and Bhutto between them succeeded in breaking the back of the administrative elite which, they failed to realise in time, was their own best guarantee, to the extent that such guarantees exist in power politics, of relative security, stability, and success.

On 14 August 2001, a new local government scheme with elected *nazims* as the heads of the districts with overall control over the district bureaucracy were constituted. Now the district administration, under the coordination of District Coordination Officers (DCOs) who replaced the deputy commissioners and the control of 'grassroots representatives' was thrown into chaos and confusion from which it has not yet emerged. Ironically, the critical element that is allowing this system to function at all is the fact that the coordination officers, drawn from the DMG, have become more powerful vis-à-vis the other departments even as their magisterial and police supervisory powers have been taken away. The monitoring committees set up to check the *nazims* and administration 'exist mostly on paper' while the DCOs, as the heads of the District Development Committee which can approve schemes up to five million rupees, have tremendous powers of patronage.[202] Not surprisingly, the level of corruption has increased, while local infrastructure in terms of education, health, and social services has declined and the administration is utterly politicised.[203] There has also been a multiplication of bureaucratic posts with, for instance, separate officers for different kinds of education, and with this 'Coordination has grown worse' than under the old system where the divisional and deputy commissioners had powers of enforcement under law.[204] For instance, prior to devolution, the deputy commissioner had powers to control prices of food, settle property disputes, and supervise the police. Now, local government officials 'find it nearly impossible to enforce their writ without the enforcement powers previously exercised by the executive magistrates backed by the police.'[205]

Even those who were initially eager participants in the devolution and decentralisation exercise have, five years too late, come to appreciate 'the institutional anarchy that results from the parallel systems for local government and hence the non-rational jurisdictions that are currently in place.'[206] Ominously, whereas under the old system the most powerful official in the district was a university-educated professional from a middleclass background, now the districts are headed by landlords immersed in local rivalries and traditions with, on average, a high school level of education (11-13 years), while their councillors, are smaller landholders with matriculation level education (8-9 years).[207] Perhaps the most damning indictment of the new local government and administrative system is the fact that it has not been extended to the forty-one military cantonments, which continue to be run under 'anti-people' and 'colonial' rules and regulations, or the federal capital, Islamabad. Ironically, given Islamabad's high level of development, recent origins, and large number of professional and middleclass residents, it is quite possibly the only part of the country where a system of elected local government on the present plan could actually work. Far from 'empowering citizens, the devolution scheme has exacerbated the

Pakistani state's institutional crisis by rooting the military in local politics.'[208]

For the civil administration and higher bureaucracy Musharraf's resignation in August 2008 due to a combination of political pressure, civil disobedience and loss of support within the military high command has raised the possibility of the termination of many of his reforms including the devolution of power to local governments. The idiosyncrasies and opportunism of Pakistan's political leaders aside, they are all compelled at some level to operate within a structure not of their making. That structure has civilian as well as military sides. Under Musharraf, ten billion dollars of US military assistance combined with his administrative and fiscal reforms further imbalanced the structure in favour of the military. The Pakistani military is today better equipped, better trained and wealthier than ever before. Its visible entrenchment in the larger socioeconomic context has increased dramatically over the past decade. Relatively and absolutely the military is in a far stronger domestic position today than it was in 1988.

Musharraf's devolution of power to local governments, reliance upon military officers for administrative and political tasks and constant interference in petty details far beneath the dignity of a head of state has meant that the civil administration has run aground. A stage has now been reached where the higher echelons of the central bureaucracy cannot even efficiently privatise state lands for its own benefit. That the once effective bureaucratic *qabza* group that raised Islamabad from the wilderness and colonised it for good measure has failed to develop a single new Capital Development Authority (CDA) sector in eighteen years is a testament to how disorganised and demoralised the civil administration has become.

For the politicians this is an extremely worrisome development. If the higher bureaucracy has become so lethargic and ineffective in the pursuit of its own material group interests it cannot be reasonably expected to display greater vigour in serving the rulers or implementing complex policies. In 1988, the politicians had at their disposal a quasi-medieval semi-effective civil administration that could, properly guided, deliver on the ground. In 2008, the politicians have at their disposal a highly politicised, dangerously divided and substantially ineffective civil administration that has spent the past seven years catering to the almost wholly primitive whims of local politicians. The task of systematically reviving the bureaucracy as an institution is probably beyond the capacity of the PPP-led coalition government at the centre or the assorted provincial governments. That said, without an effective civil service the ability of the politicians to get things done and prevent the rapid haemorrhaging of their credibility will remain compromised. History furnished little reason for optimism.

3.8 THE ECHOES OF EMPIRE

At the thematic level, the history of the Pakistani bureaucracy can be divided into four broad categories. First, the years in which an elected civilian executive exercised control over the bureaucracy (1947-1953, 1972-1977, and arguably 1997-1999). Second, years during which the civilian bureaucracy more or less dominated policy making (1953-1969, 1985-1990). Third, years in which the military assumed more or less direct command of all policy making (1969-72, 1977-85, and 1999-present). Then there were years when no body was really in charge (1990-1999). In terms of performance the period between 1947 and 1969 is probably the best. Pakistan overcame severe initial challenges and embarked upon an impressive modernization program. As one retired civil service officer remarked, the post-1969 generation has the misfortune of never having seen Pakistan in relatively 'good shape'. That said, this period of high performance had an opportunity cost.

Prolonged authoritarian rule left a huge void in Pakistan's political leadership which, in the first decade, for all its flaws, was capable of giving a lead to the civil service. The working relationship between the politicians and the bureaucracy (i.e. the former make policy, the latter assist, advise and implement) suffered irreparably. The politicisation of the local bodies and the Ayub regime's excessive reliance on the civil service to formulate and carry out directives in every field led to a decline in its prestige, impartiality, and legitimacy. It also led to the first serious rumblings and concerns about corruption at the higher levels. The increase in the level of development work affected the ability of the civil service to perform its principal functions, i.e. order and taxation. Amongst the two major structural shocks to the civil service administered by the Ayub Regime in its initial flush of success was the purge (albeit through due process) of one thousand three hundred civil servants and the abolition of the foreign training component (in England and Continental Europe) that CSP trainees underwent.

The period between 1969 to 1977 witnessed a powerful reaction to authoritarian and elitist pretensions of the Ayub regime. This reaction severely impinged upon the performance of the Pakistani bureaucracy. While the institutional cohesion of the bureaucracy was undermined by arbitrary interference, Bhutto nationalised industries and services and standardised the pay scales into twenty-two national grades (known as National Pay Scale/NPS and Basic Pay Scale/BPS) in place of the old system, which had over six hundred pay scales. These measures had a tremendous negative impact on the bureaucracy. On the one hand, the total number of government employees expanded rapidly. On the other hand, because the pay scales were standardised it became impossible to selectively revise pays. Either everyone would get a marginal increase which wouldn't make much difference or else no one would get an increase. This also led to corruption on a day to day basis and public morality deteriorated rapidly. The state became a personal estate operated as a criminal enterprise and the loss of self-respect experienced by the members of state apparatus has never been recovered from.

The Zia era saw a stabilisation and marginal recovery of the condition of the bureaucracy. Zia thought that for whatever its faults the civilian bureaucracy represented the best and brightest of what Pakistan had to offer. There was a reduction in the level of arbitrary interference by the executive and service conditions improved and in-service training was tied to promotion for the first time. However, Zia's policies of supporting the Afghan *Jihad* against the USSR and Islamisation within Pakistan did much to make society even more ungovernable. Pakistan was flush with foreign currency, drugs, arms and a crusading ideology, and the administration faced unprecedented challenges that would have proved difficult to surmount even with capable and committed leadership.

The 1988-1999 period saw in many respects a defective system becoming a non-system. The politicians did not make policy and the administration of the country languished for want of direction. Each change of government was accompanied by shuffles and reshuffles of the bureaucracy. Benazir Bhutto, for instance, established a Placement Bureau to try and induct her protégés into the civil service during her first term. Nawaz Sharif and his brother, Shahbaz Sharif, were notorious for running the government by verbal diktat, on occasion having the paper work filed retrospectively. Having already lost its *esprit de corps*, sense of competence, prestige and self-respect, the bureaucracy curried favour and sought to please the boss.

Post-1999 the military government's principal innovation as regards the bureaucracy was the system of elected local governments. Although it is too early to tell what the final impact of this system will be, certain indicators of the system's performance can be commented upon. There has been a glaring increase in ordinary criminal activity. It is widely believed that elected local leaders are highly criminalised and beyond securing favours, the elected counsellors and their leaders have little understanding of or inclination towards learning the role of an elected executive in a modern state. The powers of the DCO over departments other than law and order (police) and revenue are much greater than those of the old CSP/DMG. Elimination of the magistracy has removed an important element of control over the police without putting in place a better system. There is a perception that the devolution of power to the grassroots is a farce as the centre controls the purse strings and will be packed up as soon as the incumbent departs. This fuels uncertainty, corruption and mismanagement.

The Musharraf regime did not seem interested in introducing the local government reforms in Islamabad or in the cantonments. Evidently, for those who matter, the 'colonial' system of bureaucratic control is to be maintained. Under present conditions, an assessment from inside the higher bureaucracy is that about four-fifths of the new recruits to the superior services range in quality from mediocre to actually being worth the minimal pay they take home. The lack of enthusiasm for the state service is testified to by the small number of candidates appearing for the central services exams (around four thousand per year in the 2000s against about five thousand per year in the 1960s), making it harder for the state to fill vacancies and drying out the recruitment pool. The decline in the intellectual and moral quality of the civil servants has translated directly into deterioration in the quality of governance. It has also drawn the military into routine administration in a way not countenanced before. The military's journey into the politics and administration of the country and the attendant reassertion of the praetorian nature of the subcontinent's culture of power is the subject that is dealt with next.

NOTES

1. Wellesley was particularly conscious of the need to ensure the highest quality of civil servant possible. Arguing in favour of compulsory college education for all recruits, Wellesley identified 'general knowledge of those branches of literature and science which form the basis of the education of persons destined to similar occupations in Europe' plus Indian 'history, languages, customs...the Muhammadan and Hindu codes of law and religion' and 'the political and commercial interests of Great Britain in Asia' as the minimum acceptable standard for the civil service. It was in this context that Wellesley ordered, on 10 July 1800, the foundation of Fort William College. Cited in, Malleson, *Administration of British India under Lord Wellesley*, 103.
2. That is from Nomos, the Ancient Greek god of laws.
3. Courtenay Ilbert, *The Government of India* (London: Humphrey Milford and Stevens & Sons, Ltd., 1916), 138.
4. Ibid., 138-9.
5. Ibid., 140.
6. Ibid.
7. *Report on the Administration of the Punjab and its Dependencies for the year 1875-76* (Lahore: Government Civil Secretariat Press, 1876), 21.
8. Roy Jenkins, *Gladstone* (London: Macmillan-Papermac, 1996), 165.
9. Ibid., 166.
10. George C. M. Birdwood, *On Competitions and the ICS* (London: W. J. Johnson, 1872), 5.
11. Ibid.
12. Ibid., 9-10.
13. Philips, ed., *The Correspondence of Lord William Cavendish Bentinck: Governor-General of India 1828-1835*, vol. I, *1828-1831*, xxiii.
14. Birdwood, *On Competitions and the ICS*, 26.
15. Ibid.
16. David Gilmour, *The Ruling Caste: Imperial Lives in the Victorian Raj* (London: John Murray, 2005), 63.
17. Ibid., 68.
18. Ibid., 113-4.
19. Ibid., 149.
20. Ibid.
21. Ibid., 148.
22. A. N. Wilson, *The Victorians* (London: Hutchinson, 2002), 10.
23. That is, the politicians make policy while the higher bureaucracy advises and executes in accordance with the law.
24. Rowland Egger, *The Improvement of Public Administration in Pakistan: A Report with Recommendations* (Karachi: Government of Pakistan Press, 1953), 24.
25. Ibid.
26. *Report of the Pakistan Pay Commission*, Vol. I (Karachi: Governor-General's Press and Publications, 1949), 27. Salaries were reduced: For Secretaries the reduction was from Rs 4,000 pm to 2,500 pm. For Joint Secretaries, Rs 3,000 pm to 1,800

pm; Deputy Secretaries, Rs 2,000 pm to 1,500 pm; for Under Secretaries, Rs 1,500 pm to 1,200 pm; and for Assistant Secretaries, from Rs 1,000 pm to 900 pm.

27. Saeed Shafqat, 'Quaid-i-Azam and the Bureaucracy' in K. M. Yusuf, ed., *Politics and Policies of Quaid-i-Azam* (Islamabad: National Institute of Historical and Cultural Research, 1994), 255.
28. Ibid.
29. Ibid., 257.
30. Ibid., 258.
31. Rana Saleem Iqbal, ed., *The Quaid on Civil Servants: Speeches and Statements, October 1947 to August 1948* (Islamabad: National Documentation Centre, 2007), 17.
32. Ralph Braibanti, 'Public Bureaucracy and Judiciary in Pakistan' in Joseph LaPolambara, ed., *Bureaucracy and Political Development* (Princeton: Princeton University Press, 1963), 380.
33. Ibid., 382.
34. Ralph Braibanti, 'The Higher Bureaucracy of Pakistan', in Ralph Braibanti, ed., *Asian Bureaucratic Systems Emergent from the British Imperial Tradition* (Durham: Duke University Press, 1966), 243.
35. National Documentation Centre, Islamabad. Folder Three, 1948. File No. 2(2)-PMS/48, 23.
36. Ibid., 44.
37. Ibid.
38. Ibid., 45.
39. Ibid.
40. Ibid., 109.
41. Ibid.
42. Ibid., 113.
43. Ibid., 114.
44. Bernard L. Gladieux, 'Reorientation of Pakistan Government for National Development' (Karachi: Government of Pakistan, 1955), 2. Gladieux spent four months in Pakistan before submitting his report.
45. Egger, *The Improvement of Public Administration in Pakistan*, 1.
46. Ibid., 3.
47. Ibid., 7.
48. Ibid., 9.
49. Ibid.
50. Braibanti, 'The Higher Bureaucracy in Pakistan', 294.
51. Ibid., 330.
52. 332 in 1960.
53. Braibanti, 'The Higher Bureaucracy in Pakistan', 331.
54. In the long run there was merit in inter-wing parity. West Pakistan's population would have overtaken East Pakistan's by the early or mid-1980s. It is easy to see how had that eventuality materialised East Pakistan may have become a staunch proponent of inter-wing parity.
55. *Report of the Provincial Administration Commission, February 1960* (Islamabad: Printing Corporation of Pakistan, 1962), 6.

56. Ibid., 7.
57. Ibid., 14.
58. 1955, File No. 256/CF/55, Government of Pakistan, Cabinet Secretariat, Cabinet Branch, 'Standards for Appointments of Secretaries to Provincial Government', 1.
59. 1955, File No. 111/CF/55, Government of Pakistan, Cabinet Secretariat, Cabinet Branch, Cabinet Meeting, 21 May 1955, Case No. 356/51/55, 'Punjab Situation', 1.
60. Ibid.
61. Ibid., Cabinet Meeting, 25 May 1955, Case No. 371/52/55, 'Dismissal of Noon Ministry', 1.
62. Ibid.
63. Craig Baxter, ed., *Diaries of Field Marshal Mohammed Ayub Khan, 1966-1972* (Karachi: Oxford University Press, 2007), 116. Ayub had dined with Munir on 12 July 1967, at which time and place he learnt of this.
64. Ibid.
65. 1958, File No. 651/CF/58, Government of Pakistan, Cabinet Secretariat, Cabinet Branch, Cabinet Meeting, 18 December 1958, Case No. 1152/71/58, 'Trial of Martial Law offences by Magistrates; Procedure for Confirmation and Review of Sentences', 1.
66. 1958, File No. 595/CF/58, Government of Pakistan, Cabinet Secretariat, Cabinet Branch, Cabinet Meeting, 15 November 1958, Case No. 1020/61/58, 'Self-help', 1.
67. Ibid.
68. Ibid.
69. Ibid.
70. Ibid.
71. 1959, File No. 467/CF/59, Government of Pakistan, President's Secretariat, Cabinet Division (Cabinet Branch), 'Concept of the Future Central Government', 1.
72. *Report of the Administrative Reorganisation Committee*, (Karachi: Efficiency and O&M Wing, President's Secretariat, 1960), 1.
73. Ibid.
74. Ibid., 148.
75. Ibid.
76. Ibid., 148-149.
77. It was evidently merged with the Ministry of Information.
78. Braibanti, 'The Higher Bureaucracy in Pakistan', 303.
79. Ibid., 297.
80. Ibid.
81. Ibid., 298.
82. *Report of the Provincial Administration Commission, February 1960*, 183.
83. Ibid.
84. Ibid., 183-184.
85. *Report of the Constitution Commission, Pakistan, 1961* (Karachi: Government of Pakistan Press, 1961), 107.
86. Ibid.

87. *Report of the Pay and Services Commission, 1959-1962* (Karachi: Government of Pakistan Press, 1962), 14.
88. Ibid., 14-5.
89. Ibid., 16.
90. Ibid., 53.
91. Ibid.
92. Ibid.,
93. Ibid., 53-4.
94. Ibid., 57.
95. Tasneem Ahmad Siddiqui, *Towards Good Governance* (Karachi: Oxford University Press, 2001), 11.
96. Ibid.
97. *Report of the Working Group on the Reorganisation of the Public Service Structure in Pakistan In Light of the Fulton Report* (Islamabad: Government of Pakistan, 1969), 2-3. The three CSP members, D. K. Power, Aslam Abdullah Khan, and Nusrat Khan, withdrew formed their own working group and submitted their own report, arguing against a separate officer for development.
98. Ibid., 6.
99. Hasan Zaheer, *The Separation of East Pakistan: The Rise and Realisation of Bengali Muslim Nationalism* (Karachi: Oxford University Press, 1994), 113.
100. Ibid., 116.
101. Ibid.
102. Ibid., 122.
103. *White Paper on the Performance of the Bhutto Regime*, Vol. II, *Treatment of Fundamental State Institutions* (Islamabad: Printing Corporation of Pakistan Press, 1979), 122.
104. Ibid., 123.
105. Ibid.
106. Ibid., 123-4.
107. Ibid., 124-5.
108. Ibid., 122.
109. Ibid., 128.
110. Ibid.
111. Ibid., 129.
112. Ibid., 136.
113. Ibid.
114. Ibid., 136-7.
115. Ibid., 138.
116. Ibid.
117. Ibid., 141-2.
118. Ibid., 144.
119. Ibid., 'Statement of Vaqar Ahmed, ex Cabinet Secretary', 25 November 1977, A-17.
120. Ibid., A-18.
121. Ibid.
122. Ibid., 159.

123. Bhutto's approach towards the management of his party was the same. 'Distrustful of his own party men, and particularly of the leftists in the organization, Bhutto himself systematically weakened the party and purged it of its cadre of activists and ideologists.' This effectively turned the PPP 'into an extension of the Bhutto family.' Sayed Wiqar Ali Shah, 'Pakistan People's Party: The Twin Legacies of Socialism and Dynastic Rule' in Subrata K. Mitra, Clemens Spies and Mike Enskat, eds., *Political Parties in South Asia* (London: Praeger Greenwood, 2004), 165.
124. *White Paper on the Performance of the Bhutto Regime*, Vol. II, *Treatment of Fundamental State Institutions*, 159.
125. Rafi Raza, *Zulfikar Ali Bhutto and Pakistan, 1967-1977* (Karachi: Oxford University Press, 1997), 265.
126. Ibid.
127. *Report of the National Pay Commission 1970-1972* (Islamabad: Government of Pakistan Press, 1972).
128. 1985, Estt. Divn. U.O. No. 10(1)/84-CPI (Vol. 1), Syed Ijlal Haider Zaidi, Zaidi Papers, Secretary Establishment, Summary for the Prime Minister Mohammad Khan Junejo: 'Reorganisation of Services Structure', 4.
129. Ibid., 5.
130. Ibid., 6.
131. Ibid., 5.
132. Ibid., 9.
133. Ibid.
134. Ibid., 10.
135. Ibid., 14.
136. Ibid., 12.
137. Ibid.
138. Ibid.
139. Ibid.
140. Ibid.
141. Ibid., 60.
142. *White Paper on the Performance of the Bhutto Regime*, Vol. II, *Treatment of Fundamental State Institutions*, A-7.
143. Ibid., A-8.
144. Syed Ijlal Haider Zaidi, Zaidi Papers, Summary for the Cabinet: 'Civil Service Commission Report', 1981, 13.
145. 'Report of the Committee for the Study of Corruption, 1986', (Islamabad: Cabinet Secretariat, Establishment Division, 1986).
146. Jamilur Rehman Khan, ed., *Government and Administration in Pakistan* (Islamabad: Pakistan Public Administrative Research Centre, O&M Division, Cabinet Secretariat, Government of Pakistan, 1987).
147. One major change was that while in 1969 the CSP had accounted for 93 per cent of posts of joint secretary and above in the federal government by the mid-1970s their share was about 44 per cent. Charles Kennedy, 'Zia and the Civilian Bureaucrats: Pakistan's Bureaucracy in the 1980s', in Baxter and Wasti eds., *Pakistan Authoritarianism in the 1980s*, 91.

148. It amounted to thirteen military officers inducted into Grade 17 and 15 into Grade 18 every year against over ten times as many vacancies. Ibid., 95.
149. S. M. Haider, 'The Political and Constitutional System of Pakistan', in Jamilur Rehman Khan, ed., *Government and Administration in Pakistan*, 16.
150. Ibid., 14.
151. I. A. Imtiazi, 'Organization, Structure and Working of the Federal and Provincial Government in Pakistan', in Ibid., 57-58.
152. Agha Iftikhar Hussain, 'The Civil Services', in ibid., 186.
153. Ibid., 147.
154. Zaidi, Zaidi Papers, 'Reorganisation of Services Structure', 33.
155. Zaidi, Zaidi Papers, 'Civil Services Commission Report', 14.
156. Ibid.
157. Ibid.
158. Iftikhar Hussain, 'The Civil Services', 188.
159. Syed Ijlal Haider Zaidi, Summary for the Cabinet: 'Provincial Administration', 1981, 18.
160. Ibid.
161. Ibid.
162. Ibid., 19.
163. Ibid.
164. *Report of the Committee on Revitalization of Revenue Administration*, Vol. 1, July 1978 (Islamabad: Government of Pakistan, 1978), 3.
165. Ibid.
166. Ibid., vi.
167. Ibid., 3.
168. Abdul Qayyum, 'Land Revenue Administration', in Jamilur Rehman Khan, ed., *Government and Administration in Pakistan*, 318-319.
169. Ibid., 329.
170. Ibid., 341.
171. S. K. Mahmud, 'District Administration', in Ibid., 215.
172. Ibid.
173. Ibid.
174. 1978, No. 57/1/MLA, Note by General Ziaul Haq, 18 January 1978, addressed to all Martial Law Administrators (MLAs), governors and chief secretaries, cited in *Report of the Committee on Revitalization of Revenue*, Vol. 1, July 1978, 10.
175. Azhar Hassan Nadeem, *Pakistan: The Political Economy of Lawlessness* (Karachi: Oxford University Press, 2002), 74.
176. Ibid., 76.
177. Siddiqui, *Towards Good Governance*, 37.
178. Ibid.
179. Ibid.
180. Ibid., 200.
181. Rasul Bakhsh Rais, 'Building State and Nation in Pakistan', in Charles H. Kennedy, Kathleen McNeil, Carl Ernst, and David Gilmartin, eds., *Pakistan at the Millennium* (Karachi: Oxford University Press, 2003), 11.
182. Ibid.

183. Maleeha Lodhi, *Pakistan's Encounter With Democracy* (Lahore: Vanguard, 1994), 18.
184. Ibid., 21.
185. Ibid.
186. Ibid., 63.
187. Mushahid Hussain and Akmal Hussain, *Pakistan: Problems of Governance* (Lahore: Vanguard Books, 1993), 85.
188. Ibid.
189. Iqbal Akhund, *Trial and Error: The Advent and Eclipse of Benazir Bhutto* (Karachi: Oxford University Press, 2000), 53.
190. Ibid., 78.
191. Ibid., 77-8.
192. Lodhi, *Pakistan's Encounter with Democracy*, 243-4.
193. Ibid., 245.
194. Ibid., 44.
195. Ibid., 43.
196. Siddiqui, *Towards Good Governance*, 11.
197. Mohammad Yasin, ed., *District and Police Systems in Pakistan* (Lahore: Vanguard, 1999), 20.
198. Mushahid Hussain, *Pakistan: Problems of Governance*, 11.
199. Yasin, ed., *District and Police Systems in Pakistan*, 20.
200. Ibid., 22.
201. 'Structural Analysis of National Reconstruction', National Reconstruction Bureau (NRB), Islamabad, 27 May 2000. Cited in *Devolution in Pakistan: Reform or Regression* (Islamabad: International Crisis Group, 2004), 7.
202. Ibid., 17.
203. Ibid., 17-8.
204. Ibid., 15.
205. Ibid.
206. Shahrukh Rafi Khan, Foqia Sadiq Khan and Aasim Sajjad Akhtar, *Initiating Devolution for Service Delivery in Pakistan: Ignoring the Power Structure* (Karachi: Oxford University Press, 2007), 4.
207. Ibid., Chapter 6 'Local Government Elections: Power Dynamics in Smaller Land Holding Constituencies', 100-39.
208. *Devolution in Pakistan: Reform or Regression*, 10.

4 Praetorians

4.1 The Sword and the Spirit

From the ancient centres of civilisations in Egypt, India, Persia, and China, to the classical Hellenic and Roman imperia and the feudal domains, medieval aristocracies and more recent enlightened despotisms of Europe, it was the sword that dominated the spirit. Across the world and through history the rulers were military men and states were organised around a military patronage complex[1] although the modalities of the military organization varied considerably. We thus find that the first Mauryan emperor, Chandragupta Maurya was the former army chief of the dynasty he overthrew. The last Maurya was ultimately deposed by his army chief. The same can be said of the Roman and Byzantine empires from whose historical experience the term 'praetorian' is derived as well as for the Persian, Ottoman and Arab empires whose strength came from the practice of military slavery.

Maintaining control over military instruments was no easy task for the ruler. The ruler's arbitrary power exacerbated the apparatus's insecurity and led to frequent rebellions. The apathetic and atomised nature of societies governed arbitrarily as the ruler's personal estate meant that any rebellion that was successful became legitimate.[2] The official priesthood, a sub-sector of the state, would bow before the successful upstart and proclaim him the new Shadow of God or Heaven's Mandated. Under such conditions the ruler had to take an active interest in the affairs of the apparatus, employ espionage extensively, mercilessly punish or outwardly forgive acts of defiance and reward loyal and effective servants. In an environment dominated by arbitrariness, conspiracy and violence, survival for both master and servant required great moral dexterity and enormous amounts of animal cunning. As soon as the ruler lost the ability or will to dominate and awe his servants, the empire and its apparatus fragmented into petty rival estates. The military machine was the first casualty of this fragmentation and experienced inflation in numbers and decline in effectiveness as evidenced by the Roman, Ottoman, Timurid and Sikh, experiences.

At its height in AD 180 the Roman Empire, governed as an absolute monarchy since 27 BC, comprised forty-five provinces and stretched from Scotland in the north to the Sahara and Mesopotamia in the south and southeast. Some fifty to seventy million subjects lived in this empire and the total strength of the military was approximately three hundred thousand. In AD 180, with the death of Marcus Aurelius, the succession of wise sovereigns ended. From the reign of Octavian Augustus (27 BC–AD 14) the Roman emperors had to manage a delicate balancing act with the sovereign 'elected *by the authority of the senate* and *the consent of the soldiers.*'[3] The anxieties of the emperor were very real:

> When he [Augustus] framed the artful system of the Imperial authority, his moderation was inspired by his fears. He wished to deceive the people by an image of civil liberty, and the armies by an image of civil government.
>
> During a long period of two hundred and twenty years from the establishment of this artful system to the death of Commodus, the dangers inherent to military government were, in a great measure, suspended. The soldiers were seldom roused to that fatal sense of their own strength, and of the weakness of the civil authority, which was before and afterwards, productive of such dreadful calamities.[4]

After Marcus Aurelius the Roman Empire ran through seventy emperors, each raised and liquidated at the caprice of the military faction in control of Rome and Italy. Each imperial accession was accompanied by lavish donations to the military, especially the elite Praetorian Guard stationed at Rome since the fall of the republic in 27 BC. Convulsed by civil wars in which military commanders and provincial governors embarked on campaigns to conquer Rome and proclaim themselves, or their civilian stooges, emperor, the Roman Empire experienced a general social and economic catastrophe. Taxes, fines, confiscations, and internal dislocation spread over a century of chaos caused the population of the Roman Empire to fall by as much as half. Eventually, a military saviour restored order to what was left of the empire. At the end of this period, however, the size of the military stood at half a million men.

A similar pattern manifests itself in the Ottoman Empire. During the period of Ottoman ascendancy (1300-1600) the sultan's slave soldiers, or janissaries, numbered no more than twenty thousand. After the succession of effective rulers failed in the late-1600s the number of janissaries rose steadily and reached one hundred and fifteen thousand in 1826. In times of war and crisis barely one-sixth of the men on the payroll showed up for service. Once the protectors of the sultan and the vanguard of Ottoman expansion, the janissaries became a mafia dominated by conspiracy and internecine violence that lived comfortably in the cities, terrorised imperial subjects, and murdered reform-minded sultans at will. It was their massacre at the hands of an exceptionally cunning and ruthless ruler, Sultan Mahmud III, which enabled the Ottoman Empire to limp along until the early twentieth century when, once more, the sultan lost control of the military and became its captive after the Young Turk Revolution of 1908.

In the Timurid Empire in India imperial servants were classified as *mansabdars* or rank-holders against a numerical value indicative of the number of troops each was supposed to maintain. There was no distinction between the military and civil administration for *mansabdars* could be, and were, assigned any function the emperor deemed fit. From their coercive powers flowed immense wealth. In the late-sixteenth century Akbar's approximately one thousand seven hundred *mansabdars* received about 80 per cent of the empire's annual revenues of one hundred and thirty million rupees with the top twenty-five securing about 30 per cent of the revenue.[5] As the empire weakened in the latter half of the seventeenth century, the number of *mansabdars* rose to nearly fourteen thousand five hundred, of whom half received assignments of land and half cash salaries, against total revenues of about three hundred and eighty million rupees extracted through heavy taxation.[6]

In the context of the Sikh kingdom founded by Ranjit Singh the army numbered about eighty thousand during his reign (1799-1839) and consumed some 40 per cent of the empire's revenues.[7] This military force was trained and equipped along European lines though little else by way of modernisation was carried out.[8] Between Ranjit Singh's death in 1839[9] and the first Anglo-Sikh war in 1846, the Sikh kingdom descended into civil war as rival military factions fought for power.[10] During that period of internal dissolution the Sikh military grew in strength from eighty thousand to over one hundred and twenty thousand and would have continued to grow in numerical strength and capriciousness if the British had not intervened.[11]

The British understanding of the relationship between the military and civilian branches of the state reflected the liberal and constitutionalist bias of their own culture of power which was both admired and envied by Enlightenment-era thinkers. Carl von Clausewitz, the great nineteenth century Prussian philosopher of war and military history, understood warfare and the structures that support it as emanations of 'an act of policy.'[12] The actual application of physical force was the method while the objective was to 'compel our enemy to do our will.'[13] Ideally, the political objective or the state's 'motive for the war' would 'determine both the military objective to be reached and the amount of effort it requires.'[14] In drawing the distinction between a superior moral and intellectual entity that laid down policy and the instruments of violence used to execute the sovereign's will Clausewitz expressed an idea shared somewhat self-contradictorily by Napoleon:

> Napoleon might have been expected to give the army a privileged position within France. Two examples from many show what actually happened. General Cervoni, commanding the 8th division, ordered that 'anyone found carrying arms will be imprisoned in the Fort St Jean in Marseilles'; on 7 March 1807 Napoleon reproved him: 'A general has no civil function unless specially invested with one *ad hoc*. When he has no mission, he cannot exercise any influence on the courts, on the municipality or on the police. I consider your behaviour madness.'[15]

The other example involved cadets at the Metz artillery training school who rioted and abused the civilian population:

> Napoleon called them to order: 'The Prussian army used to insult and ill-treat burghers, who were later delighted when it suffered defeat. The army, once crushed, disappeared and nothing replaced it, because it did not have the nation behind it....' Constantly Napoleon drove home the point that a Frenchman is a citizen first and a soldier second, that every offence committed by a soldier in peacetime must first be referred to the civil authorities. As he remarked in 1808: 'There are only two forces in the world: the sword and the spirit; by spirit I mean the civil and religious institutions; in the long run the sword is always defeated by the spirit.'[16]

In expressing these views Clausewitz and Napoleon were doubtless aware that even in their own countries the power of the sword could not be underestimated. Prussia was Germany's most militaristic state and it would not be until after the Second World War that civilian supremacy would be established in that part of the world. France struggled throughout the nineteenth century to banish Bonaparte's praetorian legacy. Much of Europe remained under military or quasi-military one-party rule until the liberalizing waves of the 1970s and late-1980s.[17]

It is in this broader context that the measure of the British achievement in reforming the principles of civil-military relations ought to be viewed. During British rule several important developments took place as regards the role of the military. First, the army ceased to be the private possession of the ruler and was constituted as an institution under the law. Second, the army was insulated from politics and thus the medieval-conspiratorial soldier mindset gave way to a more professional and apolitical world view. Third, except for certain regions of the country, a disproportionate number of which were inherited by Pakistan due to its location,[18] the military gradually ceased to be an administrative instrument. Fourth, the size of the military declined as a percentage of the population. On the eve of the First World War the army's numerical strength in British India was one hundred and fifty thousand out of a population of two hundred million. On the eve of the Second World War the army numbered two hundred and fifty thousand out of a population of three hundred and fifty million (British India). Last, by the time the British left India a network of meritocratic and democratic institutions operated by civilians was in place. Power itself was transferred to constituent assemblies that comprised elected politicians upon whose sagacity rested the perpetuation of 'the most outstanding contribution of the British rule in India...a theory of civil-military relations which emphasised an over-all civilian control and the military's aloofness from politics.'[19]

4.2 Marching Orders

Between 30 June and 30 October 1947, the armed forces of British India were partitioned along communal lines. The total strength of this military was about four hundred and sixty thousand inclusive of nearly twelve thousand Indian officers and defence officials. Pakistan's share of this military was fixed at one-third, or one hundred and fifty thousand men, of whom ninety thousand were already deployed in its territory. Due to the concentration of recruitment areas in the Punjab, which contributed six-tenths of the combatant strength of the British Indian armed forces in 1927,[20] the Pakistani military was well-placed to replenish and expand its numerical strength. The critical shortage was in the officer corps where of the four thousand officers needed about half were available.

This was to be expected given the rate of progress in Indianisation targeted by British policy-makers.[21] Their objective was that by 1952 'half the total cadre of officers in the Indian Army would be Indians.'[22] Therefore, it was hardly surprising that in August 1947 some thirteen thousand five hundred of the twenty-two thousand officers in the Indian military were British.[23] In managing their imperial decline, the British seemed to be subconsciously targeting the late-1960s or early-1970s as the period in which Indianisation of the covenanted services and armed forces would be completed and power transferred to a united and self-governing India.

For the new national government in Pakistan retaining British officers into the 1970s was out of the question even though Muslims made up only one-fourth of the total strength of the officer corps of the British Indian military on the eve of independence. Liaquat Ali Khan took the defence portfolio in addition to the premiership and as the chairman of the Defence Committee of the Cabinet (DCC) relentlessly pushed ahead with a program that sought complete nationalisation of the armed forces by January 1951. As a temporary measure about five hundred British officers were retained. The pace of recruitment was increased and accelerated promotions given so that majors and colonels rose to senior command positions in a few years time. Short-term commissions were also given against vacancies while voluntary retirement was restricted. The committee constituted by the cabinet to report on nationalisation confidently asserted that the target date of 1 January 1951, would be met insofar as the army was concerned 'except in technical branches which could not carry on unless British or other foreign personnel could be obtained on contract.'[24] Such rapid change was being accomplished without significant harm to efficiency which was defined 'as the ability of the Armed Forces to defend the borders of Pakistan against aggression from neighbouring countries.'[25] The task of formulating the country's defence policy was firmly in the hands of the cabinet committee and subcommittees constituted by the prime minister under his own chairmanship.[26] Given that 'the danger of war was imminent, it was essential that speedy decisions should be taken' to ensure preparedness for military conflict and determine Pakistan's defence needs.[27] Thus, the defence committee and its subcommittees were tasked to 'deal specifically with these matters.'[28]

The principal neighbour from whom a credible threat was perceived was India. Of the one hundred and seventy thousand tons of engineering stores and machinery due to be sent to Pakistan from India only about a thousand tons were received. Of the one hundred and sixty thousand tons of ordnance stores some twenty thousand tons arrived. Against the sixty thousand tons of ammunitions and explosives and two hundred and forty-nine armoured vehicles, nothing was received.[29] The military conflict in Kashmir and the pressure exercised by India meant that military infrastructure developed along the Afghan border by the British to counter the Russians became substantially irrelevant to the defence needs of Pakistan. While much can and has been made of Jinnah's futile overtures to the United States of America for economic and military assistance, the fact is that if India had provided Pakistan with its lawful share of military assets as per the agreement between the two countries things would have turned out differently and for the better. Pakistan would have neither had to spend an average of six-tenths of its budget for 1947-1958 on defence nor would it have sought to involve itself in an alliance with the United States. It is evident that without implacable Indian hostility Pakistan would, like India itself, have adopted a neutral position and tried to play both the United States and the Soviet Union for as much aid and technical assistance.

Locked into an unwanted conflict against an adversary five times its size and rebuffed by foreign powers, Pakistan evolved a defence policy which in its initial years boiled down to raising an infantry army that could hold on to territory through physical occupation. The lack of firepower was painfully driven home in 1951 when Liaquat Ali Khan learnt that Pakistan 'had only thirteen tanks with limited engine life left in them.'[30] It was hardly surprising that the thinking of Pakistan's civilian leadership became highly militarised and the army came to occupy an increasingly influential role in policy-making.[31] Ayub Khan's ascent to the post of commander-in-chief of the army on 17 January 1951, from being a colonel on 14 August 1947, was a consequence of Liaquat Ali Khan's policy of rapid nationalisation. In effect, it meant that officers with experience of regimental command were elevated to positions of strategic importance. Those passed over in the dash to the top fumed and fretted about the injustice done to them by the corrupt politicians who raised their colleagues above them. One of these jilted aspirants who hungered for the top slot was Major General Akbar Khan who conspired to overthrow the government but whose intentions were discovered well in time.

After the conspiracy was unearthed, Liaquat Ali Khan pushed through the Constituent Assembly the Rawalpindi Conspiracy Act. This Act set up a Special Tribunal empowered to violate essential principles of law and justice. Amongst other violations, the Conspiracy Act made lawful the submission of a confession or statement as evidence 'made before the magistrate by any person...without any opportunity for the defence to confront such a person and rebut him.'[32] It also cut the 'three stages of judicial scrutiny' for capital crimes to one.[33] The Conspiracy Act thus joined PRODA and the Public Safety Act as Liaquat Ali Khan's contribution to Pakistan's expanding 'corpus of arbitrary and repressive laws, rules and practices....'[34]

Akbar Khan's thinking was revealed in the documents seized by the authorities and his own testimony. He believed all of Pakistan's problems were due to corrupt and self-seeking politicians and their bureaucratic accomplices. They had to be liquidated and 'replaced by military rule.'[35] The nationalisation of the army was condemned as 'a farce and nothing more than the filling of some chairs vacated by the British by some Pakistanis.'[36] Akbar Khan expounded his vision of a socialist Pakistan 'under a military system which creates national uniformity' and a just distribution of the fruits of nationalisation.[37] The cost of this revolution and the proposed liquidation were dismissed because 'it is the ultimate future that counts and not the period in between.'[38] The coup, its proponents believed, could act as a 'catalyst' and bring together the resentments of those passed over for promotions with those suffering from economic neglect and backwardness and the left-leaning progressive intelligentsia and become 'the herald of the new era.'[39] While a superficial communist layer was incorporated into the conspirators' thinking, in effect the program was to use 'blood and fire to obtain power' for themselves.[40]

By the time the Special Tribunal handed down its judgment on 5 January 1953, against those who sought to plunge the country into the abyss of ideocratic arbitrary rule, the situation had changed. Liaquat Ali

Khan was dead. Khwaja Nazimuddin was the new premier. Ghulam Mohammad, 'the leader of the bureaucrats' was the new governor general and poised to cut the politicians down to size.[41] These bureaucrats included a group of audits and accounts officers including Said Hassan, S. A. Hasni, and Abdul Qadir, plus Iskander Mirza, and other CSP and PSP officers.[42] In order to be successful in his manoeuvres against the politicians, however, Ghulam Mohammad needed the support of the military and that meant Ayub Khan and his clique of senior generals and loyalists.

As the commander of an army with two hundred thousand men but only thirteen operational battle-tanks, Ayub Khan shared Ghulam Mohammad's eagerness to acquire more firepower. With British supplies waning after 1951 and Indian hostility showing no indications of abatement, the United States was the only realistic option. Compounding Ayub's difficulties was the political power vacuum created by Liaquat Ali Khan's death, Khwaja Nazimuddin's ineptitude and Ghulam Mohammad's machinations. Already the military had been deployed against Kalat (1948), and used to suppress riots in Karachi (1949) and Dhaka (1950). In 1952 it was called out again in East Bengal. In March 1953 it responded to religious riots in Lahore, restored order under the umbrella of martial law and stayed in control of the city until May. In these two months Nazimuddin was arbitrarily dismissed and Mohammad Ali Bogra, then ambassador to Washington, flown in and inducted as the new prime minister.

As the chief, Ayub had a 'personal approach to running the army' and 'he took more interest than would be usual in officer appointments.'[43] This led to a rise in and of Ayub's supporters[44] which, in turn, made the army chief even more useful to Ghulam Mohammad who had decided to bring him into Bogra's 'ready-made cabinet' as the defence minister.[45] By making Ayub part of a patently illegal cabinet in which the premier and the defence minister were not elected representatives the governor-general hoped to bind the army to his will. Ayub was rewarded with extensions leading to the peculiar situation that whereas Pakistan had seven prime ministers between January 1951 and October 1958, the army chief remained the same person. In politicising the senior officers of the army and patronising its chief, Ghulam Mohammad had created a very dangerous situation for himself (had he lived) and his successors. With American dollars flowing into Pakistan from May 1954, the military leadership began thinking in terms of national restructuring and solutions to Pakistan's numerous and highly complicated problems. An essential component of the diagnosis arrived at by the praetorian mind when it contrasted the 'efficiency' of the military with the inefficiency and corruption of the civilians was that Pakistani society lacked the army's greatest asset—the unity of command.

4.3 THE UNITY OF COMMAND

An army is a strange organism. At a functional level it aspires to be a highly efficient technocracy of violence, trained and equipped with the latest methods and weapons its country can afford. At a tactical level an army appears, at least to an untrained observer, to be a vast agglomeration of feudal castes and martial tribes with each fighting unit animated by an acute sense of honour, ever sensitive to the weight of its past performance, and exuberantly idiosyncratic. At a strategic level, however, it is the unity of command and a culture of obedience to its dictates that ensures order within the mass. A military officer is thus a technocrat in the sense that he possesses highly specialised skills that can only be acquired through years of effort and practice. But because the ultimate task is to apply these skills in conditions of extreme stress or violence he is drilled into believing in his own superiority, the wisdom of his commanders, and the loyalty of his subordinates. A conscious effort is made by his trainers to harness what Plato described in *The Republic* as *thymos*—a spirited but irrational pride and desire for recognition that can overcome the fear of death. The superior *thymos* of the warrior inevitably leads him to view his non-martial counterparts as weak, soft, and inferior.[46]

On 4 October 1954, a few weeks before the arbitrary dismissal of the first Constituent Assembly and Ayub Khan's induction into the cabinet as defence minister, he wrote a memorandum that purported to present a solution to Pakistan's problems.[47] In it the rising praetorian asserted that the provincial boundaries and states of West Pakistan were artificial and sustained by the interests of politicians, for whom he had nothing but contempt. In strategic and economic terms West Pakistan was a single entity and therefore it should be merged into a single provincial unit in order to unleash its latent potential for development. East Bengal should be renamed East Pakistan, existing ministries and legislatures abolished, and each of the two provinces to be divided into smaller and relatively homogeneous administrative units. At the centre a unicameral legislature elected on the basis of inter-wing parity with an effective president was needed while at the local level full emphasis was to be laid on economic development.

In essence, what Ayub was saying was that the country ought to be organised like the army. The centre would operate as the GHQ establishing overall unity of command. The two provincial governments would serve as regional headquarters. The relatively homogeneous districts and subdivisions would be analogous to regiments and battalions. And at all levels of the chain of command the uniform national effort was to achieve excellence in technocratic developmental efficiency just as the military devoted itself to technocratic martial efficiency. These were not idle thoughts. Within a year of this program being penned, One Unit in West Pakistan and inter-wing parity were realised. The 1956 Constitution established a unicameral legislature with the president exercising real power. Soon after overthrowing Iskander Mirza on 27 October 1958, a Basic Democracies scheme suitable to the genius of the Pakistani people was imposed.[48] This scheme neatly divided Pakistan into eighty thousand ward committees that were directly elected and formed the base of an indirect electoral pyramid the tiers of which included nine thousand union councils and town committees, seven hundred and fifty-four sub-district and municipal committees, seventy-nine district and agency councils, and sixteen divisional councils. Since the eighty thousand ward committee members also acted as the electoral college for the presidential elections many 'openly sold their votes to the highest bidder.'[49] Development expenditure funnelled through the local committees by the centre facilitated the 'spread of corruption into every nook and corner of the country'[50] though its dimensions were nothing compared to what would happen later. The promulgation of the 1962 constitution with its concentration of powers in the hands of the president provided the structure introduced by Ayub with constitutional cover.[51] Ayub's diagnosis and prescriptions of 4 October 1954, became an integral component of the Pakistani praetorians' mental and moral landscape.[52]

Yahya Khan formally re-established four of West Pakistan's provinces, destroyed Ayub's basic democrats through martial law regulation, and did away with inter-wing parity. He had, however, no intention of handing power over to a civilian dispensation and was quite keen to perpetuate rule from his military headquarters without any civilian input. For this purpose hundreds of military officers were deputed to civilian positions and the higher bureaucracy was utterly marginalized:

> Rather than drawing senior civil servants into his inner circle, Yahya relied upon his trusted military staff to handle matters for him, with two brigadiers, reporting to [Lt. General] Pirzada [the Principal Staff Officer to the President], who decided on issues that senior civil servants brought to their attention. Rarely did the president see these civilians. But the decision making was marked by a paucity of paperwork, analysis, and thought, and, as colleagues observed, the decisions were impulsive and sometimes contradictory. Yahya would often tell his audiences: 'I am a soldier,' as if to absolve himself of responsibility for the wider role that he had assumed or as an excuse for his political missteps.[53]

Ziaul Haq retained martial law from 1977 to 1985, created a powerless consultative assembly at the centre and toothless local bodies at the grassroots level. In the second elections to these local bodies in 1983-1984 some seventy thousand councillors were elected to four thousand one-hundred union councils, eighty-four district and agency councils, twelve municipal corporations, one hundred and seventeen municipal committees, two hundred and eighty-eight town committees and thirty-nine cantonment boards.[54] After each set of local government elections large-scale training of the elected councillors was undertaken on the model introduced by Ayub. In 1984, some seventy-thousand councillors were trained by the government to provide them 'with the necessary professional knowledge and expertise of rural administration during their four-year terms of office.'[55] Though allergic to terms such as autonomy, Zia proved more intelligent in the pursuit of unity of command than his praetorian predecessors or successor. Unlike Ayub, Zia opted against politicising the local bodies by turning them into an electoral college. Unlike Yahya or Musharraf, he quickly grasped that the higher bureaucracy represented the most competent element in Pakistani society and should be relied upon to carry out the civil administration.

The Musharraf regime also pursued a similar line of action and called for a 'unified command' to deal with Pakistan's problems and 'grassroots' empowerment to usher in 'true' democracy. To indicate its sincerity in this regard, Omar Asghar Khan, a leading grassroots developer with what passes for credibility[56] in NGO circles was offered the local government and rural development portfolio after the 12 October 1999 coup. He accepted and the Sustainable Development Policy Institute (SDPI) and Asia Foundation in Pakistan, combined with the United Nations Development Program (UNDP), the Asian Development Bank (ADB), the World Bank (WB), the British Department for International Development (DFID), the Canadian International Development Agency (CIDA), and the Norwegian Agency for Development (NORAD), assisted the NRB in unleashing a revolution through devolution upon Pakistan. The infantile enthusiasm and remorseless naïveté of the reformers was expressed by a senior DFID official who confidently asserted in the manner of a latter-day Gladieux that 'mass empowerment was the real motivation behind devolution. Colonialism and centralisation, twin evils of Pakistan's bureaucratic institutions can't be abolished overnight—101 elected districts are the answer.'[57] Musharraf himself proclaimed that the local government reforms introduced by his regimes represented a major positive change and 'did away with the vestiges of the colonial era, when a deputy commissioner and a superintendent of police ran districts like lords. With the stroke of the pen they were both subordinated to the elected mayor.'[58] Declaring himself an incurable optimist, who sees the glass as half full, perhaps even when it is more than half empty, Musharraf dismissed criticism of the plan.[59]

Musharraf's objective was to establish unity of command that would enable the praetorian centre to exercise direct control at the local level circumventing the higher bureaucracy as well as the provincial and national politicians and assemblies. During the early months of his rule Musharraf installed one hundred and four senior (lieutenant generals and major generals) serving and retired military officers and one thousand middle ranking and junior officers in the civil administration, foreign service, and academia.[60] In the longer run, though enormously wasteful, confusing and corrupt, the devolution scheme enabled for the first time the sustained penetration of local administration by the military. The army 'bargained opportunistically along' caste, clan and kinship lines and 'unleashed equally divisive forces.'[61] Like Ayub and Zia, Musharraf appreciated that a 'multitude of scattered' local governments dependent on patronage were far 'easier for the military to deal with than four relatively more cohesive provincial governments.'[62]

The destruction of the DMG's role as collector-magistrate and police supervisor, and its subordination to local elected officials, completed the operation. Musharraf attained the unity of command through the decapitation and demoralisation of the higher bureaucracy and the undermining of the provincial and national assemblies. The provinces and local governments could both be controlled through fiscal centralisation. The provinces receive about 80 per cent of their funds from the centre, which collects 90 per cent of all taxes. This allows the centre to compel the provinces to transfer funds to the local governments and manipulate the antagonisms between these two tiers. The finishing touch was, in Yahya's fashion, 'The insertion of 3500 military people into civilian bodies [usually in important positions] at the national, provincial, divisional and district levels.'[63]

The impact upon the body-politic of the relentless pursuit of unity of command and the application of the military mind to non-military problems has been negative. Repeated attempts to reinvent the wheel have deprived Pakistan of administrative stability without improving efficiency. Each period of praetorian-led national reconstruction has intensified internal conflict and weakened the integrity of the federation. Moreover, as military rule continues and challenges mount, the senior layer of officers are exposed to criticism, civil disobedience increases, and the risk of the politicisation of the lower ranks grows. This, in turn, leads to complete or partial withdrawal from the political minefield and in the end the image projected is that Pakistan's praetorians are ultimately reluctant in their pursuit of power. This image is in part reality and needs to be understood.

4.4 Reluctant Revolutionaries

Some of Pakistan's military officers can be legitimately described as politicians manqué who prefer the 'cut-and-thrust of political manoeuvring to that of the battlefield' and rise by practicing the art of the courtier.[64] The fact remains that confronted with moderately determined civilian opposition, such as the anti-Ayub agitation of the late-1960s or the judicial crisis that ended with the temporary restoration of the Supreme Court Chief Justice in July 2007, the Pakistani military has shown little appetite for Burmese or Indonesian-style repression.

One important reason for this is Indian hostility. The Pakistani military has an enemy and while this animosity has facilitated the military's rise to prominence it also places practical limits on its capacity for political intervention. The military can ill-afford permanently to engage a substantial portion of its serving troops and officers in civilian duties. Occasional assistance, such as Operation Jute (1952-1953), Operation Close Door (1957-1958), internal security operations in aid of civil authority, emergency response and rescue in case of floods or earthquakes, and carrying out specific tasks such as the 1998 census, is as far as the military is willing to go. Pakistani military officers readily concede that for them 'to take part in running a country, especially involving petty detail in settling land disputes, lawsuits and so forth, debilitates the martial ethos....'[65] Unlike other militaries, Pakistan's armed forces actually need to keep this ethos as high as possible and their psychological orientation is squarely outwards and directed towards India and the troubled borderlands of Afghanistan. Related to this external threat are the high levels of professionalism that characterize the officer corps and the low level of overall politicisation.

About three-fourths of Pakistan's officers retire after twenty-three years of service. Army chiefs from Ayub Khan onwards have been quite 'aware that a barrack-bound army could be a breeding-ground for malcontents' and have followed his prescription of keeping the men busy with field training exercises.[66] That the ability of officers to rise depends upon their demonstrable competence until the very senior levels when political considerations may play a role circumscribes the prospects of politicisation of the officer corps. This translates directly into the apolitical nature of the average soldier whose mental horizons are shaped by a clannish sense of regimental honour, training and the prospect for modest economic advancement. In political terms this means military coups in Pakistan take place when the incumbent regime is already discredited and perceived by the public as leading the country towards anarchy. The same logic ensures that military regimes negotiate and compromise when opposition elements reassert themselves.

The patience of the preponderantly apolitical officer corps with praetorian elements at the senior levels is finite, as Yahya Khan discovered to his discomfort after the 1971 defeat at Indian hands. His protégés got such a hostile reception at GHQ Rawalpindi on 19 December 1971, that General Hamid was left 'shocked beyond speech.'[67] Military units garrisoned at Gujranwala, a major city near Lahore, were 'near mutiny' and incensed by the poor war leadership of the politicians in uniform.[68] The pervasive distaste for politics within the Pakistani military is also attested to by the failure of all coup attempts other than those launched by the army chief. In 1973, twenty-one army and fourteen air force officers were arrested on suspicion of conspiracy against the state. Of the thirty-five, one army officer and seven air force officers suffered no penalty, in the latter case at the insistence of the government which reversed their retirement orders leading to the air chief's resignation in protest. In 1995, a coup attempt by Major General Zaheerul Islam Abbasi and thirty-five other officers was thwarted. Other attempts, such as the abortive one against Zia in 1984, also met with failure.

What is fascinating about Pakistan's praetorians is their timidity.[69] All of them came to power through bloodless coups. All of them sought an accommodation with political elements soon after coming to power, though in Yahya's case the attempt failed miserably. Except for Zia, who perished in an air crash in suspicious circumstances at a time when he was transparently fumbling and losing ground, all have been bloodlessly forced from power by a combination of civil disobedience and loss of support within the military. No military ruler has carried out purges of the officer corps to eliminate perceived political rivals and install political allies. All have worked through the regular system of promotions, transfers, and postings, and sought to influence appointments through the existing procedures, rules and mechanisms for inputs though quite naturally such evaluations are partially subjective. While politics is a privilege reserved for the miniscule praetorian elite, the power exercised has secured for a large number of officers and men economic wealth and social mobility and consolidated a neo-*mansabdari* system in Pakistan.

4.5 THE NEO-*MANSBARDARI* SYSTEM

In continental bureaucratic empires wealth flows from the exercise of state power or favourable proximity to it. Such states redistribute wealth coercively extracted through taxation and confiscation and are often engaged in a mafia-style distribution of spoils amongst members of the apparatus. Force, opacity, and arbitrariness being the key ingredients in this enterprise it follows quite logically that the instruments of violence—the military, police, and intelligence agencies, the lines between which are often blurred in these states—reap the lion's share. The ruler feels that by morally and economically compromising his servants his personal will shall be blindly obeyed. Hitler, was thus fond of rewarding his loyal generals without reference to their military performance with personally signed grants of half a million pounds sterling (in current value), 'huge tracts of land', estates, presents, titles and the like.[70] In contrast, Churchill 'respected people who stood up to him' and 'he appointed Alanbrooke precisely because he knew he would stand up to him.'[71] After the war, the victorious general Alanbrooke 'found himself so impoverished' that he had to sell his house and ornithological books.[72]

Before 1947, the policy of the imperial government was to reward the enlisted men, NCOs and JCOs, with grants of lands in newly irrigated territories of the Punjab while the officers were paid sufficiently well in cash to obviate the need to remunerate them in kind. For ordinary peasants and cultivators the prospect of owning their own plot of land made the small pay they received as soldiers well worth it. The ownership of land was a mark of great distinction and source of honour. For the state the expansion of cultivation meant more land revenue and greater stability. From 1880 onwards hundreds of thousands of acres were brought under the plough and in 1900 the Land Alienation Act 'prohibited the transfer of land to non-agricultural classes' thus countering the prospect of absentee landlordism by Hindu moneylenders.[73]

Partition and the transfer of large numbers of soldiers and officers across the new divide meant that provision had to be made for resettlement and compensation. In addition to compensating the military officers for losses suffered en route to Pakistan by extending home loans it was decided to lease sites in cantonment areas 'for house building to refugees' and officers who had opted for the Pakistan armed services.[74] The proposal was for residential plots ranging from one thousand to two thousand square yards to be given in the light of need and seniority from the cantonment lands. Curiously, the service chiefs, led by Ayub Khan, demanded that the size of the plots be increased to one acre, three-fourths of an acre, and half an acre.[75] The finance ministry shot down this proposal stating that it 'did not share the views of the C-in-Cs as contained in their note' which was in flagrant violation of 'the procedure followed by all the House Building Societies.'[76] It was observed that land in cantonment areas was already developed and constituted a very valuable asset that may be required for military purposes and 'therefore be conserved as much as possible.'[77] However, about two hundred military officers were given land in cantonment areas by 1952 and some two hundred more acres were readied for lease.[78] In 1954, the provincial authorities in the Punjab were tasked with the reservation of one thousand acres of land for navy personnel.[79] To begin with the rule was one plot per officer but as senior commanders secured the authority through the defence housing societies to 'autonomously allocate plots in the cantonments' multiple plots in different schemes enabled officers to build considerable urban landholdings at throwaway prices in Pakistan's urban centres.[80]

This understandably upset those who were not refugees and in 1952 Ayub Khan launched a welfare directorate at GHQ. It immediately undertook five schemes to acquire land for military personnel along the India-Pakistan border and parcelled it out in units of twenty-five to two hundred and fifty acres. In Sindh some three hundred thousand acres were thus acquired and distributed.[81] On 7 April 1955, the chief minister of Sindh ingratiatingly informed the governor general in the context of the Ghulam Muhammad Barrage that 'as Your Excellency is aware, we have made a categorical commitment to earmark an area of hundred thousand acres for men and officers of the armed forces. This reservation may have to be increased later, if circumstances justify it.'[82] It was decided to place the land at the disposal of the defence ministry.

Ayub Khan, acting in his capacity as the concerned minister, pushed through the cabinet, on 4 May 1955, his proposals for the distribution of the hundred thousand acres. No one was to get more than two hundred and fifty acres; about fifteen thousand acres were reserved for officers and eighty-five thousand for JCOs and other ranks.[83] Officers who had already received more than fifty acres of land under the previous schemes were not eligible for a share of the one under consideration.[84] Simultaneously, Ayub helped secure civil employment for three retired officers and seven hundred and twenty-nine JCOs.[85] Ayub also took a keen interest in the appointment of Major General

Anis Ahmad Khan as the Rehabilitation Commissioner of Karachi and wrote to the premier on 21 May 1954 'introducing the officer and recommending that he might be suitably assisted to find a job.'[86] He got the job and kept it as Ayub felt 'that the employment of Muslim ex-Indian Army officers who had retired or left the Indian Army after partition was likely to affect adversely the Morale of Muslim officers at present serving with the Indian Army.'[87] He would continue in that capacity 'until a suitable senior officer became available from the CSP cadre.'[88]

Ayub was trying to quite transparently create a personal base of support in the military through the distribution of patronage amongst the officers and men.[89] After he took over as president in October 1958, he continued the 'policy of appeasement of the Army by giving them lands, increased pay and pension benefits and other venues of employment after retirement' which 'tended to create a feeling of resentment' amongst civil society at large.[90] In addition to the quotas for induction of serving and retired servicemen into the support staff of civilian departments, Ayub stripped the business community of its autonomy, such as it was, and reinforced the patron-client relationship:

> ...modern business associations were at first largely free of government control and regulation, this too came to an end with the Ayub era. Under a government reorganisation scheme adopted in 1958 and given legal effect by an ordinance in 1961, the government secured total power over the recognition and regulation of all associations in Pakistan representing trade and industry. Any organisation not recognised by the government was illegal.[91]

Furthermore, the Directorate of Trade Organizations possessed sweeping arbitrary powers over the internal management and functioning of business associations which included the power to appoint administrators if it was unsatisfied with the performance of these associations. Intriguingly, at the time of his overthrow in March 1969, Ayub Khan's family was one of Pakistan's two dozen richest with an estimated worth of as much as twenty million dollars (in 1969 currency).[92] While Ayub and his senior praetorians may have been, like Clive after the conquest of Bengal, astounded at their own modesty and perplexed by the vicious public attacks being launched on their conduct, it is interesting to see the transformation of the military officer son of a *Risaldar* Major into the leader of one of Pakistan's richest families between 1955 and 1968. Ayub's legacy was that the military's influence was felt in all sectors of the state and economy. Industrialists who employed more than one hundred workers were required to reserve one-fourth of their posts for ex-servicemen. Half the posts in the civil defence forces from September 1959 were reserved for servicemen, while in the West Pakistan provincial government half of all vacancies in Class IV and one fourth in Class III were reserved for military retirees. On the agricultural side the military had become a medium through which members of the educated middleclass and lower-middleclass could become landlords, industrialists, and urban proprietors extraordinaire. That said, even the most prosperous concerns founded by Ayub were peripheral to the economy. The Fauji Foundation (1953) was worth one hundred and fifty-two million rupees in 1970, though, by 1982 the same foundation had total assets of two billion rupees inclusive of twenty-nine industrial projects.[93] Ayub had laid the foundations of the neo-*mansabdari* system but its development into the vast and varied economic empire catering to everything from the production of breakfast cereal, the provision of education, and the welfare needs of over ten million ex-servicemen and their dependents, was made possible by the Bhutto regime.

Amongst Bhutto's first acts was to establish a Federal Security Force (FSF) that answered personally to him. One reason given for the raising of the FSF was that Gul Hassan, Bhutto's first army chief, was being non-cooperative and obstructing attempts by senior advisers to order the army around in order to quell protests.[94] It was therefore decided to constitute a paramilitary force under the direct control of the prime minister.[95] Whatever the original motivation, by the end of 1976, the FSF had over eighteen-thousand five hundred men, nearly seven hundred and fifty vehicles, and a 'modern wireless network.'[96] The FSF was equipped with semi-automatic rifles, machine guns, grenades, and rocket launchers, and tanks had been ordered but their operational use was prevented by high financial costs.[97] The FSF had direct access to the Intelligence Cell and Secret Service Fund as authorised by Interior Division.[98] In effect the FSF was Bhutto's praetorian guard and was used to intimidate and disrupt his political opponents and keep his colleagues in their place. The re-absorption of military personnel from East Pakistan as well as Bhutto's desire to make the military an instrument of his personal rule created contingencies that could be met by sharing the fruits of nationalisation with the armed forces.

Some three thousand ex-servicemen were inducted into the FSF and the nationalised banks, insurance companies and industries, were opened to military personnel.[99] Agricultural land was to be offered to military personnel for development with which the Fauji Foundation could also assist.[100] In addition to approving these schemes the feasibility of the Fauji Foundation to have a 'separate organisation to deal with small scale industries' was looked into.[101] Bhutto lavished funds on the military and army welfare-related activities raising the defence budget from about three billion rupees in 1971-1972 to over eight billion rupees in 1976-1977. Higher salaries, allowances, better insurance, as well as 'plots of land at give-away prices to Junior Commissioned Officers', were thrown in for good measure.[102]

Under Zia the neo-*mansabdari* system gained ground at an accelerating rate as a military government found itself in possession of billions of rupees in nationalized industrial and commercial assets. De-nationalisation of some of these assets helped create pliant political front-men, such as the Ittefaq Group lead by Nawaz Sharif. The system also benefited enormously from the billions of dollars pumped into the country in the form of economic and military aid as well as the drugs and arms trade networks set up to lubricate the anti-Soviet struggle in Afghanistan. The growth of a hyper-autonomous military was reflected in Zia's unsurpassed generosity in allowing the wholesale privatisation of cantonment lands. The worth of such land in the Karachi, Lahore, Peshawar, and Quetta cantonments alone, at 'conservative estimate' is half a trillion rupees (eighty-six billion US dollars).[103] It is hardly surprising that the assets of a Pakistani general are at present estimated in the range of two to five million US dollars.[104] The Fauji Foundation, in 2005, had assets of ten billion rupees, up from two billion in 1982 and one hundred and fifty-two million in 1970.[105]

The opposition to this kind of economic extraction has inspired everyone else, from politicians and bureaucrats, to judges, corporate employees, academics and journalists to set up shop and lobby for a share of state land at rates well below market value. They too want to become neo-*mansabdar*s and their criticism of the military is one of the clearest manifestations of the flagrant hypocrisy of the Pakistani group mind comprised as it is of the expressions of moral equals operating from unequal positions of power. The impact of this mentality has on civil-military relations is that neither side knows quite when to stop.

4.6 Civilian Overreach and Military Overstretch

In Pakistan the military rapidly acquired political importance and by 1958 was directly ruling the country. This initial reversion to a medieval power configuration stemmed from a number of factors. The major structural variables were conflict with India, American military assistance, excessively rapid promotions in all sectors of the state, including the military, to fill the void left by departing British officers, the breakdown of the Pakistan Muslim League's cohesion, and the remarkably high ethnic-class cohesion of the Pakistan army owning to the concentration of pre-independence recruitment grounds in West Pakistan. The major idiosyncratic contribution to the evolving mess was the failure of successive civilian leaders and civil servants, Ghulam Mohammed and Iskander Mirza in particular, to understand the requirements for the perpetuation of a State of Laws.

Pakistan's westernised civilian and political elite did not realize that in destroying the autonomy of the institutions inherited from the British (the Constituent Assembly, the provincial assemblies, local governments, the higher judiciary, political parties, etc.) and inviting the army chief into the cabinet as defence minister, they were preparing the ground for their own downfall. There was a fundamental intellectual failure at the highest levels to grasp that the broad spectrum of institutions developed by the British over many centuries were designed, at their core, to contain and subordinate military power to civilian authority. It is often forgotten that it was Iskander Mirza, the civilian and constitutional head of state, who abrogated the constitution and declared martial law, not Ayub Khan.

Once the military reacquainted itself with the taste of political power the entire fabric of constitutional development came crashing down. The inability of the military leadership to perpetuate its hold provided the civilian leadership with a second chance in 1973 and a third chance in 1988. On each occasion the civilian leadership demonstrated that it had learnt nothing from its own and the country's tragic experience. On the one hand the wise and measured exercise of arbitrary power can provide a degree of performance legitimacy. On the other hand the capricious and unenlightened exercise of power lawfully acquired rapidly depletes the reservoirs of legitimacy. The military did not prevent Zulfikar Ali Bhutto or Benazir Bhutto or Nawaz Sharif from exercising power in accordance with law, reason, and compassion. Between the persistent inability of the military to produce a wise and effective sovereign—a real Bonaparte rather than substandard pretenders like Ayub, Yahya, Zia and Musharraf, and the equally dogged determination of the civilian leadership to exercise even the smallest scrap of lawfully acquired power as arbitrarily as possible, Pakistan is trapped in a cycle of instability with the military and civilian political leadership destabilising each other.

The military leadership is intolerant of even the pretence of civilian control over its finances, weapons procurement, and its conduct of foreign policy. The civilian political leadership perceives the military as a potential instrument of their own arbitrary rule and wants a servile military leadership. It was the pursuit of this kind of servility that led the elder Bhutto to appoint Zia as army chief superseding seven more senior generals. Nawaz Sharif's farcical handling of senior civil and military appointments culminating in his attempted dismissal of Musharraf and replacement by an openly loyalist general on 12 October 1999, was precipitated by his desire to place the army and the Joint Chiefs of Staff Committee (JCSC) 'in the hands of one pliable individual who would do precisely what he wanted.'[106]

Musharraf, for his part, established a National Security Council (NSC) in which the service chiefs sit directly opposite elected representatives and thus by design has dragged the military formally into politics and robbed his civilian protégés of the regime of even the pretence of autonomy. The federal cabinet was patently held together by patronage with a record-breaking seventy-seven federal ministers and ministers of state out of a ruling coalition of two hundred Members of the National Assembly (give or take ten). The transfer of military pensions to the civilian side of the budget, the summoning of prime ministers and senior state officials to 'brief' or 'meet' the president and corps commanders at military headquarters of the army chief's camp office indicate an approach to politics comparable to a military brass band's performance of classical European music. Although forced to resign after his decision to manhandle an increasingly uncooperative judiciary backfired and led to an anti-government movement that was joined by political forces and spurred by Benazir Bhutto's assassination and a severe economic crisis, Musharraf's legacy will be felt for some time. The Pakistani military has received over US $ ten billion in direct assistance between 2002 and 2008 and entrenched itself more firmly than ever in the civil administration and Pakistan's socioeconomic landscape. Musharraf's reforms have also brought the quality and effectiveness of the civilian higher bureaucracy to their nadir. This means that the most important instrument for containing the military's ability to dominate the state apparatus is no longer able even to manage itself. The politicians who have been restored to power, moreover, are more or less the same lot who were thrown out, with a sigh of relief from the people, a decade ago. The absence of new, and therefore superficially credible, leadership means that patience with the present civilian dispensation is likely to be exhausted sooner rather than later paving the way for the restoration of military rule. Pakistan's military leadership, like its civilian counterpart, has failed to comprehend the difference between a medieval state, in which the country is the estate of a ruler legitimised by divine sanction or ideology, and a State of Laws.

In the Pakistani context the United States has also played a less than admirable role. Its enormous economic and political power have repeatedly been put at the service of Pakistani military strongmen—Ayub Khan, Yahya Khan, Ziaul Haq, Pervez Musharraf. These resources have, among other things, produced grave distortions in the Pakistani state and rendered Pakistani society even more ungovernable. For instance, both Pakistan's *jihadis* and the tens of thousands of NGOs are the direct outcome of American largesse. American advice, ranging from the Harvard Advisory Group of the 1960s to the present day devolution plan, has practically annihilated the capacity of Pakistan's westernized elite to think rationally about its own predicament. While the numerical strength of the army is a response to the Indian threat, the economic privileges enjoyed by its officers are made at least in part possible by American largesse. They are also disproportionate, the cause of immense resentment, and ultimately not in the military's own interest.

The direction in which successive cycles of civil-military mutual destabilisation have taken Pakistan in is down.[107] At the conclusion of each cycle the effectiveness, credibility, and quality of the state decreases substantially. So far, the institutional framework left behind by the British Empire has continued to provide life-support. There is, however, a limit to punishment that any state can take. The past few years have witnessed the liquidation of the civil service as a meaningful instrument of order and the creation of a class of incipient warlords dependent on handouts from the military-dominated centre in the name of devolution and 'grassroots' empowerment.

Most disturbing, however, is the invidious impact that Musharraf's desire to prolong his personal rule had on the military itself though, fortunately, the army high command withdrew its support when the popular resentment risked bringing the army into direct conflict with the people. One must bear in mind that successive military rulers were forced out by the actions of their immediate subordinates which, potentially, could have led to violence. Were it not for civilian interruptions the military may well have already broken down into rival factions locked in armed struggle for control of the levers of power and patronage. The military cannot in any seriousness think that it is somehow immune to the contradictions that afflict Pakistani society. Indeed, the military has exploited and aggravated many of these fault lines. The impact of this instability is felt in terms of the decline of the rule of law and the collapse of the state of order.

NOTES

1. Andrew J. Major, *Return to Empire: The Punjab under the Sikhs and British in the mid-Nineteenth Century* (Karachi: Oxford University Press, 1996), 224.
2. A 'recurring theme' in the history of continental bureaucratic empires is the rise 'of a new autocratic ruler from more or less obscure origins, taking power by force after a period of disorder, and claiming the decision of God for his victory and his justification.' Axworthy, *Empire of the Mind*, 46.
3. Edward Gibbon, *The Decline and Fall of the Roman Empire*, abridged and with and introduction by Frank C. Bourne (New York: Dell Publishing Co., Inc., 1963), 69.
4. Ibid., 68.
5. Abraham Eraly, *The Mughal World: India's Tainted Paradise* (London: Weidenfeld & Nicolson, 2007), 242.
6. Ibid., 244.
7. Major, *Return to Empire*, 19.
8. The *Khalsa Raj* collected about one-half of the agricultural output as taxes and 'Ranjit Singh did not make any changes in the agricultural system or land revenue that had prevailed since Mughal rule. Khushwant Singh, *Ranjit Singh*, 47.

9. At Ranjit Singh's death the total annual revenues of his kingdom were about thirty millions rupees. Ibid., 50.
10. Ranjit Singh had tried and to a substantial extent succeeded in suppressing the Sikh *misls* and at his death 'only the Ahluwalia household' retained its former autonomy. No sooner had Ranjit Singh died that the peace secured by his personal clout and vigilance collapsed and factionalism once again reigned supreme. Ibid., 156.
11. Tan Tai Yong, *The Garrison State: The Military, Government and Society in Colonial Punjab, 1849-1947* (Lahore: Vanguard, 2005), 34.
12. Carl von Clausewitz, *On War*, ed., and trans., Michael Howard and Peter Paret (Princeton: Princeton University Press, 1989), 87.
13. Ibid., 75.
14. Ibid., 81.
15. Vincent Cronin, *Napoleon* (London: HarperCollins Publishers, 1994), 201.
16. Ibid., 202.
17. For more on the transformation of Europe and the emergence there of 'civilian states' see James J. Sheehan, *Where Have All the Soldiers Gone? The Transformation of Modern Europe* (New York: Houghton Mifflin, 2008). The classical opinion was that war was the reason that states existed both at a causal level and at a teleological level. Ibid., 3-21.
18. Yong, *Garrison State*, 309.
19. Rizvi, *The Military and Politics in Pakistan*, 33.
20. Yong, *The Garrison State*, 185.
21. A. O. Mitha, the founder of the Pakistan Special Services Group (SSG) and a Major General in the Pakistan Army, lauded the British Sergeant Majors at the Indian Military Academy (IMA) who, in his opinion, were the ones who actually trained the officer recruits. Mitha felt that these Sergeant Majors 'were the best professional soldiers' he had ever encountered and that 'Neither the Pakistan Army nor the Indian Army has ever produced their like.' A. O. Mitha, *Unlikely Beginnings: A Soldier's Life* (Karachi: Oxford University Press, 2003), 48.
22. *Report of the Indian Sandhurst Committee, 14 November 1926* (London: His Majesty's Stationery Office, 1927), 22.
23. Brian Cloughley, *History of the Pakistan Army: Wars and Insurrections* (Karachi: Oxford University Press, 2006), 1. This meant that about 60 per cent of the officers were British and 40 per cent Indian.
24. 1949, File No. 173/CF/49, Government of Pakistan, Cabinet Secretariat, Cabinet Branch, 'Nationalisation Committee's Report', 8.
25. Ibid., 2.
26. 1948, File No. 172/CF/48, Government of Pakistan, Cabinet Secretariat, Cabinet Branch, 'Constitution and Procedure of Defence Committee of Cabinet.'
27. Ibid., Cabinet Meeting, 22 September 1948. Case No. 524/70/48 'Implementation of the decisions of the Defence Committee of Cabinet', 1.
28. Ibid.
29. For more see Fazal Muqeem Khan, *The Story of the Pakistan Army* (Karachi: Oxford University Press, 1963). This work may be regarded as a valuable early history of the army from official sources.

30. Pervaiz Iqbal Cheema, *The Armed Forces of Pakistan* (Karachi: Oxford University Press, 2002), 58.
31. In August 1951 it was decided to include the armed forces chiefs in those cabinet meetings that discussed defence policy. By the end of 1954 the army chief had become the minister for defence.
32. Hasan Zaheer, *The Times and Trial of the Rawalpindi Conspiracy 1951: The First Coup Attempt in Pakistan* (Karachi: Oxford University Press, 1998), 19.
33. Ibid.
34. Ibid.
35. Ibid., 249.
36. Ibid., 250.
37. Ibid.
38. Ibid.
39. Ibid., 251.
40. Ibid.
41. *The Report of the Hamood-ur-Rehman Commission of Inquiry into the 1971 War: As Declassified by the Government of Pakistan* (Lahore: Vanguard, 2003), 32.
42. Shuja Nawaz, *Crossed Swords: Pakistan, its Army, and the Wars Within* (Karachi: Oxford University Press, 2008), 163.
43. Cloughley, *History of the Pakistan Army*, 34.
44. Ibid., 35.
45. *The Report of the Hamood-ur-Rehman Commission of Inquiry into the 1971 War*, 33.
46. A great deal has been made of the so-called 'martial races' theory that was, it is popularly believed, introduced by the British. More learned observers, however, have noted that while the British did use the term and alter recruitment patterns post-1858 in doing so they were following 'a tradition that goes back to pre-British India....' Nawaz, *Crossed Swords*, 3. A more forceful and less politically correct formulation of the same point is that 'The British did not create the notion of 'martial races' in India as they have often been accused of doing. The notion of 'martial races' was well-established in India well before the White man arrived... Hinduism always accepted that Kshatriyas and Rajputs were born for war and Vaishyas were not. Muslim Princes preferred Afghan and Uzbek soldiers to Indian Muslims. And in South India the Hindu kings paid their Arab and Afghan mercenaries much more than they paid their own Hindu soldiery.' Reginald Massey, *India: Definitions and Classifications* (London: Hansib Publications, 2007), 149.
47. Amanullah Memon, ed., *The Altaf Gauhar Papers: Documents toward the Making of the Constitution of 1962* (Lahore: Sang-e-Meel Publications, 2003). The title of the note is 'A Short Appreciation of Present and Future Problems of Pakistan.'
48. Iskander Mirza, as a leading member of the governing corporation had done much to destabilise and undermine the democratic process in Pakistan. He also continued Ghulam Muhammad's policy of relying on the military to buttress his political position. It was perhaps a case of poetic justice when the long-time intriguer was outplayed by his own military protégé.
49. *The Report of the Hamood-ur-Rehman Commission of Inquiry into the 1971 War*, 49.

50. Ibid.
51. 1962, File No. 38/CF/62(2)-V, Government of Pakistan, President's Secretariat (Cabinet Division), Cabinet Section, 'Fortnightly Summary of the activities of the Ministry of Defence for the period ending the 15 March 1962', 4. The ministry reported that the constitution was 'very well-received' and suited the 'needs' of Pakistani citizens while 'everyone' was 'confident' that it would 'be understood and worked by our people' and act as a 'direct instrument for the unity, progress and prosperity of Pakistan.' Ibid.
52. As did a sense of surprise when the political clients of the military regime failed to show sufficient enthusiasm. Evidently, except for the defence minister, 'none of the members of the National Assembly, had a word of praise' for the armed forces 'which had saved the country from ruination' while '...the debate' on the defence budget 'even betrayed indifference on the part of Assembly members towards the armed services.' Ibid., 'Fortnightly Summary of the activities of the Ministry of Defence for the period ending the 31 August 1962', 3.
53. Nawaz, *Crossed Swords*, 251.
54. Muhammad Afzal, 'Local Government', in Jamilur Rehman Khan, ed., *Government and Administration in Pakistan*, 644.
55. Ibid., 657.
56. Shahrukh Rafi Khan, *Initiating Devolution for Service Delivery in Pakistan*, ix.
57. *Devolution in Pakistan*, 23.
58. Pervez Musharraf, *In the Line of Fire: A Memoir* (London: Simon & Schuster, 2006), 172.
59. Ibid., 174.
60. Nawaz, *Crossed Swords*, 532.
61. *Devolution in Pakistan*, 2.
62. Ibid., 6.
63. Ibid., 8.
64. Cloughley, *History of the Pakistan Army*, 138. This is a reference to Lt. General Peerzada, MS and Adjutant General to Ayub Khan and Principal Staff Officer to Yahya Khan.
65. Ibid., 132.
66. Ibid., 27.
67. Ibid., 213.
68. Ibid., 212.
69. One prescription for making the army coup-proof is that the unity of command ought to be abandoned. Instead, the army ought to be re-organised into three to six regional commands each headed by a four-star general appointed directly by the political executive. This, it is asserted, will make the Pakistan Army resemble the United States Army after the Tile X reforms. Nawaz, *Crossed Swords*, 582. Nawaz does not seem to realise that dividing the Pakistan Army into regional commands headed by generals of equal rank would increase the likelihood of fighting between rival military commanders. The potential level of political interference would also increase and lead Pakistan in the direction of a system resembling that of the turbulent Sikh *misls*. Nawaz also seems oblivious to the fact that in Pakistan the army chief does directly command troops. He issues orders to military commanders who obey him out of respect for seniority and the reverence that is inculcated for

the supreme importance of unity of command. Musharraf, for instance, was not even in the country when the corps commanders reacted to the attempt by the political executive to arbitrarily appoint a member of his own kinship group to the post of army chief. After having overthrown the political government, the military commanders handed power over to Musharraf. Of the ten military coup attempts in Pakistan's history only the coups sanctioned by the army chief have succeeded. The strength of his narrative granted, Nawaz's blind acceptance of American-style reforms marks him out as just another highly articulate but most unwise representative of Pakistan's heedless and unreflective westernized elite.

70. Andrew Roberts, *Hitler and Churchill: Secrets of Leadership* (London: Phoenix, 2003), 163.
71. Ibid., 134.
72. Ibid., 164.
73. Yong, *The Garrison State*, 93.
74. 1951, File No. 92/CF/51, Government of Pakistan, Cabinet Secretariat, Cabinet Branch, Summary for Cabinet, 'Leasing of Sites in Cantonments for House Building to Refugees/Optees Officers of the Armed Forces', 1.
75. Ibid.
76. Ibid., 'Note by D.M. Finances', 1.
77. Ibid.
78. Ibid., Ministry of Defence Summary, 'Leasing of Sites in Cantonments for House Building to the Officers of the Pakistan Armed Forces and Civilians Paid from Defence Estimates', 3.
79. 1954, File No. 8/CF/54-55-XIII, Government of Pakistan, Cabinet Secretariat (Main) Cabinet Branch, 'Fortnightly Summary for the period 1 April to 15 April 1954', 1.
80. Nawaz, *Crossed Swords*, 253.
81. Saeed Shafqat, *Civil-Military Relations in Pakistan from Zulfikar Ali Bhutto to Benazir Bhutto* (Boulder, Colorado: Westview Press, 1997), 36.
82. 1955, File No. 17/CF/55, Government of Pakistan, Cabinet Secretariat, Cabinet Branch, Chief Minister, Sind, to Governor General, 7 April 1955, Karachi, 'Allotment, Distribution, Sale, Lease of the Land in West Pakistan', 3.
83. Ibid., Cabinet Meeting, 4 May 1955, Case No. 295/41/55, "Allotment, Distribution, Sale, Lease of the Land in West Pakistan', 1.
84. Ibid.
85. 1955, File No. 1955-56-XII, Government of Pakistan, Cabinet Secretariat (Main), Cabinet Branch, 'Summary of the Activities of Ministry of Defence from 1 April 1955 to 30 September 1955', 3.
86. 1954, File No. 214/CF/54, Government of Pakistan, Cabinet Secretariat, Cabinet Branch, Summary for the Cabinet, 'Appointment of Major General Anis Ahmad Khan as Rehabilitation Commissioner Karachi', Ref. Case No. 864/88/54, 1.
87. Ibid., Cabinet Meeting, 5 January 1955, Case No. 11/1/55, 'Appointment of Major General Anis Ahmad Khan as Rehabilitation Commissioner, Karachi', 1.
88. Ibid.
89. Mitha, reflecting on his experience in Lahore in 1961, noted that 'The Cantonment Act clearly states that when any land is leased for building a bungalow, it must be so built that the army can afford to rent it.' No objection

certificates (NOCs) were needed to begin construction and ensure that the buildings being raised were not excessively lavish. These and many other rules and regulations were being flouted by those 'very high in the hierarchy, both in the army and the CSP.' Mitha, *Unlikely Beginnings*, 229.
90. *The Report of the Hamood-ur-Rehman Commission of Inquiry into the 1971 War*, 48.
91. Stanley A. Kochanek, *Interest Groups and Development: Business and Politics in Pakistan* (Karachi: Oxford University Press, 1983), 70-1.
92. Shafqat, *Civil-Military Relations in Pakistan*, 57.
93. Ibid., 37.
94. Nawaz, *Crossed Swords*, 324.
95. Ibid.
96. *White Paper on the Performance of the Bhutto Regime* Vol. III, *Misuse of the Instruments of State Power* (Islamabad: Printing Corporation of Pakistan, 1979), 26.
97. Ibid.
98. Ibid., 27. The authorization was communicated via Interior Division Letter No. 20/10/72-PP.
99. 1974, File No. 382/CF/74, Cabinet Division, Progress Section, 'Measures for Resettlement in Civil Life of the ex-Servicemen', 2.
100. Ibid., 3.
101. Ibid., Cabinet Division, Case No. 167/35/74, 'Measures for Resettlement in Civil Life of the ex-Servicemen', 2.
102. Cloughley, *History of the Pakistan Army*, 236.
103. Ayesha Siddiqa, *Military Inc.: Inside Pakistan's Military Economy* (Karachi: Oxford University Press, 2007), 189. The exchange rate in 2007 was approximately sixty Pakistani rupees for one US dollar.
104. Ibid., 174.
105. Ibid., 119.
106. Cloughley, *History of the Pakistan Army*, 332.
107. Stephen Cohen characterizes the military's relationship with politics as a five-step dance. The first step involves warning the civilian government of the impact its lack of competence and whimsicality is having on the country. Second, a crisis emerges that is deemed too great for the civilian regime to handle and precipitates military intervention. Third, a period of trying to sort out the country's problems through direct military control of the state and society ensues. The problems remain unsolved and thus the fourth step involves bringing on board politicians and reviving the forms of civilian rule. Finally, the army carefully reasserts itself 'behind a façade of civilian government' and remains poised to regain overt control. Stephen P. Cohen, *The Idea of Pakistan* (Washington D.C.: The Brookings Institution Press, 2004), 124.

5 Guardians

5.1 Theseus and Solon

Theseus the demigod was a great Athenian hero of legend. Amongst other great feats of valour and courage, Theseus slew the dreaded Minotaur, Periphetes the Club-bearer, Sinis the Pine-bender and Phaea the wild sow. Theseus was a great lover of justice and went out of his way to seek and punish the wicked. He would mete 'out to them the same violence that they had inflicted upon others, so that they were forced to submit to a justice that was modelled on their own injustice.'[1] His fellow Athenians were 'struck with admiration at his courage and delighted at his public spirit.'[2] Solon was another Athenian leader who demonstrated a greatly admired public spirit, although in his case it arose from a very different source.

Solon believed, much to his friend Anarcharsis's amusement, 'that his countrymen's injustice and greed could be kept within bounds by means of written laws' arrived at through reasoned argument in the public interest.[3] Anarcharsis dismissed Solon's fondness for the sovereignty of laws and compared them to a 'spider's web' that 'would hold the weak… but would be torn to pieces by the rich and powerful.'[4] Solon's response was that people 'abide by their agreements' not because of any inherent goodness but 'when neither side' had 'anything to gain by violating them.'[5] The challenge was to harness the propensity for excess intrinsic in men and channel it so that its most pernicious effects were mitigated.

In 594 BC, Solon's reputation for wisdom and the mutual exhaustion of the contending parties led the Athenians to ask him to arbitrate and accept the position of tyrant. Solon agreed to arbitrate in the official capacity of archon but refused to become a tyrant. His 'intimate friends' were furious with him for 'turning his back upon absolute power' and pleaded that he ought to consider the offer for his numerous virtues were so well-admired that everyone had confidence in his ability to wield arbitrary power justly.⁶ It did not dawn on his friends and admirers that the truly virtuous do not seek absolute power and Solon's harshly realistic assessment of human nature led him to put little faith in his own ability to resist the temptations that would doubtless flow from the acquisition of such power. Solon proceeded to prepare for Athens in consultation with the feuding parties a sovereign law or constitution that would remain in effect, depending on one's source, for ten years or one hundred, before being subjected to fundamental revision.⁷

Solon's first step was to secure the repeal of the Draconian laws which prescribed death as the penalty for more or less all serious transgressions and had contributed much to Athens becoming ungovernable. Athenian society was divided into four classes with the top three property-owners of varying degrees and the fourth comprising those without property. The first three classes could hold office in the council while the fourth could vote in the great Assembly (Ecclesia), sit in juries, and enjoy legal protection as citizens. Solon allowed property-owners to execute wills that enabled them to bequeath their assets to anyone they wanted to and thus 'showed that he rated friendship above ties of blood and free choice above necessity, and the effect of his law was to make every man's possessions truly his own.'⁸ While creating popular courts and granting citizenship to the Athenian poor, Solon retained the aristocratic judicial council, or Areopagus, as a check on the assemblies and juries. Once the parties agreed to abide by Solon's laws a copy was made on tablets, mounted, and kept at the Acropolis for all to see. Solon himself decided to leave the city for a decade in order to allow the new Athenian State of Laws to find its feet. He felt that if he stayed then he would become an extra-constitutional source of authority. Later, Solon when 'asked whether he provided the best laws for the Athenians' replied 'The best that they would accept'.⁹

Solon knew all too well that 'men are by nature both ambitious and suspicious, and know not how to use moderation where their fortunes are concerned.'¹⁰ The concessions granted by Solon emboldened the party of the Hill which found leadership in Solon's cousin, Peisistratus. Solon had warned against his cousin's tyrannical ambitions to no avail. Peisistratus and his followers staged a coup and promised to do even more justice with the poor and oppressed.¹¹ The other parties banded together and drove the tyrant out only to come to blows amongst themselves allowing him and his followers to stage a comeback. Soon

Peisistratus anointed his sons as his successors and converted Athens into an aspiring monarchy. For a while tyranny secured for Athens an uneventful and placid prosperity.[12]

In 514 BC, a powerful reaction began that in six years brought forward another outstanding statesman in the Solonian mould. This was Cleisthenes, who shared his name with his grandfather the tyrant Cleisthenes of Sicyon. Fortunately for Athens, Cleisthenes did not share his grandfather's politics. Cleisthenes reformed the legal structure of Athens and abolished the old tribes based upon kinship, location and economic status, and replaced them with ten tribes subdivided into thirds taken from different parts of the country. Each tribe elected fifty representatives to the council and each group thus constituted acted as the standing committee for thirty-six days of the year. The Ecclesia was tasked with voting upon legislation, taxation, and defence proposals made by the elected representatives in the council. The Ecclesia met every ninth day and had the power, if at least six thousand citizens thus decided, to exile any citizen perceived to be a danger to the state. The Areopagus was retained though its power remains a matter of speculation. The fact that Pericles the demagogue condemned it and overthrew it with the support of the people indicates that it had some nuisance value. Other states in the classical Mediterranean, such as Rome which wrote down its laws in 450 BC, imitated the Athenian example with greater or lesser success. Although in the case of both Athens and Rome imperial expansion eroded the authenticity of their representative institutions, this digression into classical Greek history helps illustrate the difference between the rule of justice and the rule of law. Theseus and Peisistratus represent the former while Solon and Cleisthenes are manifestations of the latter. The two conceptions flow from understandings of human nature at considerable variance with each other.

The belief in the rule of justice is derived from a profoundly optimistic assessment of the malleability of human nature. Power, it is maintained, if exercised by good and righteous people, will have beneficial effects and the pursuit of justice requires that such individuals be elevated and empowered to allow their virtue to express itself freely. Such goodness can only be produced by faith, ideology, or some other kind of metaphysical inspiration capable of motivating the power-wielder to behave righteously. Once this is achieved, public morality shall flow naturally from the heightened personal morality of the individuals that comprise society.

The belief in the rule of law is at its roots pessimistic and puts little stock in the capacity of the human race to act in a collectively positive manner. It maintains that power is innately debasing and arbitrary power unleashes the darkest and the most destructive human propensities. These propensities are rendered even more dangerous if they are reinforced by religious or ideological dogmas that generate self-righteousness and accomplish the fusion of the arrogance of power with the arrogance of piety. Although highly imperfect, a device that can be used to control human nature, mitigate its most deleterious effects and push societies towards stability and prosperity, is the rule of law. By that is meant rational laws based upon empirical appreciation of human nature that balance the interests of the governed with those of their rulers, allow for change, and express themselves through institutions and a constructive or virtuous public ethos.

The essential difference between Britain and the Greco-Roman civilisation was that the civil wars and conflicts of the former ended in triumph for the rule of law while those of the latter in the rule of arbitrary justice by despots posing as divinity incarnates.[13] Britain stood out by the eighteenth century as the exemplar of a neo-classical State of Laws where the executive and legislative powers balanced each other and were in turn checked by a powerful judiciary.[14] In Britain the 'idol of arbitrary power' was 'drowned in seas of blood' and though other lands and peoples had 'shed as much blood; but then the blood they spilled in defence of their liberty served only to enslave them the more.'[15] In other parts of the world, be it Iberia or Anatolia, the rule of arbitrary justice prevailed and should a locality take up 'arms in defence of its privileges' it stood to be 'stormed by mercenary troops' and 'punished by executioners' leaving 'the rest of the nation' to 'kiss their chains.'[16] Indeed, while the State of Laws was a Solonian enterprise the continental bureaucratic empire with its concentration of sovereign authority in the executive and ideocratic pretensions was animated by the spirit of Theseus.

One such state was the Ottoman Empire. In the fourteenth and fifteenth centuries, the Ottoman Turks brought order to the prevalent chaos in their region through the creation of a body of slave soldiers (the janissaries) and a single-minded pursuit of centralisation. By the end of the fourteenth century, the Ottoman Empire encircled the Byzantines. Within the Ottoman domain 'Only the decree of the sultan could establish any income or privilege' and 'a centralised administration' supplanted 'feudal decentralisation' in the Balkans.[17] As the Ottoman Empire expanded in the 1300s 'the bureaucratic traditions of near eastern states' came to dominate 'statecraft and administration.'[18] At the heart of the Ottoman Empire was the organising principle that the subjects and all their land belonged to the sultan.[19] The purpose of the state structure was to ensure the effective exercise of the sultan's universal proprietorship. The system of military and administrative slavery meant that the army and bureaucracy were also 'owned by the ruler.'[20]

Wise sultans, like Mehmed the Conqueror (reigned 1444-1446 and 1451-1481) and Suleiman the Lawgiver (1520-1566), understood that the effectiveness of their writ and quality of governance within their estate depended upon the intellectual and moral calibre of their servants. The slaves from whom the bureaucracy and military officers were recruited received specialised education and training. Enslaved in childhood, these trainees were taught mathematics, prose, philosophy, literature, religion, history, administration, arts, crafts, military science and law, up to the age of about twenty-five. Given their aptitude, assignments were made to judicial, administrative and military posts. The most competent were attached to the Palace, which had about seven hundred officials in the sixteenth century. The Ottoman rulers were particularly concerned with doing justice to their flock and the imperial proprietorship was regarded as a guarantee that the arbitrary power of the sultan would protect the meek. If injustice occurred it was because the sultan was not informed and periodic purges of senior officials and theocrats reinforced the sultan's image as just.

In the subcontinent it was the monarch's supreme duty to dispense justice and for this purpose he had to demonstrate both his omniscience as well as temporal omnipotence. In the Timurid Empire, like its predecessors, a number of cases were regularly brought to the emperor's notice so that they may do justice to their subjects.[21] It was held that 'only an absolute ruler' could provide 'absolute justice' being so far above the petty concerns of the rest of humanity that he would never 'moderate justice with expediency'.[22] To the Timurids, as to Theseus, 'it was essential that the punishment should match the crime', symbolically, if not literally.[23] Such justice was often administered in a fit of righteous wrath.[24] Akbar, who believed himself to be absolutely just with a great sense of the *jaza* and *saza* (reward and punishment) due to those brought before him in the tradition of his illustrious justice-dispensing ancestors, had a lamp-keeper flung to death for falling asleep on the job. His finance minister, Khwaja Mansur, was executed when compromising letters fell into imperial hands. *After* the execution an investigation was ordered which found the letters to be forged. Jahangir put up a belled-chain outside his palace so that the poor could ring it and awaken the emperor to any injustice perpetrated in the realm. This farcical exercise was a purely symbolic ornament—in an empire of a hundred million subjects distributed across hundreds of thousand of villages with practically no means of communications not many could benefit. Jahangir also kept poisonous snakes at the ready to bite officials found to be unjust and while on a hunt ordered a groom executed for disturbing the prey. To the Timurids 'crime was what offended the emperor' and similar arbitrariness and outright confusion 'prevailed at the lower levels of the…judicial administration.'[25] The organisational chaos of the judicial administration reinforced the arbitrary power of the emperor and his officials. Imperial arbitrariness and self-righteousness set the tone for those lower down the chain of command in the administration of justice and maintenance of order. Bribery was endemic, perjury a given, forgery a practicality. The judiciary, servile, incompetent and corrupt, was openly held in contempt by other officials and society at large for 'What one got in the' justice-loving Timurid system 'was not justice, but one's fate.'[26]

A similar, if not worse, situation prevailed in the successor states to the Timurid Empire. In Ranjit Singh's Punjab, as well as in other parts of the subcontinent, crimes were punished by mutilations for the poor and fines for those who could afford to pay them. Often jails were maintained exclusively for political prisoners guilty of crimes against the ruler. The arbitrariness of the justice administration notwithstanding, many highly intelligent people in the post-colonial era seriously believe that in pre-British India while justice was 'crude' it was also 'cheap, expeditious and in conformity with tradition.'[27] Tradition, evidently, had no problem with chopping off the body parts of the poor on a whim or letting the rich off with fines. The safeguard in this system was the justice loving nature of the monarch. Tipu Sultan was, and is, widely admired for having ordered his servants to delay the execution of sentences he had passed in a fit of righteous wrath for half an hour and ask him upon the time having elapsed if the decision was confirmed or rescinded. Ranjit Singh, for instance, had restricted capital punishment to acts of rebellion and anyone who was unhappy with the justice meted out by the governors could approach the ruler at his palace or during one of his tours.[28] Ranjit Singh dealt with such petitions 'summarily' or delegated to his officers.[29] It is rumoured that Ranjit Singh appointed Bahadur Singh Hindustani to prepare civil and criminal codes a decade before Macaulay set foot on Indian soil. That said, 'No record of the written code has, however, been found.'[30]

British imperial rule brought changes to the administration of justice and maintenance of order. The core principles of the reorganisation were to professionalise the officer corps of the police, codify and clarify laws and procedures with reference to local conditions, and judicial autonomy from the executive at the middle and higher levels. The civil service acted as a critical link in the entire system as it exercised limited magisterial powers subject to appeal to the sessions court and supervised the police. The greater prestige and importance of the civil service, however, meant that it had greater freedom of action than the statutory positions may indicate. A percentage of the ICS opted for judicial posts and although life in the judiciary was not as glamorous as in the executive branch the pay was 10 per cent more. This added to the prestige of the judicial service and also helped attract more talent from the private sector. The judiciary exercised the power to inspect police diaries, reverse decisions taken by executive magistrates and adhered to a proud tradition of functional autonomy from the executive dating back to the first regulating acts and reforms of the 1770s and 1780s.

This autonomy was partially secured by the dual linkage enjoyed by the judiciary. One third of the judges at the high court level were drawn from the ICS whereas the rest were recruited from the Bar. The effect of drawing into its ranks a large number of highly qualified people was that the judiciary was remarkably efficient. By the late nineteenth century it disposed of nearly five million civil and criminal cases annually. What made this possible was that the integrity and probity of the Indian judges such as *munsifs*, itself a relatively recent development, was 'a cause for thankfulness' that judicial corruption and delinquency had been mitigated.[31] The growth of public virtue applied 'equally to the superior members of the native Bar' whose prestige made them the leaders of Indian society.[32] In Bengal alone the total number of civil suits in 1893 was six hundred and fifty thousand out of which five hundred and fifty-four thousand were instituted that year and some five hundred and sixty thousand were disposed of by the courts by 1894.[33] Experience had validated the hypothesis that properly remunerated, trained, tested, and organised 'the natives, in respect to integrity and diligence, may be trusted with the administration of justice.'[34]

The police administration was in many ways the *enfant terrible* of the British Empire in India. The 1855 Commission for the Investigation of Alleged Cases of Torture in the Madras Presidency received in response to its notice nearly two thousand complaints.[35] The mandate of the Torture Commission included abuses by police and the revenue department and it noted that the vast majority of the complaints probably went unheard.[36] What perturbed greatly was the public perception that the cruelties perpetrated by the subordinate staff and Indian officials must be on the orders of British officials.[37] When it came to torture it was the near 'universal opinion among the natives themselves that in Criminal cases the practice' was 'not only necessary but right.'[38] The use of torture against alleged criminals to extract confessions and provide prompt justice excited 'no abhorrence, no astonishment, no repugnance' amongst the Indians.[39] The locally constituted police was 'a terror to well disposed and peaceable people, none whatever to thieves and rogues' and accurately regarded as 'the bane and pest of society.'[40]

The basic problem was that the regular police lacked sufficient numerical strength, was inadequately supervised, and stretched thin by the vastness of the territory they had to account for. Compounding these technical impediments was the overall nature of policing in the centuries that had preceded British rule. In pre-British India the function of the police 'was not to prevent or to detect crime' but to 'put down disorder and facilitate the movements of the army' and keep official channels of communications open.[41] The police force was an amorphous mass of armed men—retainers, officials, inspectors, spies, paramilitaries—deployed in order to help extract as much revenue as possible, keep a share for itself, and quell the resultant disorders. It may or may not have also drawn a regular pay. While we must be wary of the Timurid tendency to class all non-specialist (i.e. other than cavalry and artillery) employees as infantry, Abul Fazl asserts that some four million four hundred thousand armed men were in the service of the *zamindars*.[42]

Policing was thus primarily an exercise in deterrence and suppression through military means.

The British found that altering the formal structure of the police by dividing it into deterrent and detective wings deployed across individual provinces, introducing new laws such as the Indian Penal Code (IPC) in 1861, instituting new methods for recruitment and evaluation or gradually civilianising the police force was comparatively easy. What was terribly difficult was altering its ethos. When it came to dealing with the poor, especially when investigating suspects, the police made haste to produce someone or the other before the courts. Since a list of the local *badmash* elements was maintained this was not too hard. The impression prevailed that a competent policeman was the one who secured a high number of convictions under the law. When the suspect had some wealth the police took their time, applied pressure, and hoped for monetary inducements. The result was that the police stood correctly charged with both arresting suspects too quickly as well as abstaining longer than necessary from arrest.[43] Constables and subordinate officers routinely asked for tips, which, in many cases, were offered without asking, for the performance of their statutory duties. The division of crimes and offences into cognizable and non-cognizable (which required a summons by a magistrate) led to certain problems:

> ...the work of the Superintendents of Police is known and judged by other standards than statistical tests, and all those who work conscientiously and honestly invariably come in for a full amount of praise. But to return to the non-cognizable cases: the amount of work performed in these cases is immense, and for it the Police get little credit; What with summoning and arresting 20,155 persons and the enquiry into 14,205 attempts at burglaries, an Indian policeman's life is not one of ease and comfort.[44]

An Indian prisoner's life was even less comfortable given that lockups in many police stations were 'worse than any 'black hole' of Calcutta.'[45] During the warm and rainy season detention amounted 'to a sentence of slow death by suffocation.'[46]

In Bengal, where the regular police numbered eighteen thousand five hundred and fifty by 1875 as compared to about twenty thousand in the Punjab and twenty-one thousand in the Bombay Presidency, it was found that the majority of Indian inspectors were held in esteem 'by their superiors and their countrymen.'[47] Many of the sub-inspectors (SI) were good though as a group they suffered from malpractices much like the 'old police'.⁴⁸ The sub-inspector's 'neglect, collusion, or concealment' could ruin a case at its inception making 'subsequent rectification by superior officers' a most arduous process.⁴⁹ The SI was identified as the key to the improvement of the overall policing function. The constables and head constables were qualitatively indifferent and routinely indulged in corruption such as destroying evidence, mistreating prisoners and engaging in 'the constant receiving of petty gratifications.'⁵⁰ The village police though capable of effective policing if properly supervised was too numerous, ill-paid and spread out. They were prone to becoming 'the principal promoters and abettors of crime.'⁵¹

While these were very real problems the British Indian state had broken the back of 'the spirit of agrarian lawlessness' that had enveloped the subcontinent.⁵² In the Punjab the 'interior of most of the frontier districts' were by 1876 'as tranquil and orderly as that of any districts to the west of the river Indus.'⁵³ As chaos gave way to order exercised under laws through the ICS, IPS and judiciary, new exams for the subordinate executive services and judicial appointments encouraged merit and provided the state with a solid bureaucratic middle-order. Of the one thousand seven hundred posts in the un-covenanted Bengal provincial services in 1875 over nine hundred were held by Indians.⁵⁴ What was especially notable was that many people of landlord backgrounds had taken to professions such as law and public service thus converting the most lawless elements into servants and protectors of law and order.⁵⁵ By 1875, the *zamindars* no longer kept armed retainers and owing to this there was a decrease in gang-robbery.⁵⁶ This particular change was therefore 'not creditable to our organised police.'⁵⁷ Although the rate of prisoner mortality fell to about thirty-two per hundred thousand in 1893-1894 from twice that amount twenty-five years earlier, it was still excessive as compared to other parts of the country.⁵⁸

After 1893 Indians were allowed into the IPS through competitive exams within the ranks of inspectors and from 1921 onwards regular induction was started with separate exams for the IPS and ICS. As a covenanted service the IPS enjoyed prestige comparable to the ICS and after the deputy commissioner it was the deputy superintendent of police (DSP) or 'captain sahib' who mattered the most. The British achievement was that over a very large part of the subcontinent a regular police force constituted under laws and administered through a rational legal framework within which the judiciary enjoyed and deserved public esteem had been established. People and the servants of the state obeyed the law not because they had become morally good but because the interplay of institutions, consistency, and autonomy, had created an environment in which it was substantially in their interest to do so. The role of the Indians in the judiciary and police was on the whole commendable and the self-criticism of the official reports and commissions was itself the sign of a healthy discourse. The challenge for the leaders of India and Pakistan was to extend the regular justice system to those areas where imperial interests had deemed otherwise and infuse the apparatus and those it affected with a progressive, liberalising, and modernising spirit. Indeed, outside of Western Europe the 'law and order' administration of the subcontinent was possibly the best and could be reformed into something even better. In Pakistan, however, Solon's victory over Theseus proved evanescent.

5.2 IN THE STATE OF EMERGENCY

The rule of law has its juridical, legislative and administrative dimensions. Though these cannot be neatly compartmentalised the first concerns itself with constitutional issues and disputes that require deliberation, the second with the drafting and passage of laws, while the third is more commonly identified with the executive functions of the state. Taken together the effort is to restrain the arbitrary and unlawful exercise of power by applying, interpreting and enforcing the sovereign and ordinary laws of the land. If successful the effect is that those elected to office or appointed to senior positions such as the army chief, chief justices, chairmen of national corporations etc., under the law will be prevented to a substantial degree from acting unlawfully. In Pakistan by October 1958 the juridical and legislative aspects of the rule of law were effectively subordinated to an aggrandising executive power. This process was not undertaken with violence or bloodshed but carried through to fruition with the active collusion of senior members of the judiciary led by the Chief Justice of the Federal Court, Muhammad Munir.

The greatest casualty of this collusion was the Constituent Assembly which had unquestionably proceeded slowly with the framing of a new constitution for Pakistan. This slow rate of progress had something to do with the desire of the members of the assembly to prolong their own tenures and it had a great deal to do with the complexities inherent in framing a constitution for a state as diverse and geographically divided as Pakistan. In March 1954, the United Front in East Bengal trounced the Muslim League in provincial elections and secured two hundred and thirty-two seats out of a house of three hundred and nine. The Muslim League secured a mere ten seats which led to the charge that the Constituent Assembly in which it enjoyed a majority had lost the confidence of the people. Some demanded that the Constituent Assembly be dissolved and a new assembly be convened. The counterargument was that in a federal system defeat in provincial elections did not invalidate the ruling party's position in other provincial legislatures or the central legislature. This argument, though legally tenable, seemed a morally hollow ruse perpetrated by the members of the first Constituent Assembly to stay in office after so many years of delay.

At any rate, differences 'among the heterogeneous elements of the United Front' surfaced almost immediately and even at 'the swearing in ceremony' at the Government House on 3 April 1954, 'a group of pro-Awami League students' were demonstrating against the chief minister designate Fazlul Haq 'for including a relative of his in the cabinet.'[59] The allocation of ministerial portfolios sent shockwaves through the increasingly disunited Front and by May 1954 the province descended into violence, labour unrest, and the targeting of non-Bengalis, with hundreds killed and thousands injured at the Adamjee jute mills.[60] On 30 May 1954, the United Front ministry was dismissed, governor's rule imposed, and Iskander Mirza sent to assume charge of the province.

Back in Karachi, the Constituent Assembly picked up the pace and Premier Bogra tried to loosen the grip the governing corporation had on him since his installation in April 1953 following Nazimuddin's dismissal. Bogra's objective was to get the new constitution approved so that it would enter into effect on 1 January 1955. For once, the assembly proceeded ahead of schedule and appeared by the end of October 1954 to be on course for a passage of the draft Constitution Bill. Fearing that the governor-general would react badly to the provisions in the draft constitution which practically reduced the head of state to a cipher and established a bicameral legislature in which East Bengal would dominate the lower house, Bogra moved to protect himself. On 20 September

1954, the Constituent Assembly repealed PRODA and amended the 1935 Government of India Act to take away the head of state's powers of dismissal over ministers.

On 24 October 1954, the governing corporation struck back days before the final debate on the Constitution Bill was to take place. Ghulam Muhammad proclaimed a state of emergency and dissolved the Constituent Assembly on the grounds that it could 'no longer function'. The non-functionality of the Constituent Assembly was challenged by its president Moulvi Tamizuddin Khan at the Sindh Chief Court. The public reaction was mixed though on balance it was 'acclaimed in both wings; messages of congratulations to the Governor-General poured in by the hundreds and continued to be published in the newspapers well into the second week of November.'[61] Earlier, the dismissal of Khwaja Nazimuddin's government and his betrayal at the hands of his ministers and the members of the party 'though generally considered illegal, was welcomed by the people.'[62] As the Constituent Assembly fell it was felt that 'the country...had been saved.'[63] Politicians and members of the public who had 'challenged the democratic legitimacy of the Constituent Assembly'[64] and poured scorn upon it for having 'misused and abused the power delegated to it by the people'[65] now looked forward to justice being done.

Tamizuddin Khan managed to sneak into the courts and evade the intelligence personnel deployed to intercept him by 'arriving in a rickshaw through the side gate clad in a burqa.'[66] When the intelligence personnel realized that they had been outsmarted they tried to seize the petition but the timely intervention of 'the Registrar of the Sindh Chief Court' and the Chief Justice George Constantine 'saved the situation.'[67] The Chief Court asserted that 'There now resides in the Constituent Assembly the sovereign power' and given that the British monarch's 'own intervention to give validity or force to measures of the Constituent Assembly was not required', it was 'anomalous to say that the intervention' of the governor general in his capacity as the monarch's representative was required.[68] The Chief Court stated that there was 'no case throughout the Commonwealth outside England', which did not have a formal constitution, 'where the dissolution of a Legislature takes place except by express provision in the Constitution, whether granted by Statute or order in council.'[69] Consequently, the purported dissolution or declaration of non-functionality was 'a nullity in law.'[70] Moreover, as previously the Federal Court had decided cases arising from laws passed by the Constituent Assembly that had not received the head of state's assent, the judiciary clearly did not think such assent to be necessary for laws to be passed. Therefore, Section 223A of the modified Government of India Act under which Tamizuddin had asked for relief against the governor-general's actions was as lawful as say the 1951 Act that extended universal adult franchise which had also not received his formal assent. Ghulam Muhammad had acted under no law and therefore the new cabinet, which included Ayub Khan as defence minister, was illegal. Tamizuddin was still the president of the assembly which did not stand dissolved under law. The governing corporation appealed this decision to the Federal Court where a five-member bench comprising Chief Justice Munir and justices Sharif, Rehman, Akram, and Cornelius,[71] heard the case.

Munir, Sharif and Rehman upheld the dissolution of the assembly and overturned the Sindh Chief Court's verdict. They asserted that it was wrong 'to suppose that sovereignty in its larger sense was conferred upon the Constituent Assembly' and all acts 'passed by it required the Governor-General's assent.'[72] Since Section 223A of the Government of India Act as modified by the non-functional Constituent Assembly that gave the courts powers to review the head of state's decisions and issue writs of *quo warranto* and mandamus had not been formally approved by the governor-general the Sindh Chief Court had no authority to countermand his orders. While Akram abstained, Cornelius dissented and observed that such consent had not been considered necessary and bills became laws through assembly votes followed by the president of the assembly signing them and sending them for notification in the Official *Gazette*.[73] The granting of universal adult franchise and forty-five other acts had not received the governor-general's assent and had led to litigation in the courts and 'produced extensive effects.'[74]

Having saved his mentor, Munir's decision plunged the country into a legal limbo as dozens of acts stood repudiated by virtue of the lack of the governor-general's assent. Ghulam Muhammad issued in the manner of an imperial edict the Emergency Powers Ordinance-IX of 1955 that allowed him retrospectively to validate laws passed by the Constituent Assembly. This ordinance was challenged before the Federal Court in the *Yusuf Patel versus the Crown* case. The executive was challenged on the grounds that it did not have the power under law to make changes to the constitution of its own free will. Having created a legal vacuum, the Federal Court now *rejected* the governor general's exercise of emergency powers and thus plunged the country into an even more intractable crisis. The legal machinery of the state faced ruin as challenges to its legality mounted.[75] Indeed, the conundrum was that only an assembly could validate laws, but since the adult franchise was granted under an act that did not have the governor-general's consent, legally, elections would have to be held on the basis of limited franchise as in 1946.

Ghulam Muhammad responded by filing a reference with the Federal Court, convened a new Constituent Assembly due to meet on 10 May 1955, asked the court to advise the government on how exactly validation of laws could take place, and went ahead with the validation of over thirty laws subject to judicial review. The terms of the reference were enlarged on Munir's advice to include the legality of the dismissal of the first Constituent Assembly lest the new one be challenged on the grounds that it was illegally replacing the previous one. Having almost single-handedly plunged Pakistan into a legal quagmire through criminal collusion and incompetence, Munir's reply to the governor-general's reference, delivered on 16 May 1955, applied the doctrine of individual necessity to the state as a whole:

> ...subject to conditions of absoluteness, extremeness and immanence, an act which would otherwise be illegal becomes legal if it is done bona fide under the stress of necessity, the necessity being referable to an intention to preserve the constitution of the State or the Society...necessity knows no law and that...necessity makes lawful which otherwise is not lawful. Since the address expressly refers to the right of a private person to act in necessity, in the case of Head of the State justification to act must...be clearer and more imperative.[76]

Unrepentant and heedless of the greater consequences, Munir declared that the first Constituent Assembly had become non-functional, unrepresentative and failed to get proper assent from the governor-general:

> The disorder that stared the Governor-General in the face, consequent on the illegal manner in which the Constituent Assembly exercised its legislative authority, is apparent from the results described in the Reference as having

followed from the Court's decision in Mr Tamizuddin Khan's case and the subsequent case of Yusuf Patel. The Governor-General must, therefore, be held to have acted in order to avert an impending disaster and to prevent the State and Society from dissolution.[77]

There was little substantive difference between Munir and his judicial collaborators and the *qazi*s of the Timurid or Ottoman empires who bent over backwards to demonstrate that the executive could legitimately do what it pleased.[78] When Iskander Mirza and Ayub Khan, both of whom Munir advised and consulted with on matters of national importance and politics, staged a coup in October 1958 and issued an ordinance allowing laws under the 1956 constitution, which was technically abrogated, to continue in force until further notice, the judgment to the court challenge was a foregone conclusion. Munir, invoking Hans Kelsen's obscure theory of law and state, held that if a coup or revolution was successful then it stood legitimated and the new regime became the ultimate sovereign body. Its subsequent actions and edicts were lawful by virtue of its success. This logic had been used many times before in pre-British India where the victor in a war of succession was proclaimed legitimate by virtue of his success which, to the pre-Enlightenment mind, was possible only through divine favor. The *Dosso* case established that legitimacy flowed from success and the superior judiciary could be counted upon like their medieval equivalents to bring forth all their 'semantic sophistry' to the aid of unlawful and arbitrary acts:

> We are afraid to face the truth about ourselves; we are ingenious in our rationalization of the lies that we tell, so that we may not fall in our own self-esteem.... Our leaders lie on a grand scale; the rest of us lie, some more some less, within the radius of our humbler stations in life...We cover truth with falsehood and knowingly conceal the truth, not only at the individual level but also at the institutional level.... Even our highest court of justice has repeatedly failed to uphold the truth, calling semantic sophistry to the aid of moral self-deceit: in 1955, legitimizing the overthrow of the then Constituent Assembly by the then Governor-General; in 1958, raising a coup to the status of a 'revolution'; in 1972, exhibiting a spasm of conscience on the last day of that martial law; in 1977, falling back on the 'doctrine of necessity'....[79]

To these we may add the validation of Musharraf's coup of 12 October 1999, as well as the swearing of a new oath under a provisional constitutional order or PCO and the legitimacy extended to the 2002 referendum that secured five more years in office for the president. Like Theseus and Peisistratus, Pakistan's rulers, judges, administrators and reformers have been enamoured with the rule of justice that would flow naturally from their personal virtues.

5.3 THE RULE OF JUSTICE

Speaking on the centenary of the West Pakistan High Court in February 1967 Ayub Khan asked the assemblage 'Why can't our courts become the courts of justice instead of courts of law' and insisted that 'something be done to make justice cheaper and speedier.'[80] Ayub asserted that the laws of Pakistan 'and the ways they' were operated were not 'in consonance with our historical, ideological, cultural background' and the people did not 'have faith in them.'[81] The entire system introduced by the British to administer and uphold laws was alien and had corrupted the people of Pakistan and been corrupted by them 'to make it work at all.'[82] This corruption had created a society 'where truthfulness is not practised', thus 'no system of detection' could work with reasonable accuracy and 'no norms enforced with certainty.'[83] The colonial laws in trying to protect witnesses and the accused had contributed to a situation in which confessions made to the police could be denied with impunity before the court.[84] The courts had 'actually departed from the rule of best evidence' and 'considered it safe to act on the second best evidence.'[85] In the investigation of cases the system did not seek truth so that justice could be done but exerted itself to generate 'evidence in an admissible form.'[86] In order to serve the law forgery and perjury were thus committed while 'the supposed ends of justice' were abandoned.[87] It was only logical that the inherently corrupt, unjust, and alien system of laws had created a situation in which 'subordinate court officials who have to deal with the public' extorted 'illegal gratification from the litigants before condescending' to perform their statutory function.[88] The rule of law as expressed in the imperial legacy was 'most expensive, ineffective, dilatory, tyrannical and totally unsuited to our genius.'[89]

What was suitable to the genius of the Pakistani people was 'having a 'Jirga' style judicial system' without complicated evidence and 'procedural laws with only one right of appeal.'[90] A similar system had operated in pre-British India before being corrupted by the alien rule. The great cause of its success in the heyday of the Timurid Empire was that 'the emperors took the administration of justice very seriously.'[91] Though defective in terms of organisation, laws, jurisdiction and hierarchy, none of which were properly defined or consistently applied, justice, it is insistently maintained, was dispensed satisfactorily.[92] The singular reason for this success 'was that the emperor himself constituted the highest appellate court' and 'also heard cases and complaints against high government officials.'[93] Inspired by the personal example set by the emperor the Timurid courts and officials did not seek 'to decide a case on the basis of the record of evidence produced before it, but to make enquiries and investigations, find the truth' and, above all else, do justice.[94] It was therefore fitting that Pir Ali Mohammad Rashidi, an Ayub Khan loyalist posted as ambassador to the Philippines, advised, on 12 June 1961 in favour of establishing a monarchy in Pakistan.[95] If only Ayub Khan became the king of Pakistan 'all the fissiparous tendencies, uncertainties and conflicts' would be at an end.[96] Ayub Khan responded that a monarchy was not practical in Pakistan ignoring, perhaps, the possibility that political parties may become vehicles of dynastic rule in the near future and that a generation later an elected prime minister would seriously consider becoming the 'commander of the faithful' or *amir-ul-momineen* of Pakistan.[97]

What was remarkable about this discourse in the context of introducing the rule of justice to Pakistan was that following the introduction of the West Pakistan Criminal Law (Amendment) Act of 1963 that expanded the scope of the indigenous system there was 'a marked increase in the incidence of crime.' This was contrary to the claim that *jirga*s would act as deterrents 'against the commission of heinous crimes.'[98] In 1962, in the Peshawar division there had been five hundred and twenty-six murders, four dacoities and six hundred and ninety-eight attempted murders.[99] In 1967, there were six hundred and nineteen murders, sixteen dacoities and nine hundred and eighty-five attempted murders in the same division.[100]

The love of justice was also deemed the natural consequence of the 'Islamic system of administration of justice' which laid greater emphasis upon the 'personal character of all those who are involved, the witnesses, the prosecuting agencies and the police officers.'[101] The entire Timurid apparatus, it was maintained, was motivated by love and fear of the divine which in its Islamic variant elevated the moral virtue of justice as second only to piety.[102] Occasional instances of Muslim rulers, especially from the Pious Caliphate (632-661) but also from other times with Jahangir's belled-chain of justice exercising a most powerful hold over the neo-medieval Pakistani group mind, paying respect to judges or making a show of submission were taken as proof that the 'rule of law' as exercised in the corrupted and pessimistic Solonian institutions of the West was in fact indistinguishable from the rule of absolute justice emanating from personal morality that was the 'foundation of the entire Islamic religious, social, cultural, economic and political structure.'[103] It was hardly pointed out that if these rulers had *chosen* not to submit, as their successors did with absolute impunity, there was no institutional force that could have compelled them to do so. The conflict between the Ummayads and the Hashimites that brought down the Pious Caliphate saw the latter party rejecting the results of an arbitration that went against its political interests. The extraordinary morality of great and virtuous men does not automatically translate into a system workable by ordinary and highly fallible people.

Since only a supreme and omnipotent executive can dispense true justice the transparent contempt that successive Pakistani rulers have demonstrated by their actions for the superior judiciary is perfectly understandable. The mental and moral landscape of Pakistan's Anglophone elite is far less modern or liberal than appearances alone would indicate. This landscape is also scarred by underlying layers of insecurities, complexes, utopian delusions, unremitting cynicism and a tremendous desire to convince itself that the Mandate of Heaven is still within its grasp. Iskander Mirza, during his governorship of East Bengal, 'would often surprise the people' through 'unexpected informal' appearances at cinemas, schools, hospitals and the like.[104] To show the people his sincerity and love of justice and equality, Mirza 'stood in the queue' to purchase tickets for the movies at the Gulistan Cinema in Dhaka.[105] On other occasions Mirza travelled incognito to ascertain for himself the true state of affairs.[106] Like all lovers of justice Mirza 'employed both conventional and unconventional methods for keeping himself informed', including the intelligence agencies, personal contacts and foreign operatives.[107]

Ayub Khan's 1962 Constitution 'did not contain any Fundamental Rights' though that did not stop 'the Judges of the Supreme Court' from swearing 'the oath to uphold the Constitution.'[108] The court had earlier ruled that Ayub's Security of Pakistan Act 'could not be challenged in the courts.'[109] Later, it extended recognition to the Defence of Pakistan Rules (DPR) introduced by a presidential ordinance in September 1965 in response to war with India. The DPR allowed detention on grounds that the individual or party concerned *might* disturb internal order. The Supreme Court of Pakistan's 'judgment was therefore a bonanza for the Government to legalise an instrument of oppression used by it to silence and terrorise its citizens.'[110] When Ayub was overthrown in March 1969 and his constitution abrogated, the judiciary quietly shifted its allegiances to the new regime forgetting its earlier oath.

Yahya Khan extraordinary superficiality and crassness shone through on 3 April 1969, when, as the new president, he addressed the federal secretaries. The gathering was a nervous one given that many had been very close to Ayub Khan. In that address Yahya outlined 'his favourite concept' which was, as it turned out, *jaza* and *saza* (reward and punishment).[111] Some idea of Yahya's utterly subjective standards of reward and punishment can be gauged by his decision to elevate Abdul Rehman Siddiqui, then a mere colonel, as the de facto in charge 'for all matters of higher policies' of the Ministry of Information and Broadcasting, or by raising other middle ranking officers to posts substantially above both their seniority and their competence.[112]

With the *jaza* out of the way Yahya Khan proceeded to inflict *saza* on those he thought merited it. Yahya Khan's tribunals, set up to purge the 'corrupt' from public service 'on the basis of the report of scrutiny committees', were his contribution to the pursuit of justice.[113] The dismissal of three hundred and three senior officials was Yahya's attempt at dispensing speedy justice and 'people were delighted that they had at last found a dictator who believed in fighting corruption.'[114] Later, Yahya 'in his evidence was strongly' of the view that 'whenever a military commander, however low ranking, finds that the ordinary government cannot be carried on in the area in his command' possesses 'both the right and the obligation to impose Martial Law.'[115] It was as if in its self-perception the military sincerely believed that it possessed 'an authority superior to the Constitution.'[116]

Zulfikar Ali Bhutto's attitude towards the dispensation of justice was characterised by arbitrariness although some effort was made to maintain constitutional norms. In addition to legislation by executive ordinances, a total of two hundred and nineteen of which were passed (twenty-four between January and July 1977), the continuation of the emergency meant that fundamental rights remained suspended. Bhutto's self-styled revolutionary regime wanted to do justice by raining vengeance upon the exploiters of the poor masses with business interests and the higher bureaucracy, especially its CSP component, the principal targets. It had no time to bother with British state morality and the rule of law. The FSF existed to mete out justice to the enemies of the regime while the judiciary had to bend before the will of the sovereign people. Special courts and tribunals were created to circumvent the regular judiciary. The rules 'governing the appointment and superannuation of Chief Justices were changed by constitutional amendment to ensure the subservience of the superior courts to the political executive.'[117] The Sixth Amendment Act allowed the prime minister to grant extensions to the Chief Justice of the Supreme Court beyond the retirement age of sixty-five and Justice Yaqub Ali, who had declared that Bhutto had 'great respect for the judiciary', 'was granted an extension' when he was due for retirement. [118]

The tone had been set during the martial law period in which Bhutto was the president, when, in April 1972, the district judge of Sanghar in Sindh 'was arrested because he had given bail to a minor politician on the basis of a judgment' of the High Court.[119] The Supreme Court's intervention secured the release of the arrestee but 'this attempt to prosecute a District Judge for performing his duties...had a traumatic effect on the subordinate judiciary of Sindh.'[120] Further evidence of Bhutto's 'respect' for the judicial system included the withdrawal, on 24 April 1974, of 'the legal protection available to the citizen against *malafide* arrest on a criminal charge.'[121] On 13 September 1976, under the Fifth Amendment Act, the high courts lost their powers to grant bail.[122] The continued employment of DPR and special tribunals, the Suppression of Terrorist Activities law of 1975 and the special courts at Karachi, Peshawar, and Lahore under one high court judge apiece, meant summary trials, the presumption of guilt, the effective repeal of Habeas

Corpus, bail, and in a number of cases, appeal. The accused did not even have to be produced for formality's sake in court before a magistrate. Bhutto also promised to consider sympathetically the demand that plots of land should be 'allocated to lawyers for the construction of houses.'[123] Pliant lawyers 'were appointed legal advisers to various' nationalized 'banks on the strength of their political affiliation.'[124] By May 1976, the PPP estimated that one hundred members of the High Court Bar Association (HCBA) of Lahore were loyal to Bhutto though the situation at the district level, with only one hundred and fifty-eight loyal followers out of one thousand nine hundred members of the District Bar Association, left much to be desired.[125] As Bhutto became more desperate to hang on to power the distinction between sin and crime was sacrificed with the introduction of prohibition and bans on gambling and horse racing. Earlier, in 1973, Bhutto had established a Ministry of Religious Affairs and in 1974 had the Ahmedis declared non-Muslims by an amendment to the constitution. The ban on alcohol and gambling were imposed as part of a desperate gambit during the final days of the PPP government. Their objective was to deflect criticism of the un-Islamic nature of Bhutto's popular but increasingly embattled government. These sops to traditionalist sentiment did not alter the fortunes of the government and after being overthrown, Bhutto was put on trial before the Supreme Court for conspiracy to murder and executed on 4 April 1979 with four votes to three in favour of guilt.

Zia kept Pakistan under martial law between 1977 and 1985 and came down hard on his opponents. The martial law authorities flogged, searched, imprisoned, and confiscated 'without having to give reasons.'[126] Brutal punishments such as public floggings graced Pakistan's tortured landscape and the state poured its energies and resources into moulding society supposedly in a just and assertively Islamic frame of mind. The lawyers' associations were prohibited on pain of twenty-five lashes from inviting anyone to address them. On 25 March 1981, the judges of the supreme and high courts were invited to swear an oath of loyalty to the CMLA under the PCO or stand dismissed. An acting judge of the Supreme Court and eleven judges of the high courts were not invited to take the oath and 'their summary dismissal had a traumatic effect on the entire judiciary.'[127] Zia abstained from making permanent appointments to the supreme and high courts and 'thought it prudent to keep' the judges 'in a state of suspense and insecurity.'[128] By setting up separate *shariat* benches, appointing *qazi*s, constituting a Federal Shariat Court (FSC), rendering the Objectives Resolution an operative part of the constitution, and introducing blasphemy and adultery laws, Zia revived the 'monarch-mullah combination' that had existed for centuries prior to the advent of British rule.[129] The clerical establishment, now patronised by *zakat* funds, bestowed upon Zia in the tradition of the Timurid rulers 'divine rights to rule ruthlessly' in exchange for continued patronage.[130] Zia set a personal standard for piety by giving funds and support to mosques, such as the Lal Masjid in Islamabad, inserting a column for religious observance in the evaluation reports of state employees, providing for prayer breaks in offices and sticking to a religious routine.

Islamisation was expected to produce good people and that would allow justice to reign supreme without the artificial, alien, Godless, and heretical, innovations of the post-Enlightenment State of Laws. In order to promote a suitable Islamic world view Zia poured state resources into funding the growth of religious seminaries (*deeni madaris*). Thanks to the boost the seminaries received during Zia's rule their numbers rose from one thousand in 1980 to thirteen thousand in 2000, with a total enrolment of nearly two million students.[131] By 2000 there were one thousand seminaries with two hundred thousand students in Karachi alone.[132] The mass production of religiously motivated, sect conscious, young men with little to no employability and social mobility provided the demographic base from which the drugs trade, small arms proliferation and sectarian militias that emerged in Zia's time drew strength. The impact upon the country of such thinking was that between 1981 and 1990 the total number of crimes registered rose from one hundred and seventy-three thousand per year to three hundred and ten thousand per year.[133] The office of Ombudsman introduced in 1983 to hear complaints against the administration was in the same breath deprived of powers to act upon the results of its inquiries. Complaints, however, poured in by the tens of thousands every year. Although Zia's regime enjoyed stability, society at large was rendered increasingly ungovernable as resources from home and abroad were poured into arming, training and launching legions of Islamic militants into Afghanistan to fight the Soviets.

Zia's death brought in Benazir Bhutto and Nawaz Sharif and between 1988 and 1999 the PPP and PML-N governments rotated into and out of office. Both parties tried to concentrate as much power as possible in their own hands and inflicted one-sided accountability upon each other. Sharif, on balance, was more consciously and unapologetically medieval than Benazir Bhutto, and was fond of roaming around the country and holding open courts, sometimes televised live, in which people could personally approach him and secure justice. One of the finest manifestations of Sharif's justice was his handling of the public meeting at the Faisalabad Development Authority on 10 March 1997. Three officers 'appeared to be party to the purchase of defective water meters and to have misappropriated large sums of government funds.'[134] In a fit of righteous wrath, such as the one in which Akbar ordered the feet of a man who had stolen slippers amputated, Sharif 'ordered their arrest and they were in fact handcuffed by the police and taken into custody in his presence.'[135] The Supreme Court assumed jurisdiction in this particular case.[136] The Shariat Bill was another manifestation of the executive's desire to become the medium through which divine justice could rain down upon society.

Benazir Bhutto, for her part, elevated Sajjad Ali Shah to the post of Chief Justice of Pakistan in violation of the seniority principle hoping to secure a pliable crony in office. This was the first time since the appointment of Munir in 1954 that the seniority principle was ignored. The new appointee soon established personal links with the president and helped facilitate Benazir's dismissal in November 1996. Sajjad Ali Shah, like Munir, expected to be consulted on matters of national importance by the army chief, the president, and the prime minister. Nawaz Sharif, however, returning to power with a two-thirds majority, criticised the court and contempt charges were brought against him and his associates. Sharif rapidly proceeded to introduce changes to laws and planned to pass a Contempt of Parliament Act directed at the judiciary. After making a huge deal of personally attending the contempt hearings and comparing himself to the Pious Caliphs, Sharif revived the issue of Sajjad Ali Shah's seniority and fomented a judicial insurrection. On 28 November 1997 the Supreme Court building was attacked by ruling party members by which time the Quetta Bench had already rebelled against Sajjad Ali Shah's leadership. By 1 December 1997, ten of the justices of the Supreme Court fell in line and on 23 December 1997, Sajjad Ali Shah was dismissed in effect for thinking that the prime minister could be compelled to discuss important issues with him while leaving him a free hand to make appointments and transfers within the judiciary.[137]

The rhetoric of justice did not translate into improvements in the efficiency and competence of the judiciary. By the mid-1990s even the simplest case took an average of four and half years to resolve while more complicated cases could and did drag on for decades.[138] At the sessions court level the average pending period for cases was alarming especially for crimes against the social fabric and public order. On average, cases pertaining to the disturbance of order remained pending for two hundred and four days; illegal possession of arms and ammunition two hundred and fifty-three days; murder two hundred and fifty-one days and narcotics one hundred and sixty-eight days.[139] In 1992, at the Peshawar High Court it took an average of twenty-one months to dispose of a civil suit and eighteen months to complete a criminal case.[140] On 1 January 1994, the total number of cases pending before the Supreme Court stood at six thousand one hundred and six.[141] In the meanwhile, the speedy trial courts were a bad joke upon the justice system.[142] For the people who get trapped in the process of civil litigation or criminal investigation the consequences were and are dire. Under these circumstances the desire to avoid contact with the justice system is strong among law abiding citizens. About six out of ten prison inmates in 1986 were under-trial prisoners.[143] There, the 'generally barbaric and brutal behaviour of the jail staff' produced hardened criminals instead of repentant sinners.[144] Although there are instances of individual brilliance and courage, such as Aitzaz Ahsan and Hamid Khan, the quality of the members of the legal fraternity leaves much to be desired. Standards are lax, exams often a formality, and the lawyers are almost as dishonest as the criminals and policemen they interact with. There is also an acute shortage of properly trained public prosecutors and successive attempts at reform have yielded little beneficial change. The results are 'an expanding circle of alienation of the credibility of the national judicial system.'[145] The situation, however, on the executive side of the administration of law, order, and justice, reached a far more advanced degree of deterioration quicker and more surely.

5.4 THE FORCES OF ORDER

As a greater proportion of the All-India Services came to be recruited from the Indian subjects of the British Raj, the Joint Committee on Indian Constitutional Reform for the 1933-1934 Session advised that in continental bureaucratic states such as India 'the executive function' was of 'overriding importance.'[146] A core component of this function was the police. The characteristics of an effective police force were 'discipline, impartiality and confidence in its officers' all of which would be 'most quickly undermined' if 'political interference' and 'pressure' was introduced into its operation.[147] It would be 'disastrous' for all concerned if the police 'were to be sacrificed to the exigencies of a party or to appease the political supporters of a Minister.'[148] The administrative autonomy of the police and its related agencies and departments was essential to the preservation of the state of order in society. On the other hand the politicisation of the core executive function would diminish its legitimacy and effectiveness and given enough time unleash chaos.

By January 1933, there were one hundred and fifty-two Indian IPS officers out of a total cadre of six hundred and sixty-five which made it one of the least Indianised of the AIS.[149] In contrast, the ICS had four hundred and seventy-eight Indian officers out of a total cadre of one thousand two hundred and ninety-seven while in the Service of Engineers there were two hundred and ninety-two Indians out of a total of five hundred and ninety-six.[150] Since partition had not been figured into the equation the numerical strength and seniority of Muslim officers who opted for Pakistan in 1947 was very low. Pakistan had to make do with a mere twelve Muslim IPS officers and fourteen British IPS officers who opted to stay.[151] In contrast there were eighty-three Muslim ICS officers available to Pakistan in 1947.[152] While the middle and lower ranks of the police were reasonably well staffed the officer corps of the PSP had to be rebuilt around a tiny nucleus of British and British-trained officers. In the aftermath of partition the effort was to try and recreate the police as it had existed in British India. Even as quantitative adjustments were made and order successfully restored the capacity of the police force to resist political pressure was undermined.

By 1953, the 'impression' that members of the legislature engaged in 'undue interference with police' had 'gained ground in the public mind.'[153] Some legislators had gone so far as to instigate public disturbances and then secure bail or leniency for their followers.[154] While the CSP and PSP officers were thus far 'able to withstand the influence' exerted by politicians there was great 'danger' that 'subordinate officers' were failing to 'stand up' and resist successfully.[155] If such interference by 'Ministers' and members of the legislature continued 'unchecked' the 'virus' could infect the senior officers and lead to the erosion of the credibility and effectiveness of the state.[156] Elected representatives were circumventing officers and breaking-up the discipline of the police force which had barely recovered from the chaos of partition.[157] If the 'interference with the ordinary course of rules and law' by the politicians was not effectively stopped Pakistan would soon have 'the police it deserves and not the police it needs.'[158] Pressure was effectively exercised by the politicians to secure the recruitment of large numbers of constables who duly proceeded to become a public nuisance and administrative headache. In their desire to distribute jobs amongst their supporters the elected representatives seemed oblivious to the reality that it was 'far better to have 50 men well trained, well equipped and in perfect health than 500 men trained indifferently and housed indifferently.'[159]

Successive regimes failed to reform the principles of police organisation and contended themselves with tinkering with an early-twentieth century institutional framework. The Police Commission constituted by Ayub Khan in 1960 found that it was the functioning of the ordinary constable that determined the public perception of police.[160] Those promoted from constable to more senior positions carried with them 'the habits and modes of thought acquired in the constable grade.'[161] The key to winning the battle was to get productive and efficient sub-inspectors[162] and the training given to all ranks laid far too much emphasis on ceremonial drill.[163] These prescriptions would be repeated ad nauseam by subsequent commissions and committees.

A decade later the police numbered seventy thousand in West Pakistan (population fifty-two million) and thirty thousand in East Pakistan (population sixty-two million) and had a network of training schools and centres for traffic, wireless communications and criminal investigation as well as an academy for officer training. It was however noted that respectable people tended to keep 'their complaints to themselves for fear of being humiliated' by the police.[164] The faculty at the training centres and the academy were for the most part the 'problem children' or rejects from the main cadre.[165] Instead of looking forward to the opportunity to influence entire generations of future police officers in a positive manner the faculty regarded their postings as cruel and unusual punishment. The state's neglect of the social sciences in Pakistan also helped ensure that the instruction imparted at the training institutions did little to cultivate the critical thinking and learning skills of the police officers.

Lawlessness and corruption within the police force had become matters of grave concern at both the lower and higher levels. Police officers were engaged in the illegal acquisition of property, making deals with local businesses, manipulating cases, and living beyond their means.[166] The senior officers were protecting and facilitating corrupt and servile subordinates, acquiring property, and accepting hospitality from local notables in exchange for favours.[167] This in turn meant that the restraining influence of a clean officer corps upon the intermediate and lower ranks of the police had significantly diminished. Constables and sub-inspectors now operated in an increasingly pervasive atmosphere of corruption with little fear of their superior officers whose powers of dismissal and discipline over the lower ranks had been reduced since independence.[168] Since during Ayub's rule the inspector-generals (IG) had been in more or less complete control of postings and transfers of subordinate officers, they bore great responsibility for the state of affairs.[169]

General A. O. Mitha, the chairman of the 1969-70 Police Commission and the vice-chairmen, brigadiers Muhammad Jamshed, Malik Abdul Majid, and Ghulam Jilani Khan, opined forcefully that 'Ours is no longer an alien government interested and involved in the continuation of the 'RAJ' through police methods that bind and subjugate the people and its politicians.'[170] The problems with the police were the lack of inspiration, honesty and 'man-management'.[171] The police must 'not be shy of seeking the assistance of recognised organisation and methods consultants' to overcome these deficiencies.[172] Advancement within the police should be based upon character as well as seniority and efficiency and for this purpose 60 per cent of the assessment value for promotions should be reserved for honesty.[173]

Subsequent to the collapse of Yahya's regime under the weight of its own ineptitude and the restoration of democratic rule under Bhutto, it was hoped that the democratically elected governments would prove more responsive to public opinion and reduce the level of police high handedness as well as bureaucratic oppression.[174] This naïve expectation was brutally punctured by the unprecedented arbitrariness of the Bhutto government and the overall tangent of administrative reforms it pursued. In 1972, the police was still capable of being culturally modernised and though in a decaying orbit had enough energy left to pull itself together and change course. By 1977, the shocks administered through purges, lateral induction, equalisation and standardisation of pay-scales and destruction of service guarantees, had almost reduced it to its 1850s conditions—a dangerous and lawless force, politicised, corrupt, and a threat to peaceful and law abiding citizens. While resources that should have gone into the modernisation of the police force were poured into building the eighteen thousand strong FSF and increasing the pays and benefits of the military, the constant shuffling around of officers from one post to another vitiated the ability of the police to maintain a semblance of administrative stability.

In 1976, the Subcommittee on Law and Order observed that 'too many transfers or postings of working level officers were ordered on political considerations at the cost of partial/complete sacrifice of service requirements.'[175] PPP workers and leaders kept 'cutting across the proper flow of command and control in the executive line' while complaining that the civil service and police did not duly 'acknowledge the role of the political arm in day-to-day administration.'[176] Evidently, the 'political arm' did not understand that it had no role to play other than determining policy and overseeing its execution. The Subcommittee conceded that at the district and station jurisdiction levels 'corruption was really rampant' and 'was by far the major cause of decrease' in the prestige and effectiveness of the state.[177] The inspections of police stations had become matters of 'routine' with little attempt to actually make sure that the law was being obeyed.[178] As the state sank into demoralised ineffectiveness the district administration was far too busy catering to VIPs and giving due protocol to elected representatives and their sycophantic minions.[179] In essence, the law enforcement, supervision, and reporting apparatus was doing political work and trying to please PPP members instead of upholding the law and dealing with crime.[180] These views were politely corroborated by a team of Romanian police experts who toured the country from 10 March to 10 June 1976. They found a 'lack of functional specialisation' and a rank structure that bore 'no relation to job specifications generally.'[181] The non-seriousness of the approach towards ensuring the effectiveness of the state's core function was chilling. The political leadership seemed to take the law and order administration for granted.

Equally astonishing was that senior police officers themselves thought, in a sad though unintentional admission of their limited knowledge of the history of policing, that 'the police system of Pakistan is a colonial legacy and that the British used it to maintain law and order in a country in which they were considered unjust alien rulers.'[182] Forty years after independence 'the executive-police relations' effectively 'reduce the police to the position of a pawn in the hands of the executive.'[183] The perception of successive rulers was that the police was 'a non-development department' and so investment in its modernisation was unnecessary.[184] Blaming the British for this failure may have eased a few consciences, assuming the senior police leadership had any left, but it did not alter the reality that by 1986 the police was thought to be the most corrupt institution in the country with only 43 per cent of some twenty-one thousand respondents willing to turn to the police for help 'in the event of a personal grievance.'[185] Half the respondents said that they would probably not contact the police even if they witnessed anti-state activities.[186] Seventy-five per cent stated that those in power were entirely above the law.[187]

The police behaved as an 'aggressive' and 'para-military' organisation that had missed out on the post-1945 reforms and retrogressively committed itself to the theory of policing through force and weight of numbers.[188] Interrogation and investigation techniques were forced and haphazard and the police image was in tatters owing to the low quality of the constables who made up '95 per cent of the force.'[189] The public's transparent fear of the police and reluctance to cooperate made its tasks even harder to execute.[190] That recruitment to this force at the lower levels was arbitrary, with, in some cases, five thousand men given posts every year, and thus served to overwhelm training facilities, led to the induction of large numbers of unfit candidates, and made the police harder to manage.[191] At the training centres hardly any of the faculty possessed 'specific instructional qualifications' and, with a few exceptions, they were 'posted against their wishes.'[192] The result was that new recruits, especially in the officer corps who were most intelligent[193] and had sound reasoning and communication skills stood to be demoralised by the assortment of incompetent and/or out of favour faculty and an unimaginative curriculum which placed excessive emphasis on physical drill and not enough on law, theory, and police technology.[194] The one year of common training at Lahore prescribed by Bhutto and continued by his successors was of 'little value' though the opportunity to interact with students of other departments was 'most useful' for making friends in the right places.[195]

By 1992, the total strength of the police force stood at one hundred and ninety thousand distributed across one thousand three hundred and sixty-four police stations.[196] The total expenditure on the police was nearly five and a half billion rupees which worked out to per capita expenditure of sixty rupees for a population of about one hundred and twenty million.[197] The police to population ratio stood at one to six hundred with per capita expenditure on maintenance of police personnel varying from over thirty-two thousand rupees in the Punjab to twenty-three thousand rupees in Sindh.[198] The total size of the police force in the territories that now comprise Pakistan had risen from seventy thousand in 1970 to one hundred and ninety-thousand twenty-two years later. In spite of this numerical increase the national crime rate grew alarmingly at an annual average of 8 per cent per annum, 12 per cent in the Punjab, between 1981 and 1990.[199] Against this numerical increase in the police force the 1990s witnessed arbitrary transfers of police personnel occur at a viciously debilitating rate. In Karachi, which accounted for some six-tenths of the state's revenues in the 1990s,[200] the average tenure of the officer in charge of a police station was two months and three days.[201] At a wider level the average DSP could look forward to being in one posting for five months and twelve days.[202] The numerical strength of the police in Sindh, which stood at twenty-four thousand in 1975, and sixty thousand in 1992, rose to over ninety-three thousand five hundred by 1999-2000.[203] Given that law and order in Sindh, especially Karachi, was handed over to the army in the mid-1990s, the continuous increase in the numerical strength of the police force demonstrated its inability to perform its functions. By October 1999, Pakistan stood on the verge of the collapse of the state of order.

5.5 The State of Order

Pakistan's rulers have not been as ill-advised as one may infer from their actions. Had Khwaja Nazimuddin taken G. Ahmad's note on the internal situation seriously he may have been able to save his government and in doing so placed limits on the power of the governing corporation. Zia, Junejo, and Ghulam Ishaq Khan, were provided at no cost to themselves an accurate and rational diagnosis of the state's problems and a thoroughly sane proposal for administrative reform by Ijlal Haider Zaidi, then establishment secretary. Had they considered it seriously they may well have secured for themselves the status of saviours and prolonged their stay in power. It is perhaps the mark of debility that even when sound advice is rendered the ruler fails to recognise its merits and either blindly defends the status quo or heedlessly takes the advice for sale on the international market and its local franchises.

In February 2000, Zafar Iqbal Rathore, a police officer who retired as interior secretary and was asked to chair the Focal Group on Police Reform constituted by the Musharraf regime submitted a note titled 'State and Order' to the interior minister Moinuddin Haider. This three page note accepted that the police leadership had been 'unimaginative at the best of times and arbitrary in the bargain.'[204] Rather than seriously applying itself to reform and understanding the need for it in a rapidly changing and turbulent society the political and bureaucratic leadership had 'massively subverted' the inherited system through 'large scale arbitrary interference'.[205] The basic principles of police organisation remained that of an early-twentieth century force, the ethos of this force had become utterly medieval, and it had become more dangerous as it had acquired some of the material trappings of modernisation. Rathore added that the rulers either tried to throw money at the problem or were scared into doing nothing and did not work to deal with the collapse of 'the state of order' in a firm and rational manner:

> Briefly speaking we have a Criminal Justice System...staffed mostly by people who are generally recruited, trained, promoted and posted without any reference to merit, and almost entirely by their subservience to people in power. *It is imperative that we take steps to improve the quality of the police personnel. Therefore, the first and basic reform which is necessary is to insulate the management of the police from the arbitrary interference of the powerful members of the executive. This can be done by creating a neutral body of eminent*

persons to manage the police. This body will also undertake accountability of the police. Since the Second World War this has been successfully done in almost all the countries of North America, Western Europe and Japan. The modalities of establishing these neutral bodies, depends on the legal and institutional conditions of different countries...but the objective is the same,—insulate the police management from arbitrary interference from the powerful members of the executive...

...As the state of order has nearly collapsed throughout the society, some areas being more affected than others, instead of trying for sustained improvement, we seem to panic, to react by promising huge funds and powers to individuals and departments who promise to rid us of this nightmare. This solution has neither worked before nor is it likely to work now.[206]

Instead of ensuring the autonomy of the police the devolution of power to elected local governments dominated by landlords with five to twelve years of education turned it into the servant of the elected district heads, the *nazims*. The police reforms required that the district police officer submit an annual policing plan to the district *nazim*.[207] This plan must be approved by the *nazim* and copies sent to the sub-districts, towns and provincial government.[208] The *nazims* have the power to inspect police stations and hold the district police accountable.[209] They also write the manuscript portion of the performance evaluation report of the district police officer and coordinate between the district coordination officer and the police.[210] To oversee the police and the *nazims* safety committees and complaints commissions drawing a third of their members from the ranks of national and provincial assembly members, a third from the district councils, and a third through selection by a panel, have been constituted,[211] for the most part on paper. Members of these committees and commissions are to elect their chairmen and submit annual reports to the government.[212] The same structure is replicated with modifications at the provincial and national levels with an assortment of commissions and authorities endlessly stumbling over each other.

In the meantime, the abolition of the commissioner system with police supervisory powers in the hands of the DMG combined with the non-functionality of the other 'institutional mechanisms' have produced dire consequences:

Since the promulgation of the Police Order, a corrupt and violence-prone force has been allowed a free hand without external accountability. In fact, selective implementation of the order in an overall environment of the absence of rule of law has resulted in a sharp rise in reported police excesses, crimes, and deteriorating law and order.[213]

In districts where the personal relationship between the *nazim* and the police head is good a degree of efficiency is attained, otherwise coordination has broken down and the police 'are widely accused of running a parallel government.'[214] By the end of 2002, it was found in a survey of ninety-seven districts and fifty-seven thousand households that only about one in four people would seek police assistance in the event of threat to life or property.[215]

A sample of case records from all four provinces found that 'in not a single case had the public safety or *insaf* [justice] committees played their prescribed role in monitoring the police and the courts, along with grassroots participation, to ensure an improved dispensation of justice.'[216] Studies of districts such as Toba Tek Singh in the Punjab and Larkana in Sindh revealed a picture of delay and confusion. In the former cases 'were pending three or fourfold more than the prescribed standard'[217] while in the latter police harassment, judicial neglect and flight of the accused 'led to prolonged delays of up to eight years.'[218] A mere 18 per cent of some four hundred respondents in an SDPI survey indicated confidence in the ability of the police to help resolve problems, against 22 per cent who preferred the judiciary.[219] On the other hand, a mere 10 per cent thought the new local government institutions capable of redressing their grievances and worthy of their preference for dispute resolution.[220]

With local governments raising a mere 8 per cent of their own finances and caste and kinship pressures running amok the 'state' is itself in danger of becoming extinct. The growing anarchy has begun affecting the areas thus far spared the devolution plan, such as Islamabad and the cantonments in the NWFP and Baluchistan. The softening of the state in the hinterlands at the precise moment when extremism and religious militancy are climaxing are crises that are beyond the capacity of a fractious and fragmenting police organisation to confront. The reality of an ungovernable country with a non-functional executive capable of establishing its writ only through the direct application of military force more than offsets any advantages that may accrue from the partial restoration of the judges sacked by Musharraf in his final though unsuccessful gambit to hang on to power.

The enormity of the challenge that confronts the democratically elected post-Musharraf dispensation does not seem to have sunk in as the PPP-led coalition at the centre struggles to assert its own authority and deal with other inherited crises such as the power shortage and the fiscal crisis against the backdrop of continuing terrorist attacks and insurgency in large parts of the North-West Frontier Province. With the core executive function in a state of ruin the other institutions cannot realistically stem the rising tide of 'terminal chaos' threatening the subcontinent in general and Pakistan in particular, in a manner comparable to the aftermath of the Timurid imperial eclipse.[221]

NOTES

1. Plutarch, *The Rise and Fall of Athens: Nine Greek Lives*, trans. Ian Scott-Kilvert (London: Penguin Books, 1964), 20.
2. Ibid., 23.
3. Ibid., 47.
4. Ibid.
5. Ibid.
6. Ibid., 65.
7. Herodotus states that Solon left Athens for ten years '…under the pretence of wishing to see the world, but really to avoid being forced to repeal any of the laws which, at the request of the Athenians, he had made for them.' Herodotus, *Histories*, 13.
8. Plutarch, *The Rise and Fall of Athens: Nine Greek Lives*, 63.
9. Ibid., 57.
10. Niccolo Machiavelli, *The Discourses*, trans. Leslie J. Walker, ed., Bernard Crick, rev., Brian Richardson (London: Penguin Books, 2003), 181.
11. H. B. Cotterill, *Ancient Greece: Myth and History* (New Lanark: Geddes & Grosset, 2004), 200.
12. Ibid., 202.
13. Ben Ray Redman, ed., *The Portable Voltaire* (New York: Viking Penguin Inc., 1977), 'Selections from the English Letters', 513.
14. Montesquieu, *The Spirit of Laws*, 151-62.
15. Redman, ed., *The Portable Voltaire*, 'Selections from the English Letters', 514.
16. Ibid.
17. Halil Inalick, *The Ottoman Empire: The Classical Age 1300-1600* (London: Phoenix, 2000), 13.
18. Ibid., 65.
19. Ibid., 73.

20. Daniel Goffman, *The Ottoman Empire and Early Modern Europe: New Approaches to European History* (Cambridge: University Press, 2002), 49.
21. The standard had been set by Amir Taimur himself. In 1404, upon returning to Samarkand, Taimur learned that the city administrators had been amassing wealth. Taimur order the chief mayor executed and instructed the imperial treasury to confiscate his property as an example to the others. One of the chief mayor's friends tried to plead for the condemned man's life. Taimur ordered the chief mayor's friend executed for offending his sense of justice. One of the imperial servants, who felt himself to be in Taimur's good graces, also begged the sovereign to spare the chief mayor's life. Taimur had him arrested and put to torture so as to determine the chief mayor's total wealth. After the torturers reported back that they had extracted all the information they could, Taimur ordered the official executed as well. Marozzi, *Tamerlane*, 82. Presumably, as was the custom, the properties of the chief mayor's friends and associates who tried to intercede on his behalf would have also been confiscated.
22. Eraly, *The Mughal World*, 237.
23. Ibid.
24. Ibid., 238.
25. Ibid.
26. Ibid., 266.
27. Khushwant Singh, *Ranjit Singh*, 161.
28. Ibid.
29. Ibid.
30. Ibid.
31. *Report on the Administration of Bengal 1874-1875* (Calcutta: Bengal Secretariat Press, 1876), 33.
32. Ibid.
33. *Report on the Administration of Bengal 1893-1894* (Calcutta: Bengal Secretariat Press, 1894), 14.
34. *Selection of Papers from the Records of the East India House*, Vol. II, 13.
35. *Report of the Commissioners for the Investigation of Alleged Cases of Torture in the Madras Presidency* (Madras: H. Smith at the Fort St. George Gazette Press, 1855), 23.
36. Ibid.
37. Ibid.
38. Ibid., 49.
39. Ibid. The 1872 Evidence Act made confessions in police custody or to officials of the police inadmissible in court.
40. Ibid., 62.
41. R. Bosworth Smith, *Life of Lord Lawrence*, Vol. I (London: Smith, Elder & Co., 1883), 290.
42. Abul Fazl Allami, *A'in-I Akbari*, trans. H. Blochmann (Calcutta: Calcutta Madrassah, 1873; reprint, Lahore: Sang-e-Meel Publications, 2003), 225.
43. E. Tyrwhitt, *Report on the Administration of the Police of the North-Western Province for the Year 1873* (Allahabad: North-Western Provinces' Government Press, 1874), 8.
44. Ibid., 20.

45. Ibid., 23.
46. Ibid.
47. *Report on the Administration of Bengal 1874-1875*, 24.
48. Ibid.
49. Ibid., 24-5.
50. Ibid., 25.
51. Ibid., 26.
52. Ibid., 30.
53. *Report on the Administration of the Punjab and its Dependencies for the year 1875-1876*, 30.
54. *Report on the Administration of Bengal 1874-1875*, 4.
55. Ibid., 15.
56. Ibid., 28.
57. Ibid.
58. *Report on the Administration of Bengal 1893-1894*, 14. The prisoner mortality rate was about thirty-two per thousand in the Punjab in 1875-76.
59. S. G. Jilani, *Fifteen Governors I Served with: The Untold Story of East Pakistan* (Lahore: Bookmark, 1979), 9.
60. Ibid., 10.
61. Inamur Rehman, *Public Opinion and Political Development in Pakistan 1947-1958*, 151.
62. Jilani, *Fifteen Governors I Served With*, 1.
63. Inamur Rehman, *Public Opinion and Political Development in Pakistan 1947-1958*, 151.
64. Ibid., 146.
65. Ibid., 150.
66. Syed Sharifuddin Pirzada, ed., *Dissolution of Constituent Assembly of Pakistan and the Legal Battles of Moulvi Tamizuddin* (Karachi: Asia Law House, 1995), i.
67. Ibid.
68. Ibid., 118.
69. Ibid., 126.
70. Ibid.
71. For more on Cornelius see Ralph Braibanti, ed., *Chief Justice Cornelius of Pakistan: An Analysis with Letters and Speeches* (Karachi: Oxford University Press, 2000). Intriguingly, Cornelius 'wanted to extend the jirga system' into the settled districts and praised it as a means of controlling the crime rate. Ibid., 35. In 1965, at the Third Commonwealth and Empire Conference on Law 'he suggested a modern variation of the amputation of limbs as a deterrent.' Ibid.
72. Pirzada, ed., *Dissolution of Constituent Assembly of Pakistan and the Legal Battles of Moulvi Tamizuddin* 214.
73. Ibid., 216.
74. Ibid., 217.
75. Jan Mohammed Dawood, *The Role of the Superior Judiciary in the Politics of Pakistan* (Karachi: Royal Book Company, 1994), 18.
76. Pirzada, ed., *Dissolution of Constituent Assembly of Pakistan and the Legal Battles of Moulvi Tamizuddin,* 294.
77. Ibid., 307.

78. In the original Timurid dominion, 'The priestly entourage owed its position to Temur, and in return for his generous patronage' made sure that whatever he did was explained as a perfectly just emanation of divine will. Indeed, the debate over whether Taimur adhered to Islamic or Mongol precepts of law and justice 'misses the point.' Taimur 'was interested in either code insofar as it supported' his policies and decisions. Marozzi, *Tamerlane*, 95-97. Pakistan's rulers have an analogous relationship with British, Islamic and customary laws and have created a bewildering constitutional and legal mess from which they can pick and choose whatever principle or detail in consonance with their arbitrary and self aggrandising behaviour.
79. 'Report of the Committee on the Study of Corruption, 1986', 68-9.
80. Baxter, ed., *Diaries of Field Marshal Mohammed Ayub Khan, 1966-1972*, 62. 17 February 1967.
81. Ibid.
82. Ibid.
83. 1960, File No. 178/CF/60, Government of Pakistan, President's Secretariat, 'Note on the Administration of Justice and Procedural Reforms', 2.
84. Ibid., 4-5.
85. Ibid., 3.
86. Ibid., 5.
87. Ibid.
88. *The Report of the Law Reform Commission 1958-59* (Karachi: Government of Pakistani Press, 1959), 101.
89. Memon, ed., *The Altaf Gauhar Papers*, 53.
90. Ibid.
91. Mohammad Yasin and Tariq Banuri, eds., *The Dispensation of Justice in Pakistan* (Karachi: Oxford University Press, 2004), 76.
92. Ibid., 89.
93. Ibid.
94. Nasim Hassan Shah, 'Judicial Administration', in Jamilur Rehman Khan, ed., *Government and Administration in Pakistan*, 258.
95. Memon, ed., *The Altaf Gauhar Papers*, 183-4.
96. Ibid., 183.
97. Ibid., 232.
98. *The Report of the Law Reform Commission 1967-1970* (Karachi: Government of Pakistan Press, 1970), 149.
99. Ibid.
100. Ibid.
101. Nasim Hassan Shah, 'Judicial Administration', 294.
102. *The Report of the Law Reform Commission, 1967-1970*, 113.
103. Hassan Shah, 'Judicial Administration', 255-6.
104. Jilani, *Fifteen Governors I Served With*, 19.
105. Ibid.
106. Ibid.
107. Ibid.
108. Dorab Patel, *Testament of a Liberal* (Karachi: Oxford University Press, 2000), 79.

109. Ibid., 78.
110. Ibid., 95.
111. Abdul Rehman Siddiqui, *East Pakistan: The End Game, An Onlooker's Journal, 1969-71* (Karachi: Oxford University Press, 2004), 17.
112. Ibid., 16.
113. Ibid., 98.
114. Patel, *Testament of a Liberal*, 95.
115. *The Report of the Hamood-ur-Rehman Commission of Inquiry into the 1971 War*, 63.
116. Ibid.
117. *White Paper on the Performance of the Bhutto Regime*, Vol. II, *Treatment of Fundamental State Institutions*, 44.
118. Ibid., 70.
119. Patel, *Testament of a Liberal*, 121.
120. Ibid.
121. *White Paper on the Performance of the Bhutto Regime*, Vol. II, *Treatment of Fundamental State Institutions*, 47.
122. Ibid., 51.
123. *White Paper on the Performance of the Bhutto Regime*, Vol. II, *Treatment of Fundamental State Institutions*, 107.
124. Ibid., 113.
125. Ibid., 108.
126. Asghar Khan, *We've Learnt Nothing from History: Pakistan Politics and Military Power* (Karachi: Oxford University Press, 2005), 175.
127. Patel, *Testament of a Liberal*, 180. Justice Dorab Patel refused to take the oath and was consequently dismissed.
128. Ibid., 181.
129. Ibid.
130. Ibid.
131. Zahid Hussain, *Frontline Pakistan: The Struggle With Militant Islam* (New Delhi: Penguin Books India, 2007), 79.
132. Ibid.
133. Yasin, ed., *District and Police Systems in Pakistan*, 200.
134. Nasim Hassan Shah, *Memoirs and Reflections* (Islamabad: Alhamra Publishing, 2002), 124.
135. Ibid.
136. Ibid.
137. In the period prior to his removal Sajjad Ali Shah reveals that he considered it perfectly normal for himself to be consulted on matters of national importance. When the crisis between the executive and judiciary came to a head Shah asked the president to provide security and deploy paramilitaries and military units to protect the Supreme Court from the prime minister. Sajjad Ali Shah, *Law Courts in a Glass House*, 508-509.
138. Yasin and Banuri, eds., *The Dispensation of Justice in Pakistan*, 172.
139. Ibid., 102.
140. Ibid., Appendix 13.
141. Ibid., Appendix 19.

142. Ibid., 90.
143. 'Report of the Committee for the Study of Corruption, 1986', 239.
144. Ibid.
145. Ibid.
146. *Joint Committee on Indian Constitutional Reform Session 1933-34*, vol. I, part I (London: His Majesty's Stationery Office, 1934), 13.
147. Ibid., 50.
148. Ibid.
149. Ibid., 174.
150. Ibid.
151. Braibanti, 'Public Bureaucracy and Judiciary in Pakistan' in Joseph LaPolambara, ed., *Bureaucracy and Political Development*, 347.
152. Ibid.
153. *Report of the East Bengal Police Committee* (Dacca: East Bengal Government Press, 1954), 7.
154. Ibid.
155. Ibid.
156. Ibid.
157. Ibid., 8.
158. Ibid.
159. Ibid., 47.
160. *Report of the Pakistan Police Commission, 1960-61* (Rawalpindi: Government of Pakistan Press, 1961), 48.
161. Ibid., 23.
162. Ibid.
163. Ibid., 62.
164. *Report of the Pakistan Police Commission 1969-70* (Rawalpindi: Police Commission Secretariat, 1970), 32.
165. Ibid., 53.
166. Ibid., 93-94.
167. Ibid., 94-95.
168. Ibid., 96.
169. Ibid., 13.
170. Ibid., 14.
171. Ibid., 13.
172. Ibid.
173. Ibid., 100.
174. *G. Ahmad's Committee on Police Organisation and Reforms in Pakistan* (Islamabad: Government of Pakistan, 1972), 6.
175. *Report of the Subcommittee on Law and Order 1976* (Islamabad: Government of Pakistan Press, 18.
176. Ibid., 19.
177. Ibid., 15.
178. Ibid., 13.
179. Ibid., 8.
180. Ibid., 9.

181. *Appraisal of Police Administration in the Islamic Republic of Pakistan by Romanian Police Experts* (Rawalpindi: Government Press, 1976), 2.
182. S. D. Jamy, 'Police Administration' in Jamilur Rehman Khan, ed., *Government and Administration in Pakistan*, 441.
183. Ibid., 442.
184. Ibid.
185. 'Report of the Committee for the Study of Corruption, 1986', 34.
186. Ibid., 34.
187. Ibid.
188. A. J. Giles, *Final Report of Chief Superintendent A. J. Giles, British Police* (Islamabad: Interior Division, 1984), 24.
189. Ibid. In Britain all police officers joined as constables and rose through intra-department exams to higher positions. In Pakistan, the class structure had been retained even with the introduction of Unified Grades under Bhutto. The structural flexibility of the police had been greater under the old system.
190. Ibid.
191. Ibid., 9-10.
192. Ibid., 11.
193. Ibid., 9.
194. Ibid. 11.
195. Ibid., 14.
196. Yasin, ed., *District and Police Systems in Pakistan*, 165-166.
197. Ibid., 162.
198. Ibid., 164.
199. Ibid., 200.
200. Nadeem, *Pakistan: The Political Economy of Lawlessness*, 163.
201. Siddiqui, *Towards Good Governance*, 43.
202. Ibid.
203. Ibid., 40.
204. Zafar Iqbal Rathore, Chairman of the Focal Group on Police Reform. Rahore Papers, 'State and Order'. Paper presented to the Interior Minister, Lt. General Moinuddin Haider, February 2000, 2.
205. Ibid.
206. Ibid., Emphases in the original.
207. *The Police Order 2002, Updated Version* (Islamabad: National Reconstruction Bureau, 2007), 17.
208. Ibid.
209. Ibid.
210. Ibid., 17-18.
211. Ibid., 20.
212. Ibid., 23.
213. *Devolution in Pakistan*, 20.
214. Ibid.
215. A. Cockcroft, N. Anderson, K. Omer, et. al., 'Social Audit of Governance and Delivery of Public Services: Base Line 2002 National Report'. Paper Presented at Conference on State of Social Sciences and Humanities: Current Scenario and Emerging Trends, December, 2003.

216. Shahrukh Rafi Khan, *Initiating Devolution for Service Delivery*, 202.
217. Ibid.
218. Ibid., 216.
219. Ibid., 200.
220. Ibid.
221. Eraly, *The Mughal World*, 382.

6 Diwans

6.1 Tax Imperia

The pre-modern continental bureaucratic empire was not so much a state as it was an agency engaged in the extraction of revenue through all means at its disposal from the society it governed. The mandarins, guardians, praetorians and ideocrats through whom power was exercised and mediated, needed to be fed, trained, equipped, motivated and, above all else, remunerated. Martial and artistic aggrandisement required funds as did the confidential servants of the sovereign. The sovereign also had to appear as a benevolent entity and there being little moral relationship between himself and his servants and subjects, ceremonial occasions necessitated acts of generosity such as the remission of tax revenues, festivals, bazaars and the giving away of gifts in the form of land grants, titles and expensive jewellery. The ruler and servants also maintained lavish lifestyles and lived in unrivalled splendour and grandeur. All of this required wealth.

Kautilya understood the relationship between power and wealth and proclaimed that 'From wealth (*kosa*) comes the power of the Government (*danda*).[1] With the treasury and the army the earth is acquired with the treasury as the ornament.'[2] The state depended upon the 'power of its Treasury' which in turn made possible a stronger state capable of acquiring more territory and extracting greater revenues.[3] Kautilya advised the ruler to take great care in selecting his taxation officers. An overzealous officer who extracted more than the assessed revenue would ruin the country while a generous spendthrift would make unreasonable programs for expenditure and spoil the people while wasting the emperor's revenues. Especially dangerous were those officers who ate up the imperial revenues and colluded with locals. In order to keep the financial administration in check, the chancellors, ministers and *adhyakshas* or departmental heads that corresponded to the rank of federal or union secretaries in Pakistan and India, were enjoined to 'employ the secret agents to ensure that the servants of the State perform their duties.'[4] The senior officers were themselves under surveillance and subject directly to imperial wrath the objectives of which included rendering them compliant before the emperor and turning them into instruments for the projection of the emperor's omniscience and omnipotence lower down the bureaucracy. The emperor was thus advised in his own interest to act as a rational parasite so that the gathering of taxes worked smoothly without excessive damage to the cultivator, artisan and merchant. It is fitting that *artha* means wealth and the *Arthashastra* translates roughly as the 'Science/Discipline of Wealth'. Theoretic pieties, however, did not prevent continental bureaucratic empires from becoming insatiable leviathans.[5]

The Timurid Empire was a remarkably effective revenue generating machine. It extracted between a third and a half of GNP as revenue and distributed this wealth amongst the administrative elite.[6] At its peak efficiency in 1647, the Timurid Empire generated two hundred and twenty million rupees of revenue. Almost six-tenths of this revenue, or one hundred and thirty-two million rupees, was received by the four hundred and fifty-five highest *mansabdar*s.[7] If we accept the lower estimate that the total revenues were one-third of GNP, then it would equal six hundred and sixty million rupees. This in turn would mean that four hundred and fifty-five individuals were allocated one-fifth of the Timurid Empire's GNP. About three-fourths of total revenues were spent on the maintenance of the military, paramilitary and militia forces while the rest was spent on the lifestyle of the administrative elite. The military assisted the provincial revenue authorities headed by provincial *diwan*s who rivalled the governors and were answerable directly to the emperor. A large number of troops were worthy but poor and so received a horse and lands from the state with Turks and Persians paid twenty-five rupees per month, Indians twenty rupees a month, and if employed to collect revenues the troops got only fifteen rupees per month.[8]

The concentration of revenue resources and the absence of a clear or enforceable distinction between personal and public expenditure meant that only a fraction of the total revenues was actually translated into assets that could be deployed by the state. *Mansabdar*s routinely cheated the emperor by failing to maintain the requisite number of troops, horses, and stores. The emperor cheated the *mansabdar*s by assigning overvalued *jagir*s, delaying salary payments and appointments, transferring them too frequently, and confiscating their assets when they fell from favour or died. When the central agency weakened from 1660 onwards, it became harder for the state to manage its resources. The number of officers increased while the value of assignments in land as well as salaries decreased. Rather than working to improve the quality of the administration, rates of taxation were increased and taxes abolished by earlier emperors, such as the poll-tax on non-Muslims, were levied. These increases were self-defeating for they destroyed the productive base of the Timurid Empire, rendered it harder to govern, and led to the emergence of tax-farming. Many of the tax-farmers and *mansabdar*s carved out estates for themselves, levied additional taxes and extorted as much as they could. Even the most powerful successor states to the Timurid Empire, such as the Sikh kingdom and the Maratha Confederacy, failed to develop a regular system of revenue administration and relied heavily on plunder as opposed to regular taxation.

The rise of the British Empire in India in these chaotic conditions led to significant changes in the financial administration and political economy of India. Three aspects, in particular, stand out in the case of what has been referred to as the 'Tax Britannica.'[9] The first was the introduction of parliamentary financial control and regular budgeting and accounting procedures.[10] The second was the low ratio of taxes to GDP and the underlying changes to India's sources of revenue. And the third was the remarkably high proportion of what would today be called development expenditure.

The 'modern budgeting system' was 'developed in the West' in response to the growth of representative institutions in both their classical and feudal incarnations over a long period of time with many breaks and checks in the process.[11] Although in England parliamentary institutions steadily gained control of public finances, from 1200 onwards it was Robert Walpole who used the term budget for the first time to describe his annual plan for revenue and expenditure.[12] Ultimate supervision of the Indian budget, first introduced in 1860, rested with the British Parliament and the India Office while the system of financial controls 'were primarily characterised by a concern to ensure accountability of expenditure.'[13] The system was also highly centralised under the finance member of the vice-regal council.[14] The auditing system was based on 'regular scrutiny' with 'periodic and percentage checks of governmental financial transactions.'[15] The effort was to detect cases of breach of rules, wastage, 'loss of funds or violations of financial propriety' and 'unearth procedural deficiencies and system failures.'[16] From 1921, a Public Accounts Committee was constituted to oversee the auditing process and review its reports.[17] In April 1924, the Central Board of Revenue (CBR) was established to collect revenues from growing non-provincial sources such as customs, excise, and income tax, as the share of land revenue in total revenues steadily diminished.

The tax-to-GDP ratio in British India varied between 5 and 10 per cent.[18] The share of land revenue in total revenues declined from 53 per cent in 1900 to 7 per cent in 1946.[19] The share of the salt tax declined from 16 per cent in 1900 to 2 per cent in 1946.[20] On the other hand the share of customs, excise, and income tax revenues rose from 9, 10, and 3 per cent respectively in 1900 to 22, and 37 per cent in 1946.[21] Of the total revenues about 40 per cent were collected by the provinces and though the relative decline in land revenue and increase in total expenditures produced dislocation the power to raise and levy sales tax meant that the provinces possessed a viable and growing source of revenue that could allow them to retain significant fiscal autonomy.

A curious feature of what is characterised as the status quo and law and order oriented British Raj was its high level of development expenditure, especially on infrastructure. In 1900, the total percentage of the budget spent on defence was 22 per cent against 21 per cent on health, education, and capital outlay. In 1946, defence received 26 per cent of the budget while health, education, and capital outlay accounted for 31 per cent of the budget. Debt servicing remained well below 10 per cent of the budget for the most part and the total expenditure on the administration fell from 24 per cent in 1900 to 15 per cent in 1946. This freed up resources for financing activities as diverse as village cooperatives and heavy industries. Even more remarkable was the fiscal stability maintained through two world wars and a global economic depression with the unintended result that Britain ended up owing India money while the latter gained independence with a robust positive sterling balance. The modest levels of total collection combined with effective checks on expenditure meant that money was spent against items of real value and thus did not fuel inflation, corruption and wastage, until the speculative boom of the Second World War.[22] The challenges before the Indian and Pakistani leaderships included the mopping-up of the ill-effects of the war, increasing the tax-to-GDP ratio, the reorientation of the taxation system from indirect taxes on consumption to direct taxes on incomes, improving the quality of the taxation personnel, and effective modernisation of the land revenue administration.[23] The latter sector in particular affected nine-tenths of the population even though it no longer generated a large share of total revenues.

6.2 A Free Country

Between 1952 and 2006, Pakistan's tax-to-GDP ratio ranged between 8 and 15 per cent with an effective median range of 10 to 12 per cent. Within the taxes about four-fifths of tax revenues came from indirect taxes such as customs, excise, sales tax and withholding taxes (WHT), technically counted as direct taxes but effectively indirect and regressive in operation.[24] Income and corporation taxes which accounted for 16 per cent of total revenues in 1952-1953[25] had, by 1988, fallen to about 10 per cent of total revenues.[26] The aversion to raising taxes on income was explained in terms of their supposed tendency to punish the honest taxpayer and their insufficient redistributive impact.[27] The 'issue of direct versus indirect taxes' was dismissed as being 'largely of academic interest' as an 'indirect tax system' could attain a high degree of progressiveness through applying different rates on separate categories of items.[28] It is fascinating that when these words were written Pakistan's tax-to-GDP ratio was 13 per cent while government spending stood at 25 per cent of GDP.[29] The difference was made up through foreign loans with $4 billion worth raised between 1972 and 1977.[30] That said, in 1960-1961 the tax-to-GDP ratio stood at 9 per cent.[31] Ayub's greatest economic asset was ready access to foreign funds on favourable terms and in 1962 73 per cent 'of the total resources available to spend in Pakistan...were external funds' while in 1966 this figure was 74 per cent.[32]

From a very early stage, Pakistan's rulers took to loans and aid as convenient devices for avoiding substantial reform and rejuvenation of the tax administration. Without making the effort to raise tax collection they splurged on defence and development and took loans to make up the difference. In 1990, Pakistan's debt was $20 billion and by May 1998 it increased to $43 billion.[33] While in 1990, 36 per cent of government revenues were spent on paying interest, by mid-1999, 61 per cent had to be spent on interest payments.[34] The tax-to-GDP ratio fell from 14 per cent in 1994-1995 to 13 per cent in 1999-2000 and 11 per cent in 2005-2006. Even the most competent financial administrators defined success in terms of securing foreign loans on whatever terms possible. In the context of the political instability of the late-1980s and 1990s, the rotation of governments led to nine agreements being signed between Pakistan and the International Monetary Fund (IMF).[35] Given that the IMF 'enjoys excessive concentration of power, and has virtual monopoly of knowledge and ideas in prescribing what are the right policies'[36] it pushed Pakistan along the path of trade liberalisation and structural adjustment. This meant a reduction in customs receipts which the state made good by raising the sales tax and withholding taxes, especially on transactions and withdrawals. It also meant that Pakistan's ratio of taxes to GDP remained low while dependency on external funding was reinforced.

As of June 2006 Pakistan, had one and half million income tax payers (population one hundred and sixty million) and one hundred and seventeen thousand sales tax payers.[37] Direct taxes were estimated at 30 per cent of the seven hundred and twelve billion rupees ($12 billion at the exchange rate prevalent at the time) of revenue collected but of these 60 per cent were withholding taxes with 'deductions...made at the source' on twenty-five heads including contracts, telephones and cash withdrawals.[38] The criticism of the withholding taxes notwithstanding they were 'regarded as an effective mechanism to improve the tax net given the large segment of informal/undocumented economy.'[39] In June 2006, the direct taxes amounted to 3 per cent of GDP. Relative to the size of GDP and its commitments Pakistan is less able today to generate revenue through taxation of its own land, people, and resources than in the crisis-ridden mid-1990s. Without the generous influx of American aid and the rescheduling of debts in exchange for cooperation with US strategic objectives and loans from international financial institutions, which amounted to $15 billion between 2003 and 2007, Pakistan's financial administration would simply collapse. This dismal fiscal performance has contributed to Pakistan's ungovernableness and is the consequence of the structure and ethos of the financial administration.

6.3 To and From the Centre

The central government in Pakistan collects 90 per cent of all revenues. The one dynamic source of revenue the provinces had in the form of the sales tax was taken from them in 1948 to meet the challenges of the state of siege. While some senior officers, such as A. G. N. Kazi, argued that the sales tax and proposed income tax on agriculture should be handed over to the provinces and that provincial fiscal autonomy would allow *more* taxes to be collected and *reduce* provincial liabilities, no changes were made in the structure of taxation.[40] Simply increasing the size of the divisible pool, Kazi argued, would only result in more political pressure 'being built up for its division.'[41] This scramble for resources doled out by the centre fuelled provincial discord and could be dealt with if the sales tax was 'placed in the provincial sphere of taxation.'[42]

The disparity between central and provincial revenues is plainly evident. In 1987 and 1994, the centre raised from the sources under its control, eighty-nine billion rupees and two hundred and fifty-seven billion rupees in tax revenues, respectively.[43] Against this, the provincial revenues from taxation amounted to four and a half billion rupees in 1987 and nine and a half billion rupees in 1994.[44] Thus the provincial tax revenues as a percentage of central tax revenues stood at 5 per cent in 1987 and about 4 per cent in 1994. This was the trend from the late 1980s to the mid-1990s and it was therefore hardly surprising that in 2006, the centre accounted for 92 per cent of total revenue collection and financed the provincial and local governments through a system of awards and transfers that begin and end with the central government.

As the centre collects taxes and negotiates deficits by borrowing from home and abroad it is natural that it should control and directly administer expenditure in areas that affect local and provincial interests. One of the fundamental imbalances in Pakistan's financial administration is that while almost everything that materially affects the quality of life of the average citizen, such as health, education, law and order, municipal services, and conciliation, falls under the statutory purview of provincial or local governments, almost the entire allocation and spending is done through the central government. In 1979 the centre accounted for some three-fourths of the total state expenditure while in 1989 it accounted for seven-tenths of the total.[45] After federal expenses were met the balance was shared amongst the provinces through central award and transfers. Current expenditure rose from 10 per cent of GDP to 18 per cent of GDP in between 1971 and 1994, development expenditure peaked at 11 per cent of GDP in 1976 and thereafter went into decline until 2002.[46] By 1994, development expenditure stood at about 4 per cent of GDP against nearly 6 per cent for defence and 5 per cent for interest payments.[47]

The wastage that an over-centralised, often incompetent, and utterly unaccountable financial administration engages in is enormous. Revenues are raised through indirect taxes on consumption, which punish the poor and middle classes, or through withholding taxes and taxes on savings which, again, hit the lower income groups the hardest. The rich get away with minimal taxation and to make up the difference between its tax revenue and expenditure the government borrows from any and all sources and prints money thus fuelling price inflation that again crushes the urban poor and middle classes and rural wage labourers.[48] Since the borrowed amount has to be paid back through tax revenues, it effectively means that the poor will be taxed disproportionately to raise the requisite funds. The borrowed funds are often allocated for development spending and projects intended for the benefit of the poor. Planning and execution by remote control, however, means that only 'a small ratio' of what is spent or budgeted actually reaches the 'earmarked target groups'.[49] Most of the money spent by the centre on development 'has either lined the pockets of the consultants, contractors, and engineers or has simply been wasted.'[50] Central expenditures and transfers for development represent a terrible haemorrhage of largely borrowed funds that the Pakistani poor will have to repay through the indirect taxation pitilessly visited upon them and the direct taxation imposed on the middleclass professionals who operate in the formal sector.[51] On balance, 'only 30 per cent of the benefit of development funds actually reaches the target groups.'[52] Other officials put the leakage at as high as 80 or 90 per cent but hardly anyone would be prepared to admit in private to more than a third of development funding actually reaching the intended beneficiaries. If we accept the conservative estimate it means that if Pakistan spends 6 per cent of GDP on development, 4 per cent of GDP would be wasted. Given the low tax-to-GDP ratio this translates into the direct wastage by the centre of about a third of the tax revenues it generates through an overwhelmingly regressive taxation regime. Since the rich make do for themselves, it may be advisable that the state reduces development expenditure to 2 per cent of GDP, rigorously supervises its disbursement and eliminates indirect taxes on items such as edible oils, tea, cigarettes, medicines, and other items of daily consumption and try to curtail its propensity to hurt the poor by superficially trying to help them. The undermining of the inspectorial controls on the administration as a whole were and are precisely the cause of general decay in the ability of the apparatus to raise and spend revenues. Qualitatively, however, centralisation of the revenue collection and expenditure has a singular advantage in that the CBR is the institution primarily responsible for collecting taxes and thus by improving its performance the financial administration can be salvaged.

Taking stock of the situation the Taskforce on the Reform of Tax Administration constituted by the Musharraf regime, reflected that Pakistan's financial administration had evolved along five mutually reinforcing lines. The most important was the sheer arbitrariness and frequency with which 'legal and administrative changes were made.'[53] Whereas between 1947 and 1988, the CBR had fifteen heads making for an average tenure of two years and ten months, it had thirteen heads between 1988 and 1999 making for an average tenure of ten months. Even the status of the CBR changed from one government to another. With such arbitrariness governing the status and leadership of the CBR it was not surprising that 'major policy changes' were 'not accompanied by adequate changes in the administrative framework.'[54] The relationship between the tax payers and collectors was substantially adversarial, while the collection machinery had failed to keep pace 'with the growing demands on tax administration.'[55] The CBR itself was pinned down by its own mass and lack of efficiency in personnel management. The tax officials were simply 'not paid a living wage' while honesty was an almost impossible proposition with the bulk of the 33,000 persons employed in the tax administration locked in 'the lower ranks with low productivity' which made for an immense 'drag on the system.'[56] Since 1947 the tax-to-GDP ratio 'varied narrowly around 11 per cent' and income tax payers were 'less than 1 per cent of the population.'[57] The Taskforce warned:

> Pakistan's fiscal crisis is deep and cannot be easily resolved. Taxes are insufficient for debt service and defence. If the tax to GDP ratio does not

increase significantly, Pakistan can not be governed effectively, essential public services can not be delivered and high inflation is inevitable.[58]

Pakistan's Old Regime, like its French counterpart two centuries earlier, had reached a point where it had to either raise more taxes, or hope for a miracle, or await its inevitable demise. As it happened, the revival of strategic and economic ties with the United States of America following the 11 September 2001 attacks, gave the Pakistani ruling elite a respite. Instead of taking the opportunity to reform it soon reverted to its old habits and allowed the tax-to-GDP ratio to remain stagnant at around 11 per cent.

About 70 per cent of the direct taxes collected were withholding taxes and many of these were presumptive taxes levied on transactions and could not in any honesty 'qualify as income tax.'[59] Thus, *real* taxes on earned income accounted for 1 per cent of GDP. Of the one million tax payers four hundred and forty thousand were salaried persons, many of them government servants, and 'subject to little scrutiny.'[60] About two hundred and seventy-five thousand fell under the self-assessment scheme and only about 25 to 30 per cent of income tax payers received more detailed scrutiny.[61] Whereas in 2000, 0.7 per cent of the population paid income tax,[62] in June 2006, 0.9 per cent of the population paid income tax.[63] The income tax collectors and assessors routinely lost files or tampered with them and were 'ill equipped for the job, particularly to deal with complex tax returns of businesses.'[64] These poorly trained and remunerated collectors would 'arbitrarily fix the taxpayer's income and expenses' and also being involved in the appeals process could effectively coerce the honest and collude with the dishonest.[65] All too frequently the taxes were 'negotiated, with substantial loss to the treasury' and profit to the collectors and payers.[66] At the stroke of a pen a low grade employee can substantially increase or decrease the tax liability of a businessman or industrialist. If, however, the taxpayer opted for collusion with the taxation staff they became subject to blackmail. If they refused to collude then over-assessment could ruin them financially and open the door to endless litigation.

The sales tax generated revenues equal to 4 per cent of GDP albeit with only sixty-two thousand registered taxpayers in 2000.[67] In June 2006, the number of registered taxpayers under this head had risen to one hundred and seventeen thousand[68] although a mere seventeen industries contributed 80 per cent of all indirect taxes with half of them accounted for by petroleum, automobiles, machinery, cigarettes, telecom and iron and steel.[69] The auditing mechanism had broken down with productivity reduced to '1.2 audits per auditor per month' as against the international standard of '5 audits per auditor per month.'[70] Twenty-nine per cent of the audit staff was 'conducting work other than audit and refund scrutiny.'[71] In terms of effectiveness this meant that 93 per cent of general sales tax (GST) payers would not be audited in any given year making detection of malpractice an accidental occurrence.[72]

Between 1952 and 1991, the customs department, which was the major revenue generator, was steadily declining in relative importance due to international trade liberalisation. By 2000, its contribution to tax revenues stood at 18 per cent. Even in its declining role the customs maintained 'a large number of low paid employees' who demanded 'speed money' for moving documents from one desk to another or retrieval of any document from congested and chaotic record rooms.'[73] The lot of the supplicant was characterised by inordinate and unpredictable delays and addition to compliance costs.[74] The system was tedious, wasted time and lent itself admirably to collusive malpractice between businessmen and customs agents.[75] Customs procedures had changed little from the early twentieth century and were defensive relics of an age when the volume of trade was relatively small and trade policies were restrictive.[76] The introduction of greater automation and computerisation under electronic governance initiatives displaced a proportion of the obstruction and corruption to the data entry and control staff and actually made such illicit activities faster and more efficient as senior officers often lacked the supervisory skills. One senior official remarked that in the absence of governance, attempts to introduce electronic governance were laughable as even of the tiny percentage of citizens with computers most would simply not trust the state with their credit card numbers. Ultimately, it would appear, it was the quality of the tax administration personnel, not the electronic equipment at their disposal, which mattered.

The quality of the tax administration personnel was poor and characterised by demoralisation, internecine rivalries and general incompetence. Seventy-five per cent of the officers were recruited though the Central Superior Services (CSS) examinations for the income tax and customs groups and 25 per cent through promotion from the lower grades. The CSS, being a general exam in which higher aggregate marks determine the cadre into which successful candidates are inducted, did not bring in people with requisite background knowledge of economics, public administration and humanities, while the 'recruitment of non-officers is heavily influenced by interest groups and has resulted in the employment of a large number of unqualified and incompetent people.'[77] Promotions were too slow and based primarily on seniority which led to mediocre and corrupt timeservers moving up with competent officers, breeding a sense of entitlement amongst the former and exasperation amongst the latter. With the ratio of one officer to ten non-officers in the direct taxes administration and one officer to thirty-nine non-officers in the indirect taxes administration, effective supervision was next to impossible.[78]

Intriguingly, the post-2002 reforms have not improved the actual performance of the CBR even relative to its performance between 1995 and 2000. During these five immensely difficult years the number of income tax returns rose from two hundred and fifty thousand to one million. Since 2000 only five hundred thousand new income tax payers have been added. The rate of increase in the case of income taxes is thus absolutely and relatively inferior to 1995-2000. On the sales tax front the number of returns filed rose from thirty thousand in 1995 to sixty-two thousand in 2000, while by June 2006 the total was one hundred and seventeen thousand. The absolute increase is impressive but the relative increase is inferior to that achieved in 1995-2000. The difference is probably due to the non-availability of easy money from abroad during the 1990s. Post-2001, when foreign funds became available on relatively easy terms, the government allowed the tax-to-GDP ratio to remain stagnant in the 10 to 11 per cent range and avoided taking politically difficult decisions to redress the structural weaknesses in the financial administration.

The CBR had gradually been converted into an instrument of 'the rulers and their interest groups.'[79] Successive regimes beginning with the import substitution industrialisation policies of the 1950s and 1960s used the taxation system to reward favourites and cronies with bonuses, exemptions, tip-offs, and other forms of policy manipulation. The beneficiaries of this largesse were trader-merchants such as the Adamjees, Dawoods, Saigols, Isphahanis, Karims, etc., who were first given industrial assets out of the evacuee pool or built by the PIDC and then patronised by the state through protective barriers and special treatment in order to convert them into industrial capitalists.[80] Later rulers resorted to cruder devices such as the issue of special temporary exemptions on customs duties on individual items or industries. In this manner temporary reductions on duties along with the intended beneficiaries given adequate forewarning were granted for luxury cars, sugar, computer parts and scrap metal during the 1990s.[81] Those who stood up to the rulers 'had to pay a price' in terms of transfers and circumvention and the executive's consistent effort since the 1950s was to place 'handpicked officers in key positions in the tax administration to get their work done.'[82]

With the rulers treating the revenues and the institutions and officers responsible for their collection in an arbitrary and proprietorial manner, the scribes and accountants were liable to do the same, some enthusiastically, other cautiously, and quite a few out of sheer desperation. An officer testified to this effect:

> I joined service with great enthusiasm and a mission to serve the people. Unfortunately, I had to start my career with breaking a law and it has been the same ever since. I was forced to break the law as the State conveniently ignored its responsibilities towards it employees. My bosses were completely indifferent to our situation. Islamabad, in its wisdom, simply directs us to open two more offices and then expects to fend for ourselves. The situation is so bad that one has to be dishonest just to keep ones people honest.
>
> I am expected to pay for my petrol when I go for official rounds. I am expected to pay for paper, typing, photocopying, even postage. All of this is official work. It adds up to Rs 6000 per month. Am I mad to pay it from my pocket? What do they (Islamabad) expect? They know everything.[83]

In April 2009, eight years after the Taskforce on Reform of Tax Administration submitted its report the basic pay of a junior officer in grade eighteen is approximately fourteen thousand rupees per month. Including all other allowances the amount reaches twenty-two to thirty thousand rupees per month. With inflation in the range of nearly 20 per cent it is simply surreal to expect that the tax administration will not, like its medieval equivalents, live off the land. The instances 'where tax collectors are expected to deliver by 'living off the land' are innumerable.'[84] This practice 'has led to massive' disheartening effects and shattered the junior officers' trust in the competence and sincerity of senior officers dissolving institutional cohesion and *esprit de corps*. The predator-prey mindset that this mode of tax administration has encouraged has led as many people as possible to try and escape contact with collectors and find that it is more economical and less stressful to evade taxes than to actually pay them.[85]

The environment within the CBR was vitiated by the politicised manner of recruitment of the lower staff and the role of vested interests in filling up the ranks of promoted officers. The officers who came via the CSS exams were often too old to be trained in the highly technical and complex profession they found themselves in. The Common Training Program was too short, irrelevant, and of little professional value though it did allow the new entrants to network with those in other occupational groups. The Specialised Training Program was hampered by inadequate faculty, a lack of professional orientation, and was of little utility to the officers insofar as their actual duties were concerned. These new recruits, most of them lacking the proper educational background, and having received woefully inadequate training, were thrown into battle against thirty thousand entrenched clerks, accountants, assistants and support staff, often without support or guidance from their senior colleagues.

Whether on the direct or indirect taxes side, officers were surrounded by colleagues divided into those who cannot work and those who do not work. In the case of the direct taxes administration there were fourteen thousand staff in grades one through fifteen while in the indirect taxes administration there were about sixteen thousand five hundred, or 90, and 92 per cent of the total establishment strengths, respectively.[86] When the non-officers in grade sixteen were added the percentage of officers was 6.5 per cent in the direct taxes administration and 2.5 per cent in the indirect taxes administration.[87] The patently 'irrational manpower recruitment policy' had immersed the CBR in a 'clerical culture' that infected and overwhelmed officers.[88] The majority of the employees were 'unproductive' but their maintenance in terms of salaries and benefits resulted in 'inadequate salaries for all employees.'[89] With far too many officers 'paying almost their entire salaries for house rent' thanks to the equalisation and democratisation of public sector salaries pursued by successive regimes, the CBR was plagued by demoralisation, poor performance, and corruption.[90]

While the system has been tinkered with no fundamental reform has been attempted. The 2005-2006 year book for the CBR proclaimed that the tax administration had been 'transformed into a modern, progressive, effective and credible organisation' and boasted that its 'new LOGO and FLAG' inaugurated by the then prime minister Shaukat Aziz, were of great significance and thus 'both these events have been given due prominence.'[91] This self-congratulatory rhetoric is a manifestation of the state apparatus's desire to please the boss and engage in crude self-deception. Rhetoric about promoting a better tax culture aside, reform of the financial administration needs to confront the propensity of the rulers and their servants to act arbitrarily and unaccountably. Another manifestation of the same tendency is the neglect of the rural administration, particularly the land revenue administration, which directly affects seven-tenths of the Pakistani population that lives in the countryside.

6.4 Forgotten Lands

Even in 2006-2007, agriculture directly accounts for one-fourth of Pakistan's GDP and employs the bulk of the workforce. Its capitalist side provides Pakistan's textile, tobacco, food processing and leather goods industries with raw material. In between harvests agricultural labour is often used for such backbreaking work as cleaning canals and waterways or less strenuous activities such as domestic help in the urban areas. With only 1 per cent of landowners in possession of over fifty acres of land, the vast majority of rural denizens are subsistence farmers, tenants, or serfs. With as much as 70 per cent of the population living in the countryside trying to eke out a meagre existence from increasingly uneconomic landholdings, it is *their* interaction with the state that constitutes the preponderance of Pakistan's experience of governance. To the policy planners, development experts, and senior officials, the agriculturalist is a victim of history and part of the collateral damage of the war for industrialisation. Through the interplay of the cynical indifference of officialdom and the utopian certainties of the development community there remains the unmitigated bleakness of existence in the hinterland. Other than attacking the land revenue administration as a relic of the colonial past and loudly proclaiming that it must make way for development or dismissing it as irrelevant to the financial administration as land revenue accounts for less than 1 per cent of total revenues, little has been done to improve it.[92]

Some argue that this neglect has been a good thing for Pakistan. This is so not because the land revenue administration is efficient or just or not in need of reform but given the hatchet-job reformers have inflicted upon other parts of the state they would only make things worse by turning their gaze towards the countryside. The consequences of tampering with the land revenue administration, it is warned, could include mass rural unrest, upsurge in criminal activity, and violent internal migrations. The land revenue administration acts as an anchor and enjoys the support of the better off segment of the rural population. Given Pakistan's tragic reformative experience this line of argument cannot be lightly dismissed.

In 1977, the Committee on Revitalisation of Revenue Administration noted that the abolition of land taxes on holdings of less than twenty-five acres of irrigated land meant that 90 per cent of land owners accounting for 68 per cent of 'total privately owned land in the country' were no longer subject to taxation.[93] Before the 1975 reforms, land revenue was collected from eleven million landowners accounting for six and a half million acres and generated one hundred and twenty million rupees of revenue.[94] After the reforms one million two hundred thousand landowners with three million four hundred thousand acres were taxed though with changes made in 1977 this figure declined to four hundred and forty thousand landowners with two million acres of land liable to pay taxes.[95] This meant that by 1977, 1 per cent of the landowners accounted for 18 per cent of the cultivated area and paid 64 per cent of the land revenue.[96]

Other than reducing the level and scope of taxation or changing the formula through which taxes were to be calculated, successive governments did not appreciate that disputes arising from rights in lands and land revenue brought the largest number of people into contact with the state apparatus and was therefore one of the most important determinants of how people perceived the state.[97] Most citizens had never seen, nor, perhaps, would ever see, an income tax or customs officer. To the average citizen the state *was* for all practical purposes the *patwari*, the *tehsildar* and deputy-*tehsildar*, the assistant collector, the assorted agricultural and irrigation staff and the police constable. The combination of political pressure and development work left 'the already harassed District and Divisional heads' little time to supervise the land revenue administration or attend to the complaints of the rural masses.[98] This had led to pervasive 'insecurity and instability' with the 'efficiency and objectivity of revenue and district administration' gravely undermined.[99] It was generally admitted that since 1947 there was 'progressive deterioration in the maintenance of the revenue record.'[100]

The pivot of the land revenue administration was the deputy commissioner in his capacity as district collector. It was his responsibility to collect the land revenue, maintain statistics and act as the 'guardian and registrar of the rights in the soil enjoyed by private persons.'[101] The collector also adjudicated disputes between tenants and landlords and acted as the 'custodian of state property.'[102] The increased emphasis on development work had led to a 'growing neglect of touring', with a greater concentration of work in the district headquarters and the 'intimate contact with the rural masses' vital to the efficient and just operation of the revenue administration was being lost.[103] The tremendous imbalances in the countryside between the larger and smaller landlords and between landlords and tenants necessitated the 'interdependence of judicial and executive functions' in the land revenue administration.[104] Proposals to separate land revenue from the general administration would diminish the 'career prospects' of revenue officials and lead to great demoralisation.[105] The land revenue administration 'would lose the umbrella of the prestige and influence of the Deputy Commissioner and Commissioner' if a separation of functional powers were implemented and once the strong hand was removed 'inefficiency and corruption' would increase.[106]

In the 1980s the collectors, assistant collectors, *tehsildar*s and *patwari*s were kept so busy with 'miscellaneous' work that they had 'hardly any time [left] to attend to their real work.'[107] Under the devolution scheme implemented in 2001, landlords with more than fifty acres came to dominate the districts as elected *nazim*s and use the revenue administration now separated from the general administration and under its own revenue officers as an instrument of power and patronage. With the general administration decapitated and floundering 'Dispute and factionalism between' kinships and castes often characterised by 'obsessive' compulsions to diminish a rival party's *izzat* (honour/prestige) and establish one's own '*chaudhrahat* (dominance)' have been exacerbated by the now overtly politicised land revenue administration.[108]

The seriousness of land revenue administration and its relationship to the overall governability of an overwhelmingly rural country cannot be underestimated. And yet, those who matter in the power structure simply do not care. Those who ostensibly care are subservient to American tutelage with its desire to transform the rural administration and society with 'a systematic research for democratic social technology'[109] and do not understand the motivations, needs, and requirements of rural society and how these are embedded in the structure of land revenue administration and related areas. Those who understand, or have the capacity to do so, do not matter and are isolated from and demoralised by the generously donor-funded public discourse.

6.5 Golden Sovereigns and Economic Governance

If Kautilya or Shang Yang were to examine Pakistan's financial administration, several of its facets would strike them as incomprehensible and self-defeating. The first is the absence of consistent, meaningful, and effective efforts to raise revenues from within the state's frontiers given the availability of sufficient resources. The second is the eagerness of the Pakistani elite to enter into tributary-mercenary relationships with other states in order to spare itself the hardship of generating tax revenues. The third is the weakness of the apparatus even in securing and distributing enough resources for its own sustenance while it wastes funds on luxuries and favours. And finally, the lack of seriousness with which financial administration, one of the core areas of governance, was and is approached would probably appal them. The essence of economic governance, which is to live within your means or acquire the means to live, has been lost on Pakistan's rulers. Indicative of this transparent combination of ineptitude and complacency was that by 1990 Pakistan direct taxes accounted for less than 2 per cent of GDP, or not even half the percentage for countries with per capita incomes of less than $360.[110] Collection of indirect taxes as a share of GDP was no better than other low-income countries.[111]

Pakistan has muddled through sixty years in a state of permanent underdevelopment without a financial administrative policy worth the name. It does not seem that any regime seriously considered the material and psychological requirements of an effective financial administration. They also appeared indifferent to the impact that prolonged failure to collect and spend taxes efficiently and justly would have on the overall credibility of the state. The CBR and land revenue administration were perceived as instruments, the former for national leaders the latter for provincial and local leaders, through which favours, punishments, and inducements could be dispensed. Just as the centre depended on handouts and loans from abroad that ultimately crippled its fiscal flexibility the provinces and local governments depended on loans and grants from the centre. National, provincial, and local self-government are all the consequences of fiscal autonomy the erosion of which leads the debtors and dependants into an asymmetrical relationship with their creditors and patron. At the highest levels from an early stage the effort was to attract by any means necessary foreign aid and patronage:

> Increasing importance is now being attached to the operation of centralised planning organisations, especially by the aid-giving countries which tend to judge an aid-receiving country's competence by the standing and quality of its planning agency. It has been suggested, therefore, that the status and operational strength of the Planning Commission should be brought to a higher level than at present.[112]

There is no intrinsic moral difference between the senior bureaucrat who defines his competence in terms of the foreign currency loans he negotiates and the minister who signs the agreement into effect on the one hand and the professional beggars on the streets of Pakistan. Indeed, begging is a national pastime. Pakistani diplomats beg for credits, development assistance, and visas. Businessmen and the eternally infant industries beg for protection, subsidies, and easy loans. NGOs beg international donors and the State of Pakistan to fund their pursuit of 'democratic social technology' and 'just and democratic governance'.[113] Clerics beg for alms, and lately arms, along with lands and subsidies from local and foreign sources. With mere ten or eleven out of every hundred rupees going into the state's coffers Pakistan could double the tax-to-GDP ratio with great benefit to both citizens and the state without overburdening the economy. That, however, would require stable law and order conditions, effective supervision of the collection machinery, inspection, audit, and a qualitative and quantitative reform of the principles as well as details of the entire financial administration.

Substantially responsible for the woes of the financial administration are the sheer arbitrariness and irresponsibility with which the economic governance of Pakistan has been carried out. This arbitrariness was in evidence during the desperate early years although between 1953 and 1969 the governing corporation did achieve a measure of stability. After Yahya's brief but disastrous rule, Bhutto replaced the 'centralised economic planning and its technical/institutional competence with a highly personalised and ad hoc approach.'[114] In the case of the nationalisation of two thousand eight hundred and fifteen units of the agricultural processing industry there was 'no evidence on record' that indicated any careful consideration.[115] Evidently, it was a 'one-man decision' with 'even the cabinet' informed after the confiscations had 'already been set in motion.'[116] The confiscation of large-scale manufacturing units led private investment to fall from one billion three hundred million rupees in 1971 to less than half a billion rupees in 1976 while public sector investment rose from sixty-three million rupees to nearly one billion two hundred million rupees during that same period.[117] In the planning of the nationalisation of the banking sector, carried out on 1 January 1974, the State Bank of Pakistan (SBP) was not even consulted.[118] While a bloated and inefficient public sector was established, little attempt was made to improve the financial administration whose audit function was now hugely increased owing to the growth in the number and size of public entities. In January 1976, the CBR identified seventy thousand potential taxpayers and they were threatened with severe consequences which led to four thousand new income tax returns.[119] Combined with inflation, this led to a 56 per cent increase in income tax collection as compared to 1974-1975.[120] That said, enforcement was lax and there were merely thirty-four prosecutions for income tax related offences.[121] With the flow of aid from the West reduced, the state was forced to borrow from its erstwhile patrons causing total external debt to rise between 1972 and 1977 from three billion seven hundred million dollars to six billion three hundred million dollars.[122] The real impact was felt in terms of the shattering of confidence in Pakistan's financial institutions and the atmosphere of distrust and subterfuge that it bred. The state was ill equipped to manage productive assets and though privatisation began soon after Bhutto's overthrow in 1977 it was a restricted and often politically motivated process. Ever since the Bhutto-era reforms Pakistan's financial administration has been saddled with public sector enterprises that it can neither manage profitably nor sell off to buyers interested in anything more than strip mining the assets in question.

Zia's years in power coincided with rapprochement between the United States and Pakistan following the 1979 Soviet invasion of Afghanistan. With remittances pouring in from the oil-rich Middle East and billions of US dollars worth of Saudi and Western money in economic, military, technical and clandestine assistance being pumped into Pakistan, Zia and his unimaginative financial team chose to govern and change nothing beyond opportunistic privatisation. Interest payments, less than 2 per cent of GDP in 1977, rose to 5 per cent of GDP by 1988.[123] Defence expenditure, about 5.5 per cent of GDP in 1977, rose to nearly 7 per cent of GDP in 1988.[124] Development expenditure fell from 10 per cent of GDP in 1977 to 7 per cent of GDP in 1988.[125] Fiscal deficits were less than 6 per cent of GDP only in 1980-1981 and 1981-1982 and otherwise ranged between 7 and 9 per cent of GDP with 8 per cent deficits in 1979, 1985, 1986, and 1988.[126] The overall tax-to-GDP ratio ranged between 11 per cent in 1978 and 14 per cent in 1988 with direct taxes stagnant at less than 2 per cent of GDP and indirect taxes rising from 9 to nearly 12 per cent of GDP.[127] Domestic debt surged from 21 per cent of GDP in 1980-1981 to 43 per cent of GDP in 1988.[128]

What followed after 1988 was more of the same minus American grants and aid and phased reduction of customs duties eating into state revenues. Although the number of income tax returns quadrupled between 1995 and 2000 while sales tax returns doubled, successive governments took loan after loan from international financial institutions and acquired a crippling foreign debt burden in addition to the burgeoning domestic debt that was Zia's legacy. Although both PPP and PML-N governments agreed with IMF programs and policies leading to a policy consensus, they also spent most of their time and energy questioning, investigating, and reversing their predecessor's policies. The combination of arbitrariness, tactical cunning, 'policy reversals and adventurous economic initiatives.' with each group trying to use the financial administration to 'establish political power and supremacy' brought the economy and the state finances to a nadir.[129] The dispute with independent power producers, the on-again off-again motorway project, the yellow cab scheme, and freezing of eleven billion US dollars worth of foreign currency accounts following the nuclear tests in May 1998, and the prime minister's housing scheme in the works in 1999, were the major 'policies' pursued between 1988 and 1999.

After 2002, the anti-terror alliance with the United States has, as was the case during the Ayub and Zia periods, temporarily resolved Pakistan financial administrative crisis. The rate of increase in the number of income tax and sales tax payers slowed during Musharraf's rule, which is strange given that the regime claims GDP and per capita income doubled between 2002 and 2007 growing at 6 to 7 per cent per year. How this was achieved confounded the policy makers who, evidently, could not do simple arithmetic. If GDP was, for the sake of argument, one hundred in 2002, growing at 7 per cent per year it would be one hundred and seven in 2003, one hundred and fifteen in 2004, one hundred and twenty-three in 2005, one hundred and thirty one in 2006, and one hundred and forty in 2007. Several Pakistani representatives abroad who questioned the data they were being asked to sell as the authentic official figures to foreign governments and investors found that senior financial managers were at a loss to explain the doubling of GDP in five years. One asserted that the government was factoring inflation into the growth rate, which would mean that if Pakistan had an inflation rate of 100 per cent its economy would double every year. Another explanation was that the depreciation of the rupee was being factored in which was also interesting given that Pakistan's currency has been more or less stable at sixty rupees to the US dollar for the past five years. With the regime engaging almost four billion dollars of external debt every year, of which fifteen billion dollars were received between 2003 and 2007 and an additional ten to fifteen billion on the cards for the next five years, Pakistan's macroeconomic stability was an illusion not backed up by the increased ability of the state to generate revenues from its domestic resources.

This illusion was shattered during the final year of Musharraf's rule. Rising costs of inputs, such as food and fuel, combined with a reckless growth model based primarily on the stimulation of consumption and driven by external transfers, brought the financial administration to its knees. The PPP-led coalition government that took shape after February 2008 spent its first six months muddling through on all fronts other than putting pressure on Musharraf to resign. This aggravated the crisis of confidence and coincided with a global economic crisis. Finally, after being rebuffed by its empathisers such as Saudi Arabia and Chinese, Pakistan went to the IMF and secured a $7.5 billion loan in order to avert default and restore a semblance of credibility to the state finances. The conditions attached to the loan require Pakistan to restrain its deficits and raise its revenues but there seems to be little stomach on part of the government to undertake serious reforms. A repeat of 1988-1999 seems to be on the cards albeit in the context of continued external economic and military aid inflows.

6.6 Lax Republica

A member of the 1992 Economy Commission had warned of the growing 'similarities' between the financial administration of the Timurid Empire under Aurungzeb and his successors and the State of Pakistan.[130] The first was the insufficiency of revenues relative to the needs of the state due to 'the unwillingness or the inability' of the state' to collect taxes more effectively and efficiently.[131] The second was the unsustainable increase in wasteful expenditure 'merely to create an effect of grandeur', not very successfully, one might add.[132] The third was the absence of 'financial discipline by either avoiding or disregarding institutional scrutiny of proposed expenditure.'[133] The fourth was the increase in the number of state employees even as the state's capacity to pay them wages commensurate with their responsibilities and discretionary powers declined.[134] Finally, the breakdown in internal discipline due to 'continuous arbitrariness' and the slackening of 'accountability' and 'scrutiny' resulted in 'a large number of state employees living off the land and in many cases making more money through corruption than their salaries.'[135]

The persistent inability of a state to raise enough tax revenue to meet its expenses when domestic resources are sufficient is cause for serious concern. The cavalier treatment of the financial administration by successive regimes has contributed to and sustained a permanent fiscal crisis. Due to greater concern with spending money than raising money to spend, expenditures have soared above revenues with the difference made good through domestic and external borrowing or outright theft and confiscation of liquid and productive assets held by Pakistani nationals. During periods of intimacy with the United States the payments for services rendered and expected, offset the fiscal crisis and cause the limited reserves of political and administrative will to reform to evaporate altogether. As an outmoded early-twentieth century financial administration limped along a highly regressive course, the quality of its personnel, organisation, and culture steadily deteriorated while its effectiveness relative to other post-colonial states declined and continues to do so. Treated as a medieval instrument by the rulers it behaves arbitrarily and malevolently towards the ruled living off the land in a predatory manner. Citizens respond through flight, concealment, misdirection and collusion with the numerous corrupt elements. Of these citizens, the rural masses are left to fend for themselves and, after the devolution plan introduced by the Musharraf regime in 2001, are now completely at the mercy of local landlords while the apparatus caters to the interests and fantasies of the Anglophone elite. This elite has become so accustomed to its role as a ridiculed and undignified supplicant abroad and a callous, effete and whimsical caricature of a ruling class at home that it lacks the resolve and perhaps even the ability to stand on its own two feet. The most ubiquitous characteristic in this elite's exercise of power is its proprietorial attitude towards the state and the tendency to treat it in the manner of the Grand Seigneur.

NOTES

1. A near contemporary and leading example of a different emergent bureaucratic tradition was Lord Shang (d.338 BC), adviser to Duke Hsiao of the state of Qin that unified China in 221 BC held views similar to Kautilya as did other Chinese legalist thinkers. *The Book of Lord Shang*, a compilation of legalist reflections and advice on statecraft, asserted that order, tax collection and the power of the state flowed in harmonious sequence through the exertion of the ruler and his highest officials. The establishment of an effective order, based on laws applied equally upon the subjects and subordinate officials, was essential to controlling the tendency of officials to privatise imperial revenues and oppress (or collude with) the taxpayers. Taxes ought to be carefully calculated and applied as a proportion of actual yield with the long-term objective of weakening the autonomy of taxpayers and subordinate officials and strengthening the central state. Shang Yang, *The Book of Lord Shang*, trans. J. J. L. Duyvendak, intro. Robert Wilkinson (Hertfordshire: Wordsworth Editions Limited, 1998), 150 and 135-144.
2. Kautilya, *The Arthashastra*, trans. L. N. Rangarajan, 254.

3. Ibid., 304.
4. Ibid., 305.
5. Raychaudhry and Habib, eds., *The Cambridge Economic History of India*, vol. 1, *c.1200 to c.1750*, 173. The Delhi Sultanate was organized along similar lines as the Timurid Empire. However, the former was relatively unstable and less economic data is forthcoming about it as compared to the latter.
6. Ibid., 178.
7. Irfan Habib, *Essays in Indian History*, 97.
8. Abul Fazl Allami, *A'in-I Akbari*, trans. H. Blochmann, 225.
9. John Keay, *India: A History* (London: HarperCollins, 2000), 414.
10. Budgeting and auditing, in their modern forms, were introduced in India by James Wilson, the founder of the *Economist*, and the first Finance Member of the Supreme Council of India. Wilson served from 29 November 1859 to 11 August 1860, fell ill during the monsoon, and died in India. In this brief period he also introduced paper currency and the income tax.
11. Hameed Akhtar Niazi, 'Financial Administration' in Jamilur Rehman Khan, ed., *Government and Administration in Pakistan*, 452.
12. Ibid., 453.
13. Ibid., 478.
14. Ibid.
15. Ibid., 506.
16. Ibid.
17. Ibid., 408.
18. Dharma Kumar, *The Cambridge Economic History of India*, vol II, *c. 1757—c. 1970* (Cambridge: The Press Syndicate of the Cambridge University, 1982; reprint, Delhi: Orient Longman, 1984), 931.
19. Ibid., 929.
20. Ibid.
21. Ibid.
22. The Indian mobilisation effort included two and a half million volunteers for the military, five million additional workers employed in war industries, and an additional one million employed in the railways. Philip Mason, *A Matter of Honour* (London: Jonathan Cape, 1974), 495.
23. In India, the adoption of centralised planning for the development of a socialist pattern of economy resulted in a perpetual 'dualism between the still limited modern industrial sector and the vast rural hinterland.' The formal sector of the Indian economy accounted for mere 3-8 per cent of employment, was centred in a few provinces and metropolises, and provided the livelihood for about 15 per cent of the total population. The average rate of growth for the period up to 1992 was also sluggish and failed to substantially raise per capita income. Many of the imbalances found in the Indian approach would also be found in Pakistan although the latter adopted a more open economic system and thus managed to sustain higher rates of economic growth. For more on India's successes and failures see Francine R. Frankel, *India's Political Economy, 1947-2004: The Gradual Revolution* (New Delhi: Oxford University Press, 2005).
24. Niazi, 'Financial Administration', 526.
25. Ibid.

26. *Pakistan Economic Survey, 1995-96* (Islamabad: Central Board of Revenue, 1996), 139.
27. *Final Report of the Taxation Commission,* Vol. I (Karachi: Printing Corporation of Pakistan, 1974), 11.
28. Ibid., 15.
29. Ibid., 19.
30. Ishrat Hussain, *Pakistan: The Economy of an Elitist State* (Karachi: Oxford University Press, 1999), 27.
31. *Final Report of the Taxation Commission,* Vol. I, 24.
32. Ibid.
33. Ishrat Hussain, *Economic Management in Pakistan, 1999-2002* (Karachi: Oxford University Press, 2003), 2.
34. Ibid.
35. Ibid., 10.
36. Ibid., 7.
37. *CBR Yearbook 2005-2006* (Islamabad: Directorate of Research and Statistics, Government of Pakistan, 2006), 16-17.
38. Ibid., 31-32.
39. *CBR Yearbook 2004-2005* (Islamabad: Directorate of Research and Statistics, Government of Pakistan, 2005), 15.
40. *Report of the Finance Commission, 1962* (Karachi: Government of Pakistan Press, 1962), 24.
41. Ibid., 26.
42. Ibid., 25.
43. *Pakistan Economic Survey, 1995-1996* (Islamabad: Government of Pakistan, 1996), 138.
44. Ibid.
45. S. Akbar Zaidi, *Issues in Pakistan's Economy*, 208.
46. Ibid., 206.
47. Ibid.
48. Subsistence farmers as they grow their own food are in part insulated from food inflation. In discussion with capitalist farmers I found that the inflation in food prices does not translate into higher prices for the ordinary farmer.
49. Siddiqui, *Towards Good Governance*, 16.
50. Ibid.
51. Ibid., 29.
52. Ibid., 30.
53. *Report of the Taskforce on Reform of Tax Administration, 14 April 2001* (Islamabad: Central Board of Revenue, Government of Pakistan, 2001), i.
54. Ibid.
55. Ibid.
56. Ibid.
57. Ibid.
58. Ibid.
59. Ibid., ii.
60. Ibid., iii.
61. Ibid.

62. Ibid., iv. 1 million out of a total population of 140 million.
63. *CBR Yearbook 2006-2006*, 16. Or 1.49 million out of a total population of 160 million.
64. *Report of the Taskforce on Reform of Tax Administration, 14 April 2001*, iv. A contradiction in this statement is that if the taxation staff were genuinely that ignorant of the rules and procedures involving businesses it would be a lot easier for businessmen to dupe them and get away with minimal pay-offs.
65. Ibid.
66. Ibid.
67. Ibid., vi.
68. *CBR Yearbook for 2005-2006*, 17.
69. Ibid., 33-34.
70. *Report of the Taskforce on Reform of Tax Administration, 14 April 2001*, vii.
71. Ibid.
72. Ibid.
73. Ibid., x.
74. Ibid., xi.
75. Ibid.
76. Ibid. The coast guards are poorly trained and ineffective against smuggling.
77. Ibid., xv.
78. Ibid., xvi.
79. Ibid., 166.
80. Shafqat, *Civil Military Relations in Pakistan*, 41, 45.
81. *Report of the Taskforce on Reform of Tax Administration, 14 April 2001*, 167.
82. Ibid.
83. Ibid., 175. Six thousand rupees equalled about one hundred US dollars at the time of the Taskforce's deliberations.
84. Ibid.
85. Ibid., 177.
86. Ibid., 195.
87. Ibid., 196.
88. Ibid.
89. Ibid.
90. Ibid., 197.
91. *CBR Yearbook for 2005-2006*, i.
92. Massey dissects the pretensions of South Asian elites and observes: 'The Brown sahib has proved to be unscrupulous bloodsucker; the White sahibs who represented a distant imperial power could on a personal level be just, even benign. Many British district officers had an acute sense of *noblesse oblige*. This statement will not be greeted with applause by the rulers of either India, Pakistan, Sri Lanka or Bangladesh. Even the good White Liberal will chip in with the trite slogan: 'Good government is no substitute for self government.' But go to any part of South Asia and speak to any poor landless labourer in his seventies or eighties. Ask only one question: Were you happier under British rule? I am quite sure of the answer you will get.' Massey, *India*, 13.
93. *Report of the Committee on Revitalization of Revenue Administration*, Vol. 1, July 1978, 31.

94. Ibid., 73.
95. Ibid.
96. Ibid., 74.
97. 1959, File No. 196/CF/59, Government of Pakistan, Cabinet Secretariat, 'Standardisation of Land Revenue throughout West Pakistan', 1. In April 1959, for instance, the government of West Pakistan separated the land revenue from the water rate. Ibid.
98. Ibid., 18.
99. Ibid.
100. *Report of the Provincial Administration Commission, February 1960*, 161.
101. Ibid., 167.
102. Ibid.
103. Ibid., 171.
104. Ibid., 164.
105. *Report of the Committee on Revitalization of Revenue Administration*, Vol 1, *July 1978*, 22.
106. Ibid.
107. Qayyum, 'Land Revenue Administration', 336-337.
108. Shahrukh Rafi Khan, *Initiating Devolution*, 181.
109. M. A. K. Beg, 'Rural Development', in Jamilur Rehman Khan, ed., *Government and Administration in Pakistan*, 667.
110. S. Akbar Zaidi, *Issues in Pakistan's Economy*, 211.
111. Ibid.
112. *Report of the Administrative Reorganisation Committee*, 223. This committee deliberated between 1958 and 1960.
113. In their own defence, the intellectual dependents cultivated by American patronage believe that their ideas, though 'imported' had been 'spontaneously adopted, internalised, and brought into the public sphere' by the NGOs. Shahrukh Rafi Khan, ed., *Fifty Years of Pakistan's Economy: Traditional Topics and Contemporary Concerns* (Karachi: Oxford University Press, 1999), 3. What is remarkable is that the Anglophone leaders of the social sector in Pakistan define their competence in terms of their ability to mimic the movements of American academia as it devises prescriptions to its own problems. Decentralisation, structural adjustment, empowerment, grassroots mobilisation, sustainable development, etc., are thus imitated without empirical appreciation of the realities on the ground in Pakistan.
114. Ishrat Hussain, *Pakistan: The Economy of an Elitist State*, 25.
115. *White Paper on the Performance of the Bhutto Regime*, Vol. IV, *The Economy* (Islamabad: Printing Corporation of Pakistan, 1979), 30.
116. Ibid.
117. Ibid., 52.
118. Ibid., 63.
119. *Federal Taxes Administration Report, 1975-76* (Islamabad: Central Board of Revenue, 1977), 6.
120. Ibid., 7.
121. Ibid.
122. *White Paper on the Performance of the Bhutto Regime*, Vol. IV, *The Economy*, 1.

123. S. Akbar Zaidi, *Issues in Pakistan's Economy*, 206.
124. Ibid.
125. Ibid.
126. Ibid., 205.
127. Ibid., 211.
128. Ibid., 223.
129. Ishrat Hussain, *Pakistan: The Economy of an Elitist State*, 35.
130. Zafar Iqbal Rathore, Rathore Papers, 'State and Economy', Note submitted to the 1992 Economy Commission, March 1992, Islamabad, 9.
131. Ibid.
132. Ibid.
133. Ibid.
134. Ibid.
135. Ibid., 10.

7 Grand Seigneurs

7.1 Sovereign-Proprietors

The rulers of continental bureaucratic empires, great and small, were sovereign-proprietors and effectively owned the lands, peoples and instruments of power under their command.[1] Their servants received an inferior right of possession over a portion of the ruler's wealth in the form of lands, rents and salaries. Local notables would be confirmed by the apparatus which retained the right to intervene in their internal disputes and politics if they militated towards overt defiance. In some cases, such as that of the Rajputs in the Timurid Empire, local notables may have been assimilated into the official hierarchy. As for the ordinary cultivators and artisans the output of their labour was at the mercy of the apparatus either directly in the form of the emperor or indirectly in the form of his slaves, servants and favourites. While in Old Regime France, Louis XIV boldly overrode feudal prerogative and aristocratic privilege and declared 'that all the lands in the kingdom had been originally leased on terms by the state which thus remained the sole real owner',[2] the Timurid Empire with four and a half million square kilometres of varied territory, a hundred million subjects and two hundred million rupees of average annual revenues was 'the property of one man, the emperor.'[3] Almost two millennia earlier Megasthenes, a Greek ambassador to the Mauryan court, found that the sovereign was the proprietor of his empire which was in effect an imperial estate.

The proprietorial nature of sovereign power in continental bureaucratic empires meant that the servants of imperial rule were highly insecure in their possession of lands, rents and salaries. Dependent on the caprices of an arbitrary master for the preservation of their wealth, dignity, status and even titles, the servants tried to steal and cheat their employer out of his wealth as much as possible. Kautilya found that just as it was 'impossible to know when a fish moving in water is drinking it, so it is impossible to find out when government servants in charge of undertakings misappropriate money.'[4] The sovereign-proprietorial state was to its servants like 'honey or poison that one may find at the tip of one's tongue' and it was 'impossible' for the official 'not to take, at least a little bit, of the King's wealth.'[5] It was easier to understand and predict 'the paths of birds flying in the sky' than it was to investigate 'government servants who hide their income.'[6] The universal insecurity felt by the servants of the sovereign-proprietor meant that they found ways to try and take as much as they could out of the royal wealth that came into their hands and live ostentatiously while they could. From the ruler's perspective such activities increased his powers over his subordinates so long as he was able to punish enough of his servants to keep most from undermining the stability of his rule. Spies and informers were necessary so that the ruler may know who was taking what and how and this knowledge could be used to blackmail officers into doing the royal bidding. Corruption to the ruler was the pilferage or wastage of imperial wealth by his servants. As for the ruler, he may be guilty of oppression, injustice, or harshness but he could hardly be accused of stealing from himself. Understandably, the ruler did get upset if subordinates usurped imperial authority or took excessive advantage of structural flaws. The remedy was extraordinary personal exertion to punish those who stole more than the ruler was willing to tolerate.

Akbar[7] was particularly incensed when he learnt that the *qazi*s in the ecclesiastical department responsible for grants of land, scholarships and inquisitions, were, like many of the officials in the other departments 'in the habit of taking bribes from the grant-holders' or stealing the funds and lands put at their disposal by the emperor.[8] The emperor denounced 'these men, who wear a turban as a sign of respectability, but are bad at heart, and who wear long sleeves, but fall short in sense.'[9] Akbar ordered the dismissal of most of the serving *qazi*s, had Persian and Turkish women who colluded with the clerics to steal from the emperor and acquire tax-free lands under false pretences convicted of fraud, and ordered inquiries into all grants of over one hundred *bigha*s (subsistence units of land).[10] Senior ecclesiasts were forbidden on pain of imprisonment and dismissal from making any grants of more than fifteen *bigha*s without imperial approval.[11] The emperor was equally offended by the manner in which those grants of land which had been converted into gardens and orchards and so generated profits were subjected to 'the greediness of Government officers' and extortion.[12]

Akbar personally intervened and 'commanded that such profits should not be interfered with' by officials unless they wished to make enemies of their master.[13] When it was found that the grant-holders were guilty of bribery and collusion with officials in order to get a better deal for themselves, the emperor ordered them brought before him so that he may administer justice in such cases directly.[14] The emperor, 'with the view of teaching wisdom and promoting true piety' took keen interest in the personnel management of the ecclesiastical department and personally appointed ecclesiasts who struck him as 'disinterested' at the central and district levels.[15] Between 1578 and 1605, the period in which Akbar exercised direct personal supervision of the ecclesiastical affairs 'there is only one case of irregularity' concerning the 'charge of corruption and bribery' against the head of province of Gujrat's religious establishment.[16] The accused 'was tried, found guilty and imprisoned.'[17] The continuous personal effort required to make examples and prevent things from getting out of hand meant that whereas a Chandragupta Maurya or Akbar could manage the tour de force, less competent rulers would rapidly find themselves isolated, surrounded by sycophants and end up allowing their servants to carve out petty estates of their own resulting in loss of control and the break-up of the empire.

There also existed a number of structural parallels between the states of the subcontinent and the English East India Company that ultimately displaced many of them in the mid-eighteenth century. The first parallel was that the corporation, like the continental bureaucratic empire, was dominated by 'the drive for monopoly control'.[18] For the former this implied the ability to control the market through horizontal as well as vertical consolidation. For the latter monopoly control meant the absolute power of the sovereign over the territory, wealth, and status of his servants and through them over the country at large. Neither liked competition and both possessed a totalitarian outlook. This drive for corporate or imperial monopoly over profits and power, or power and profits, was balanced by the speculative propensities of officials, investors, and other associates.[19] It was as difficult for the corporation to regulate employees that were physically removed from the headquarters as it was for sovereign-proprietors to supervise their distant subordinates. Within headquarters or in the imperial palace intrigue and conspiracy clouded the atmosphere and made it harder to relate decisions and policies to ground realities. All the way up and down the chain of command the tendency was for corporate employees and imperial servants to report things as fine lest the shareholders or the emperor and his advisers get upset. The third similarity was that neither the corporation nor the continental bureaucratic empire possessed an automatic remedy for abuse and thus generally failed to attain stability.[20]

Against these similarities there were several great differences as well in terms of motivation, structures and objectives. Statecraft was a divinely inspired pursuit and the apparatus of empire saw itself not as a business venture but as a great and virtuous enterprise well worth sacrificing life for. In terms of structure the continental bureaucratic empire was organised so as to provide public services such as order, justice, infrastructure, defence, charity and humanitarian assistance, all of which were not profit generating ventures. Governance of a state meant balancing land, people, power, wealth, culture and imperial idiosyncrasies, against the generation of revenue required to sustain the entire process. It was an immeasurably more difficult and exhausting task than selling fabrics or buying tea. The differences in motivation and structure translated in different objectives. The corporation had a single objective in the generation of sufficient profits to sustain the appreciation of its own stock value. The state had many different objectives and required a tremendous amount of energy and vision upon the part of the ruler and the administrative elite to give coherence to it.

After the conquest of Bengal in 1757, the East India Company went berserk in its pursuit of profits for its shareholders. It was also polarised between the 'Bengal Squad' led by Clive and their opponents led by Laurence Sullivan leading to 'Civil war...among the shareholders.'[21] Each side created artificial stockholders to win more votes with Clive spending a substantial portion of his ill-gotten wealth on purchasing over two hundred votes while Sullivan managed to muster a hundred and sixty. In the numbers game Clive and his supporters won and by 1764 were in full control. Their objective, the same as that of all private corporations, was to increase share value by any means necessary. Clive resorted to insider trading to fuel increases in the stock value and through a 'tiny group of 60 executives simply engrossed the whole of the inland trade, excluding not just Asian merchants, but also junior executives and independent European traders.'[22] Thanks to these devices the share price rose from one hundred and twelve pounds sterling in

1762 to two hundred and twenty three pounds sterling by 1766 and the following year the Company agreed to pay the authorities at home four hundred thousand pounds a year in exchange for freedom to operate as it deemed fit. Though the Company's own officials, such as Hastings, admitted that their profit-driven governance was ruining the country they just could not stop until a combination of meteorological and management disasters between 1769 and 1771 brought both Bengal and the Company to its knees. A million two hundred thousand may have perished in the famine of 1769-1770[23] while the Company responded by actually *increasing* the revenue rates. Share prices tumbled and by 1773 the Company ended up with liabilities almost twice the value of its assets. It needed a loan to save itself but by now the popular mood and government hostility were such that it would come only with strings attached.

These conditions paved the way for the projection of the core organising principle of the British State of Laws, that the state was not the personal estate of the ruler, into the administration of its Indian territories. Successive governors-general cracked down upon patronage, bribery and the privatisation of public functions and enforced separation of the corporate and governmental aspects of the British Indian state. By 1813, the Company had effectively lost its monopoly and, a generation later, its trading activities were further curtailed. The combination of executive vigilance, competitive recruitment and the abolition of sovereign-proprietorship brought about a substantial shift in the culture of power of the administrative elite and to a fair extent the Indianised middle-order.

For instance, the taking of bribes by senior officials was a fact of life in 1770 with Clive and Hastings setting the standard for gift-taking, bribery and forgery. It was a matter of some embarrassment by 1800, a serious danger to career and reputation by 1830, and a freak occurrence by 1860. This was not because the British officers had become innately moral men in the course of a couple of generations but because of the changes in the incentive structure and discipline, thus explained A. Hamilton on 19 November 1813:

> The probity of persons whose decisions affect the lives and fortunes of the natives, in a station remote from the presidency, is exposed to strong temptations. It may be useful to enumerate the restraints which, in such a

case, are likely to operate on the mind of a Company's servant and of a native Commissioner. A detection in judicial corruption exposes the former to the loss of a large salary in possession, he sees all his prospects in life vanish, the influence of his family which procures him the nomination to the service, the sums expended in a liberal education...the many years he has spent in acquiring experience and languages, now no longer available, all are sacrificed. He has to begin the world again, but with a ruined character; and the eminence in which he once stood he can never hope to regain. On the other hand, the salary of the native Commissioner is trifling. If the bribe is accepted, he trusts to his address to escape discovery; but should the worst happen, and he lose his office, the sum he has received is equivalent to many years purchase of his former salary. His family and friends are far from considering him in the light of a degraded person, and he resumes his former habits, without experiencing any other mortification than that of discovering that his address was unequal to the occasion.[24]

In other words, the combination of good pay, prestige, high qualifications and reasonable certainty of discovery in the event of wrongdoing, security of service during good behaviour and freedom from presumptive suspicion and arbitrary interference, was what made the senior British officials relatively honest. Moreover, if they seriously transgressed, senior officials could not count on their colleagues to bail them out. John Lawrence, writing on 16 July 1853, admonished a colleague found taking a bribe that 'It is useless my trying to help you. There is no remedy for the error you have committed other than to bear the penalty and express your contrition.'[25]

The British achievement was that at the level of principle the sovereign-proprietorial mode of governance was dead. Public property and private property both existed under laws enforced by the corruption-free executive elite headed by the ICS and adjudicated upon by a superior judiciary that enjoyed tremendous prestige. The officers were servants of the law not the personal appointees of the sovereign. The bureaucratic middle order was substantially honest although here it was often more out of fear of their superior officers who possessed considerable disciplinary powers over them. At the lower levels the habitually corrupt were perhaps a third of the total while another fifth was opportunistically corrupt using their official positions to extract the means of livelihood. In the countryside as well as in the cities, it was not considered wrong to tip low-level functionaries or provide a helpful constable with a good meal. In the engineering service and public works department, contractors and engineers received commissions set at less than 10 per cent of the total contract value.[26] What mattered was that the corruption that did take place did not constitute a serious threat to the survival of the state and was not of concern at the policy-making and senior executive or judicial levels. Even under the pressure of the Second World War, the British did not relax financial controls and disciplines and constituted anti-corruption departments tied to the Special Branch of the Indian Police.[27]

The British administrative elite 'were men notable for high intellectual status' possessed great capacity for leadership and management and 'enjoyed a high reputation for personal morality' and probity in the conduct of public affairs.[28] By extending the principles of pay, prestige, accountability and *esprit de corps* the British had during their final seventy years of rule established institutions staffed primarily by Indians and in so doing transmitted a substantial portion of their idiosyncratic state morality.[29] And yet, it seemed that a decade after the British withdrawal from the subcontinent corruption had infected every segment of the apparatus even at the senior levels even though 'In the period of British rule' the AIS in general and ICS in particular were almost completely free from this disease.[30] The challenge for the leaders of free India and Pakistan was to extend the application of the principles of the British-era reforms to the lower tiers of the state apparatus and improve the investigative and disciplinary functions of the apparatus.[31] Instead, they proceeded to treat the state as a vast personal estate and headed back, some unconsciously, others consciously, to the pre-Enlightenment sovereign-proprietor configuration.[32]

7.2 Partisans

Corruption is a social activity.[33] In an administrative state it is not possible for the rulers be they elected politicians or military dictators to engage in the privatisation of public funds and assets, the violation of laws and procedures, and the arbitrary use of power without the collaboration of a large number of civil servants, subordinate officials, or military and intelligence personnel. Under the British imperial nomocracy the freakishly divergent culture of power of the administrative elite meant that the incentives and pressures for the unlawful and proprietorial tendencies inherent in continental bureaucratic empires were steadily rolled back. In a very important sense the culture of power of the British Indian state was an alien imposition and imported restraint on the sovereign-proprietorial instincts of the Indian subjects.

The effects of these instincts were already in evidence between 1919 and 1947 when the representative principle was introduced at the provincial and national levels. Suhrawardy, as the premier of Bengal before partition 'would receive [even] the most respectable man be he a merchant' or civil servant while 'lying on his bed with his legs outstretched and people seeing him in his bed room had to talk to him standing by his side.'[34] Khwaja Nazimuddin, the Adamjees and Dawoods, among others, were subjected to the same humiliation.[35] Once the supplicant had approached the premier's bed Suhrawardy would 'show his authority by shouting at people' or then address them in 'a bantering tone.'[36] When out of power Suhrawardy rediscovered his manners and social graces and courted those who could get him back into a position of authority.[37] Fazlul Haq, another luminary of the freedom struggle and Pakistan movements who served as governor of East Pakistan from March 1956 to April 1958, used to sign all applications brought before him and thought it good to give people 'spontaneous pleasure even if it was temporary.'[38] He also defended his choice of mediocre, corrupt and non-serious colleagues as ministers on the grounds that such people were the 'true representatives' of the masses in terms of their intellectual aptitude and understanding of state morality.[39]

In West Pakistan, in April 1950, a bench of the Lahore High Court found that the former chief minister, the Nawab of Mamdot, was guilty of corruption, abuse of power and obstruction of justice. Mamdot had obtained on 20 September 1947, for himself nearly nineteen hundred acres of land in the Montgomery district out of evacuee property.[40] He was also found guilty of having 'conspired with Raja Hassan Akhter, PCS' through whom he 'had obtained the allotment, to destroy the evidence.'[41] On 25 January 1949, Mamdot had put his 'signature to a very good report relating to Raja Hassan Akhter', though he knew 'of the irregularities committed' by the officer in question.[42] Moreover, these favourable remarks on the personal files of administrative collaborators such as Raja Hassan Akhter and Khwaja Abdur Rahim (PAS/CSP) were made immediately *after* Mamdot's dismissal though the files carried earlier dates 19, 20, and 23 January.[43] Mamdot's objective was to protect his partisans from the governor and other civil servants angered by his unlawful and arbitrary conduct.[44]

The 'root-cause of all corruption' represented by the combination of abuse of power and privatisation of state resources in the subcontinent was the region's 'arbitrary culture of power' formed over millennia of anarchy, warlordism and despotism.[45] In the subcontinent the wielders of power perceived it as 'a personal acquisition and prerogative' while those subjected to its exercise saw power 'as residing in the person of high officials' and not in such artificial colonial-era trivialities as laws, procedures, or constitutionalism.[46] In *azad* (independent, free) Pakistan if the rulers so wished they could override the law and do as they pleased and it was only when they did not want to do something that legal or constitutional propriety were invoked. The rulers sought arbitrary power while the people wanted this power to be used to advance their own personal or sectional interests. Leadership was based on a combination of force, deception, and charisma and it sought to use the instruments of state power to perpetuate personal rule.[47] After 1947, the British-era veneer wore off and the rulers as well as the ruled regressed 'to the original structure' of the subcontinent's 'group mind and group behaviour.'[48] Partition and the disposal of evacuee property in land and capital facilitated this regression. Frosty relations between India and Pakistan also made it harder for verification procedures to be pursued effectively.

On 10 March 1949, A. M. Khan Leghari, the Punjab's secretary for refugees and rehabilitation, warned all the commissioners that the governor was 'deeply concerned over the difficult question of wrong allocation of Evacuee Property.'[49] A very large number of 'Locals' were passing themselves off as refugees 'for securing evacuee property.'[50] Refugee status was a much sought after commodity as locals were prohibited from occupying evacuee property.[51] Many non-Punjabis settled in the province were presenting themselves, often armed with forged papers and false testimonials, as migrants or members of the landed gentry who were now cut off from their lands in India.[52] Some simply occupied properties at will, moving into vacant houses, grabbing plots of land, and taking advantage of the chaos to reinvent themselves.[53] Tragically, senior government officials were also involved in this process of creative genealogical rewriting and asserting that they had left behind properties in India.⁵⁴ A 1954 inquiry by the Special Police Establishment (SPE) reported that 'about 50 building sites which were evacuee properties had been acquired in Karachi by Government Servants, some of them of very senior status.'⁵⁵ The SPE observed that 'it was common talk in Karachi' and in the rest of the country that senior officials had used their administrative powers and connections to acquire evacuee properties 'when they had left no property in India' and help their relatives and clients do so as well.⁵⁶ Some of the plots acquired were 'of considerable value' and many of the officers engaged in the appropriation of state property were doing so in contradiction of 'the declarations filed by them on solemn affirmation' that 'they abandoned no immovable property in India' with absolute impunity.⁵⁷

The central government's seizure of Karachi and its refusal to compensate the Sindh provincial authorities for the loss of their properties was itself in direct violation of British-era rules that categorically required the state to compensate any private or public institution or individual in exchange for the acquisition of their property. Having unlawfully seized Karachi, the central government ministers had taken it upon themselves to carry out personal inspections of its environs, receive deputations, and interfere at will with the administration of the city.⁵⁸ The ministers thought that their task was to personally intervene, in the manner of Timurid potentates, to remedy abuses brought to their notice by aggrieved residents.⁵⁹ The Administrative Enquiry Committee advised that ministers should concern themselves with more serious issues relating to excessive government expenditures in the absence of sufficient tax revenues and framing laws and policies to ensure the autonomous and transparent operation of the growing number of departments, and stop interfering in the routine affairs of the administration. It warned, for instance, that 'the leakage of revenue under the main heads like customs, excise and income-tax' was already in the range of fifteen to twenty per cent and needed to be urgently redressed if the increases in government spending on development were to be sustained without heavy borrowing.⁶⁰ It was in the politicians' own best interest to 'impose a self-denying ordinance' so that they could cease direct interference in the administration and simply inform those who came to them that they did not have any lawful power to get things done for them.⁶¹ If administrative autonomy was allowed to take root 'the public and all concerned' would be the winners in the long-run and the ministers could take credit for the improved efficiency.[62] As the complexity and numerical strength of the administrative apparatus grew the subjective, personalised and proprietorial attitude of the ruling elite boded ill for the ability of the state to maintain internal discipline.

Undaunted by these prognostications, the elected representatives continued interfering with the result that by July 1956, the Karachi Municipal Corporation 'was in very bad shape.'[63] In addition to 'several cases of embezzlement' the corporation's cashier had run away and official documents were being deliberately destroyed.[64] A major corruption scandal involving the faulty construction of thousands of quarters for refugees in the Malir and Landhi areas of Karachi had rocked the city at about the same time.[65] The concerned minister took note of the complaints and launched a personal initiative leading to the formation of an enquiry committee.[66] After the committee had deliberated action was taken against those suspected of involvement.[67] On 6 August 1956, it was reported that two executive engineers, seven assistant engineers and twelve overseers had been charged while the contractors were blacklisted and had paid eight hundred thousand rupees in damages.[68] The government then allocated an additional one million rupees for construction of the quarters along improved lines.[69] During this episode the 'Secretary, Ministry of Refugees and Rehabilitation was ignoring his Minister and policy directives', was 'not loyal to his Minister and was encouraging a controversy in the press.'[70] Of course, it was not possible for a commission of enquiry to be set up every time a scandal occurred and routine and departmental accountability had to be given priority over such extraordinary and politically motivated interventions.

Against this backdrop of ministerial interference and slackening intra-administrative accountability, officials 'were plunging too deeply into house building activities' having received in many cases allotments of plots of land from the state.[71] Some of the officials had 'embarrassed themselves by building houses beyond their means.'[72] The special provision of allowances to officers meant that they could avail of themselves considerably greater sums than the ten thousand rupees borrowing limit of the House Building Finance Corporation that ordinary citizens were allowed.[73] Given that at the time ten thousand rupees was a small fortune and the prices of land, construction materials and house rents were well within the means of officers on their regular

Grand Seigneurs **249**

salaries, such practices represented the triumph of greed over need. It was a matter of some concern than within a few years of independence Pakistan's civil and military officers had perfected and institutionalised the mechanism through which state lands and resources could be privatised even as their salaries were in real terms reduced. The state would acquire land or sell off its own land at below market rates to its civil and military officers. Loans and advances would then be offered to develop these properties without there being any bar on the ability of officers to acquire multiple plots over a period of time. While the civil and military officers acquired and developed an appetite for landed wealth their political masters took to living off the land. While on tour ministers expected to be lavishly entertained ignoring instructions to the contrary.[74] Ministerial ostentation was infectious and the files of the period are at times consumed by alarm over lavish expenditures on gifts, ceremonial occasions, dinner receptions, and outdoors entertainments by officers and attempted without success to reverse the trend.[75]

Equally worrisome was the association of public representatives with private concerns, business houses, and industrialists who created multiple conflicts of interests and brought the state into disrepute. This was hardly surprising given the hundreds of industrial units handed over to businessmen out of evacuee property. Rising development expenditure and industrial development projects undertaken by the industrial development corporation increased that impression. The 1949 Development of Industries (Federal Control) Act, for instance, established the central government's patronage over the cement, coal, electrical goods, power generation, glass, ceramics, textiles, steel, machine tools, telephone, paper, leather, tobacco and fishing industries. It was therefore perfectly understandable that businessmen identified material success not with the actual profitability of their companies or the quality of their entrepreneurship and management but with proximity to the politicians and bureaucrats in control of the levers of patronage.

In order to cultivate politicians and bureaucrats, a number of inducements were offered. Marriage alliances, post-retirement employment of officials in senior positions, jobs for the children of bureaucrats and political leaders, shares in the company, and membership of governing bodies and boards of directors, were just some of the inducements offered. Businessmen would go to great lengths to create and sustain the impression that they were under the protection and favour of Pakistan's sovereign-proprietors. By August 1950, the attempts of private companies to secure, or appear to have secured, state patronage were causing some embarrassment. It was vital, felt senior mandarins, to, at the very least, stop private companies from using terms such as 'Jinnah', 'Quaid-i-Azam', and 'Dominion' in their letterheads and advertisements lest 'the use of these words' be 'misconstrued to denote the patronage of the Quaid-i-Azam or any connection with the Government of Pakistan.'[76] It was also proposed that companies be prohibited 'from exercising undue influence' by publicly brandishing 'the names of distinguished shareholders.'[77] Eventually, the state gave up trying to enforce such an unpopular, and unprofitable, distinction and deemed that there would 'be no bar to a Minister holding shares in Company or to being a sleeping Partner in a Company or his serving as a Director ex-officio, on behalf of Government on the Board of Directors of any Company in which Government had invested money.'[78] To make matters worse, ministers and public representatives at all levels engaged in collusion with smugglers, grain hoarders, and even dacoits. In Sindh the members of the provincial assembly from Thar Parkar district along with 'Police and Government Officials' were staging dacoities to compel locals to hand over their stores of grain.[79] The provincial authorities also took full advantage of Liaquat Ali Khan's Safety Act to silence the opposition through arrests and intimidation.[80] Even former ministers 'were arrested under the Safety Act' which indicated that the authorities did not have sufficient grounds for arrest under the ordinary criminal laws.[81] The political nature of the charges was apparent when the prime minister urged the Sindh chief minister to withdraw 'the cases against Talpur and others' and abstain from the 'victimisation of officers.'[82]

In their desire to get re-elected politicians rode roughshod over democratic and legal norms. The initial enthusiasm felt at the introduction of universal suffrage in 1951[83] rapidly gave way to 'frustration and despondency' as 'malpractices perpetrated and underhand tactics used' came to light.[84] Ruling-party candidates tampered with electoral rolls, carved out 'pocket constituencies', stuffed votes, obstructed opposition candidates, and kidnapped and intimidated rivals with the support of the administrative machinery.[85] The Lahore High Court Bar Association testified that at least fifty Punjab provincial assembly members were elected due to the illegal intervention of the official machinery on their behalf.[86] The election tribunals, administrative staff, and official machinery were all under the control of the party in power and inspired little confidence.[87] Such arbitrary acts in violation of the law made the politicians dependent on the administrative machinery rather than their popularity to secure election. By favouring corrupt subordinates and undermining their own popular legitimacy, the politicians presided over the liquidation of their own authority and facilitated the rise of the governing corporation.

The politicians may have opened the doors to the sovereign-proprietorial mode of governance but it was their partisans, and later masters, in the mandarin and military castes that benefited the most. While the politicians visibly and highly unintelligently acted in a corrupt, acquisitive and power-hungry manner singularly motivated by the desire to be re-elected at any cost, the permanent employees set about a more systematic privatisation of state resources.[88] This was accomplished scientifically and quietly through house building schemes, special allotments of lands, assumption of policy-making and policy manipulation, prioritisation of infrastructure development activities towards lands in which they had investments to push up the market value thereof, and the passage of laws and regulations that provided legal cover to their theft of state resources. The impression created that the politicians were more corrupt while the bureaucrats and military officers were relatively clean helped the governing corporation gain the moral ascendancy over elected representatives. This impression was at one level correct in that the fractiousness of politics, the buying and selling of votes, the use of criminal tactics to punish rivals, hoarding of essential commodities and the politicisation of the administration, were very real aspects of political corruption. That said, the governing corporation contributed to political instability, interfered in the making and breaking of parties and governments, and manipulated the political scene to serve its own interests and deflect attention from its own privatisation of state resources. The governing corporation was also willing to pay a high price to its clients and stooges in the form of ministerial posts, contracts, and favours, to keep up democratic pretences and thus fuelled political corruption and the politics of patronage. Corruption was a tool that the governing corporation used to bind politicians to its will through the selective application and retrospective annulments of PRODA and through the provision of intelligence and administrative assistance to the king's party, such as Iskander Mirza and the Republicans, in order to get their members re-elected. The Pakistani ruling elite began to 'look upon the state as their personal estate' and sought to operate by 'spreading wide a network of patron-client relations' based on the principle that advancement in all walks of life was 'possible only through the patronage of powerful patrons.'[89]

7.3 POWERFUL PATRONS

The assumption of direct control by the governing corporation in 1958 and the purges of state employees, including eighty-four from the Class I officer rank, the crackdown on smuggling and hoarding, and the disqualification of an entire generation of Pakistan's politicians under the Electoral Bodies Disqualification Order (EBDO), did not actually diminish the growth in corruption though restrictions on the press and politics did help convey the *impression* that it had been reduced. Reflecting on the growth of corruption between 1958 and 1967, the Special Committee for the Eradication of Corruption from Services of 1967 asserted that under British rule 'for almost a hundred years public services at…the upper and middle echelons were by and large honest.'[90] Twenty years after independence, 'the misuse of official power for private gain', bribery, theft of state assets, nepotism etc., were a constant nuisance.[91] Honest citizens and public servants lived 'in a continuous state of displeasure and frustration' while the ranks of the corrupt were being steadily increased by the demoralisation of those who saw 'no purpose in swimming against a strong tide.'[92] The martial law of 1958 to 1962 had secured an initial reduction in the level of corruption but the aggravated insecurity of civil servants combined with strong demand quickly translated into a situation where the greater risk was 'covered by greater price.'[93] The local government system introduced by Ayub was characterised by the buying and selling of votes and had pulled the district administration into the web of local intrigue and pressure that corrupted and politicised the services.[94] Corruption in the land revenue administration at the lower levels was out of control as district officers concentrated on development, the generous allocations for which further fuelled corruption, wastage, and inflationary pressures.[95] The Public Works Department (PWD) was now a consolidated vertical combination of corruption from the labourers and clerks 'up to the Executive

Engineer and often higher.'⁹⁶ The police and taxation agencies were the 'most corrupt' at the middle and lower levels with extortion, bribery, faulty assessments, delays in registrations of cases and complaints and other irregularities taking a heavy toll on the ability of the state to dispense its core functions and keep a check on its elaborated activities.[97] The subordinate staff in the judiciary was 'regularly paid' by litigants and, shockingly, even judges had started taking bribes.[98] In industries, commerce, semi-government bodies and infrastructure departments 'illegal gratification' was 'received at all levels' with 'high officials' and lowly technical staff alike accepting bribes, doing favours, and crafting out of the body of the state their own petty estates.[99]

The anti-corruption establishment comprising the Special Police Establishment at the centre, the Directorate of Anti-Corruption in West Pakistan, the Bureau of Anti-Corruption in East Pakistan, and its provincial and district anti-corruption councils, were practically non-functional relative to the massive increases in expenditure and the sheer number of state employees. The intra-departmental controls had also eased significantly. Between 1948 and 1966 only three Class I officers in East Pakistan 'were successfully dealt with departmentally' for corruption.[100] The level of intra-departmental accountability was much better in West Pakistan with seventy Class I officers disciplined for corruption between 1948 and 1966.[101] The centre fared the best with one hundred and two Class I officers disciplined departmentally between 1948 and 1966.[102] While there was much left to be desired in the accountability of officers, the administrative support staff and low-paid employees of the state were also increasingly difficult to control. While in British India tipping was 'glossed over as a fact of life', twenty years after independence 'the rapacity of the class of inferior and subordinate officials' had 'assumed a disturbing proportion.'[103] The deterioration in the land revenue administration affected the largest number of people. The 'acts of corruption and rapacity on the part of the *patwari* and the hierarchy up to the level of the supervisory officers like Revenue Assistant' that occurred in the rural areas were practically innumerable.[104] With a mere seventy-one Class I officers in the anti-corruption establishment in the *entire* country responsible for maintaining accountability in an officer corps numbering over five thousand and total officials and employees of over a million in the context of a twenty-five fold increase in development expenditure between 1951-1952 and

1968-1969, the contagion was spreading almost unchecked.[105] Far too many of the cases failed to hold up in court. Of the total of twenty-three thousand six hundred and fifty-eight cases brought against government employees by the anti-corruption establishment between 1948 and 1966, only six thousand ended in convictions.[106]

Convictions that did take place most often resulted in reduction in pay, transfer, suspension, or an adverse report. These were of little deterrent value given the volume of money to be made. A part of the problem was that as officers carved out estates for themselves and patronised each other and subordinates they protected those who were guilty of even heinous acts of violence such as murders and robberies as well as less brutal offences. Given that neither the public nor officials had much regard for 'police integrity' there was little chance that the anti-corruption departments staffed by police could inspire much confidence.[107] Since the police stations in West Pakistan got 'only two rupees per annum for stationery' there was no way to operate police stations unless the officers and men, even the honest ones, lived off the land.[108] With superintendents of police increasingly corrupt and senior ranks protecting subordinates, the middle and lower ranks were getting harder to control. The officers and subordinate ranks were, in effect, imitating their most powerful patron, Ayub Khan.

In addition to the curious increases in the fortunes of his family after he became defence minister in 1954, Ayub Khan set the personal standard for corruption and patronage. The founding of Islamabad, in 1959, opened the doors to massive institutionalised corruption that has benefited three generations of Pakistani military and civilian officials through the allotment of plots at below market prices and heavy investment in infrastructure development in the capital territory. At another level deputy commissioners were expected to deliver basic democrat votes for the presidential elections. And then Ayub generously privatised public wealth to bind the hired clique of politicians, courtiers and ministers at his command to his will. During Zulfikar Ali Bhutto's 'tenure as Minister in the Ayub Cabinet' some nine million rupees were spent out of development funds on his two thousand acre Nasrat Farm.[109] Government expenditure on the sinking of private tube-wells cost two million rupees.[110] In his dealings with leading business houses, such as the Saigols, Ayub Khan would, if they required, personally approve their use of foreign exchange 'on the telephone.'[111]

Grand Seigneurs 255

Paraphrasing Confucius, Ayub reflected that 'Not more surely does the grass bend before the wind than the masses yield to the will of those above them.'[112] Ayub was also fascinated by the teachings of one professor Parkinson who asserted that 'In any organisation' there was the 'Abominable No Man' who should be bypassed in favour of the 'Yes Man' who got things done.[113] In dealing with the elected representatives of the masses in the assemblies, Ayub found that large numbers sought audiences and began by eulogising his services, insinuated that his advisers were not keeping him properly informed, ridiculed 'their rivals and detractors' and then ended by asking for a personal favour or request.[114] As the political tide turned against him in 1968, Ayub complained that his generously financed 'Muslim League is inactive and is not pulling its weight' leading to a political vacuum on the street which the opposition parties were filling.[115] In order to bail out his clients, Ayub ordered the 'administration down to the *tehsil* level' to maintain 'contact with the local Muslim League leaders' and help them in any way they asked.[116] A month later, Ayub fumed that he was 'surrounded by senior officials' who were disloyal to him and governors who were 'ineffective and incapable'.[117] His advisers were sycophantic to the point of making the regime and its leader an object of ridicule by obsequiously celebrating a 'Decade of Development' in the midst of widespread discontent that was boiling over onto the streets.[118] The cabinet ministers were non-entities and the king's party was inactive and ineffective and melting away in the face of opposition protests in spite of all he had done for it.[119]

What Ayub Khan's undergraduate debater level intellect failed to grasp was that a clique of bureaucratic yes men and political invertebrates bound to him by personal acts of generosity and patronage were the equivalent of grass in the Confucian analogy.[120] Now that the wind was blowing in the opposite direction the grass would bend in that direction as was its nature. Those willing to be bought are always keen to be resold for a higher price or will renounce their earlier allegiance in exchange for the forgiveness of the ascendant ruler if he lets them quietly enjoy the fruits of their earlier collaboration. Under Ayub Khan, efficiency was 'synonymous with irregularity' and the yes men who produced 'short term results by irregular methods' were 'generally considered more competent.'[121] In order to get things done and spend the money being pumped into development, government departments and officers were actually bribing each other to move things along.¹²² Ayub's basic democracies were particularly prone to having a large portion 'of the money allocated for development' appropriated 'by the officials and basic democrats.'¹²³ The 'phenomenal material prosperity' achieved by the corporate sector, industrialists, and other crony-capitalists thanks to the state patronage directed their way through the bureaucracy, infected the bureaucratic medium with 'the desire to try and keep pace' with the lifestyles of the entrepreneurs and managers in the private sector.¹²⁴ By the time the governing corporation was eclipsed and elected political rule restored, corruption was a serious problem at the lower levels, a significant one in the middle ranks and a growing cause for concern at the senior levels, especially in the development arm. Enough of the old ethos, however, remained so that the situation was neither hopeless nor beyond redemption and could be retrieved by a political leadership sufficiently enlightened to realise that by tolerating corrupt servants it would only undermine its own stability.

7.4 THE ESTATE OF PAKISTAN

While Bhutto was probably less personally acquisitive and certainly far more intelligent than Ayub Khan, he more than compensated by being vastly more arbitrary and contemptuous of the law. Although 'a façade of democracy' was retained from 1973 to 1977, Pakistan experienced 'authoritarian rule at its worst: capricious, tyrannical, Machiavellian.'¹²⁵ The government established 'transcendental control' over the various sections of the economy through its indiscriminate policy of 'nationalisation'.¹²⁶ In his pursuit of absolute power Bhutto undermined 'the operational autonomy of almost every organ of the state' and thus 'spread insecurity all around.'¹²⁷ The consequences included the spiralling increase in 'corruption within the government' presided over as it was by an 'increasingly omnipotent, arbitrary and corrupt central authority.'¹²⁸ Before Bhutto, corruption was a serious problem. By the time he was overthrown, it was a way of life.

The expenditure of six million rupees of state funds on Bhutto's private residences at Karachi and Larkana, payments of some two million rupees out of the Secret Service Funds to party workers and the illegal 'import of foreign goods for personal use of the approximate value of one and a half million rupees with the 'evasion of customs duty and sales tax estimated at nearly three million rupees were some of the more prominent personal instances of corruption.[129] The Z. A. Bhutto Trust was set up on 31 October 1973 and the People's Foundation Trust on 19 August 1974 to acquire assets and effectively put them at the disposal of the family. In this regard, a three thousand five hundred square yard plot valued at the market price of one thousand five hundred rupees per square yard was acquired from the Karachi Metropolitan Corporation for two hundred and thirty-five rupees per square yard with Afzal Said Khan, Bhutto's principal secretary, writing the official letters to 'get the necessary details tied up.'[130] On this plot a multi-storey building was constructed without an approved plan at the cost of twenty-five million rupees and rented out to several state-owned enterprises.[131] It appeared that the trusts were 'treated as family property' and 'in a fit of anger, during the enquiry' Mrs Bhutto admitted as much.[132] While Bhutto augmented his family wealth, his associates and subordinates, political and administrative, feasted upon the vast estate that Pakistan was now converted into and the residual hesitations of the Ayub period vanished.

Maulana Kausar Niazi, the religious affairs minister, spent nearly two million rupees of public money on the purchase of his own books.[133] Mumtaz Bhutto, the Sindh governor, compelled the Pakistan Shipping Corporation to take 'an expensive tied loan' of thirteen million US dollars against which three and a half million rupees were paid as commissions and brokerage.[134] This was accomplished 'through his trusted Additional Secretary and, in the process, received full support as a collaborator from Mr Saeed Ahmad of the Pakistan Shipping Corporation.'[135] Ghulam Mustafa Khar, the Punjab governor, transferred thirty-five acres of land to his brother Ghulam Meladi without any payment to the previous owner and gave one hundred and twenty-five acres to his brother Ghulam Arbi for payment of fifty-two thousand rupees.[136] Sadiq Hussain Qureshi, Punjab's chief minister, appropriated and sold one hundred and fifty-seven acres of state land for nearly one million eight hundred thousand rupees.[137] Jam Sadiq Ali in Sindh approved in his own hand one hundred and twenty-three applications for allotment of plots in Karachi meant to be auctioned and inducted one hundred and forty-five persons in the provincial Agricultural

Supplies Organisation 'at a time when it had not even a single vacancy.'[138]

The politicisation of the administration at all levels, its insecurity aggravated by the withdrawal of statutory protection and repeated purges and arbitrary transfers undermined autonomy and integrity. With remuneration levels cruelly cut by inflation and indifferent political leadership, the administration's powers were vastly increased by nationalisation and repressive laws. Combined, these factors led to the breakdown of state's already precarious inner moral balance. State employees were now consciously servants of their political masters and dependent on them for patronage and support. The internal discipline eroded as politically connected subordinates attacked senior officers who gave them adverse reports, got their postings through lobbying and currying favour, and victimised their subordinates with impunity. Busy courting favour and trying to save themselves departmental heads abandoned 'hierarchical supervisory inspections', collaborated in the concealment of corruption,[139] and even stopped cooperating with the auditing process.[140] The anti-corruption institutions were converted into instruments of intimidation and basically sought to find complainants 'ready and willing to relentlessly pursue' cases against individual officers.[141] The anti-corruption machinery, still functional though in decline in 1966, was all but incapacitated a decade later:

> The Income Tax bar of Karachi was asked by a visiting Member CBR to name or identify suspect officers. The short answer given to him was to go and just have a casual survey of the Income Tax Offices, noting the cars the officers were using, the persons to whom they belonged and their life style…This yawning gap between facts widely known and facts officially known has generally created the impression that Anti-Corruption Agencies have been corruptly quieted into not seeing the facts which can readily be seen and verified and not feeling what everyone else feels. It is this incapacity of the anti-corruption agencies which has evoked the suggestion that they should be completely done away for they add to the corruption instead of reducing it.[142]

Insofar as the private sector was concerned, its most successful members thought corruption 'useful and necessary' for the generation of profits, evasion of taxes and quick disposal of cases.[143] Even clerics were aggressively using religion in order 'to advance unjust causes and to protect ill gotten gains' such as the illegal construction of mosques and seminaries on unlawfully occupied land.[144] Over-centralisation at the secretariat combined with the reluctance of junior officials to take decisions at their own levels had created powerful incentives to pay bribes in order to get things done on time as otherwise cases could be kept pending for five to ten years. The abandonment of touring by district officers led to the further loss of control over the land revenue administration and law and order. The district-level centralisation at headquarters meant that people found it increasingly difficult to get access to the deputy commissioners without having to deal with corrupt intermediaries and lower staff. In the public sector corporations and nationalised industries management was haphazard and posts considered sinecures by the employees. The massive discretionary powers of officials combined with their depreciating pay made for a corrosive mixture of apathy, mediocrity, desperation, corruption and time-serving. Amazingly, a mere forty-nine officers[145] were convicted on charges brought against them by the special police establishment between 1967 and 1978 although thousands were arbitrarily dismissed, appointed, transferred and disciplined during the same years.[146]

Even as the state degenerated into an estate the reformers asserted that 'disparity between the incomes of the lowest and the highest officials militates against the development of an egalitarian society, free from economic and social injustices.'[147] In British India the state 'had neither in theory nor in practice, accepted the responsibility for housing' or the provision of conveyance for the personal use of its employees.[148] Instead, it *paid* in *cash* officers at a generous rate and middle ranks at a respectable rate. In Pakistan, 'housing and children's education' and 'expenditure on transport' were increasingly 'beyond the means of a Government Servant.'[149] The state was forced to provide tens of thousand of housing units and vehicles for private use and nationalised educational institutions relaxing quality control and reducing fees even as it poured borrowed and printed money into development schemes most of which was wasted and all of which fuelled inflation that further reduced the purchasing power of public sector salaries and reinforced the dependence of state employees on remuneration in kind. By standardising the pay scale into twenty-two grades the flexibility of the remunerative system was shattered and the marginal increases in everyone's salaries failed to keep pace with the increase in real prices. At the same time the state was providing more incentives in terms of plots, facilities and concessions that employees took advantage of to make ends meet in many cases and prosper in some. The corruption and wastage this engendered added to toxicity levels within the state apparatus. By 1977, the servants of the state were treated and compensated as they had been in pre-British India. It was only logical that they would also behave in the manner of their medieval and ancient antecedents. No body in a position of real authority seemed to understand that a single corrupt officer could do more damage to the state than many dozens of low level functionaries or that a properly remunerated, disciplined, and motivated officer corps was the key to keeping administrative subordinates in check.

Perceiving the state as estate, Bhutto's successors unabashedly took to privatising public assets. Zia presided over the privatisation of cantonment lands worth hundreds of billions of rupees as well as the distribution of billions of dollars of international military and economic assistance. Benazir Bhutto and Nawaz Sharif 'awarded lands worth $166.6 million (Rs 9.7 billion) to friends and cronies.'[150] Bribery and involvement in land development schemes as partners and collaborators became almost routine in the public sector as the distinction between personal and public wealth was blurred even further. Privatisation, like nationalisation, became a major vehicle of corruption while arbitrariness in decision-making multiplied delays and inefficiency. After 1972, so great was the increase in the levels of corruption that it could 'be declared an industry.'[151]

7.5 NEMESIS

Muhammad Khan Junejo, premier from 1985 to 1988, continues to be regarded as an honest and competent leader who could have done some good had he not been hampered by Ziaul Haq's interference. Junejo's government did, however, attempt to understand corruption and it found that by 1986, 70 per cent of citizens believed that they could not get what was legitimately due to them unless they paid bribes, called in favours, or used a combination of both.[152] Eight per cent thought police reform could possibly stem the increase in corruption, 5 per cent put their faith in elected representatives and a mere 3 per cent felt that political parties could fight the menace.[153] Seventy-five per cent believed that state officials and elected representatives placed themselves above the laws of the land and thus could not be expected to take steps to tackle corruption or enforce the rule of law.[154] Forty-six per cent thought that tax money collected by the state was stolen or wasted.[155] The apathy that prevailed was revealed by the lack of response to special questionnaires sent to members of the national and provincial assemblies as well as private citizens and government departments. Of the two hundred and forty-one questionnaires sent to the Punjab assembly only one reply was received while from the other provincial assemblies no replies were received.[156] Out of thirty-nine federal ministers and advisers one replied, of eighty-nine senators four replied, and of one hundred and ninety-four National Assembly members five replied.[157] From private citizens and government departments the showing was much better though still low with thirty-eight replies received against one hundred and twenty-eight questionnaires sent.[158] The Council of Islamic Ideology (CII) merely reproduced some extracts from an earlier study and remained silent thereafter.[159]

Interviews with leaders of public opinion revealed them superficially knowledgeable of the ways of corruption but most of them 'were long on talk and short on clarity.'[160] There was a strong tendency to generalise from personal experience. What was striking was that 64 per cent of the respondents operated on the assumption that corruption was unavoidable and a fact of life that one had to accommodate.[161] Twenty-four per cent thought that corruption was the intelligent thing to engage in while honesty was patently 'stupid'.[162] Thus, 88 per cent of the respondents thought corruption was either unavoidable or intelligent. This pointed 'to the mentality of the people at large' and indicated that corruption had become socially acceptable.[163] Intriguingly, people were no longer incensed by what they saw happening around them. In the 1970s the frustration with the growth of corruption was so great that even knowledgeable and experienced people talked 'of shooting a few hundred, may be a thousand suspected' of large-scale corruption as an example.[164] It appeared that outrage at those who abused public office for private gain had been transformed into apathy balanced by a desire to join the ranks of the corrupt if the opportunity arose.

In 2000, the Taskforce on the Reform of Tax Administration conducted its own survey of citizens, civil society representatives and government servants. Respondents were asked questions that required them to quantify on a scale of one to five with five indicating extreme concern and one indicating no concern. Overall, 79 per cent of respondents were extremely concerned or very concerned about corruption and the impact it was having on the country.[165] Amongst taxpayers, 65 per cent were extremely concerned and 18 per cent were very concerned about corruption.[166] The respondents felt sadness, frustration and hopelessness about corruption with about a third opining that corruption was caused by and had contributed to the 'collapse of moral values.'[167] While 27 per cent were worried about corruption due to its perceived link with underdevelopment and 21 per cent were concerned about it because of its negative impact on Pakistan international image, a mere 13 per cent made the connection between corruption and the breakdown of law and order, while only 19 per cent linked it to the failure in financial administration and the spectre of bankruptcy.[168]

Eighty-one per cent of the respondents, and 68 per cent of tax officials, regarded the state institutions as corrupt while 59 per cent overall felt the private sector to be corrupt.[169] The police was ranked as the most corrupt, followed by the lower courts, the Water and Power Development Authority (WAPDA), income tax, land revenue administration, customs, passports and ID, municipalities and sales tax.[170] Corruption was perceived to be particularly rampant in the criminal justice system and financial administration and substantially out of control in the other departments. Eighty-six per cent of the respondents thought corruption levels had either increased or remained constant between 1995 and 2000, and 78 per cent expected corruption to either continue increasing or stabilise, rampant though it was, at 2000 levels between 2000 and 2005.[171] Eighty-nine per cent of respondents were dismissive of 'corruption reduction initiatives' and harboured no expectations of improvement.[172]

At the CBR headquarters, 59 per cent of the respondents thought that corruption was fairly, very, or extremely widespread while in its self-assessment nearly half of CBR employees were considered corrupt.[173] That said the tax offices down the line were considered far more corrupt than the headquarters owing to greater public dealing. Overall, 78 per cent of income tax department employees, 76 per cent of customs employees and 68 per cent of sales tax staff were considered corrupt.[174] According to tax administrators, for 'each hundred rupees of genuine income tax payments' due to the state, it collected only about forty rupees due to corruption.[175] The remaining sixty rupees were divided between the assessment staff, the tax payer and the supervising officers. The ratio of collection was fifty-one out of every hundred rupees in customs and fifty-two out of every hundred rupees in sales tax.[176] Because of corruption, the state collected only *half* the legitimate amount of revenues from the *existing* tax base. Thus, if the tax-to-GDP ratio was in the range of 10-12 per cent the same percentage was not being collected due to corruption. To quantify the ratios, if the total taxes collected amounted to about two hundred and fifty-billion rupees in 1995, the amount collected should have been four hundred and fifty to five hundred billion rupees. By the same token, if we assume that half the tax administration personnel engaged in corruption as did half the tax payers, it would translate into a tenth of Pakistan's GDP being appropriated through corruption by twenty thousand government servants and half a million taxpayers. The real impact of this corruption is greater than the simple addition and subtraction of a tenth of total GDP when one factors in the borrowing at high rates of interests that the state resorts to in order the close the gap between its income and expenditures.

Since 2002, corruption in Pakistan has grown although, as in the Zia period, a robust rate of economic growth fuelled by remittances and transfers from abroad temporarily eased the resource squeeze of the 1990s. The devolution plan, which was the Musharraf regime's central reform of the state, has displaced a greater proportion of the corruption to the district levels with the *nazim* and DCOs responsible between the two of them for hundreds of millions of rupees of unchecked expenditure. Coordination has worsened, redundancies have multiplied and the quality of service delivery in almost every area has declined. At the centre a record-breaking seventy-seven member cabinet nominally presided over the distribution of largesse to the lower levels. Scandals ranging from the privatisation of the steel mills to the Pakistan-owned Roosevelt Hotel in Manhattan, the 2006 stock market crash which wiped out twelve billion dollars, the economic collapse of the national airline are only some of the cases that have come to light. In the meanwhile, the expenditure on the president's household and staff rose from seventy-five million rupees in 1999 to three hundred and nine million rupees in 2007 while the prime minister's personal expenses rose from ninety-eight million rupees in 1999 to three hundred and sixty-seven million in 2007.[177] Expenditure on the National Assembly rose from two hundred and fifty million rupees in 1999 to one billion rupees in 2007 while the Senate's expense increased from one hundred and eleven million rupees to five hundred and seventy-seven million during the same period.[178] Ministers, assistants and advisers that cost the exchequer twenty-four million rupees in 1999 cost it one hundred and fifty-five million in 2007.[179] Senior government servants have repeatedly allotted themselves additional plots of land with the government's blessing at about one-fourth of the market value while expenditure on their perks and privileges mean that secretary rank officers cost as much as four hundred thousand rupees or nearly seven thousand dollars per month to maintain. Their take home salaries are equal to perhaps a tenth of this amount. Lower ranked employees clamour for the privatisation of their state-owned residential units.

With the National Accountability Bureau (NAB) little more than an instrument of political harassment and intimidation, routine accountability procedures were severely neglected. The regime does not seem to appreciate the difficulty that any serious attempt to detect, prosecute and secure convictions under the laws of the land must take into consideration. By one guesstimate, five to ten thousand individuals have made more than ten million rupees through corruption over the past seven years. Even if the state wishes to bring one thousand of these individuals to justice given the complexity of white-collar crime and the rules of evidence and procedure, it would take an investigative team of three or four officers to handle a single case from its inception to a court decision. In effect, that means a trained and highly motivated cadre of about five thousand anti-corruption officers would be needed to deal with only the major instances of corruption.

The PPP-led government that came to power at the centre after the February 2008 elections forced Musharraf from power six months later through a sustained political campaign that interfaced with the lawyers' protests against the military ruler's arbitrary dismissal of sixty senior judges. Rumours of corruption and maladministration have abounded, fuelled in part due to the break-up of the grand coalition that forced Musharraf from power. The ascent of Benazir Bhutto's widower, Asif Ali Zardari, to the presidency, has done little to inspire public confidence. Zardari is widely believed to be corrupt and is popularly known as 'Mr

Ten Per cent'. He is also held responsible for much of the bad name that the two Benazir Bhutto governments (1988-90, 1993-96) earned for alleged corruption. Zardari denies the allegations and points out that he was kept in jail for a total of eleven years on different charges inclusive of corruption without a single case resulting in a conviction. That in itself is an indicator of the weakening of the state and the open politicisation of its anti-corruption institutions in that it cannot legally convict through a fair judicial process persons widely perceived to be corrupt.

As of 2006, Pakistan is ranked in the same range as Nigeria and Sierra Leone by Transparency International's Corruption Perception Index (CPI). Its score on the corruption scale with ten indicating low levels of corruption and one indicating extremely high levels is 2.2/10 which makes it the twenty-first most corrupt (out of one hundred and sixty-three countries in the survey) country in the world.[180] Over one hundred and ten countries on the survey scored four or less on the CPI and in 2005 the World Bank estimated the global annual cost of corruption at one and a half trillion US dollars.[181]

Continental bureaucratic empires are intensely proprietorial entities that blur the distinction between private and public wealth. In Pakistan, the reassertion of the proprietorial attitude transcends the formal divisions within the state apparatus as well as the alternation of democratic, oligarchic and dictatorial regimes. This reversion has cost Pakistan dearly in material as well as moral terms eroding the effectiveness and legitimacy of the state even as it renders the society increasingly ungovernable. Without reform of the culture of power and sustained improvement in the quality of the bureaucracy it is difficult to see any positive change taking place. The attrition to which the state's credibility is subjected combined with the steady accretion to fatalism and fractiousness of those governed by it, and the inadequacy of reform efforts past and present, have facilitated and been reinforced by the reversion to an arbitrary, delusional and proprietorial culture of power. The reassertion of the pre-British norms of exercising power have accelerated the decline of the state and evoked 'in the people arbitrary and corrupt responses.'[182] This behaviour is ultimately self-defeating for the 'arbitrary culture of power among the ruling elite destroys social solidarity, promotes internal chaos and 'invites external aggression'.[183] A ruling elite characterised by intellectual stagnation that presides over a society driven into public apathy and fear of the rational through decades of arbitrariness and corruption of every conceivable kind can do little but await the arrival of its Nemesis.[184]

NOTES

1. On 27 November 1900, while on campaign in China, Major Amar Singh of the Jaipur State forces received 'the shocking news that the Jaipore Durbar had confiscated the three jagirs, leaving barely anything at all' for his clan of Kanota Rajputs. The British intervened on his behalf as the premier of Jaipur, Babu Kanti Chander Mookerjee disliked the Kanotas was pursuing a vendetta against them. It was only after Mookerjee died in February 1901 that the dispute, which had dragged on for many years, came to an end. Amar Singh, *Reversing the Gaze: Amar Singh's Diary, A Colonial Subject's Narrative of Imperial India*, Susanne H. Rudolph, Lloyd I. Rudolph and Mohan Singh Kanota, eds., (Boulder, Colorado: Westview Press, 2002), 133-50. The Rajput nobles dared not speak out, unless they had British support, against such arbitrary treatment 'for fear of the state officials' who were by and large Brahmans, Banias, and Kashmiris from outside the Rajputana. In Jaipur 'not a single Rajput' aristocrat held a high administrative post. Ibid., 428. Thus, the princely states preserved the pre-British practices and norms including the sovereign-proprietorial exercise of power and were far more arbitrary than the directly administered territories (British India).
2. Alexis de Tocqueville, *The Old Regime and the Revolution*, trans. Alan S. Kahan, eds., François Furet and Françoise Mélonio (Chicago: University of Chicago Press, 1998), 231.
3. Eraly, *The Mughal World*, 42.
4. Kautilya, *The Arthashastra*, trans. L. N. Rangarajan, 282.
5. Ibid.
6. Ibid., 283.
7. Abul Fazl draws a distinction between a 'true king' and a 'selfish ruler.' The principles of government and the apparatus of empire, comprising armies, treasuries, imperial servants, slaves, courtiers etc., were similar in both cases. The difference lay in the spirit that animated the ruler's deployment of these assets and his enlightened self-interest. The true sovereign possessed sufficient detachment from the spectacle and manifestations of power to work diligently to make it enduring and great. The selfish sovereign, however, confused the spectacle with the substance and spent his time and energies revelling in the former to the neglect of the latter and in doing so hastened his own downfall and inflicted calamities on his subjects. Abu'l Fazl Allami, *A'in-I Akbari*, trans. H. Blochmann, 58.
8. Ibid., 252.
9. Ibid.
10. Ibid.
11. Ibid.
12. Ibid.

13. Ibid.
14. Ibid.
15. Ibid.
16. Ibn Hasan, *The Central Structure of the Mughal Empire*, 269.
17. Ibid.
18. Nick Roberts, *The Corporation that Changed the World: How the East India Company Shaped the Modern Multinational* (Hyderabad: Orient Longman Limited, 2006), 35.
19. Ibid.
20. Ibid.
21. Ibid., 84.
22. Ibid., 86.
23. Rajat Datta, *Society, Economy and the Market: Commercialisation in Rural Bengal c. 1760-1800* (New Delhi: Manohar, 2000), 264.
24. *Selection of Papers from the Records at the East India House Relating to the Revenue, Police and Civil and Criminal Justice under the Company's Governments in India*, Vol. II, 17.
25. Bosworth Smith, *Life of Lord Lawrence*, 408.
26. One can see the decline in construction standards in Pakistan almost anywhere. The buildings that date from the British Raj, though badly maintained and extensively abused, are generally in better shape than those built in the 1950s and 60s. Those buildings that date from the 1950s and 60s are in turn in better shape than those built post-1972. The deterioration in construction standards in the public sector is matched by deterioration in the private sector. Even the higher income groups, who typically invest $100,000 to $500,000 in the acquisition of residential property and home construction, suffer at the hands of dishonest contractors and construction companies. One major reason for this is the abandonment of quality controls and inspections by the state and the corrupt collusion of public officials.
27. The distorting effects of the war were felt primarily in the form of war-profiteering, some thing that also took place in Britain on a larger scale and inflation eating into the purchasing power of the millions of additional employees hired by the government in railways and war industries.
28. *Report of the Pay and Services Commission, 1959-1962*, 11.
29. Ibid.
30. Ibid., 18.
31. Mitha, whose first assignment as a military officer was famine relief in Bengal (1943) was horrified by the '…complete lack of concern at the lower levels of bureaucracy for the agony of those who were dying.' The callousness of wealthier Indians and the indifference of the provincial (Muslim League) government, which was responsible for food and agriculture and controlled the lower rungs of the administration, were appalling. They also stood in sharp contrast to the integrity and compassion of the steel frame: 'Despite these obstacles, the famine relief succeeded, chiefly due to the hard and dedicated work of the Deputy Commissioners and Superintendents of Police who managed to control the corruption successfully.' Mitha, *Unlikely Beginnings*, 68.

32. For the past several years, officer trainees at the Civil Services Academy at Lahore have been taught to think of the citizens as consumers of public services and themselves as providers of public services. This is meant to help them develop a customer-friendly corporate culture towards the citizen-consumers. The transparent shallowness of this approach means that it is not taken seriously by anyone though it represents a tragic waste of time and resources. It is also yet another example of how American tutelage has robbed Pakistan of the ability or the will to develop rational training programs for its own officers based on indigenous social sciences research. That the quality of this research is generally quite poor while the quantity is inadequate are also reflective of the non-seriousness of the Pakistani ruling elite. Without a rational and effective social sciences base of its own, Pakistan's rulers cannot comprehend, let alone positively change, the realities of their own country. They are also rendered subservient to irrational foreign tutelage or ideological delusions and quick fixes.
33. It also employs different methods and can often be eased into due to the cultural parameters within which it operates. Alexander Evans examines these parameters and finds that in different cultures, from Nigeria to China, an important manifestation of corruption is influence. These go by different names and have slightly different connotations depending on the context. Thus in China, *guanxi* indicates a hierarchically but mutually dependent patron-client relationship that promotes the interests of all concerned. In Russia, *blat* serves much the same purpose and its connotations include official clout and personal contacts that can help get things done. In Pakistan, *sifarish* indicates patronage or help with securing official favour. In Nigeria, *dash*, or tipping/bribery, refers to the ability to use money or clout to help kinsmen in need of government favour and is an integral part of the local Big Man culture. Alexander Evans, 'The Utility of Informal Networks to Policy Makers', in Anne Lane et al., *Terrorism, Security and the Power of Informal Networks* (Cheltenham: Edward Edgar, 2008).
34. National Documentation Centre, Islamabad, Folder Eight. 1950, File No. 2(1)-PMS/50, Government of Pakistan, Prime Minister's Secretariat, 'Correspondence with the Governor, East Bengal', 189.
35. Ibid.
36. Ibid.
37. Ibid.
38. Jilani, *Fifteen Governors I Served With*, 48.
39. Ibid., 49.
40. National Documentation Centre, Islamabad, Folder Eight. 1950, File 2(2)-PMS/50, Government of Pakistan, Prime Minister's Secretariat, 'Correspondence with the Governor Punjab', 288.
41. Ibid., 289.
42. Ibid., 291.
43. Ibid., 292.
44. Ibid.
45. 'Report of the Committee on the Study of Corruption, 1986', 76.
46. Ibid.
47. Ibid., 78.
48. Ibid., 84.

49. 1949, File No. 20/CF/49, Government of Pakistan, Cabinet Secretariat, Cabinet Branch, No. 2300-Reh.-49/1676, 'Policy Regarding Allotment of Evacuee Property', 1.
50. Ibid.
51. Ibid., 16.
52. Ibid.
53. Ibid.
54. Ibid.
55. Ibid., No. 108/CW/54, Karachi, 20 December 1954, 'Allotment of Evacuee Plots in Karachi to Government Servants', 1.
56. Ibid.
57. Ibid.
58. *Report of the Administrative Enquiry Committee* (Karachi: Government of Pakistan Press, 1953), 18. Its members were the Establishment Secretary, T. B. Creagh Coen, the Finance Secretary, Mumtaz Husain, and the Joint Secretary Establishment, E. A. Franklin.
59. Ibid.
60. Ibid., 43.
61. Ibid., 18.
62. Ibid.
63. 1956, File No. 314/CF/56, Government of Pakistan, Cabinet Secretariat, Cabinet Branch, Cabinet Meeting, 11 July 1956, Case No. 590/37/56, 'Administration of the Karachi Municipal Corporation', 2.
64. Ibid.
65. 1956, File No. 192/CF/56, Government of Pakistan, Cabinet Secretariat, Cabinet Branch, 'Report of the Enquiry Committee set up by the Government to Examine Defective Construction of Quarters in the Refugees Colonies in Karachi', 1.
66. Ibid., 4.
67. Ibid.
68. Ibid., No. F.3(17)/55-R.III, Government of Pakistan, Ministry of Refugees and Rehabilitation, Karachi, 6 August 1956, 1.
69. Ibid.
70. 1956, File No. 299/CF/56, Government of Pakistan, Cabinet Secretariat, Cabinet Branch, Cabinet Meeting, 5 July 1956 Case No. 573/36/56, 'Action against the Secretary, Ministry of Refugees and Rehabilitation', 2.
71. 1949, File No. 317/CF/49, Government of Pakistan, Cabinet Division, Note by T. B. Creagh Coen, Chairman Administrative Enquiry Committee, April 1953, 2.
72. Ibid.
73. Ibid.
74. Ibid., 'Public Entertainment for Hon'ble Ministers when on Tour', 1.
75. Ibid., Notification No. 4/12/49-SE.II-11 July 1951, 1.
76. 1949, File No. 10/CF/49, Government of Pakistan, Coordination Branch, P.U.C. D.O. Letter No. 365/337, 10 August 1950, Secretary Commerce and Education to Secretary-General, 1.
77. Ibid.

78. Ibid., Cabinet Meeting, 7 January 1955, Case No. 28/2/55, 'Association of Central or Provincial Ministers with Private Concerns', 1.
79. National Documentation Centre, Islamabad, Folder Three. 1948, File No. 7(2)-PMS/48, Government of Pakistan, Cabinet Secretariat, Prime Minister's Secretariat Karachi Branch, 'Correspondence with the Premier, Sind', 285-286.
80. 1954, File No. 245/CF/54, Government of Pakistan, Cabinet Secretariat, Main Cabinet Branch, Cabinet Meeting, 15 December 1954, Case No. 1012/104/54, 'Victimization of the Members of the Opposition by the Present Sind Ministry', 1.
81. Ibid.
82. Ibid., Cabinet Meeting, 11 April 1955, Case No. 219/27/55 'Withdrawal of Cases against Mr Talpur and Others', 1.
83. In India, adult suffrage displaced the urbanised Anglophone elite from the political process and brought to power dominant caste and kinship leaders whose attitude towards the state was, even at the theoretic level, proprietorial. Frankel, *India's Political Economy*, 21. India's Planning Commission estimates that 70-90 per cent 'of rural development funds are siphoned off by a web extending from the *panchayat* head to the local MP, with officers too claiming their share.' Ramchandra Gupta, *India After Gandhi: The History of the World's Largest Democracy* (London: Macmillan, 2007), 683.
84. *Report of the Electoral Reform Commission, 1956* (Karachi: Government of Pakistan Press, 1956), 1.
85. Ibid.
86. Ibid., 6.
87. Ibid., 5.
88. In India corruption is as bad, if not worse, than in Pakistan. The difference lies in the share of the loot and plunder. In India the criminality and rapaciousness of the politicians is far greater than that of the civilian or military bureaucracy and more entrenched in the system. In most provinces at least one-fifth of the members of the provincial legislatures are indicted criminals, with some states, such as Rajasthan, boasting assemblies where two-fifths of the members are indicted criminals. After the 2004 general elections, nearly one fifth of both Congress and BJP MPs at the centre were indicted criminals. Some 45 per cent of Congress MPs and 23 per cent of BJP MPs owed money to public institutions. Indeed, a Gallup survey indicated that on the eve of the sixtieth year of independence 91 per cent of the citizens believe their political leaders to be corrupt. Political parties had for all practical purposes degenerated into dynastic estates, communal or caste-based fascist organisations, and criminal mafias. Ramchandra Gupta, *India After Gandhi*, 684-6. What is clear from the Indian experience is that democracy is only incidentally relevant to the quality of leadership.
89. 'Report of the Committee on the Study of Corruption, 1986', 94.
90. *Report of the Special Committee for Eradication of Corruption from Services, 1967* (Rawalpindi: Government of Pakistan Press, 1967), 4.
91. Ibid., 3.
92. Ibid.
93. Ibid., 5.

94. Ibid.
95. Ibid., 12.
96. Ibid., 13.
97. Ibid.
98. Ibid.
99. Ibid.
100. Ibid., 25.
101. Ibid.
102. Ibid.
103. Ibid., 27.
104. Ibid., 43.
105. Ibid., 65.
106. Ibid
107. *Report of the Pakistan Police Commission 1969-70*, 23.
108. Ibid., 31.
109. *White Paper on the Performance of the Bhutto Regime*, Vol. I, Z. A. Bhutto, His Family and Associates (Islamabad: Printing Corporation of Pakistan, 1979), 7.
110. Ibid.
111. Roedad Khan, ed., *The British Papers: Secret and Confidential India-Pakistan-Bangladesh Documents 1958-1969* (Karachi: Oxford University Press, 2002), 694.
112. Baxter, ed., *Diaries of Field Marshal Mohammed Ayub Khan, 1966-1972*, 5. 6 September 1966.
113. Ibid., 11. 23 September 1966.
114. Ibid., 114. 7 July 1967.
115. Ibid., 285. 21 November 1968.
116. Ibid.
117. Ibid., 291. 20 December 1968.
118. Ibid.
119. Ibid.
120. One of these yes men included Altaf Gauhar who, in his capacity as Ayub Khan's information secretary, was responsible for ensuring that proper respect was paid to the government.
121. *Report of the Special Committee for Eradication of Corruption from Services, 1967*, 14.
122. Ibid., 12.
123. Ibid., 16.
124. Ibid., 14.
125. 'Report of the Committee on the Study of Corruption, 1986', 89.
126. Ibid.
127. Ibid.
128. Ibid., 89-90.
129. *White Paper on the Performance of the Bhutto Regime*, Vol. I, Z. A. Bhutto, His Family and Associates, 9-10.
130. Ibid., 42.
131. Ibid., 42-3.
132. Ibid., 45.

133. Ibid., 50-51.
134. Ibid., 56-57.
135. Ibid.
136. Ibid., 71-72.
137. Ibid., 73.
138. Ibid., 78.
139. *Report of the Commission on the Eradication of Corruption, 1979* (Islamabad: Government of Pakistan, 1979), 34.
140. Ibid., 35.
141. Ibid., 46.
142. Ibid.
143. Ibid., 13.
144. Ibid., 17.
145. Class I/Grade 17-22.
146. *Report of the Commission on the Eradication of Corruption, 1979*, 202.
147. *Report of the National Pay Commission, 1976* (Islamabad: Printing Corporation of Pakistan, 1976), iii.
148. Ibid., 112, 105.
149. Ibid., 119.
150. Siddiqa, *Military Inc.*, 105.
151. Siddiqui, *Towards Good Governance*, 221.
152. 'Report of the Committee on the Study of Corruption, 1986,' 27.
153. Ibid.
154. Ibid., 34.
155. Ibid.
156. Ibid., 36-8.
157. Ibid.
158. Ibid.
159. Ibid., 39.
160. Ibid., 43.
161. Ibid., 60.
162. Ibid.
163. Ibid.
164. *Report of the Commission on the Eradication of Corruption, 1979*, 19.
165. *Report of the Taskforce on Reform of Tax Administration*, 14 April 2001, 164.
166. Ibid.
167. Ibid.
168. Ibid.
169. Ibid., 165.
170. Ibid.
171. Ibid., 166.
172. Ibid.
173. Ibid., 171.
174. Ibid., 172.
175. Ibid.
176. Ibid., 173.
177. Kunwar Idris, 'So Much of Money, So little Work', *Dawn*, 18 August 2007, 7.

178. Ibid.
179. Ibid.
180. Transparency International 2006, Corruption Perception Index. Downloadable from www.transparency.org/publications in PDF format.
181. Robert Looney, 'Profiles of Corruption in the Middle East', *Journal of South Asian and Middle Eastern Studies*, Vol. XXVIII, No. 4, Summer 2005, 2.
182. 'Report of the Committee on the Study of Corruption, 1986', 94.
183. Ibid., 95.
184. Ibid.

Conclusion

Pakistan's governance and culture of power closely correspond to the highly arbitrary, proprietorial and ideocratic pattern of continental bureaucratic empires in the subcontinent's history. Over a period of sixty years, the Anglo-Muslim elite that governed Pakistan has failed to build upon the positive aspects of the British imperial nomocracy. It has actually done worse through the subversion and destruction, both conscious and unintentional, of the structure, ethos, and discipline of the state apparatus. Unlike more successful bureaucratic states, including examples as diverse as Singapore, Malaysia, France, and Japan, the rulers of Pakistan and their administrative acolytes failed to realise that in such states it was and is the intellectual and moral quality of the servants of the state that determine, above all else, the quality of order and the capacity for progress.[1] At a macro level, the rulers and their advisers parroted the latest clichés being churned out by academic industries in the United States and its post-1945 European dependencies. This advice emphasised 'democracy' and 'development' and stigmatised law and order, taxation and general administration as 'colonial' relics that could now be safely ignored to allow for the innate goodness of man to reign free while the state 'reoriented' itself towards development work. The repetition of received wisdoms did not diminish in any way the reality on the ground that in the *actual* exercise of power the rulers became increasingly isolated from the legal, psychological and cultural inhibitions of the British period. The mental horizon of the ruling elite was fragmented into one part in which the fashionable rhetoric was regurgitated on command in order to secure aid and another major part that led it to behave in a progressively more medieval manner. The latter severely affected the entire state apparatus and rendered it dysfunctional in both principle and operation.

This dysfunction is a phenomenon that cuts across the rise and fall of governments and the performance of Pakistan's administrative institutions. Its greatest indicator is that even as components of the apparatus and the leadership fail to perform their statutory functions, they overreach into other spheres and try to concentrate the powers that lawfully belong to others into their own hands. The original breaches in the functional division of the state were made by elected representatives during Pakistan's early years. They were warned of the consequences by British governors and civil servants to the effect that such arbitrary and unlawful interference in the administrative institutions was for the politicians an exercise in self-immolation. Heedless, the politicians used and abused the apparatus to secure their personal power and wealth and drew the higher bureaucracy and the armed forces into politics while punishing opposition leaders and dissenters through repressive legislation, ordinances and the repeated imposition of governor's rule. By using the administrative institutions to secure personal and political ends, elevating bureaucrats such as Ghulam Muhammad to cabinet posts, and recklessly pushing forward with the nationalisation of the armed forces, which led to the rise of Ayub Khan to the post of army chief in 1951, the politicians opened the door to the ascendance of a governing corporation of mandarins, praetorians, guardians, and *diwan*s. There was no way that a clever bureaucrat like Ghulam Muhammad or an ambitious army chief like Ayub Khan could have manipulated their way to political power.

The governing corporation reinforced the dysfunction of the Pakistani state but reversed its polarity. Instead of politicians using the administration for political purposes it was now the politicians who were used and abused by the governing corporation. For five years (1953-1958) an effort was made by the senior officers of the higher bureaucracy and military to maintain a constitutional and democratic façade in a manner reminiscent of the East India Company's indirect rule, or 'dual government' over Bengal from 1757 to 1774. In Pakistan, as in early-colonial Bengal, this exercise met with limited initial success followed by mounting contradictions. The initial success was achieved by admitting pliant members of the superior judiciary into the charmed circle and allowing obedient politicians a free hand to exercise patronage in exchange for their support of the supreme executive. These political hydraulics further exacerbated the crisis of state through the enfeeblement of the provincial and local governments with the former in West Pakistan swept away by One Unit in 1955. The superior judiciary under Muhammad Munir became a servile instrument of the executive while the army chief was brought into the central cabinet immediately after the first Constituent Assembly was rendered non-functional just days before the final debate on the long awaited Constitution Bill. To top it all a state of emergency was proclaimed and the fate of the nascent democracy was sealed.

In their handling of politics and politicians the leaders of the governing corporation proved as arbitrary and inept as the politicians had been when it came to dealing with the administrative institutions. Political insecurity and with it fractiousness, volatility and corruption increased while, at the same time, opposition to the manipulation of politics by powerful members of the executive grew correspondingly. By 1958, it was evident that the governing corporation would have either to cede real power to elected representatives in order to maintain the credibility of the constitutional system it had forced into existence after the dissolution of the first Constituent Assembly, or be forced from power after the proposed March 1959 elections, or else assume complete and direct control. Egged on by his army chief and assured of the superior judiciary's support, President Iskander Mirza took the third option, abrogated the constitution, declared martial law and made Ayub Khan the Chief Martial Law Administrator. Having sacrificed the constitution under which he was president at the altar of unenlightened selfishness, Mirza was soon overthrown by his army chief and on 28 October 1958, slinked off quietly into exile to spend the rest of his life in pointless though richly deserved obscurity.

Over the decade that followed, bureaucratic overstretch took the shape of the higher bureaucracy performing purely political tasks, making policies, and overseeing their execution. The CSP, in particular, acted as a body of political governors and were required to deliver the Basic Democracy vote in favour of Ayub as it constituted the presidential Electoral College. The eventual revival of politics under a new constitution, formulated by the governing corporation that established an imperial presidency with vast powers exercising transcendental control over the political system and state apparatus but without any effective countervailing restraint, reduced the politicians to ciphers and courtiers. The absence of formal statutory safeguards for civil servants, as realised after the initial purges, did not affect the higher bureaucracy but Ayub's reliance on the 'yes man' who produced results and got things done, especially on the development side, led to a disruption of the administrative structure which lost its competence relative to the tasks it was being asked to perform. The linchpin of the British-era area administration was the deputy commissioner who acted as collector of land revenue, magistrate and supervisor of police. Without making adequate administrative provisions, the general administration was burdened with additional duties on the development side while most of the senior planning posts were occupied by CSP members. Order, taxation and supervision of the police were deemed passé while the area administration was deflected from its original purposes. It seemed as if the ruler and his advisers thought that the core functions of the state would take care of themselves. This reorientation led to the polarisation of the higher bureaucracy along CSP/non-CSP lines with the latter becoming envious of the unprecedented power, prestige, and patronage entrusted to the former even in areas where it lacked technical competence. For its part the CSP got carried away and abandoned its role of bureaucratic leadership. It also *prevented* any substantial reform of the administrative system, such as the introduction of a development commissioner with statutory powers to coordinate all the health, education, and public works functions of the state, and practically monopolised all important posts. In doing this the group solidarity of the higher bureaucracy was undermined and immense reservoirs of resentment were created against the domination of the CSP and its successor, the DMG, that continued to be drawn upon even after it lost its pre-eminent position. The impact on the efficiency, integrity and prestige of the state apparatus of overstretch and internal polarisation was singularly adverse.

Between 1969 and 1977 these dysfunctional tendencies were reinforced in two very different but equally pernicious ways. Yahya Khan marginalised the CSP and circumvented the higher bureaucracy by concentrating decision-making and execution powers in the hands of a military-staffed CMLA Secretariat. Cashing in on the popular antipathy towards the higher bureaucracy in general and CSP in particular, hundreds of officers were purged and subjected to humiliating inquiries which were often motivated by their closeness to Ayub. Yahya believed that the country could be administered like the army, and while he prided himself on his ability to handle politicians and sort things out, it was eventually his regime that was handled and sorted out with disastrous and irretrievable consequences for the unity and territorial integrity of Pakistan.

While Yahya and his military colleagues lost one half of the country, Zulfikar Ali Bhutto put the state apparatus in the half that remained through a series of punishments and humiliations from which it never recovered. All of the propensities towards the politicisation of the administration, the destruction of functional autonomy and the treatment of servants of the state as personal servants, in evidence amongst elected representatives during the first decade of independence, were revisited upon the apparatus with a vengeance. Bhutto consciously set about 'breaking the back' of the CSP and his objective was to transform the state apparatus into an instrument of personal rule operationally more powerful than ever before. Moreover, just as Ayub had increased the scope of administrative power without improving its competence, Bhutto did so by nationalizing industries and services and increasing the size of the public sector. This meant that civil servants untrained for the management of productive assets found themselves in charge of cotton processing plants, shipping, banks and insurance companies. In the meanwhile, their remuneration, discipline, and autonomy, were undercut on a vast scale by 'democratisation' of the pay scales, inflation, and politicisation through arbitrary appointments, dismissals, and transfers. Statutory guarantees were not incorporated into the 1973 Constitution, while the public service commissions were stripped of their autonomy from the executive and reduced to the status of exam administering bodies. The elected civilian executive proved as hostile to provincial and local autonomy as its military and bureaucratic predecessors and continued with the centralisation of fiscal power and interference in the provincial administration. The autonomy of the superior judiciary was steadily whittled down by amendments and intimidation while Bhutto sought to turn the military into a willing accomplice through the elevation of officers who did as they were told and generous increases in the share of the armed forces in the public wealth. These attempts backfired and after being overthrown by his hand-picked army chief, Ziaul Haq, Bhutto was condemned to death after being found guilty of conspiracy to murder by a majority of supreme court justices.

Zia's eleven years with its prolonged martial law (1977-1985) saw the autonomy of the provinces, local governments, judiciary and political parties being significantly reduced. There was, however, a marginal rehabilitation of the higher bureaucracy though this was more than offset by the negative impact of Islamisation at home and the holy war bankrolled by the United States and its allies against the Soviet Union in Afghanistan, on the social fabric of Pakistan.[2] While prognostications and proposals were made by senior civil servants about the long-term trends and the dire need to undertake sound reform of the state apparatus, the influx of easy money from abroad combined with the banality of Zia's senior political advisers and henchmen, led to a decade that could have been used to rehabilitate the state being squandered. The net result was that as Pakistani society became more ungovernable the state apparatus did not improve commensurately and no serious structural reforms were made, the availability of sound diagnoses and prescriptions from Zia's own establishment secretary notwithstanding. Furthermore, the structural imbalances of over-centralisation and inadequate fiscal and administrative autonomy at the levels where the state apparatus could materially affect lives for the better worsened or remained constant.

Between 1988 and 1999 political instability, often instigated by the establishment itself, combined with sheer ineptitude and lack of vision and understanding on the part of the elected representatives, brought the state apparatus to the verge of exhaustion. Once again, dysfunction was aggravated with local, provincial, and federal authorities tripping over each other. The bureaucracy was being used as a political instrument, the military relied upon to perform routine bureaucratic functions, and the superior judiciary eventually stormed into submission. The politicisation of the administration brought it to a point where it became simply ineffective in dispensing its assigned functions even as these roles were increased in number. It appeared that the elected representatives had learnt nothing from their earlier experiences and in compounding the malaise and trying to secure their personal rule at any cost they, like earlier rulers, succeeded in making the former worse while actually hastening their own departure from power.

Since 1999, the decline of the state apparatus has been accelerated by the reforms introduced by Musharraf's military regime.[3] The devolution of power to elected local governments, combined with the marginalisation of the higher bureaucracy and the undermining of provincial autonomy has steadily drawn the military into local politics and administration.

These manoeuvres have alienated and demoralised the higher bureaucracy even as fiscal centralisation translates into the ability of the praetorian-dominated centre communing directly with elected *nazim*s in charge of districts. The manner of their election is often suspicious and the politicisation of the administration under their control, inclusive of the police, land revenue, and development, is presently an uncontested fact of life. As in the Ayub and Zia periods, the availability of easy money from abroad sapped the political will to engage in serious thinking and undertake substantive reform of the state apparatus. The post-Musharraf period is still taking shape though there does not seem to be any coherent plan on part of the politicians that may enable them to restore their credibility and ameliorate the crisis of state.

Faced with the prolonged inability of Pakistani rulers, be they politicians, bureaucrats, or soldiers, to understand the imperatives of structural and operative autonomy, the resultant dysfunction has steadily undermined the ethos, *esprit de corps*, and professional integrity of the state apparatus. In terms of their behaviour the personnel and departments of the state have been converted into instruments of arbitrary and personal rule. There are substantial differences in the mental and moral outlook of a civil servant who thinks and acts as a servant of the law and one who defines his own competence in terms of his ability to do what the ruler asks of him regardless of the legality of the order. The negation of rules and procedures by the servants of the state in order to please the boss or secure their personal interests has impacted the state apparatus in several mutually reinforcing ways characterised by arbitrariness, delay, confusion and personalisation.

In terms of arbitrariness the servants of the state have increasingly adopted a behaviour pattern that revolves around doing what they please as opposed to what the law, rules and policies require of them. As long as the select cases that affect the interests of those powerful enough to do them harm or secure them favour are speedily resolved the servants of the state have a more or less free hand. But this affects the apparatus in terms of its day-to-day efficiency and objectivity. For instance, cleaning and routine maintenance are normally ignored until the day before or morning of an important meeting or a visit by a senior officer or dignitary. First Incident Reports are often not registered by the police unless the supplicant can produce a bribe or demonstrate influence with the senior officers. On the other hand, fraudulent reports and cases are registered at will as and how the rulers and their protégés deem fit or as the police themselves become party to local disputes or engage in harassment. An application for a license to do business, acquire property for an industrial project, set up a school or hospital, or simply register for a computerised national identity card, will collect dust or be lost unless a member of the bureaucracy or ruling group can be motivated to take a personal interest in the case. Officers and staff come into work late and cynically congratulate themselves in that by leaving on time they are at least being punctual about something.[4] Officers and staff, having come to work late, spend much of their time intriguing, gossiping, socialising and doing personal rather than official work. As work piles up the nuisance value of the officers and their staff increases, forcing applicants to make repeated trips. This breeds hatred of the state, apathy to its interests, demoralisation amongst honest citizens and irrepressible opportunism amongst those willing to play, or try to play, a game without rules. The state and society as a whole are the losers as the credibility of the former in the eyes of the latter declines and the body politic is subjected to the administrative equivalent of death by a thousand cuts.

The collective impact of arbitrariness, delay, confusion, and personalisation on the state apparatus is felt most tangibly in terms of its growing ineffectiveness. As the officers and staff divert their attention away from the performance of their duties under law it becomes harder for the state machinery to do anything properly, including serving the interests of the rulers in a sustainable manner. Sheer incompetence and apathy translates into sloppiness and indiscretion which bring the rulers as well as the state into disrepute. Moreover, as the state softens many orders given cannot be executed at all while others are delayed or simply lost in transmission somewhere along the line. While this mode of functioning may have worked in pre-modern times thanks to the extraordinary exertions of the sovereign, the state machinery is now too complex and vast to be managed and led through such limited and highly subjective means. The decreasing effectiveness of the state and the loss of discipline, order, and control within the apparatus leads to the infamy of the rulers, diminishes their chances of staying in power, and contributes to their unpopularity. Faced with the irrational parasitism of many of their leaders and colleagues, the fear of what might happen in case 'accountability' is arbitrarily meted out by the next ruler leads many *honest* and capable servants of the state to do nothing or spend their time recording objections on the files brought to their notice thereby further reducing the speed of the state machinery, or serving out sentences without any substantive posting as officers on special duty. This further demoralises the apparatus and depletes its slender reserves of capable and upright officers. In essence, the servants of the state, reduced to the condition of personal servants of the politically powerful, have become miniature reflections of their masters. It means that all too often, the officers with integrity do not get sufficient opportunity to gain experience in important positions while those subservient to the rulers are placed in key positions where they can effectively promote the personal interests of their masters. Thus, on the one hand Pakistan has many honest but inexperienced bureaucrats while on the other it has a greater number of dishonest ones who invest their time not in performing their statutory functions but in pleasing the boss. The moral relationships within the apparatus, and between the servants of the state, citizens, and the leadership, have, consequently, all but collapsed.

Driven by and accelerating this collapse of trust, respect, and discipline is the proclivity of the rulers and their servants to treat the state as a personal estate. This dimension of Pakistan's culture of power exercises a gravitational hold on the entire governance process. It cuts across institutional, class and intellectual divisions in Pakistani society and military rulers, elected representatives and mandarin politicians are equally held in thrall by a proprietorial attitude towards the state. Pakistani politicians try to convert as much of the public wealth into personal assets and consider it their *haq* (right) to at least recover the costs of their election campaigns from abuse of official powers. The more sophisticated bureaucrats and military officers have refined the privatisation of state resources into a science. Self-righteous theocrats have taken to the occupation of state lands and converted them into illegally built mosques, seminaries and residences. The private sector, often with official collusion, also grabs public lands and wealth even as it evades taxes and ignores standards and laws. As the state grows enervated, even the academia and media have taken to cutting the public purse and wholeheartedly joined the drive for privatisation of public wealth albeit on a more limited scale than their compatriots in other sectors.

The result of this insidious proprietorial attitude is evident from corruption, decay of the state of order and descent of society into moral and legal chaos in stark contrast to the British period and in marked resemblance to the pre-British periods. A portion of this corruption is institutionalised while a substantial percentage at the lower levels affects ordinary people and aggravates loss of order and control within the state apparatus. From the constable and the *patwari*, to the local council and lower courts, bribes must be paid in order to get the machinery to move at all. Even then, it moves slowly and ineptly and often needs further inducements. With the officers themselves party to this corruption or simply unable to perform the supervisory tasks expected of them, the subordinate staff is a disorganised, turbulent, and anarchic mass of the incompetent, the corrupt and the malevolent. Instead of improving the training, remuneration, prestige and supervision of the subordinate staff, little effort was expended even on the officers while discretionary powers, politicisation, and declining real pay created an atmosphere conducive to the promotion of two main alternatives for most public servants—corruption or destitution. The response of individuals in society has been to try and take advantage of the phenomenon for their personal benefit even as they complain about the menace of corruption. The dissolution of public morality, the growth in the social acceptability of corruption and enveloping contempt for the law and the state are some of the other responses to the 'disease'. Taken together, Pakistan has become an ungovernable and cynical society and it is generally assumed by people that the rulers and the servants of the state, from the lowly constables to the 'Honorable' ministers are stealing as much as they can and treating the state as a personal estate. This perception further reinforces the decline in trust and demoralises those public servants who are actually honest and competent. It must be borne in mind that amongst the rulers and servants of the state honesty is defined as not taking bribes or engaging in outright oppression. The privatisation of public wealth through acquisition of plots of land below the market rate, influencing decisions in favour of their clients or themselves, receiving concessions, transport, lavish gifts and other privileges open to abuse, are not considered 'corruption' by those who exercise power since it is done under legal cover or has simply ceased to arouse ire.

In the eyes of the rulers the utility of corruption in its legal and illegal forms is that it binds people to their will, at least apparently. The medieval logic is that if the ruler allows his servants and clients to take more than their fair share of the *ruler's* wealth, they can be blackmailed by threat of accountability or influenced through material inducements into doing what the ruler wishes of them. Corruption is also 'useful' for carving out of the body of the state apparatus a group of loyalists who, presumably, will do anything to keep the incumbent in power for fear of being punished by his prospective successor. By allowing political and administrative subordinates to run wild the irksome operational autonomy of the state apparatus can be converted into servile instrumentality. The price of such tactical cunning has been strategic disaster for the rulers. In addition to diminishing the effectiveness of the state apparatus and destroying their own reputations, the rulers find themselves surrounded by sycophants who tell them what they want to hear, thereby causing them to lose their grip, never particularly firm in the case of Pakistani leaders, on reality. Corruption also makes for very poor adhesive as Iskander Mirza, Ayub Khan, Zulfikar Ali Bhutto, learnt, and Ziaul Haq was beginning to learn before his death. A corrupt servant or political client is his master's worst enemy as the temporary immunity he enjoys makes him even more overbearing and incompetent than he otherwise would be. It also leads them to peddle their influence and carve out their own estate and engage in more injustice and oppression than their master would perhaps be willing to sanction. Those who can be bought will sell themselves to a higher bidder and are unlikely to stand by their master if the tide turns against him.

The inability of successive regimes to reform the state apparatus in a meaningful and constructive manner and thus secure their own long-term interests reflects the delusional facet of Pakistan's culture of power and governance. From a very early stage the rulers withdrew into a world of contagious fantasy, inspired and generously patronised by the United States. Instead of rationally comprehending the realities of governance in the subcontinent and working for slow and steady improvement in the quality of the state apparatus along trajectories in evidence before 1947, the rulers took to parroting, mimicking, and occasionally implementing solutions devised by foreign 'experts' and consultants. A remarkable testament to the faith-based approach of the United States is that there is hardly any substantial deviation in the principles of the 'anti-colonial', 'democratic' and 'development' oriented advice tendered in the early 1950s and the 'bottom up', 'people centred' and 'anti-colonial' rhetoric of the late-1990s and early twenty-first century. In the interim, most of the states in the developing world who took the US advice have collapsed into internal chaos and external penetration. That many of the states that took the Soviet advice or adopted some other ideological solution also fared as badly or worse is no consolation though the broad lesson to be derived is that governance requires great reserves of patience, reason, and the capacity to resist irrational tutelage. The heedlessness and unreason of the great powers aggravates the miseries of the weak and over-clever.

While advice and funds from the United States steadily debilitated the cognitive function of the Pakistani state apparatus, the rhetoric of religiosity added to internal divisions and accelerated the movement towards a medievalised society. Dire warnings of the ultimate impact of using religion as an instrument to secure political ends, the full force of which is now beginning to be felt, were ignored as often as they were given. The modernist Anglo-Muslim elite surrendered its credibility at home through its proximity to the United States even as it undermined domestic stability and its international reputation by appeasement of orthodox elements. In the meantime the quality, effectiveness, and public perception of the state apparatus declined with the caveat that such reforms as were implemented accelerated the descent of state and society into fragmentation and disorder.

Each major constituent of the state apparatus has been affected by and contributed to the general decline in governance. The higher bureaucracy has been reduced in stature and competence to a shadow of its former self and behaves as an auto-phage. The law and order administration has evolved into the most unlawful and disorderly component of the state machinery. This has affected the ability of the state to check corruption and make its writ run in an effective or lawful manner. The financial administration has alternated between periods of complacency when assistance from the United States, and therefore also its satellites and dependencies such as the United Kingdom and Japan, was forthcoming and utter desperation when easy access to external sources of financing dried up. The inability of the financial administration to tax domestic resources and spend such revenues with a tolerable degree of efficiency even by the standards of other countries in the same income range as Pakistan has ramifications for almost all sectors of the state and society. Insufficient tax revenues due to the corruption and incompetence of the financial administration mean greater reliance on borrowing and printing of currency to meet expenditures, a large part of them on development. The lack of financial discipline translates into the wastage of these and other funds. The public perception that the tax money is liable to be wasted or simply stolen makes citizens reluctant to pay while the poor intellectual and moral qualities of the tax administration personnel encourage evasion and bribery. As for the land revenue administration, which affects the largest number of people, scarcely a thought has been spared for it and it exists by virtue of sheer inertia, its oppressiveness and liability to abuse ignored by the policy makers. Repeated military interventions have tarnished the military's own reputation, reduced the insulation of the military from politics and administration, and multiplied internal contradictions. Attempts by military rulers to 'reform' Pakistan and engineer politics have harmed the state apparatus and produced grave distortions in the political and social environment of the country.

These policy makers, reformers and public servants have operated under the illusion that the quality of the state apparatus is of little concern and that governance and public service are 'humdrum' activities best left to the mediocre. It appears that the Pakistani elite in its understanding of the state and the exercise of power has appropriated and internalised the worst and most irrelevant lessons from the American experience and combined them with the ideocratic and arbitrary culture of power of the subcontinent. A globalisation of the discourse on the state has proceeded along with and often reinforced the reversion to pre-British modes of exercising power. Having become more contemporary and fashion-conscious in its rhetoric and material trappings, the Pakistani elite has also become more medieval, obsolescent and 'indigenous' in its actual exercise of power and competence with dire ramifications for the state apparatus. Although history does not furnish grounds for optimism there are sufficient indications of insight and vision in the records of the state itself that strongly suggest that present outcomes were not completely inevitable.

The salvation of a state to be successful must be grounded in a rational diagnosis of the central element of the crisis that afflicts it. At the heart of this crisis in Pakistan lies the exercise of power in an arbitrary, proprietorial and delusional manner at all levels of the state apparatus and government. This manner of exercise is the product of millennia of ideocratic arbitrary rule and substantially inherent in the structure and ethos of continental bureaucratic empires. Being so firmly rooted in the historical experience of governance, it cannot be easily reversed since over time the social and cultural fabric has been woven around these attitudes. Any reform must therefore accept that it will take several generations to bring about substantive change. Indeed, it took two generations for the British Indian state to reform the culture of power of its five thousand senior-most officers and an additional forty to fifty years for these reforms to take root in the bureaucratic middle order and act as a restraint on the lower ranks. Pakistan's reformers, on the other hand, in their obsession to produce quick results and inspired by absurd notions derived from American tutelage about the innate goodness and malleability of the human race, get easily demoralised when their ill-conceived efforts invariably fail.

Pakistan is a continental bureaucratic empire. The territories that presently comprise it were governed by continental bureaucratic empires long before the British advent. The British, however, reformed the state apparatus inspired and compelled by a combination of their anomalous culture of power and Enlightenment notions of governance. Thus, while bureaucracy was not a colonial invention, the modernised apparatus of the British Empire in India was a synthesis of indigenous administrative methods and Western ideas and principles. The relationship between the British Indian state and the pre-British states was analogous to the relationship between the absolute monarchy and royal bureaucracy of Old Regime France (1624-1789) and the Napoleonic bureaucracy that still administers France today, five republics, numerous upheavals, and two hundred years later.

The British in India, like Napoleon in his own country, realised that in continental bureaucratic empires the intellectual and moral qualities of the servants of the state were the major determinants of the quality of governance. It was in the ruler's own interest to ensure the highest possible median quality of civil servant, especially in the higher bureaucracy. This meant recruitment on merit, security of tenure, internal discipline, autonomy under the law, excellent pay, the cultivation of a powerful *esprit de corps* and the association of maximum prestige with service to the state. The British left behind institutions and practices that were undermined by successive regimes and their administrative collaborators in Pakistan even as the powers, patronage and financial disbursements under the control of the state apparatus increased exponentially. In principle, therefore, the rulers and the servants of the state need to realise that as an administrative state Pakistan must ensure that the best and the brightest are inducted into the officer corps of the state apparatus and that the viability of the state depends on this being done. The recruitment, discipline and transfers of the servants of the state must be entrusted to autonomous bodies constituted by acts of parliament effectively reducing the role of the rulers to the making of policies and overseeing their implementation. Given the self-inflicted disasters that successive rulers have brought upon themselves by interfering in the administration of the state they would do well to restrain themselves from such activities. An able, autonomous and motivated higher bureaucracy is also the key to gradually and peacefully restoring overall civilian supremacy over the state apparatus, reducing the level of corruption, improving the maintenance of order and ensuring the effectiveness of the writ of the state. It is also the surest way to restore the prestige of the state, act as a bulwark against obscurantism, ensure that the enormous sums spent on development are effectively used, and provide politicians with inputs that can help them formulate sound policies.

Having outlined the broad principles of reform the actual task must be entrusted to senior members of the state apparatus and political leaders. The demoralisation and degradation of the former and irrational compulsions and heedlessness of the latter render it practically impossible for substantive reform to take place. Worse, so little time has been devoted to understanding the state apparatus from within or without that the reforms embarked upon thus far have done more harm than good. With each passing year, however, the state apparatus weakens in terms of effectiveness even as internal challenges to its writ mount. The growing immensity of the challenge reinforces Pakistan's arbitrary, irrational and proprietorial culture of power. The ultimate challenge that any ruling elite can face is an existential crisis which emanates from its inherent deficiencies of attitude, mentality, experience, and competence. The Pakistani elite, as well as its counterparts in many other developing countries of whom a large proportion are in South Asia, Central Asia, and the Middle East, has singularly failed to demonstrate the ability or the will to rise above its own character. Due to this failure, it has for all practical purposes condemned itself and the society it presides over to a condition in which the pre-British past and the post-colonial present and future bear ever greater resemblance to each other.

NOTES

1. After a decade of disasters it appears that at least some of the more intelligent advocates of American triumphalism have toned down their rhetoric. Francis Fukuyama notes, for instance, that 'The difference in development outcomes between East Asia and Latin America since the 1970s is largely due to the greater competence and strength of state institutions in the former region, rather than to market-friendly policies.' Francis Fukuyama, *After the Neocons: America at the Crossroads* (London: Pacific Books, 2006), 123. Fukuyama practically commits heresy by acknowledging that 'Before you can have a democracy, you have to have a state....' Ibid., 125.
2. Abdel Bari Atwan provides a sobering perspective on the Afghan jihad's most famous offspring—al Qaeda. Writing about the cultural context from which al Qaeda emerged, Atwan states: 'Secrecy and the necessity for secrecy, or at least discretion, for survival, has historically been a part of the Arab experience, as is the ability to undermine an enemy with a patient watchfulness that will discover his secrets.' Abdel Bari Atwan, *The Secret History of al Qaeda* (Los Angeles: University of California Press, 2006), 125. Al Qaeda's strategic design is the provocation of Western or allied ground invasions of Muslim countries and then slowly grind down allied, but primarily US, military power through prolonged insurgencies. This has the added advantage of fuelling anti-West sentiment in the Muslim world and isolating the westernized Muslim elites who opt to side with the West in its struggle against militant Islam. Given the economic crisis that the United States finds itself at the centre of, and the seemingly endless conflicts in Afghanistan and Iraq, al Qaeda's grand strategy appears to be working remarkably well.
3. The downfall of the Musharraf regime was precipitated by the loss of support within the military. Although in 2008, 'The election commission had failed to stop the PML-Q [the pro-Musharraf party] from carrying out extensive pre-poll rigging before the elections...army chief, General Kayani had signalled to the administration and intelligence agencies two days before the election that there was to be no interference or rigging.' Ahmed Rashid, *Descent into Chaos: How the War against Islamic Extremism is being lost in Pakistan, Afghanistan and Central Asia* (London: Allen Lane, 2008), 390. Unsurprisingly, in the context of the struggle against the Taliban in Afghanistan, '...the international community failed to grasp early on the centrality of law enforcement and justice-sector reform...Law enforcement was left for last, was given the least funding, and commanded the least attention of the Western donors.' Ibid., 204.
4. In many departments the subordinate staff have become audacious enough to *tell* the officers come three o'clock in the afternoon that it is time to leave.

Bibliography

Private Papers from Pakistan

Rathore, Zafar Iqbal. Police Service of Pakistan, 1960-1996. Private Papers

———, 'Failure of National Integration or Regionalism in Pakistan.' Islamabad: National Defence College, 1984.
———, 'Psycho-Social Environment of Pakistan.' Undated.
———, 'State and Economy'. Note submitted to the 1992 Economy Commission, March 1992, Islamabad
———, 'State and Order'. Paper presented to the Interior Minister, Lt. General Moinuddin Haider, February 2000.
———, 'State and Society.' Paper presented to the Interior Minister, Lt. General Moinuddin Haider, February 2000.

Zaidi, Syed Ijlal Haider. Civil Service of Pakistan, 1954-1990. Private Papers

———, 'Civil Services Commission Report.' Government of Pakistan, Cabinet Secretariat (Establishment Division), 1982.
———, 'Promotion Policy.' Government of Pakistan, Cabinet Secretariat (Establishment Division), 1984.
———, 'Proposed Secretariat Group and DMG Group to be Merged Together as Pakistan Administrative Service.' Government of Pakistan, Cabinet Secretariat (Establishment Division), n.d.
———, 'Provincial Administration.' Government of Pakistan, Cabinet Secretariat (Establishment Division), 1982.
———, 'Quota System.' Government of Pakistan, Cabinet Secretariat (Establishment Division), 1982.
———, 'Reorganisation of Services Structure.' 'Secretariat Staffing.' Government of Pakistan, Cabinet Secretariat (Establishment Division), 1985.
———, 'Report of the Committee on Recruitment and Emoluments of Inspectors/Assistant Sub-Inspectors of Police and Tehsildars/Naib Tehsildars.' Government of Pakistan, Cabinet Secretariat (Establishment Division), 1984.
———, 'Secretariat Staffing.' Government of Pakistan, Cabinet Secretariat (Establishment Division), 1982.

Declassified Government of Pakistan Record

Government of Pakistan, 1947. File No. 21/CF/48. Cabinet Secretariat.
———, File No. 35/CF/47. Cabinet Secretariat.
———, File No. 224/CF/47. Cabinet Secretariat. Cabinet Branch.
Government of Pakistan, 1948. File No. 2(2)-PMS/48. Cabinet Secretariat. Prime Minister's Secretariat Branch.
———, File No. 2(3)-PMS/48. Cabinet Secretariat. Prime Minister's Secretariat Branch.
———, File No. 2(4)-PMS/48. Cabinet Secretariat. Prime Minister's Secretariat Branch.
———, File No. 3(3)-PMS/48. Cabinet Secretariat. Prime Minister's Secretariat Branch.
———, File No. 3(5)-PMS/48. Cabinet Secretariat. Prime Minister's Secretariat Branch.
———, File No. 3(6)-PMS/48. Cabinet Secretariat. Prime Minister's Secretariat Branch.
———, File No. 4(4)-PMS/48. Cabinet Secretariat. Prime Minister's Secretariat Branch.
———, File No. 5(1)-PMS/48. Cabinet Secretariat. Prime Minister's Secretariat Branch.
———, File No. 6(4)-PMS/48. Cabinet Secretariat. Prime Minister's Secretariat Branch.
———, File No. 7(2)-PMS/48. Cabinet Secretariat. Prime Minister's Secretariat Branch.
———, File No. 10/CF/48. Cabinet Secretariat.
———, File No. 29/CF/48-II. Cabinet Division. Cabinet Secretariat.
———, File No. 46/CF/48. Cabinet Secretariat.
———, File No. 148/CF/48. Cabinet Division.
———, File No. 150/CF/48. Cabinet Secretariat. Cabinet Branch.
———, File No. 163/CF/48. Cabinet Division.
———, File No. 220/CF/48. Cabinet Division. Cabinet Section.
———, File No. 231/CF/48. Cabinet Secretariat.
———, File No. 232/CF/48. Cabinet Division.
———, File No. 245/CF/48. Cabinet Division. Cabinet Section.
Government of Pakistan, 1949. File No. 2(2)-PMS/49. Prime Minister's Secretariat.
———, File No. 2(3)-PMS/49. Prime Minister's Secretariat.
———, File No. 2(5)-PMS/49. Prime Minister's Secretariat.
———, File No. 2(6)-PMS/49. Prime Minister's Secretariat.
———, File No. 2(7)-PMS/49. Prime Minister's Secretariat.
———, File No. 2(8)-PMS/49. Prime Minister's Secretariat.
———, File No. 3(1)-PMS/49. Prime Minister's Secretariat.
———, File No. 3(2)-PMS/49. Prime Minister's Secretariat.
———, File No. 3(4)-PMS/49. Prime Minister's Secretariat.
———, File No. 10(5)-PMS/49. Prime Minister's Secretariat.
———, File No. 20/CF/49. Cabinet Secretariat. Cabinet Branch.
———, File No. 173/CF/49. Cabinet Secretariat. Cabinet Branch.

————, File No. 264/CF/49. Cabinet Secretariat. Cabinet Branch.
————, File No. 317/CF/49. Cabinet Division.
Government of Pakistan, 1950. File No. 1(1)-PMS/50. Prime Minister's Secretariat.
————, File No. 2(1)-PMS/50. Prime Minister's Secretariat.
————, File No. 2(2)-PMS/50. Prime Minister's Secretariat.
————, File No. 2(3)-PMS/50. Prime Minister's Secretariat.
————, File No. 2(4)-PMS/50. Prime Minister's Secretariat.
————, File No. 3(2)-PMS/50. Prime Minister's Secretariat.
————, File No. 3(3)-PMS/50. Prime Minister's Secretariat.
————, File No. 3(4)-PMS/50. Prime Minister's Secretariat.
————, File No. 3(6)-PMS/50. Prime Minister's Secretariat.
————, File No. 3(8)-PMS/50. Prime Minister's Secretariat.
————, File No. 3(15)-PMS/50. Prime Minister's Secretariat.
————, File No. 3(17)-PMS/50. Prime Minister's Secretariat.
————, File No. 3(18)-PMS/50. Prime Minister's Secretariat.
————, File No. 3(20)-PMS/50. Cabinet Secretariat, Prime Minister's Secretariat Branch.
————, File No. 4(3)-PMS/50. Prime Minister's Secretariat.
————, File No. 5(2)-PMS/50. Prime Minister's Secretariat.
————, File No. 6(4)-Cord/50. Prime Minister's Secretariat. Coordination Branch.
————, File No. 7(1)-PMS/50. Prime Minister's Secretariat.
————, File No. 21/CF/50 Vol. V. Cabinet Secretariat. Cabinet Division.
————, File No. 53(13) Cord/49-50. Prime Minister's Secretariat. Coordination Branch.
————. File No. 80/CF/50. Cabinet Secretariat. Cabinet Branch.
————. File No. 82/CF/50. Cabinet Secretariat.
————. File No. 277/CF/50. Cabinet Secretariat.
Government of Pakistan, 1951. File No. 92/CF/51. Cabinet Secretariat. Cabinet Branch.
————, File No. 240/CF/51. Cabinet Secretariat. Cabinet Branch.
Government of Pakistan, 1952. File No. 1(1)-PMS/52. Cabinet Secretariat. Prime Minister's Branch.
————, File No. 1(4)-PMS/52. Cabinet Secretariat. Prime Minister's Branch.
————, File No. 2(1)-PMS/52. Prime Minister's Secretariat.
————, File No. 2(2)-PMS/52 Pr. III. Prime Minister's Secretariat.
————, File No. 2(3)-PMS/52. Cabinet Secretariat. Prime Minister's Branch.
————, File No. 3(2)-PMS/52. Cabinet Secretariat. Prime Minister's Branch.
————, File No. 3(3)-PMS/52. Cabinet Secretariat. Prime Minister's Branch.
————, File No. 3(5)-PMS/52. Prime Minister's Secretariat.
————, File No. 3(6)-PMS/52. Prime Minister's Secretariat.
Government of Pakistan, 1953. File No. 23(34)-PMS/53. Cabinet Secretariat. Prime Minister's Branch.
————, File No. 112/CF/53. Cabinet Secretariat. Cabinet Branch.
————, File No. 181/CF/53. Cabinet Secretariat. Cabinet Branch.
————, File No. 271/CF/53. Cabinet Secretariat. Cabinet Branch.
Government of Pakistan, 1954. File No. F. 1(1)/54-FC. Cabinet Secretariat. Cabinet Branch.

―――, File No. 8/CF/54-55-XIII. Cabinet Secretariat. Main Cabinet Branch.
―――, File No. 214/CF/54. Cabinet Secretariat. Cabinet Branch.
―――, File No. 245/CF/54. Cabinet Secretariat. Main Cabinet Branch.
Government of Pakistan, 1955. File No. 17/CF/55. Cabinet Secretariat. Cabinet Branch.
―――, File No. 111/CF/55. Cabinet Secretariat. Cabinet Branch.
―――, File No. 230/CF/55. Cabinet Secretariat. Cabinet Branch.
―――, File No. 231/CF/55. Cabinet Secretariat. Cabinet Branch.
―――, File No. 256/CF/55. Cabinet Secretariat. Cabinet Branch.
Government of Pakistan, 1956. File No. 192/CF/56. Cabinet Secretariat. Cabinet Branch.
―――, File No. 299/CF/56. Cabinet Secretariat. Cabinet Branch.
―――, File No. 314/CF/56. Cabinet Secretariat. Cabinet Branch.
Government of Pakistan, 1958. File No. 595/CF/58. Cabinet Secretariat. Cabinet Branch.
―――, File No. 651/CF/58. Cabinet Secretariat. Cabinet Branch.
Government of Pakistan, 1959. File No. 196/CF/59. Cabinet Secretariat.
―――, File No. 467/CF/59. President's Secretariat.
―――, File No. 475/CF/59. President's Secretariat. Cabinet Division. Cabinet Branch.
―――, File No. 476/CF/59. President's Secretariat. Cabinet Division. Cabinet Branch.
Government of Pakistan, 1960. File No. 79/CF/60. President's Secretariat. Cabinet Division. Cabinet Branch.
―――, File No. 178/CF/60. President's Secretariat.
Government of Pakistan, 1962. File No. 38/CF/62(2)-V. President's Secretariat. Cabinet Division. Cabinet Section.
Government of Pakistan, 1965. File No. 71/CF/65. President's Secretariat. Cabinet Division.
―――, File No. 99/CF/65. President's Secretariat. Cabinet Division.
―――, File No. 172/CF/65. President's Secretariat. Cabinet Division.
―――, File No. 208/CF/65. President's Secretariat. Cabinet Division.
―――, File No. 306/CF/65. President's Secretariat.
―――, File No. 326/CF/65. President's Secretariat.
Government of Pakistan, 1974. File No. 382/CF/74. Cabinet Division. Progress Section.

Unpublished Official Reports

Ahmad, G. 'Mr G. Ahmad's Committee on Police Organization and Reforms in Pakistan'. Islamabad: Government of Pakistan, President's Secretariat, 1972.
Dehlavi, S. K. 'Report on the Administrative Law & Courts in England, France, Germany, Switzerland, Italy, Holland, Belgium, Sweden & Spain.' Rome/Islamabad: Government of Pakistan, Ministry of Foreign Affairs, 1961.
Giles, A. J. 'Final Report of Chief Superintendent A. J. Giles, British Police.' Islamabad: Government of Pakistan, Interior Division, 1984.

Gladieux, Bernard L. 'Reorientation of Pakistan Government for National Development.' Karachi: Presented to the Planning Board, Government of Pakistan, 1955.
Hilali, Agha. 'Hilali Report, 1977: Working of three Pakistan Missions Abroad, Ottawa, New York and Ankara.' Islamabad: Government of Pakistan, 1977.
Husain, Akhtar. 'Report on the Reorganisation of the Karachi Administration, 1951.' Karachi: Government of Pakistan, Interior (Home) Division, 1951.
'Report of the Committee for the Study of Corruption, 1986.' Islamabad: Government of Pakistan, Cabinet Secretariat, 1986.
'Report of the D. K. Power Working Group, 1969.' Islamabad.
'Report of the High Powered Law Reform Committee, 1974.' Islamabad: Government of Pakistan, Ministry of Law and Parliamentary Affairs, 1974.
'Report of the Special Committee Constituted by the President to Examine the Recommendations of Mr G. Ahmad on the Police System in Pakistan.' Islamabad: Government of Pakistan, President's Secretariat, 1972.
'Report of the Working Group on Reorganisation of the Public Service Structure in Pakistan, in light of the Fulton Report.' Islamabad: Government of Pakistan, 1969.
'Report on the Working of the Central Secretariat'. Islamabad: O&M Wing, Cabinet Secretariat, Government of Pakistan, 1974.

Official Documents and Publications from British India

Census of India, 1921. Calcutta: Superintendent Government Printing, India, 1924.
India Military Budget Estimate for the year 1872-73. Calcutta: Bengal Secretariat Press, 1873.
Report of the Commissioners for the Investigation of Alleged Cases of Torture, in the Madras Presidency. Madras: H. Smith at the Fort St. George Gazette Press, 1855.
Report on the Administration of Bengal, 1874-75. Calcutta: Bengal Secretariat Press, 1875.
Report on the Administration of Bengal, 1893-94. Calcutta: Bengal Secretariat Press, 1894.
Report on the Administration of the Bombay Presidency for the year 1892-93. Bombay: Government Central Press, 1893.
Report on the Administration of the Punjab and its Dependencies for the year 1875-1876. Lahore: Government Civil Secretariat Press, 1876.
Report on the Administration of the Punjab and its Dependencies for 1893-94. Lahore: The Punjab Government Press, 1894.
Sedition Committee Report, 1918. Calcutta: Superintendent Government Printing, India, 1918.
Selection of Papers from the Records at the East India House Relating to the Revenue, Police and Civil and Criminal Justice under the Company's Governments in India. Vol. I. London: E. Cox and Son, 1820.
_____, Vol. II. London: E. Cox and Son, 1820.
_____, Vol. III. London: J. L. Cox, 1826.
_____, Vol. IV. London: J. L. Cox, 1826.

Speeches by the Earl of Elgin Viceroy and Governor-General of India 1894-1899. Calcutta: Office of the Superintendent of Government Printing, India, 1899.

Tyrwhitt, E. *Report on the Administration of the Police of the North-Western Province for the year 1873*. Allahabad: NWP Government Press, 1873.

Official Documents and Publications from Pakistan

Appraisal of Police Administration in the Islamic Republic of Pakistan by Romanian Police Experts. Rawalpindi: Government Press, 1976.

CBR Yearbook, 2004-2005. Islamabad: Directorate of Research and Statistics, Government of Pakistan, 2005.

CBR Yearbook, 2005-2006. Islamabad: Directorate of Research and Statistics, Government of Pakistan, 2006.

Constituent Assembly Debates. Karachi: Pakistan Publications, 1949.

Devolution in Pakistan: Reform or Regression? Islamabad: International Crisis Group, 2004.

Egger, Rowland. *The Improvement of Public Administration in Pakistan: A Report with Recommendations*. Karachi: Government of Pakistan Press, 1953.

Federal Taxes Administration Report 1975-1976. Islamabad: Central Board of Revenue, 1977.

Final Report of the Taxation Commission. Karachi: Printing Corporation of Pakistan, 1974.

Guidelines for Monitoring Committees of Local Governments. Islamabad: National Reconstruction Bureau, 2001.

Police Order 2002. Islamabad: National Reconstruction Bureau, 2007.

Police Reforms Committee, 1976. Rawalpindi: Government Press, 1976.

The Punjab Local Government Ordinance 2001. Islamabad: National Reconstruction Bureau, 2007.

Report of the Administrative Enquiry Committee. Karachi: Government of Pakistan Press, 1953.

Report of the Administrative Reorganisation Committee. Karachi: Efficiency and O&M Wing, President's Secretariat, 1960.

Report of the Civil Services Commission, 1978-79. Islamabad: Printing Corporation of Pakistan, 1979.

Report of the Commission on the Eradication of Corruption, 1979. Islamabad: Government of Pakistan Press, 1979.

Report of the Committee on Revitalization of Revenue Administration, July 1978. Islamabad: Government of Pakistan Press, 1978.

Report of the Constitution Commission, Pakistan, 1961. Karachi: Government of Pakistani Press, 1961.

Report of the Electoral Reform Commission, 1956. Karachi: Government of Pakistan Press, 1956.

Report of the East Bengal Police Committee, 1953. Dhaka: East Bengal Government Press, 1954.

Report of the Finance Commission, 1962. Karachi: Government of Pakistani Press, 1962.

The Report of the Hamood-ur-Rehman Commission of Inquiry into the 1971 War: As Declassified by the Government of Pakistan. Lahore: Vanguard, 2003.

Report of the Law Reform Commission, 1958-59. Karachi: Government of Pakistan Press, 1959.

Report of the Law Reform Commission, 1967-1970. Karachi: Government of Pakistan Press, 1970.

Report of the National Pay Commission, 1970-72. Islamabad: Government of Pakistan Press, 1972.

Report of the National Pay Commission, 1976. Islamabad: Printing Corporation of Pakistan, 1976.

Report of the Orientation Workshops for Executive District Officers (Literacy). Islamabad: National Reconstruction Bureau, 2002.

Report of the Pakistan Commission. Vol. I. Karachi: Governor-General's Press and Publications, 1949.

―――, Vol. II. Karachi: Governor-General's Press and Publications, 1950.

Report of the Pakistan Police Commission, 1960-61. Rawalpindi: Government of Pakistan Press, 1961.

Report of the Pakistan Police Commission, 1969-70. Rawalpindi: Police Commission Secretariat, 1970.

Report of the Pay and Services Commission 1959-1962. Karachi: Government of Pakistan Press, 1962.

Report of the Provincial Administration Commission February 1960. Islamabad: Printing Corporation of Pakistan, 1982.

Report of the Special Committee for Eradication of Corruption from Services. Rawalpindi: Government of Pakistan Press, 1967.

Report of the Standing Organsation Committee on the Reorganisation of the Functions and Structure of the Central Government in light of the New Constitution, April 1962. Rawalpindi: Central Army Press, 1962.

Report of the Subcommittee on Law and Order, 1976. Islamabad: Government of Pakistan Press, 1976.

Report of the Taskforce on Reform of Tax Administration, 14 April 2001. Islamabad: Central Board of Revenue, Government of Pakistan, 2001.

White Paper on the Performance of the Bhutto Regime. Vol. I. *Mr Z. A. Bhutto, His Family and Associates.* Islamabad: Printing Corporation of Pakistan, 1979.

―――, Vol. II. *Treatment of Fundamental State Institutions.* Islamabad: Printing Corporation of Pakistan, 1979.

―――, Vol. III. *Misuse of the Instruments of State Power.* Islamabad: Printing Corporation of Pakistan, 1979.

―――, Vol. IV. *The Economy.* Islamabad: Printing Corporation of Pakistan, 1979.

Official Documents and Publications from the United Kingdom

East India (Advisory and Legislative Councils). Vol. II, Part I. *Replies of the Local Governments, Enclosures I to XX to Letter from the Government of India, No. 21, dated 1 October 1908.* London: His Majesty's Stationery Office, 1908. Cd. 4435

———, *Replies of the Local Governments, Enclosures XXI to XXX to Letter from the Government of India, No. 21, dated the First of October 1908*. Vol. II, Part II. London: His Majesty's Stationery Office, 1908. Cd. 4436.

Forrest, G. W., ed. *Selections from the State Papers of the Governor-General of India*. Vol I. *Hastings*. London: Constable & Co. Ltd., 1910.

———, Vol II. *Hastings*. London: Constable & Co., Ltd., 1910.

The Indian Army Commission Report of Major General Hancock. London: Her Majesty's Stationery Office, 1859.

India Office List for 1935. London: Harrisons and Sons Ltd., 1935.

Indian Statutory Commission. Vol. III. *Reports of the Committees appointed by the Provincial Legislative Councils to Co-operate with the Indian Statutory Commission*. London: His Majesty's Stationery Office, 1930. Cmd. 3572.

———, Vol. IV. *Memoranda Submitted by the Government of India and the India Office to the Indian Statutory Commission*. London: His Majesty's Stationery Office, 1930. Cmd. 70-240-4.

———, Vol. V. *Memoranda Submitted by the Government of India and the India Office to the Indian Statutory Commission*. London: His Majesty's Stationery Office, 1930. Cmd. 70-240-5.

———, Vol. VI. *Memorandum Submitted by the Government of Madras to the Indian Statutory Commission*. London: His Majesty's Stationery Office, 1930. Cmd. 70-240-6.

———, Vol. IX. *Memorandum Submitted by the Government of the United Provinces to the Indian Statutory Commission*. London: His Majesty's Stationery Office, 1930. Cmd. 70-240-9.

Joint Committee on Indian Constitutional Reform Session 1933-34. Vol. I. Part I. London: His Majesty's Stationery Office, 1934.

Mansergh, N. and Lumbey, E. W. R., eds. *Constitutional Relations Between Britain and India: The Transfer of Power*. XI Vols. London: Her Majesty's Stationery Office, 1970-82.

Vol. I: *Cripps Mission, January-April 1942* (1970)

Vol. II: *'Quit India', 30 April—21 September 1942* (1971)

Vol. III: *Reassertion of Authority, Gandhi's Fast and the succession to the Viceroyalty, 21 September 1942—12 June 1943* (1971).

Vol. IV: *The Bengal Famine and the New Viceroyalty, 15 June—31 August 1944* (1973).

Vol. V: *The Simla Conference, Background and Proceedings, 1 September 1944- 28 July 1945* (1974).

Vol. VI: *The Post-War Phase: New Moves by the Labour Government, 1 August 1945- 22 March 1946* (1976).

Vol. VII: *The Cabinet Mission, 23 March—29 June 1946* (1977).

Vol. VIII: *The Interim Government, 3 July—1 November 1946* (1979)

Vol. IX: *The Fixing of a Time Limit, 3 November—2 March 1947* (1980).

Vol. X: *The Mountbatten Viceroyalty, Formulation of a Plan, 22 March—30 May 1947* (1981).

Vol. XI: The *Mountbatten Viceroy Announcement and Reception of the 3 June Plan, 31 May—7 July 1947* (1982).

Philips, C. H., ed. *The Correspondence of Lord William Cavendish Bentinck: Governor General of India 1828-1835*. Vol. I. *1828-1831*. Oxford: Oxford University Press, 1977.

———, *The Correspondence of Lord William Cavendish Bentinck: Governor General of India 1828-1835*. Vol. II. *1831-1835*. Oxford: Oxford University press, 1977.

Report of the Commissioners Appointed to Inquire into the Organization of the Indian Army, Together with the Minutes of Evidence and Appendix. London: Her Majesty's Stationery Office, 1859.

Report of the Indian Sandhurst Committee, 14 November 1926. London: His Majesty's Stationery Office, 1927.

Statement Exhibiting the Moral and Material Progress and Condition of India during the year 1907-8. London: His Majesty's Stationery Office, 1909.

Published Primary Sources and Contemporary Sources

Ahmed, Nizam-ud-din. *Tabakat-i-Akbari*. Trans. Sir H. M. Elliot. Lahore: Sind Sagar Academy, 1975.

Aijazuddin, F. S. *The White House & Pakistan: Secret Declassified Documents, 1969-1974*. Karachi: Oxford University Press, 2002.

Akhund, Iqbal. *Trial and Error: The Advent and Eclipse of Benazir Bhutto*. Karachi: Oxford University Press, 2000.

Allami, Abu'l Fazl. *A'in-I Akbari*. Trans. H. Blochmann. Calcutta: Calcutta Madrassah, 1873; reprint, Lahore: Sang-e-Meel Publications, 2003.

Allami, Abu'l Fazl. *The Akbarnama*. Trans. H. Beveridge. Vol 1. Lahore: Islamia-al-Saudia Printers, 1984.

Allana, G., ed. *Pakistan Movement: Historic Documents*. Lahore: Islamic Book Service, 1977.

Ali, Choudhri Muhammad. *The Emergence of Pakistan*. Lahore: Research Society of Pakistan, 1973.

Ambedkar, B. R. *Pakistan or the Partition of India*. Bombay: Thacker & Co., 1946.

Amery, Leo S. *The Empire at Bay: The Leo Amery Diaries 1929-1945*. Burnes, John and David Nicholson, eds. London: Hutchinson & Co. Ltd., 1988.

Arif, Khalid Mahmud. *Working with Zia: Pakistan's Power Politics 1977-1988*. Karachi: Oxford University Press, 1995.

Azad, Abul Kalam. *India Wins Freedom*. New Delhi: Orient Longman, 1988.

Battuta, Ibn. *Travels in Asia and Africa 1325-54*. London: Routledge and Keagan Paul, 1929; reprint Lahore: Services Book Club, 1985.

Bernier, François. *Travels in the Mogul Empire: AD 1656-1668*, trans. Irving Brock, revised and improved edition, Archibald Constable. London: Archibald Constable and Company, 1891; reprint, Karachi: Indus Publications, n.d.

Birdwood, George C. M. *On Competitions and the ICS*. London: W. J. Johnson, 1872.

Braibanti, Ralph, ed. *Chief Justice Cornelius of Pakistan: An Analysis with Letters and Speeches*. Karachi: Oxford University Press, 2000.

Embree, Ainslie T., ed. *Sources of Indian Tradition*, vol 1, Second Edition, *From the Beginning to 1800*. New Delhi: Penguin Books, 1992.

Fallaci, Oriana. *Interview with History*. Trans. John Shepley. Boston: Houghton Mifflin Company, 1976.

Gandhi, Arun, ed. *The Morarji Papers: Fall of the Janata Government*. New Delhi: Vision Books, 1983.

Gauhar Altaf. The Altaf Gauhar Papers: Documents toward the Making of the Constitution of 1962. Amanullah Memon, ed. Lahore: Sang-e-Meel Publications, 2003.

Godbole, Madhav. *Unfinished Innings: Recollections and Reflections of a Civil Servant*. New Delhi: Orient Longman, 1996.

Hasan, Gul. *Memoirs of Lt. General Gul Hasan*. Karachi: Oxford University Press, 1993.

Hasan, Mubashir. *The Mirage of Power: An Inquiry into the Bhutto Years 1971-1977*. Karachi: Oxford University Press, 2000.

James, Morrice. *Pakistan Chronicle*. London: Hurst & Company, 1993.

Jilani, S. G. *Fifteen Governors I Served with: Untold Story of East Pakistan*. Lahore: Bookmark, 1979.

Iqbal, Rana Saleem ed. *The Quaid on Civil Servants: Speeches and Statements, October 1947 to August 1948*. Islamabad: National Documentation Centre, 2007.

Khan, Ayub. *Diaries of Field Marshal Mohammed Ayub Khan, 1966-1972*. Craig Baxter, ed. Karachi: Oxford University Press, 2007.

———, *Friends not Masters*. Lahore: Vanguard, 2000.

Khan, Inayat. *Shahjahan-nama*, trans. A. R. Fuller, eds., W. Begley and Z. A. Desai. Delhi: Oxford University Press, 1990.

Khan, Jameelur Rehman, ed. *Government and Administration in Pakistan*. Islamabad: Pakistan Public Administration Research Centre O&M Division, Cabinet Secretariat, Government of Pakistan, 1987.

Khan, Khafi. *History of Alamgir*, trans., S. Moin-ul-Haq. Karachi: Pakistan Historical Society, 1975.

Khan, Muhammad Asghar. *We've Learnt Nothing from History: Pakistan's Politics and Military Power*. Karachi: Oxford University Press, 2005.

Khan, Roedad, ed. *The British Papers: Secret and Confidential India-Pakistan-Bangladesh Documents 1958-1969*. Karachi: Oxford University Press, 2002.

Khan, Saqi Mustad. *Maasir-i-Alamgiri*. Trans. Jadunath Sarkar (Calcutta: Royal Asiatic Society of Bengal, 1947 reprint; New Delhi: Munshiram Manoharlal, 1985).

Khan, Syed Ahmed. *The Causes of the Indian Revolt*, trans., Colonel Graham and Auckland Clovin, with an introduction by Francis Robinson. Karachi: Oxford University Press, 2000.

Khaldun, Ibn. *The Muqaddimah (An Introduction to History)*. Trans. Franz Rosenthal. Ed., N. J. Dawood. London: Routeledge and Kegan Paul, 1978.

Kautilya. *The Arthashastra*, trans, L. N. Rangarajan. New Delhi: Penguin Books, 1992.

Kautilya, *The Arthashastra*, trans, R. Shamasastry. Bangalore: Government Press, 1915.

Lewis, Primila. *Reason Wounded: A Personal Account of India's Emergency*. Lahore: Vanguard Books Ltd., 1979.

Maconchie, Evan. *Life in the Indian Civil Service*. London: Chapman and Hall, 1926.

Mazari, Sherbaz Khan. *Journey to Disillusionment*. Karachi: Oxford University Press, 1999.

Mitha, A. O. *Unlikely Beginnings: A Soldier's Life*. Karachi: Oxford University Press, 2003.
Munir, Mohammed, *From Jinnah to Zia*. Lahore: Vanguard Books, 1980.
Musa, Mohammad. *Jawan to General: Reflections of a Pakistani Soldier*. Karachi: East & West Publishing Company, 1987.
Musharraf, Pervez. *In the Line of Fire: A Memoir*. London: Simon & Schuster, 2006.
Patel, Dorab. *Testament of a Liberal*.
Pirzada, Syed Sharifuddin. *Dissolution of Constituent Assembly of Pakistan and the Legal Battles of Moulvi Tamizuddin Khan*. Karachi: Asia Law House, 1995.
Raza, Rafi. *Zulfikar Ali Bhutto and Pakistan: 1967-1977*. Karachi: Oxford University Press, 1997.
Sachau, Edward C. *Alberuni's India: An account of the Religion, Philosophy, Literature, Geography, Chronology, Astrology, Customs, Laws, and Astrology of India About AD 1030*, vol 1. Lahore: Ferozesons, 1962.
Shah, Nasim Hasan. *Memoirs and Reflections*. Islamabad: Alhamra Publishing, 2002.
Shah, Sajjad Ali. *Law Courts in a Glass House: An Autobiography*. Karachi: Oxford University Press, 2001.
Shang Yang. *The Book of Lord Shang*. Trans. J. J. L. Duyvendak. Intro. Robert Wilkinson. Hertfordshire: Wordsworth Editions Limited, 1998.
Siddiqui, Abdul Rehman. *East Pakistan: The Endgame, An Onlooker's Journal 1969-1971*. Karachi: Oxford University Press, 2004.
Singh, Amar. *Reversing the Gaze: Amar Singh's Diary, a Colonial Subject's Narrative of Imperial India*. Susanne H. Rudolph, Lloyd I. Rudolph and Mohan Singh Kanota, eds. Boulder, Colorado: Westview Press, 2002.
Tuzuk-i-Jahangiri, trans. Alexander Rogers, ed., Henry Beveridge. Vol 1. Years 1-13 (n.p. 1909-1914 reprint; Delhi: Munshiram Manoharlal Publishers, 1978).
Yusufi, Khurshid Ahmed Khan, ed. *Speeches & Messages of the Quaid-i-Azam*, Vol IV. Lahore: Bazm-I-Iqbal, 1996.
Zaidi, Z. H. ed. *Quaid-i-Azam Mohammad Ali Jinnah Papers: Prelude to Pakistan, 20 February—2 June 1947*. Vol. 1. Part 1. Islamabad: National Archives of Pakistan, 1993.
———, ed. *Quaid-i-Azam Mohammed Ali Jinnah Papers*. Vol. II. *3 June—30 June, 1947*. Islamabad: National Archives, 1994.
———, ed. *Quaid-i-Azam Mohammad Ali Jinnah Papers: The States: Historical and Policy Perspectives and Accession to Pakistan*. Vol. VIII. Islamabad: Quaid-i-Azam Papers Project, 2003.

Secondary Sources

Abbot, Freeland. *Islam and Pakistan*. Ithaca: Cornell University Press, 1968.
Afzal, Rafique. *Pakistan: History and Politics 1947-1971*. Karachi: Oxford University Press, 2001.
Ahmad, Aftab. *Beyond the Vision: A Soul-searching View of the East Pakistan Separation*. Islamabad: Dost Publications, 2007.
Ahsan, Aitzaz. *The Indus Saga and the Making of Pakistan*. Lahore: Nerh Ghar Publications, 2001.

Allen, Charles. *Buddha and the Sahibs: The Men who Discovered India's Lost Religion.* London: John Murray, 2002.

Ali, Athar M. *Mughul India: Studies in Polity, Ideas, Society and Culture.* New Delhi: Oxford University Press, 2007.

―――, *The Mughal Nobility Under Aurungzeb.* New Delhi: Asia Publishing House, 1970.

Ali, Parveen Shaukat. *Pillars of British Imperialism: A Case Study of Sir Alfred Lyall 1873-1903.* Lahore: Aziz Publishers, 1976.

Armstrong, Karen. *Buddha.* London: Phoenix, 2002.

Ashraf, K. M. *Life and Conditions of the People of Hindustan.* New Delhi: Mushiram Manoharlal, 1970.

Askari, Syed Hasan. *Medieval India: A Miscellany.* New Delhi: Asia Publishing House, 1969.

Aspinall, A. *Cornwallis in Bengal.* New Delhi: Uppal Publishing House, 1987.

Atwan, Abdel Bari. *The Secret History of al Qaeda.* Los Angeles: University of California Press, 2006.

Axworthy, Michael. *Empire of the Mind: A History of Iran.* London: Hurst & Company, 2007.

Aziz Ahmed, *An Intellectual History of Islam in India.* Edinburgh: Edinburgh University Press, 1969.

Aziz, K. K. *The British in India: A Study in Imperialism.* Islamabad: NCHCR, 1975.

―――, *Pakistan's Political Culture: Essays in Historical and Social Origins.* Lahore: Vanguard, 2001.

Baxter, Craig and Syed Razi Wasti, eds. *Pakistan Authoritarianism in the 1980s.* Lahore: Vanguard, 1991.

Bayly, C. A. *The Birth of the Modern World: 1780-1914.* Oxford: Blackwell Publishing, 2004.

Bayly, Susan. *The New Cambridge History of India: Caste, Society and Politics from the Eighteenth Century to the Modern Age.* Cambridge: Cambridge University Press, 2000.

Becher, Matthias. *Charlemagne.* London: Yale University Press, 2003.

Bernstein, Jeremy. *Dawning of the Raj: The Life and Trial of Warren Hastings.* London: Auram Press Ltd., 2000.

Bidwai, Praful. 'A Critique of Hindutva,' *South Asian Journal*, October-December 2003.

Birnbaum, Pierre. *The Idea of France.* Trans. M. B. DeBevoise. New York: Hill and Wang, 2001.

Blanning, T. C. W. *The Culture of Power and the Power of Culture: Old Regime Europe 1660-1789.* Oxford: Oxford University Press, 2002.

Bradshaw, John. *Rulers of India: Sir Thoman Munro and the British Settlement of the Madras Presidency.* Oxford: Clarendon Press, 1894.

Braibanti, Ralph ed. *Asian Bureaucratic Systems Emergent from the British Imperial Tradition.* Durham: Duke University Press, 1966.

Brass, Paul R. *The New Cambridge History of India: The Politics of India since Independence.* Cambridge: Cambridge University Press, 1992.

Braudel, Ferdinand. *A History of Civilizations.* Trans. Richard Mayne. New York: Penguin Group, 1995.

———, *Civilization and Capitalism 15th-18th Century*. Trans. Sian Reynolds. Vol I. *The Structures of Everyday Life*. London: Phoenix Press, 2002.
———, Vol. II. *The Wheels of Commerce*. London: Phoenix Press, 2002.
———, Vol. III. *The Perspective of the World*. London: Phoenix Press, 2002.
Brockelmann, Carl. *History of the Islamic Peoples*. New Delhi: Munshiram Manoharlal Publishers, 1995.
Brown, Judith M, ed. *The Oxford History of the British Empire*. Vol. IV. *The Twentieth Century*. Oxford: Oxford University Press, 1999.
Buckland, C. E. *Dictionary of Indian Biography*. Lahore: Sang-e-Meel Publications, 1985.
Burleigh, Michael. *Earthly Powers: Religion and Politics in Europe from the Enlightenment to the Great War*. London: HarperCollins Publishers, 2005.
———, *The Third Reich: A New History*. London: Macmillan, 2000.
Buruma, Ian. *Voltaire's Coconuts or Anglomania in Europe*. London, Phoenix, 2000.
Cannadine, David. *Ornamentalism: How the British Saw Their Empire*. New York: Oxford University Press, 2001.
Carsten, F. L. ed. *The New Cambridge Modern History*. Vol V. *The Ascendancy of France 1648-88*. Cambridge: University Press, 1969.
Cheema, Pervaiz Iqbal. *The Armed Forces of Pakistan*. Karachi: Oxford University Press, 2002.
Choudhury, Golam W. *Constitutional Development in Pakistan*. London: Longman Group, 1969.
———, *Pakistan: Transition from Military to Civilian Rule*. Essex: Scorpion Publishing, 1988.
Churchill, Winston S. *A History of the English-Speaking Peoples*. vol. 1, *The Birth of Britain*. London: Cassell, 2002.
———, Vol. 2, *The New World*.
———, Vol. 3, *The Age of Revolution*.
———, Vol. 4, *The Great Democracies*.
Clarke, Peter. *The Cripps Version: The Life of Sir Stafford Cripps*. London: AllenLane the Penguin Press, 2002.
Clausewitz, Carl von. *On War*. Trans., Michael Howard and Peter Paret. Princeton: Princeton University Press, 1989.
Clive, John. *Macaulay: The Shaping of a Historian*. Cambridge: The Belknap Press of Harvard University Press, 1987.
Cloughley, Brian. *A History of the Pakistani Army: Wars and Insurrections*. Karachi: Oxford University Press, 2006.
Cohen, Stephen P. *India: Emerging Power*. Washington D.C.: Brookings Institute Press, 2001.
Commager, Henry Steele. *The Empire of Reason: How Europe Imagined and America Realized the Enlightenment*. London: Widenfeld and Nicolson, 1998.
Cotterfell, Arthur. *China: A History*. London: Pimlico, 1995.
Cotterill, H. B. *Ancient Greece: Myth and History*. New Lanark: Geddes & Grosset, 2004.
Cromwell, Daniel W. *The SEWA Movement and Rural Development*. New Delhi: Sage, 2003.
Cronin, Vincent. *Napoleon*. London: HarperCollins Publishers, 1994.

Darwin, John. *After Tamerlane: The Global History of Empire since 1405*. London: Penguin Books, 2007.

Dawood, Jan Mohammed. *The Role of the Superior Judiciary in the Politics of Pakistan*. Karachi: Royal Book Company, 1994.

Danzinger, Danny and John Gillingham. *1215: The Year of Magna Carta*. London: Hodder and Stoughton, 2003.

Dewey, Clive. *Anglo-Indian Attitudes: The Mind of the Indian Civil Service*. London: Hambeldon Press, 1993.

Di Scala, Spencer M. and Salvo Mastellone. *European Political Thought 1815-1989*. Boulder, Colorado: Westview Press, 1998.

Dodwell, H. H., ed. *The Cambridge History of India, vol 5, British India 1497-1858* Cambridge: Cambridge University Press, 1921; reprint, New Delhi: S. Chand & Company (Pvt.) Ltd., 1987.

———, ed. *The Cambridge History of India, vol 6, The Indian Empire 1858-1919 with Additional Chapters 1919-1969*. Cambridge: Cambridge University Press, 1932; reprint, New Delhi: S. Chand & Company (Pvt) Ltd., 1987.

Eraly, Abraham. *The Last Spring: The Lives and Times of the Great Mughals*. New Delhi: Viking, 1997.

———, *The Mughal World: India's Tainted Paradise*. London: Weidenfeld & Nicolson, 2007.

Feiling, Keith. *A History of England From the Coming of the English to 1918*. Trowbridge & Esher: Book Club Associates., 1975.

Feldman, Herbert. *The Herbert Feldman Omnibus*. Karachi: Oxford University Press, 2001.

Ferguson, Niall. *Empire: How Britain Made the Modern World*. London: The Penguin Press, 2003.

Feuchtwanger, Edgar. *Bismarck*. New York: Routledge, 2003.

Fisk, Robert. *The Great War for Civilisation: The Conquest of the Middle East*. London: Harper Perennial, 2006.

Fukuyama, Francis. *After the Neocons: America at the Crossroads*. London: Pacific Books, 2006.

———, *Trust: The Social Virtues and the Creation of Prosperity*. New York: The Free Press, 1995.

Galantier Marc, *Law and Society in Modern India*, ed., Rajeev Bhavan. Delhi: Oxford University Press, 1988.

Gibbon, Edward. *The Decline and Fall of the Roman Empire*. Abridged and with an Introduction by Frank C. Bourne. New York: Dell Publishing Co., 1963.

Gilmour, David. *Curzon*. London: John Murray, 1994.

———, *The Ruling Caste: Imperial Lives in the Victorian Raj*. London: John Murray, 2005.

Goff, Jacques Le. *Medieval Civilization: 400-1500*, trans. Julia Barrow. Oxford: Basil Blackwell, 1984.

Goffman, Daniel. *The Ottoman Empire and Early Modern Europe: New Approaches to European History*. Cambridge: University Press, 2002.

Grant, Michael. *The Fall of the Roman Empire*. London: Phoenix, 2005.

Griffiths, Percival. *To Guard my People: The History of the Indian Police*. London: Ernest Benn Limited, 1971.

Guha, Ramchandra. *India After Gandhi: The History of the World's Largest Democracy*. London: Macmillan, 2007.

Gupta, Anandswarup. *The Police in British India: 1861-1947*. New Delhi: Concept Publishing Company, 1979.

Gupta, Ramchandra. *India After Gandhi: The History of the World's Largest Democracy*. London: Macmillan, 2007.

Habib, Irfan. *Essays in Indian History: Towards a Marxist Perspective*. New Delhi: Tulika, 1995.

Habib, Irfan, ed. *Medieval India: Researches in the History of India 1200-1750*. Delhi: Oxford India Paperbacks, 1999.

Haroon, Sana. *Frontier of Faith: Islam in the Indo-Afghan Borderland*. London: Hurst and Company, 2007.

Harle, J. C. *The Art and Architecture of the Indian Subcontinent*. London: Penguin Books, 1986.

Havell, H. L. *Ancient Rome: The Republic*. New Lanark: Geddes & Grosset, 2003.

Hayat, Sikandar. *Aspects of the Pakistan Movement*. Islamabad: National Institute of Historical and Cultural Research, 1998.

———, *The Charismatic Leader: Quaid-i-Azam Jinnah and the Creation of Pakistan*. Karachi: Oxford University Press, 2008.

Hennessy, H. F. *Administrative History of British India*. New Delhi: Neeraj Publishing House, 1983.

Herodotus. *Histories*. Trans. George Rawlinson. Hertfordshire: Wordsworth Editions, 1996.

Hiro, Dilip. *Inside India Today*. London: Routledge & Kegan Paul, 1976.

Hirschmann, Edwin. *White Mutiny: The Ilbert Bill Crisis in India and the Genesis of the Indian National Congress*. New Delhi: Heritage Publishers, 1980.

Hobsbawn, Eric. *Interesting Times: A Twentieth Century Life*. London: AllenLane the Penguin Press, 2002.

———, *On History*. London: Abacus, 1997.

Hourani, Albert. *A History of the Arab Peoples*. Cambridge Massachusetts: The Belknap Press of Harvard University Press, 1991.

Hussain Hali, *Hayat-i-Javed*. Trans. David J. Mathews. Panipat: n.p. 1902; reprint, Delhi: Rupa & Co., 1994.

Hussain, Ishrat. Economic Management in Pakistan: 1999-2002. Karachi: Oxford University Press, 2003.

———, *Pakistan: The Economy of an Elitist State*. Karachi: Oxford University Press, 1999.

Hussain, Mushahid and Akmal Hussain. *Pakistan: Problems of Governance*. Lahore: Vanguard, 1993.

Hussain, Mushahid. *Pakistan's Politics: The Zia Years*. Lahore: Progressive Publishers, 1990.

Ibn Hasan. *The Central Structure of the Mughal Empire and its Practical Working up to the Year 1657*. Karachi: Oxford University Press, 1967.

Ilbert, Courtenay. *The Government of India*. London: Humphrey Milford and Stevens & Sons, Ltds., 1916.

Inalick, Halil. *The Ottoman Empire: The Classical Age 1300-1600*. London: Phoenix, 2000.

Jackson, Peter. *The Delhi Sultanate: A Political and Military History*. Cambridge: Cambridge University Press, 1999.

Jalal, Ayesha. *Democracy and Authoritarianism in South Asia: A Comparative and Historical Perspective*. Lahore: Sang-e-Meel Publications, 1995.

Jamaluddin, Syed. *The State Under Timur: A Study in Empire Building*. New Delhi: Har Anand Publishers, 1995.

James, Lawrence. *Raj: The Making and Unmaking of British India*. London: Abacus, 2003.

———, *The Rise and Fall of the British Empire*. London: Abacus, 2001.

Jenkins, Roy. *Gladstone*. London: Macmillan-Papermac, 1996.

Karnad, Bharat. *Nuclear Weapons and Indian Security: The Realist Foundations of Strategy*. New Delhi: Macmillan, 2002.

Katouzian, Homa. *State and Society in Iran: The Eclipse of the Qajars and the Emergence of the Pahlavis*. London: I. B. Tauris Publishers, 2000.

Kaura, Uma. *Muslims and Indian Nationalism: The Emergence of the Demand for India's Partition 1928-1940*. New Delhi: Manohar Book Service, 1977.

Keay, John. *India: A History*. London: HarperCollins, 2000.

———, *India Discovered*. London: William Collins & Sons, 1988.

Kejariwal, O. P. *The Asiatic Society of Bengal and the Discovery of India's Past: 1784-1838*. Delhi: Oxford University Press, 1988.

Kennan, George F. *The Marquis de Custine and his 'Russia in 1839'*. London: Hutchinson, 1972.

Kennedy, Charles H. *Bureaucracy in Pakistan*. Karachi: Oxford University Press, 1987.

———, Kathleen McNeil, Carl Ernst, and David Gilmartin, eds. *Pakistan at the Millennium*. Karachi: Oxford University Press, 2003.

Kennedy, Hugh. *The Court of the Caliphs: When Baghdad Ruled the Muslim World*. London: Phoenix, 2005.

Kennedy, Paul. *The Rise and Fall of the Great Powers: Economic Change and Military Conflict 1500-2000*. London: Fontana Press, 1989.

Kemp, Barry J. *Ancient Egypt: Anatomy of a Civilization*. London: Routledge, 2002.

Khan, Fazal Muqeem. *The Story of the Pakistan Army*. Karachi: Oxford University Press, 1963.

Khan, Hamid. *The Constitutional and Political History of Pakistan*. Karachi: Oxford University Press, 2002.

Khan, Shahrukh Rafi, Foqia Sadiq Khan and Aasim Sajjad Akhtar. *Initiating Devolution for Service Delivery in Pakistan: Ignoring the Power Structure*. Karachi: Oxford University Press, 2007.

Kochanek, Stanley A. *Interest Groups and Development: Business and Politics in Pakistan*. Karachi: Oxford University Press, 1983.

Kosambi, D. D. *The Culture and Civilization of Ancient India in Historical Outline*. New Delhi: Vikas Publishing House, 1985.

Korbel, Josef. *Danger in Kashmir*. Princeton: Princeton University Press, 1954; reprint, Karachi: Oxford University Press, 2003.

Kukraja, Veena and M. P. Singh, eds. *Pakistan: Democracy, Development and Security Issues*. New Delhi: Sage Publications, 2006.

Kulke, Hermann and Dietmar Rothermund. *A History of India*. New Delhi: Manohar Publications, 1991.

Kumar, Dharma. *The Cambridge Economic History of India*, Vol. II, c. 1757—c. 1970. Cambridge: The Press Syndicate of the Cambridge University, 1982; reprint, Delhi: Orient Longman, 1984.

Kumar, Raj, ed. *Local Government and Administration during Muslim Rule in India*. New Delhi: Anmol Publications Pvt. Ltd., 2000.

Kuper, Adam and Jessica Kuper, eds. *The Social Science Encyclopedia*. Lahore: Services Book Club, 1989.

Lambrick, H. T. *Sir Charles Napier and Sind*. Oxford: Clarendon Press, 1952.

Lane, Anne et al. *Terrorism, Security and the Power of Informal Networks*. Cheltenham: Edward Edgar, 2008.

Lane-Poole, Stanley. *Mediaeval India Under Muhammaden Rule*. Lahore: Sang-e-Meel, 1991.

LaPolambara, Joseph ed. *Bureaucracy and Political Development*. Princeton: Princeton University Press, 1963.

Ledbetter, James, ed. *Dispatches for the New York Tribune: Selected Journalism of Karl Marx*. London: Penguin Books, 2007.

Lewis, David L. *God's Crucible: Islam and the Making of Europe, 570 to 1215*. New York: W. W. Norton, 2008.

Lindsay, J. G., ed. *The New Cambridge Modern History*. Vol. VII. *The Old Regime 1713-63*. Cambridge: Cambridge University Press, 1970.

Lodhi, Maleeha. *Pakistan's Encounter with Democracy*. Lahore: Vanguard, 1994.

Lord, John. *The Maharajas*. New York: Random House, 1971.

Louis, Roger Wm. *Ends of British Imperialism: The Scramble for Empire, Suez and Decolonization*. London: I. B. Tauris, 2006.

Luce, Edward. *In Spite of the Gods: The Strange Rise of Modern India*. London: Little, Brown, 2007.

Machiavelli, Niccolo. *The Discourses*. Trans. Leslie J. Walker. Ed. Bernard Crick. Rev. Brian Richardson. London: Penguin Books, 2003.

MacMullen, Ramsay *Corruption and the Decline of Rome*. New Haven: Yale University Press, 1988.

Mahmood, Sohail. *Bureaucracy in Pakistan: An Historical Analysis*. Lahore: Progressive Publishers, 1990.

Mahmud, Khalid. *Indian Political Scene, 1989: Main Contenders for Power*. Islamabad: Institute of Regional Studies, 1989.

Mahmud, Safdar. *Pakistan Political Roots and Development 1947-1999*. Karachi: Oxford University Press, 2003.

Major, Andrew J. *Return to Empire: Punjab under the Sikhs and British in the mid-Nineteenth Century*. Karachi: Oxford University Press, 1996.

Majumdar R. C., H. C. Raychaudri, and Kalikinkar Datta, *An Advanced History of India*, 3rd ed. Macmillan Student Editions. London: Macmillan, 1967.

Malleson, G. B. *Administration of British India under Lord Wellesley*. New Delhi: Daya Publishing House, 1988.

Man, John. *Kublai Khan: The Mongol King who Remade China*. London: Bantam Press, 2006.

Marozzi, John. *Tamerlane: Sword of Islam, Conqueror of the World*. London: Harper Collins, 2004.

McGrath, Allen. *The Destruction of Pakistan's Democracy*. Karachi: Oxford University Press, 1996.

Merne, Cecil. *The Development of Self-Government in India 1858-1914*. Chicago: The University of Chicago Press, 1922.

Metcalf, Thomas R. *The New Cambridge History of India: Ideologies of the Raj*. Cambridge: Cambridge University Press, 1994.

Milton, Giles. *Big Chief Elizabeth: How England's Adventurers Gambled and Won the New World*. London: Hodder and Stoughton, 2001.

———, *Nathaniel's Nutmeg: How One Man's Courage Changed the Course of History*. London: Hodder and Stoughton, 1999.

Mishra, Pankaj. *Temptations of the West: How to be Modern in India, Pakistan, Tibet and Beyond*. New York: Farrar, Straus and Giroux, 2006.

Mitra, Subrata K., Clemens Spies and Mike Enskal, eds. *Political Parties in South Asia*. London: Praeger Greenwood, 2004.

Montefiore, Simon Sebag. *Stalin: The Court of the Red Tsar*. London: Phoenix, 2003.

Moon, Penderel Sir. *The British Conquest and Dominion of India*. London: Duckworth, 1989.

Moore, Barrington Jr. *Social Origins of Dictatorship and Democracy: Lord and Peasant in the Making of the Modern World*. Boston: Beacon Press, 1967.

Mujeeb, M. *The Indian Muslims*. London: George Allen & Unwin Ltd., 1967.

Mukherjee, Sipra. *Indian Administration of Lord William Bentinck*. New Delhi: K. P. Begchi & Company, 1994.

Mulgan, Geoff. *Good and Bad Power: The Ideals and Betrayals of Government*. London: Allen Lane, Penguin Books, 2006.

Mumtaz, Soofia, Jean-Luc Racine, and Imran Anwar Ali, eds. *Pakistan: The Contours of State and Society*. Karachi: Oxford University Press, 2002.

Nadeem, Azhar Hassan. *Pakistan: The Political Economy of Lawlessness*. Karachi: Oxford University Press, 2002.

Naipaul, V. S. *An Area of Darkness*. London: Pelican Books, 1968.

Naqvi, Syed Nawab Haider. *Development Economics: Nature and Significance*. New Delhi: Sage Publications, 2002.

Naseem, S. M. and Khalid Nadvi, eds. *The Post-Colonial State and Social Transformation in India and Pakistan*. Karachi: Oxford University Press, 2002.

Nawaz, Shuja. *Crossed Swords: Pakistan, its Army, and the Wars Within*. Karachi: Oxford University Press, 2008.

Nayar, Kuldip and Asif Noorani. *Tales of Two Cities*. New Delhi: Lotus Collection, 2008.

Nayar, Kuldip and Khushwant Singh. *Tragedy of Punjab: Operation Bluestar and After*. New Delhi: Vision Books Pvt., Ltd., 1984.

Niaz, Ilhan. *An Inquiry into the Culture of Power of the Subcontinent*. Islamabad: Alhamra Publishing, 2006.

Nizami, K. A., ed. *Politics and Society During the Early Medieval Period: Collected Works of Professor Mohammed Habib*. Two Vols. New Delhi: Peoples Publishing House, 1981.

Noorani, A. G. *The RSS and the BJP: A Division of Labour*. New Delhi: LeftWord Books, 2000.

O'Brien, Conor Cruise. *The Great Melody*. London: Minerva, 1993.

Orwell, George. *Orwell: The Observer Years*. London: Atlantic Books, 2003.
Padamsee, Alex. *Representations of Indian Muslims in British Colonial Discourses*. New York: Palgrave MacMillan, 2005.
Palkhivala, N. A. *We, the People*. Bombay: Strand Book Stall, 1988.
Palmer, Alan. *Metternich: Councilor of Europe*. London: Phoenix, 1997.
Penner, Peter and Richard Dale McLean, eds. *The Rebel Bureaucrat: Frederick John Shore (1799-1837) as Critic of William Bentinck's India*. Delhi: Chanakya Publications, 1983.
Pipes, Richard. *Property and Freedom*. New York: Alfred A. Knopf, 1999.
Plutarch. *The Rise and Fall of Athens: Nine Greek Lives*. Trans. Ian Scott-Kilvert. London: Penguin Books, 1965.
Possehl, Gregory ed. *Harappan Civilization: A Contemporary Perspective*. New Delhi: Oxford and IBH Publishing Co., 1982.
Powell, Avril. *Muslims and Missionaries in Pre-Mutiny India*. Surrey: The Curzon Press, 1993.
Punj, Balbir K. 'Hindu Rashtra', *South Asian Journal*. October-December 2003.
Pye, Lucian W. and Mary W. Pye. *Asian Power and Politics: The Cultural Dimensions of Authority* Cambridge, Massachusetts: The Belknap Press of Harvard University Press, 1985.
Qureshi, I. H. *Akbar: The Architect of the Mughul Empire*. Karachi: Ma'aref Limited, 1978.
———, *Ulema In Politics: A Study Relating to the Political Activities of the Ulema in the South Asian Subcontinent from 1556—1947*. Karachi, Inter-services Press Ltd., 1972.
Qureshi, M. Naeem. *Pan-Islam in British Indian Politics: A Study of the Khilafat Movement, 1918-1924*. Leiden: Brill, 1999.
Rahman, Tariq. *Language, Ideology and Power: Language-Learning Among the Muslims of Pakistan and North India*. Karachi: Oxford University Press, 2002.
Rapson, E J., ed. *The Cambridge History of India*. Vol. 1. *Ancient India*. Cambridge: Cambridge University Press, 1921; reprint, New Delhi: S. Chand & Company (Pvt.) Ltd., 1987.
Rashid, Ahmed. *Descent into Chaos: How the War against Islamic Extremism is being lost in Pakistan, Afghanistan and Central Asia*. London: Allen Lane, 2008.
Raychaudhry, Tapan and Irfan Habib, eds. *The Cambridge Economic History of India*, vol. 1, *c1200 to c1750*. Cambridge: Cambridge University Press, 1982.
Read, Anthony and David Fisher. *The Proudest Day: India's Long Road to Independence*. London: Jonathan Cape, 1997.
Redman, Ben Ray, ed. *The Portable Voltaire*. New York: Viking Penguin Inc., 1977.
Rehman, Inamur. *Public Opinion and Political Development in Pakistan 1947-1958*. Karachi: Oxford University Press, 1982.
Riasanovsky, Nicholas V. *A History of Russia*. New York: Oxford University Press, 1977.
Rizvi, Hasan Askari. *The Military and Politics in Pakistan, 1947-1997*. Lahore: Sang-e-Meel Publications, 2000.
Roberts, Andrew. *Hitler and Churchill: Secrets of Leadership*. London: Phoenix, 2003.
Roberts, J. M. *History of the World*. New York: Oxford University Press, 1993.

Roberts, Nick. *The Corporation that Changed the World: How the East India Company Shaped the Modern Multinational*. Hyderabad: Orient Longman Private Limited, 2006.

Robinson, Francis. *Islam, South Asia and the West*. New Delhi: Oxford University Press, 2007.

Russell, Bertrand. *Power: A New Social Analysis*. London: Unwin Books, 1960.

Saiyid, Dushka H. *Muslim Women of the British Punjab: From Seclusion to Politics*. London: MacMillan Press Ltd., 1998.

Saran, P. *The Provincial Government of the Mughals: 1526-1658*. Allahabad: Kitabistan, 1941; reprint Lahore: Faran Academy, 1976.

Saunders, J. J. *A History of Medieval Islam*. London: Routledge, 1965; reprint, 1996.

Sayeed, Khalid B. *Political System of Pakistan*. Boston: Houghton Mifflin Company, 1967.

Schama, Simon. *A History of Britain: At the Edge of the World? 3000 BC-AD 1603*. London: BBC Worldwide Ltd., 2000.

———, *A History of Britain: The British Wars 1603-1776*. London: BBC Worldwide Ltd., 2001.

Secondat, Charles de. *The Spirit of Laws*. New York: Prometheus Books, 2002.

Sen, Amartya. *Identity and Violence: The Illusion of Destiny*. New York: W. W. Norton and Company, 2006.

Shafqat, Saeed. *Civil-Military Relations in Pakistan from Zulfiqar Ali Bhutto to Benazir Bhutto*. Boulder, Colorado: Westview Press, 1997.

Shah, Ghanshyam, ed. *Dalit Identity and Politics: Cultural Subordination and the Dalit Challenge*, vol 2. Sage Publications: New Delhi, 2001.

Shah, Ghanshyam, Mario Rutten, and Hein Streefkerk, eds. *Development and Deprivation in Gujarat*. New Delhi: Sage Publications, 2002.

Sharma, Jyotirmaya. *Hindutva: Exploring the Idea of Hindu Nationalism*. New Delhi: Penguin Books, 2006.

Sharma, Mukul, ed. *Improving People's Lives: Lessons in Empowerment from Asia*. New Delhi: Sage, 2003.

Sheehan, James J. *Where Have All the Soldiers Gone? The Transformation of Modern Europe*. New York: Houghton Mifflin, 2008.

Shelbourne, David. *An Eye to India: The Unmasking of a Tyranny*. Suffolk: Penguin Books, 1977.

Short, Philip. *Mao: A Life*. London: Hodder and Stoughton, 1999.

Siddiqa, Ayesha. *Military Inc. Inside Pakistan's Military Economy*. Karachi: Oxford University Press, 2007.

Siddiqui, Tasneed Ahmad. *Towards Good Governance*. Karachi: Oxford University Press, 2001.

Siedentop, Larry. *Democracy in Europe*. London: Allen Lane Penguin Press, 2000.

Sikand, Yoginder. *The Origins and Development of the Tablighi-Jama'at, 1920-2000: A Cross-country Comparative Study*. New Delhi: Orient Longman, 2002.

Singh, Khushwant. *The End of India*. New Delhi: Penguin Books, 2003.

———, *Ranjit Singh: Maharaja of the Punjab*. New Delhi: Penguin Books India, 2001.

Skinner, Quentin. *Visions of Politics*. Vol. I, *Regarding Method*. Cambridge: Cambridge University Press, 2002.

———, *Visions of Politics*. Vol. II, *Renaissance Virtues*. Cambridge: Cambridge University Press, 2002.
———, *Visions of Politics*. Vol. III, *Hobbes and Civil Science*. Cambridge: Cambridge University Press, 2002.
Smith, Bosworth R. *Life of Lord Lawrence*. Vols. I and II. London: Smith, Elder & Co., 1883.
Spellman, W. M. *Monarchies: 1000-2000*. London: Reaktion Books, 2001.
Srivastava, Kamal S. *Some Aspects of Indian History*. Varanasi: Sangeeta Prakashan, 1998.
Stokes, Eric. *The English Utilitarians and India*. Delhi: Oxford University Press, 1982.
Strudwick, Nigel. *The Administration of Egypt in the Old Kingdom: The Highest Titles and Their Holders*. London: KPI Limited, 1985.
Tandon, Rajesh and Ranita Mohanty, eds. *Does Civil Society Matter? Governance in Contemporary India*. New Delhi: Sage, 2003.
Talbot, Ian. *Pakistan: A Modern History*. Lahore: Vanguard, 1999.
Thapar, Romila. *Cultural Pasts: Essays in Early Indian History*. New Delhi: Oxford University Press, 2005.
———, *The Penguin History of Early India: From the Origins to AD 1300*. London: Penguin Books, 2002.
Tocqueville, Alexis de. *Democracy in America*. Trans. George Lawrence. Ed., J. P. Mayer. New York: HarperCollins, 2000.
———, *The Old Regime and the Revolution*. Trans. Alan S. Kahan. Edited and with an Introduction by François Furet and Françoise Mélonio. Chicago: University of Chicago Press, 1998.
Toynbee, Arnold J. *A Study of History*. Abridged in two volumes by D. C. Somervell New York: Dell Publishing Co., 1978.
Travelyan, Raleigh. *The Golden Oriole*. New York: Viking, 1987.
Trench, Charles Chevenix *The Indian Army and the King's Enemies 1900-47*. London: Thames and Hudson, 1988.
Tripp, Charles. *A History of Iraq*. Cambridge: Cambridge University Press, 2001.
Tully, Mark and Zareer Masani. *From Raj to Rajiv: 40 Years of Indian Independence*. London: BBC Books, 1988.
Tunzelmann, Alex von. *Indian Summer: The Secret History of the End of an Empire*. London: Simon & Schuster, 2007.
Tusi, Nizam-ul-Mulk. *The Book of Government or Rules for Kings: The Siyasatnama or Siyar al-Muluk of Nizam al-Mulk*. Trans. Hubert Drake. London: Routledge and Kegan Paul, 1960.
Vidal, Gore. *Imperial America: Reflections on the United States of Amnesia*. New York: Nation Books, 2004.
Volkogonov, Dmitri. *The Rise and Fall of the Soviet Empire: Political Leaders from Lenin to Gorbachev.* Trans. Harold Shukman. London: HarperCollins, 1999.
Waseem, Mohammad. *Politics and the State in Pakistan*. Lahore: Progressive Publishers, 1989.
Weiner, Tim. *Legacy of Ashes: The History of the CIA*. New York: Doubleday, 2007.
Wheatcroft, Andrew. *The Ottomans*. London: Viking, 1993.
Wheeler, Mortimer. *The Indus Civilization*. London: Book Club Associates, 1976.

Wheen, Francis. *How Mumbo-Jumbo Conquered the World: A Short History of Modern Delusions.* London: The Fourth Estate, 2004.
Wilson, A. N. *After the Victorians.* London: Hutchinson, 2005.
———, *The Victorians.* London: Hutchinson, 2002.
Wilson, Harold. *The Governance of Britain.* London: Book Club Associates, 1976.
Wittfogel, Karl A. *Oriental Despotism: A Comparative Study of Total Power.* New Haven: Carl Purington Rollins Printing Office of the Yale University Press, 1963.
Woloch, Isser ed. *Revolution and the Meanings of Freedom in the Nineteenth Century.* Stanford: Stanford University Press, 1996.
Woodruff, Philip. *The Men Who Ruled India.* Vol 2. *The Guardians.* Norwich: Jarrold and Sons Ltd., 1965
Yasin, Mohammad, ed. *District and Police Systems in Pakistan.* Lahore: Vanguard, 1999.
Yasin, Mohammad and Tariq Banuri, eds. *The Dispensation of Justice in Pakistan.* Karachi: Oxford University Press, 2004.
Yasin, Muhammad. *A Social History of Islamic India: 1605-1748.* Lucknow: n.p., 1958 reprint; Lahore: Book traders, n.d.
Yong, Tan Tai. *The Garrison State: The Military, Government and Society in Colonial Punjab, 1849-1947.* Lahore: Vanguard, 2005.
Yusuf, K. M., ed. *Politics and Policies of Quaid-i-Azam.* Islamabad: National Institute of Historical and Cultural Research, 1994.
Zachariah, Benjamin. *Nehru.* London: Routledge, 2004.
Zaheer, Hasan. *The Separation of East Pakistan: The Rise and Realization of Bengali Muslim Nationalism.* Karachi: Oxford University Press, 1994.
———, *The Times and Trial of the Rawalpindi Conspiracy 1951: The First Coup Attempt in Pakistan.* Karachi: Oxford University Press, 1998.
Zaidi, Akbar S. *Issues in Pakistan's Economy.* Karachi: Oxford University Press, 2000.
Zimbardo, Philip. *The Lucifer Effect: How Good People Turn Evil.* London: Rider, 2007.
Ziring, Lawrence. *Pakistan: At the Cross Currents of History.* Lahore: Vanguard, 2004.
Zurcher, Erik J. *Turkey: A Modern History.* London: I. B. Tauris & Co. Ltd., 1998.

Index

A

Abbasi, Zaheerul Islam, 153
Abbasid, 16 n. 13, 27, 55 n. 29
Abul Fazl, 33, 37, 56 n. 39, 57 n. 49, 57 n. 61, 58 n. 63, 175, 203 n. 42, 234 n. 8, 267 n. 7
Achaemenid, 14 n. 3, 28, 53 n. 2, 54 n. 18
Adhyakshas, 22, 210
Administrative Enquiry Committee, 248, 270 n. 58, 270 n. 71
Afghan(s), 31, 34, 56 n. 38, 59 n. 108, 60 n. 108, 64, 129, 164 n. 46, 290 n. 2
Ahmad, Vaqar, 111, 113
Ahmed, G., 80, 81, 82
Ahsan, Aitzaz, 53 n. 1, 192
Akbar the Great, 31, 34, 35, 36, 37, 56 n. 37, 57 n. 50, 140, 173, 191, 240, 241
Akhund, Iqbal, 123, 137 n. 189
Alanbrooke, 154
Alfred the Great, 38
Ali, Ch. Muhammad, 82
Ali, Yaqub, 188
All-India Services (AIS), 65
American, 5, 6, 10, 58 n. 71, 98, 99, 103, 108, 115, 146, 159, 161, 166 n. 69, 215, 227, 230, 237 n. 113, 269 n. 32, 287, 288, 290 n. 1
Anglo-Muslim, 64, 65, 66, 67, 275, 286
Anglo-Saxon, 38, 39, 111
Arab Empire, 16 n. 13, 27, 138
Aristocracy, 39, 40, 44, 90
Arthashastra, artha, 12, 21, 23, 31, 54 n. 8, 54 n. 9, 54 n. 10, 54 n. 15, 211, 233 n. 2, 267 n. 4
Aryan, 21
Ashoka, 24, 25, 36, 54 n. 19
Asian Development Bank (ADB), 150

Athens, 169, 170, 202 n. 1, 202 n. 7, 202 n. 8,
Aurelius, Marcus, 139
Aurungzeb, 31, 36, 37, 50, 57 n. 48, 57 n. 50, 58 n. 64, 232
Australia, 42, 118
Awami League, 110, 111, 179
Aziz, Shaukat, 224

B

Babur, 31, 56 n. 36
Baghdad, 16 n. 13, 55 n. 27, 55 n. 29,
Bahawalpur State, 70
Balban, Ghiyathudin, 27
Baluchistan, xi, 70, 75, 201
Barrage, Ghulam Muhammad, 155
Basic Democracies, 103, 104, 106, 148, 257
Bentinck, 47, 48, 59 n. 103, 61 n. 130, 131 n. 13
Bernier, 56 n. 45, 57 n. 62, 58 n. 67
Bhutto, Benazir, xii, 122, 123, 129, 137 n. 189, 160, 161, 166 n. 81, 190, 191, 261, 265, 266
Bhutto, Zulfikar Ali, 17 n. 25, 109, 111, 113, 114, 115, 116, 117, 125, 129, 134 n. 103, 135 n. 123, 135 n. 124, 135 n. 125, 135 n. 142, 157, 158, 160, 166 n. 81, 167 n. 97, 188, 189, 195, 196, 198, 206 n. 117, 206 n. 121, 206 n. 123, 208 n. 189, 229, 230, 237 n. 115, 237 n. 122, 255, 257, 258, 261, 272 n. 109, 272 n. 129, 279, 285
Bihar, 22
Bogra, 146, 179
Bombay, 50, 176

Bonaparte, Napoleon, 18 n. 31, 142, 160
Braibanti, 99, 132 n. 32, 132 n. 34, 132 n. 50, 132 n. 53, 133 n. 78, 204 n. 71, 207 n. 151
Braudel, 12, 19 n. 37, 19 n. 38
British Empire in India, ix, x, 5, 12, 13, 42, 46, 47, 48, 50, 52, 63, 64, 175, 212, 288
British, ix, x, xiv, 5, 6, 12, 13, 18 n. 31, 37, 38, 41, 42, 43, 44, 45, 46, 48, 49, 50, 52, 53, 59 n. 96, 59 n. 97, 59 n. 100, 60 n. 108, 60 n. 115, 60 n. 119, 60 n. 120, 62, 63, 64, 65, 66, 67, 83 n. 1, 89, 90, 92, 93, 94, 95, 98, 103, 105, 106, 108, 114, 140, 141, 142, 143, 144, 145, 146, 159, 162 n. 1, 163 n. 21, 163 n. 23, 164 n. 46, 174, 175, 176, 177, 180, 184, 188, 190, 193, 197, 205 n. 78, 208 n. 188, 212, 213, 236 n. 92, 243, 244, 245, 247, 248, 253, 267 n. 1, 275, 276, 284, 288
Buddhism, 24, 25, 36, 54 n. 19
Bureau of Anti-Corruption, 254
Bureau of National Reconstruction (BNR), 104
Burke, Edmund, 43, 44
Byzantine, 16 n. 13, 138, 172

C

Calcutta, 43, 46, 50, 62, 91, 176
Canada, 42
Canadian International Development Agency (CIDA), 150
Central Asia, 28, 52, 289, 290 n. 3
Central Board of Revenue (CBR), 213, 235 n. 26, 235 n. 53, 237 n. 119
Central Superior Services (CSS), 220
Chakravartin, 25, 26, 43
Charles I, 39
Chaudaries, 33
Chief Martial Law Administrator (CMLA), 102
Chingezi Turks, 31
Chundrigar, 102

Churchill, 17 n. 21, 58 n. 75, 154, 166 n. 70
Civil Service Act of 1973, 112
Civil Service of Pakistan (CSP), 72
Civil Services Academy, 99, 269 n. 32
Clausewitz, 141, 163 n. 12
Cleisthenes, 170
Commission for the Investigation of Alleged Cases of Torture 1855, 175
Committee for the Study of Corruption 1986, 118, 135 n. 145, 207 n. 143, 208 n. 185
Committee on Revitalization of Revenue Administration, 136 n. 164, 236 n. 93, 237 n. 105
Common Law, 39
Common Training Program, 223
Communist, 16 n. 16, 71, 77, 80, 145
Congress, 64, 65, 66, 67, 84 n. 23, 85 n. 24, 271 n. 88
Constantine, George, 180
Constituent Assembly, 71, 77, 82, 83, 86 n. 72, 86 n. 73, 86 n. 74, 100, 145, 147, 159, 178, 179, 180, 181, 182, 183, 204 n. 66, 204 n. 72, 204 n. 76, 277
Constitution Commission, 105, 106, 133 n. 85
Continental bureaucratic empire/empires/ state, 1, 2, 3, 4, 5, 7, 13, 15 n. 5, 16 n. 13, 20, 21, 24, 25, 26, 27, 30, 31, 36, 37, 38, 40, 41, 42, 43, 45, 46, 47, 48, 49, 50, 52, 53, 58 n. 75, 89, 93, 153, 162 n. 2, 171, 193, 210, 211, 239, 241, 242, 246, 266, 275, 288
Cornelius, A. R., also Justice Cornelius, 106, 109, 181, 204 n. 71
Cornwallis, 44, 45, 46, 47, 59 n. 83, 59 n. 91
Culture of Power, ix, xiii, 4, 5, 6, 7, 9, 11, 13, 14 n. 1, 16 n. 13, 16 n. 16, 20, 21, 26, 27, 31, 38, 40, 42, 43, 45, 48, 49, 52, 53, 68, 72, 89, 130, 141, 243, 245, 246, 247, 266, 275, 283, 285, 287, 288, 289
Curzon, 89
Custine, Marquis de, 41, 58 n. 71

D

Daula, Sirajud, 42
Daula, Yamin-ud, 32
Daultana, Mian Mumtaz, 81, 82
Deccan, 31, 55 n. 25
Defence Committee of the Cabinet (DCC), 143
Defence of Pakistan Rules (DPR), 187
Dehlavi, S. K., 11, 18 n. 30
Delhi Sultanate, 27, 28, 29, 30, 31, 35, 55 n. 25, 55 n. 28, 234 n. 5
Delhi, 19 n. 38, 27, 28, 29, 30, 31, 35, 37, 52, 55 n. 25, 55 n. 28, 56 n. 36, 234 n. 5
Deobandi, 67, 68, 82
Department for International Development (DFID), 150
Development of Industries (Federal Control) Act 1949, 250
Devolution of Power, xi, 127, 130, 200, 280
Dhaka, 80, 146, 186
Dharma, 23, 25
Dharma-mahamattas, 25
Directorate of Anti-Corruption, 254
Directorate of Trade Organizations, 156
District Coordination Officers (DCOs), 125, 126, 130, 264
District Development Committee, 126
District Management Group (DMG), 116, 118, 121, 124, 125, 126, 130, 151, 200, 278
District Rehabilitation Officers, 73
*Diwan*s, *diwan*, 13, 16 n. 13, 34, 211, 212, 276
Dosso, 183
Draconian, 169
Dundas, 69, 85 n. 34
Durand Line, 71

E

East Bengal, 7, 51, 65, 70, 71, 73, 75, 78, 79, 80, 82, 146, 147, 179, 186, 207 n. 53, 269 n. 34

East India Company, 38, 42, 46, 60 n. 115, 89, 241, 242, 268 n. 18, 276
East Pakistan, 7, 110, 111, 132 n. 54, 134 n. 99, 148, 157, 194, 204 n. 59, 206 n. 111, 246, 254
Egypt, 1, 2, 15 n. 5, 15 n. 8, 15 n. 9, 15 n. 10, 15 n. 11, 20, 21, 53 n. 2, 138
Electoral Bodies Disqualification Order (EBDO), 253
Emergency Powers Ordinance-IX of 1955, 181
En, 1, 15 n. 5,
Ensi, 15 n. 5
esprit de corps, 48, 92, 130, 223, 245, 281, 288
Establishment Division, 12, 115, 116
European, 11, 14, 38, 41, 45, 49, 53, 61 n. 127, 63, 66, 140, 160, 203 n. 20, 242, 275
Executive function 5, 7, 11, 18 n. 31, 45, 46, 47, 118, 178, 193, 202, 226

F

Fauji Foundation, 157, 158
Federal Investigation Agency (FIA), 113
Federal Public Service Commission (FPSC), 114
Federal Public Service Commissions Act 1973, 112
Federal Security Force (FSF), 157, 158, 188, 196
Federal Shariat Court (FSC), 190
Focal Group on Police Reform, 199, 208 n. 204
Folkmoot, 38
France, 11, 17 n. 20, 18 n. 30, 18 n. 31, 19 n. 38, 39, 41, 141, 142, 239, 275, 288
Fulton's committee, 114

G

Gandhi, M. K. (Mahatma), 66, 70, 271 n. 83, 271 n. 88,
Ganges, 19 n. 38, 21

Index **315**

General Head Quarters (GHQ), 109, 148, 153, 155
Germany, 11, 17 n. 21, 18 n. 30, 38, 41, 141
Governing corporation, 13, 98, 100, 101, 102, 106, 107, 110, 164 n. 48, 179, 180, 181, 199, 229, 252, 253, 257, 276, 277
Great Charter (*Magna Charta*), 40, 42
Gujranwala, 153
Gupta, Guptas, 25, 27, 30

H

Haq, Fazlul, 179, 246
Haq, Ziaul, 17 n. 22, 88 n. 112, 117, 118, 119, 121, 123, 129, 135 n. 147, 136 n. 174, 149, 150, 153, 158, 160, 161, 189, 190, 199, 230, 231, 261, 264, 279, 280, 281, 285
Harappan, 21
*Harkara*s, 35
Harvard Advisory Group, 161
Hasan, Mubashir, 10, 17 n. 25
Hastings, Warren, 43, 44, 58 n. 74, 58 n. 76, 58 n. 80, 243
Henry II, 39
Herodotus, 15 n. 3, 15 n. 8, 15 n. 11, 16 n. 11, 53 n. 2, 202 n. 7
Hinduism, 24, 36, 59 n. 108, 66, 164 n. 46

I

Ibn Battuta, 29, 55 n. 30
Ibn Khaldun, xi, 20, 53 n. 3
Ideocratic complex, 3, 24, 25, 35, 36, 50
India, ix, x, xiv, 5, 10, 12, 13, 14 n. 3, 18 n. 27, 18 n. 33, 19 n. 38, 20, 21, 26, 31, 32, 38, 42, 43, 44, 45, 46, 47, 48, 49, 50, 51, 52, 53, 54 n. 8, 56 n. 37, 56 n. 38, 57 n. 47, 57 n. 50, 57 n. 53, 57 n. 54, 58 n. 74, 58 n. 76, 59 n. 82, 59 n. 86, 59 n. 92, 59 n. 93, 59 n. 96, 59 n. 97, 59 n. 100, 59 n. 101, 59 n. 103, 59 n. 106, 60 n. 109, 60 n. 111, 60 n. 114, 60 n. 115, 60 n. 120, 61 n. 122, 61 n. 128, 61 n. 130, 63, 64, 65, 67, 68, 69, 70, 74, 76, 78, 84 n. 5, 84 n. 9, 84 n. 13, 84 n. 23, 89, 90, 93, 105, 131 n. 1, 131 n. 3, 131 n. 13, 138, 140, 142, 143, 144, 146, 152, 155, 159, 162 n. 5, 164 n. 46, 173, 175, 178, 180, 181, 183, 185, 187, 193, 203 n. 34, 210, 212, 213, 234 n. 5, 234 n. 9, 234 n. 10, 234 n. 18, 234 n. 23, 236 n. 92, 241, 242, 245, 247, 248, 254, 260, 261, 267 n. 1, 268 n. 18, 268 n. 24, 271 n. 83, 271 n. 88, 272 n. 111, 276, 288
Indian Army, 60 n. 109, 60 n. 111, 89, 143, 156, 163 n. 21
Indian Civil Service (ICS), 48, 61 n. 126, 63, 91, 92, 95, 108, 131 n. 10, 131 n. 14, 174, 177, 193, 244, 245
Indian Muslims, 34, 60 n. 120, 164 n. 46
Indian National Congress (INC), 65, 67
Indian Penal Code (IPC) 176
Indianisation 50, 63, 93, 143
Indo-Gangetic, 31, 55 n. 25
Indus, Indus Valley, 14 n. 3, 20, 21, 53 n. 1, 54 n. 6, 71, 177
Industrial Finance Corporation, 75
International Monetary Fund (IMF), 215, 230, 232
*Iqta*s, 27, 28
Islamabad, xi, xiii, xiv, 9, 126, 127, 130, 190, 201, 222, 255
Islamisation, 18 n. 29, 129, 190, 280

J

Ja'far, Qudama ibn, 16 n. 13
*Jagir*s, 32, 34, 211, 267 n. 1
Jahangir, 31, 37, 173, 186
Jallianwalabagh, 52
Jamaat-i-Islami, (JI), 71
James I, 39
Jamiat-Ulema-i-Islam, Pakistan (JUI-P), 78, 81
Janissaries, 140, 171
Jinnah, 10, 12, 18 n. 32, 66, 67, 69, 71, 72, 76, 77, 83, 84 n. 6, 84 n. 7, 86 n. 73, 88 n. 112, 94, 95, 144, 251

Jirgas, 69, 185
John, King, 39
Joint Committee on Indian Constitutional Reform for the 1933-1934 Session, 193
Junejo, Muhammad Khan, 135 n. 128, 199, 261

K

Kakul, 104
Kalat State, 70
Kama, 23
Karachi, xi, 65, 72, 75, 76, 82, 146, 156, 158, 166 n. 86, 166 n. 87, 179, 188, 190, 198, 248, 249, 257, 258, 259, 270 n. 55, 270 n. 63, 270 n. 65, 270 n. 68, 271 n. 79
Kashmir, 31, 65, 69, 70, 144, 267 n. 1
Kautilya, 21, 22, 24, 25, 26, 31, 54 n. 8, 54 n. 9, 54 n. 10, 210, 227, 233 n. 1, 233 n. 2, 239, 267 n. 4
Kazi, A. G. N., 216
Khairpur, 73, 86 n. 52
Khalji, Allaudin, 27, 36
Khan, Ayub, 10, 17 n. 22, 82, 102, 105, 106, 109, 110, 133 n. 63, 144, 146, 147, 152, 154, 155, 156, 159, 161, 165 n. 64, 181, 183, 184, 185, 187, 194, 205 n. 80, 255, 256, 257, 272 n. 112, 272 n. 120, 276, 277, 285
Khan, Azam, 82
Khan, Ghulam Ishaq, 117, 199
Khan, Liaquat Ali, 10, 68, 77, 80, 83, 143, 144, 145, 146, 251
Khan, Major General Akbar, 145
Khan, Moulvi Tamizuddin, 180
Khan, Qurban Ali, 82
Khan, Yahya, 109, 111, 148, 152, 161, 165 n. 64, 187, 278
Khan, Zafarullah, 68, 77
Khusrau, 37
*Kuttab*s 16 n. 13

L

Larkana, 114, 201, 257

Lateral Entry Scheme, 113, 114
Lawrence, John, 244
Leghari, A. M. Khan, 247
Louis XIV, 239
Lugal, 15 n. 5

M

Madras, 50, 59 n. 99, 92, 175, 203 n. 35
Magi, 54 n. 18
Mahmud III, 140
Mahmud, Khaqan, 113
Majlis-i-Ahrar, 81
Makran Coast, 21
Mandarins, 2, 13, 83, 125, 210, 251, 276
*Mansabdar*s, *mansabdari, mansab*, 32, 33, 48, 105, 113, 140, 153, 157, 158, 211, 212
Mansur, 34, 55 n. 29, 173
Mansur, Khwaja, 34, 173
Marathas, 34
Maudoodi, 78
Maurya, Chandragupta, 21, 54 n. 8, 138, 241
Maurya, Mauryan, Mauryas, 21, 22, 24, 25, 26, 29, 30, 37, 54 n. 8, 138, 239, 241
Mediterranean, 170
Megasthenes, 239
Mehmed the Conqueror, 172
Menes, 53 n. 2
Mesopotamia, 20, 139
Ministry of Economic Affairs, 75, 86 n. 62, 85 n. 65, 86 n. 68
Mirza, Iskander, 82, 101, 102, 146, 148, 159, 164 n. 48, 179, 183, 186, 252, 277, 285
MLR-114 Removal from Service Regulation, 111
Mongol, 29, 34, 56 n. 36, 205 n. 78
Montesquieu, 17 n. 20, 38, 46, 58 n. 81, 202 n. 14
Mopilla Uprising of 1921, 52,
Mu'tasim, 27, 55 n. 27
Mudie, Francis, 68, 69, 85 n. 33

Mughal, 31, 57 n. 48, 57 n. 52, 57 n. 55, 58 n. 64, 162 n. 5, 162 n. 8, 203 n. 22, 209 n. 221, 267 n. 3, 268 n. 16
Muhammad, Ghulam, 74, 82, 83, 155, 164 n. 48, 180, 181, 182, 276
Multan, 29
Munir, Muhammad (also, Justice Munir), 94, 102, 178, 181, 276
Munro, 46, 47, 59 n. 99
Musharraf (General Musharraf), xii, 6, 88 n. 113, 127, 130, 149, 150, 151, 160, 161, 162, 165 n. 58, 166 n. 69, 184, 199, 202, 218, 231, 232, 233, 264, 265, 280, 281, 290 n. 3
Muslim League, 64, 67, 68, 70, 71, 72, 76, 77, 80, 81, 82, 85 n. 24, 96, 97, 101, 179, 256, 268 n. 31

N

Nanda, 21
National Accountability Bureau (NAB), 265
National Documentation Centre (NDC), xiv, 9, 11, 85 n. 25, 85 n. 41, 85 n. 51, 86 n. 52, 86 n. 56, 86 n. 57, 87 n. 85, 87 n. 95, 87 n. 96, 132 n. 35, 269 n. 34, 269 n. 40, 271 n. 79
National Pay Commission of 1970-72, 114, 135 n. 127, 273 n. 147
National Reconstruction Bureau (NRB) 137 n. 201, 208 n. 207
National Security Council (NSC) 160
Naukarshahi, 97
Nawab of Mamdot, 68, 246
Nazi Germany, 17 n. 21
Nazims, 125, 126, 200, 226, 281
Nazimuddin, Khwaja, 80, 82, 83, 146, 179, 180, 199, 246
Niazi, Maulana Kausar, 258
Nile, 20, 53 n. 2
Nobility, 39, 57 n. 48, 58 n. 64
Noon, Firoze Khan, 102, 133 n. 61
Norman, Normandy, 38, 39, 40
North Africa, 27
North-West Frontier Province (NWFP), xi, xii, 65, 69, 70 75, 112, 201

Norwegian Agency for Development (NORAD), 150

O

Objectives Resolution, 77, 78, 86 n. 72, 190
Octavian Augustus, 139
Officers on Special Duty (OSD), 122
Official priesthood, 3, 22, 25, 26, 30, 35, 36, 50, 138
Ombudsman, 190
One Unit, 100, 101, 110, 148, 276
Ottoman, 14, 83 n. 1, 138, 139, 140, 171, 172, 183, 202 n. 17, 203 n. 20
Oxus, 20, 22

P

Pakistan Foreign Service (PFS), 106, 116
Pakistan Muslim League (PML), 122, 159
Pakistan Muslim League-Nawaz (PML-N) 122, 190, 230
Pakistan National Alliance (PNA), 117
Pakistan People's Party (PPP), 109, 111, 112, 117, 122, 128, 135 n. 123, 189, 190, 196, 202, 230, 231, 265
Panas, 23, 24
Patwari, 225, 226, 254, 284
Pay and Services Commission of 1959-1962, 106, 108
Peisistratus, 169, 170, 184
Persia, 14 n. 3, 28, 32, 53 n. 2, 54 n. 18, 138
Persian, 15 n. 3, 16 n. 13, 27, 30, 34, 46, 53 n. 2, 54 n. 18, 55 n. 29, 56 n. 36, 57 n. 54, 64, 65, 66, 138, 211, 240
Pirzada, 149, 204 n. 66, 204 n. 72, 204 n. 76
Placement Bureau, 122, 129
Plassey, 42
Police Service of Pakistan (PSP), 72, 97, 103, 116, 146, 193, 194
Post-colonial, 10, 18 n. 27, 61 n. 127, 173, 233, 290
Praetorian Guard, 139, 157

Provincial Civil Service (PCS), 96, 246
Punjab, 20, 51, 59 n. 108, 64, 65, 68, 70, 73, 75, 80, 81, 82, 84 n, 8, 85 n. 25, 96, 101, 102, 112, 120, 131 n. 7, 133 n. 59, 142, 154, 155, 162 n. 1, 163 n. 11, 173, 176, 177, 198, 201, 204 n. 53, 204 n. 58, 247, 251, 258, 262, 269 n. 40

Q

Qadeer, Mohammad A., 11, 18 n. 29
Qazi, qadi, 30, 36, 183, 190, 240, 55 n. 29
Quaid-i-Azam, xiii, xiv, 18 n. 32, 71, 72, 86 n. 73, 132 n. 27, 251
Quetta, 82, 158, 191
Qureshi, Ishtiaq Hussein, 77
Qureshi, Moeen, 123

R

Rajput, 25, 33, 34, 164 n. 46, 239, 267 n. 1
Rashidi, Pir Ali Mohammad, 185
Rathore, Zafar Iqbal, xiii, 199, 208 n. 204, 238 n. 130
Rawalpindi Conspiracy Act, 145
Rawalpindi, 75, 80, 87 n. 95, 145, 153, 164 n. 32,
Republican Party, 101
Richard II, 39
Roman, Roman Empire, 13, 38, 77, 138, 139, 162 n. 3, 171, 208 n. 181,
Roosevelt, Eleanor, 93
Russians, 52, 144

S

Safavid, 32
Samarra, 55 n. 27
Sassanid, 16 n. 13, 54 n. 18
SAVAK, 15 n. 3
Scribes, 1, 2, 222
Secretary of State for India, 89
Shah, Sajjad Ali, 17 n. 24, 191, 206 n. 137

Shahjahan, 31, 37, 56 n. 43, 57 n. 50
Sharia, 78
Shariat, 66, 190, 191
Sharif, Nawaz, 88 n. 113, 122, 123, 129, 158, 160, 190, 191, 261
Sharif, Shahbaz, 129
Siddiqui, Abdul Rehman, 187, 206 n. 111
Sikhs, 59 n. 108, 84 n. 13, 162 n. 1
Sindh, xii, 20, 65, 70, 73, 79, 87 n. 85, 112, 125, 155, 180, 181, 188, 198, 201, 248, 251, 258
Singh, Amar, 267 n. 1
Singh, Ranjit, 60 n. 108, 140, 162 n. 8, 163 n. 9, 163 n. 10, 173, 174, 203 n. 27
Solon, 168, 169, 170, 178, 202 n. 7
Spanish, 52
Special Committee for the Eradication of Corruption from Services of 1967, 253
Special Police Establishment (SPE), 248
Specialised Training Program, 223
State Bank of Pakistan (SBP), 229
State of Laws, 38, 40, 41, 42, 44, 46, 48, 50, 53, 89, 159, 161, 169, 171, 190, 243
Subcommittee on Law and Order 1976, 196, 207 n. 175
Sufi, 30
Suhrawardy, 101, 246
Suleiman the Lawgiver, 172
Sumer, 1, 15 n. 5
Sustainable Development Policy Institute (SDPI), 150, 201

T

Taimur, Amir 56 n. 36, 203 n. 21, 205 n. 78
Taskforce on the Reform of Tax Administration, 218, 262
Tax-to-GDP ratio, 213, 214, 215, 219, 221, 228, 230, 264
Tehsildars, 113, 226
Theseus, 168, 170, 171, 172, 178, 184

Timurid, x, 31, 32, 33, 35, 36, 37, 38, 46, 48, 56 n. 36, 56 n. 37, 56 n. 38, 59 n. 108, 63, 105, 113, 139, 140, 172, 173, 175, 183, 185, 186, 190, 202, 205 n. 78, 211, 212, 232, 234 n. 5, 239, 248
Tocqueville, Alexis de, 41, 58 n. 71, 58 n. 72, 267 n. 2
Trevelyan, Charles, 90
Tughluq, Mohammed bin, 36
Turco-Persian, 46, 57 n. 54, 64
Turks, 27, 31, 34, 53, 171, 211
Tusi, Nizam al-Mulk, 15 n. 6

U

Ulema, 66, 78, 79, 81, 82
Umayyad, 16 n. 13
United Front, 179
United States, 41, 58 n. 75, 114, 144, 146, 161, 165 n. 69, 219, 230, 231, 233, 275, 280, 285, 286, 290 n. 2
Universal proprietor, 1, 3, 22, 25, 26, 27, 30, 34, 36, 37, 39, 44, 172
Usmani, Maulana Shabbir Ahmad, 68, 77

V

Victorian Britain, 93
Village headmen, 24, 25, 28
Visayapati, 25
Voltaire, 17 n. 20, 38, 202 n. 13, 202 n. 15

W

Water and Power Development Authority (WAPDA), 263
Wellesley, 45, 46, 59 n. 97, 131 n. 1
West Asia, 27
West Pakistan, 64, 65, 70, 73, 83, 86 n. 54, 100, 101, 110, 111, 132 n. 54, 147, 148, 157, 159, 166 n. 82, 166 n. 83, 184, 185, 194, 237 n. 97, 246, 254, 255, 276
westernisation experience, 64, 65, 67

witena gemot, 38
World Bank, 123, 150, 266

Y

Yang, Shang, 227, 233 n. 1
Yusuf Patel versus the Crown, 181

Z

Zaidi, Ijlal Haider, xiv, 117, 135 n. 128, 135 n. 144, 136 n. 159, 199
*Zamindar*s, 33, 44, 46, 175, 177